Essentials of Removal and Relief

Representing Individuals in Immigration Proceedings

AILA Titles of Interest

AILA's Occupational Guidebooks

Immigration Options for Physicians

Immigration Options for Nurses & Allied Health Care Professionals

Immigration Options for Religious Workers

Immigration Options for Academics and Researchers

Immigration Options for Investors and Entrepreneurs

Statutes, Regulations, Agency Materials & Case Law

Immigration & Nationality Act (INA)

Immigration Regulations (CFR)

Agency Interpretations of Immigration Policy (Cables, Memos, and Liaison Minutes)

AILA's Immigration Case Summaries

Core Curriculum

Selected Fundamentals of Immigration Law

*Immigration Law for Paralegals**

AILA's Guide to Technology and Legal Research for the Immigration Lawyer

CD Products & Toolbox Series

AILA*Link CD-ROM*

The AILA Immigration Practice Toolbox

The AILA Litigation Toolbox

Treatises & Primers

Kurzban's Immigration Law Sourcebook
by Ira J. Kurzban

Professionals: A Matter of Degree
by Martin J. Lawler

AILA's Asylum Primer
by Regina Germain

Immigration Consequences of Criminal Activity
by Mary E. Kramer

Essentials of Removal and Relief
by Joseph A. Vail

Other Titles

David Stanton Manual on Labor Certification

AILA's Global Immigration Guide: A Country-by-Country Survey

Immigration & Nationality Law Handbook

The Visa Processing Guide

Ethics in a Brave New World

Immigration Litigation: Winning in Federal and Immigration Courts

Immigration Practice & Procedure Under NAFTA

Client Brochures (10 Titles)

Government Reprints

BIA Practice Manual

Immigration Judge Benchbook (Print or CD)

Citizenship Laws of the World

EB-5 Manual

Tables of Contents and other information about these publications can be found at ***www.ailapubs.com***. Orders may be placed at that site or by calling 1-800-982-2839.

*An AILA-distributed title

Essentials *of* Removal and Relief

Representing Individuals in Immigration Proceedings

Joseph A. Vail

Edited by
Stephanie L. Browning

AMERICAN IMMIGRATION LAWYERS ASSOCIATION
www.aila.org

Web Site for Corrections and Updates

Corrections and other updates to AILA publications can be found online at: ***www.aila.org/BookUpdates.***

If you have any corrections or updates to the information in this book, please let us know by sending a note to the address below, or e-mail us at ***books@aila.org***.

This publication is designed to provide accurate and authoritative information in regard to the subject matter covered. It is distributed with the understanding that the publisher is not engaged in rendering legal, accounting, or other professional service. If legal advice or other expert assistance is required, the services of a competent professional should be sought.

—from a Declaration of Principles jointly adopted by a Committee of the American Bar Association and a Committee of Publishers

Printed in the United States of America

ISBN 1-57370-178-5
Stock No. 81-78

To Vince and Babe

Marie and John

and my daughters, Tania and Aleyda

Summary of Contents

About AILA

The American Immigration Lawyers Association (AILA) is a national bar association of more than 11,000 attorneys who practice immigration law and/or work as teaching professionals. AILA member attorneys represent tens of thousands of U.S. families who have applied for permanent residence for their spouses, children, and other close relatives for lawful entry and residence in the United States. AILA members also represent thousands of U.S. businesses and industries who sponsor highly skilled foreign workers seeking to enter the United States on a temporary or permanent basis. In addition, AILA members represent foreign students, entertainers, athletes, and asylum-seekers, often on a pro bono basis. Founded in 1946, AILA is a nonpartisan, not-for-profit organization that provides its members with continuing legal education, publications, information, professional services, and expertise through its 36 chapters and over 50 national committees. AILA is an affiliated organization of the American Bar Association and is represented in the ABA House of Delegates.

American Immigration Lawyers Association
1331 G Street, NW, Suite 300
Tel: (202) 507-7600
Fax: (202) 783-7853
www.aila.org

DETAILED TABLE OF CONTENTS

PREFACE

Looking back, the decade of the 1980s was for the most part a positive period for immigrants, and their representatives. The U.S. Supreme Court found that immigrant children had a right to a public education regardless of immigration status. The 1980 Refugee Act was enacted. Solo practitioners, legal aid lawyers, religious organizations, pro bono attorneys, and others zealously defended asylum-seekers fleeing horrendous conditions around the world. In addition to the energy in asylum defense, the 1986 legalization program was passed, and millions of immigrants legalized their status. Thereafter, IMMACT90 was enacted, thus liberalizing immigration laws and granting temporary protected status (TPS) to thousands fleeing civil wars, natural disasters, and persecution. The unfair treatment of Salvadoran and Guatemalan refugees was at least partially remedied by TPS and the *ABC* class settlement.

However, in the 1990s, immigration law changed. The generosity of the 1986 legalization program was replaced with "Proposition 187-English Only" movements—calls to close off the border and clamoring by many politicians who felt that the United States had been too generous in granting amnesty. As a result, Congress passed IIRAIRA and AEDPA in 1996—two draconian immigration proposals that expanded the grounds of deportability and inadmissibility and dramatically reduced or eliminated relief. The Board of Immigration Appeals (BIA), in a series of decisions, strictly interpreted these laws, especially in regard to the criminal provisions in IIRAIRA. At the same time, Congress moved to reduce or eliminate judicial review of the agency's decisions. The Attorney General, in 2002, then moved to "streamline" (*i.e.*, drastically reduce) any administrative review of immigration judges' decisions.

Suffice it to say that the last 15 years generally have not been positive for immigrants or those advocating on their behalf. However, despite these setbacks, there have been ever-increasing numbers of new lawyers taking up the challenge of representing immigrants and refugees. Pro bono representation, in particular, is on the rise. Major law firms are championing the causes of protecting unaccompanied immigrant children and immigrant spouses who have been victimized by domestic violence. Immigration clinics that train law students to competently and energetically fight for immigrants' rights in court are opening throughout the country. The ranks of AILA itself have grown, and the solo practitioners and old veterans of immigration court have not been demoralized. Most continue to go into court daily to battle the Department of Homeland Security (DHS) for any minimal rights they can gain for their clients, and find ways to challenge wrongful denials of relief in spite of the attempts to eliminate administrative and judicial review.

It is for these individuals that this book was written. It is a book on the basics—hopefully, a helpful tool for those new to the law of immigration to learn and understand the fundamentals of immigration court practice. It is written for law students, pro bono attorneys, new lawyers, accredited organizations, and even as a refresher for grizzled immigration court vets. It is not an advanced theoretical discussion, but rather, a "how to" book. This is the first edition, and it is hoped that it will evolve as the law does.

I started as an accredited representative with Volunteers In Service To America (VISTA) and later worked as a legal aid lawyer for several years. I have worked with and learned from the best and most generous lawyers I've ever met. They have been teachers, mentors, and comrades-in-arms from the early 1980s until the present. Whether they know it, all have in one way or another helped me to gather and understand the information contained on the following pages, and have shown me what it means to be an advocate for immigrants. I want to acknowledge a few here.

Thank you, Sam and Peter Williamson, Luis Wilmot, Nancy Falgout, Dan Graney, Peter Schey, Lee Teran, Barbara Hines, Lisa Brodyaga, Charles Foster, Harry Gee, Gordon Quan, Meg Burkhart, Russ Christensen, Chava Colon, Mike Jacobsen, Regina Germain, Becky Burdette, Brian Bates, Dick Fischer, Terry Weir, Anya Sykes, Angie Kelley, Michael Coughlin, Bill Van Wyke, Rex Wingerter, Mary Brittingham, Yvonne Vega-Martinez, Martha Garza, Bob Etnyre, Nadine Wettstein, Mary Kenney, Tom Perkinson, Diana Velardo, Jenny Moya, Anne Chandler, Lawrence Rushton, and Nieves Lawrence.

I also would like to thank AILA for its efforts in bringing this book to fruition. Specifically, credit goes to Director of Publications Randy P. Auerbach for his encouragement in getting this project off the ground. In addition, this book would not have been completed without the effort, above and beyond the call of duty, of Stephanie L. Browning. Not only was she a top-notch editor on this project, but a valuable partner in challenging some of my legal conclusions and pushing me to make this a better product. Thanks, Steph!

Joseph A. Vail
March 2006

INTRODUCTION

Aside from the federal tax code, immigration law probably is the most complicated and dynamic part of the American legal system. As the huddled masses have poured into the United States over the past 200 years, the country has had to grapple with deciding who among the new immigrants would be accepted and would be rejected as residents. From the mid-19th century to the present day, each new era in American history has brought a different wave of immigrants—from Irish Catholics to Chinese to Southern and Eastern Europeans, Latin Americans, Asians, Africans, and those from the Middle East. Each wave of immigrants has brought music, food, culture, and energy from which our cultural heritage has grown.

However, each wave has also brought individuals whom the country has decided to reject for a variety of reasons, such as crime, poverty, illiteracy, illness, security threats, and violations of immigration laws. With each new class of individuals found to be undesirable as entrants to the United States, the immigration laws have been amended to add new grounds of excludability, *i.e.*, bases for denying admission. And if an individual deemed unwelcome for any of the reasons cited above had made it past our borders already, new grounds of deportability, *i.e.*, bases for removing the person, were added to make removal possible.

As a result, the laws governing exclusion of aliens seeking to enter the United States, and removal of those already here, have grown from a few basic statutes in the 19th century to a complex and byzantine web in the present day. Since 1986, there have been at least a half-dozen major overhauls of the immigration laws, with another currently on the horizon. Unfortunately, like a contractor trying to build a new edifice without removing the remains of an old one, Congress adds new immigration laws on top of old laws with little effort to harmonize them. The results are often laws that are confusing and contradictory. New lawyers and others attempting to decipher our immigration laws are often perplexed and frustrated.

This book is an attempt to simplify the laws relating to immigration enforcement. It is geared toward those who are starting in this field trying to understand the basics of immigration court proceedings. Despite the complexities of immigration law, it boils down to a few basic questions: Whom do we permit to enter the country and whom do we keep out? Who do we permit to remain here after entry and whom do we remove/deport?

Whom We Keep Out

Those who are denied entry into the country are called "inadmissible." The rules as to whom is deemed inadmissible are found at Immigration and Nationality Act

(INA) §212(a).[1] Although there are 10 different grounds with numerous sub-sections outlined, they can be narrowed down to five major areas, plus a few miscellaneous grounds of inadmissibility. The general bases for denying admission, *i.e.*, excluding an alien from admission at the land border, seaport, or airport are:

- health;
- crime;
- security concerns;
- immigration (violations); and
- public charge grounds.

Some of these individuals are turned away right at the border, or its functional equivalent, without a court hearing. This action is called "expedited removal." Others are granted entry, or manage to enter the country surreptitiously, and are given a hearing before an immigration judge (IJ) before being deemed inadmissible and made to leave the country. For some individuals, despite a finding of inadmissibility, there are waivers or pardons that may permit them to overcome the basis for exclusion. These are found at INA §212.

Whom We Remove

Many non–American citizens gain entry to the country legally or illegally. Some come legally to the United States on temporary visas (*e.g.*, tourists) or permanent visas (*e.g.*, spouses of U.S. citizens).

If, after lawful entry, they take some action that violates their previously lawful status, such as allowing a visa to expire, working without authorization, or being convicted of a crime, they become "removable." That is, they have gained admission lawfully but the government now wishes to "remove" them for violating the section of the INA that governs the reasons an individual may be removed—INA §237(a). These laws are in many ways similar to the grounds of exclusion or inadmissibility at INA §212, but are, of course, distinct in other ways. They include as reasons for removal:

- crime;
- immigration violations;
- security threats;
- lack of proper documentation or registration; and
- public charge grounds.

In addition to those who forfeit their lawful status based on an INA §237(a) ground, individuals who have managed to enter illegally, *i.e.*, without proper inspection or by fraud, are also "removable." Just as with individuals who have entered le-

---

[1] Immigration and Nationality Act of 1952, Pub. L. No. 82-414, 66 Stat. 163 (codified as amended at 8 USC §§1101 *et seq.*)

gally and later fallen out of lawful status, these individuals have a right to a removal hearing before an IJ to determine whether they will be removed.

To Whom We Grant Relief

Despite being inadmissible or removable, U.S. laws sometimes grant individuals waivers or the right to seek relief from removal. This relief is sought from the Department of Homeland Security (DHS) or, if the person is in removal proceedings (*i.e.*, has a hearing before an IJ), the Department of Justice (DOJ). There are numerous waivers of inadmissibility (most found at INA §212(d)–(l)) as well as forms of relief from removal. Many of these waivers and forms of relief depend on close U.S. citizen or lawful permanent resident family ties and/or a showing of hardship to these family members if the immigration laws are enforced. Other relief forms and waivers depend on a variety of factors, including evidence of persecution, a lengthy period of physical presence, or residence in the United States.

How All This Is Decided

In the immigration enforcement arena, there are two sources of authority—DHS and DOJ. The former Immigration and Naturalization Service is gone, replaced in 2002 with DHS. Within DHS, there are two enforcement agencies—U.S. Customs and Border Protection (CBP), which is entrusted with securing the border and keeping out individuals deemed inadmissible, and U.S. Immigration and Customs Enforcement (ICE), which works in the interior of the country and is responsible for finding, detaining, and removing those deemed to be removable.

Individuals stopped by CBP at the airport, seaport, or border are often summarily removed in expedited removal proceedings without going before an IJ. Those arrested and detained in the interior of the country are generally brought before an IJ for a removal hearing. The IJs are employees of DOJ and are under the jurisdiction of the Attorney General. Within removal hearings, there are two central questions:

(1) Is the person in proceedings removable for violating an immigration law; and

(2) If so, is the person eligible for some form of relief that will permit him or her to remain in the United States?

An ICE attorney represents the government in seeking removal of the alien, while the alien has the right to an attorney (at no expense to the government). If the IJ finds that the person is not removable, proceedings are terminated and the person is not removed. If the IJ finds the person removable but grants relief, the individual is not removed. If the IJ finds the person removable and cannot grant relief, the person is ordered removed or told that he or she may leave "voluntarily" or be ordered removed if he or she refuses this voluntary departure. Either side can appeal the decision of the IJ to an appellate body, the Board of Immigration Appeals (BIA). Depending on the type of case and the basis for the decision, judicial review of the BIA decision may be available.

Moving Forward

Immigration laws, in spite of some modern media claims to the contrary, have become exceedingly strict. While the bases for excluding and removing aliens have expanded, the possibilities of relief have been limited and, in some cases, eliminated. Obtaining relief is extremely difficult. Most present-day immigrants—Latin-Americans and Asians being the most abundant—differ very little from their Irish and European forerunners. Most are hard-working, have limited education, and are seeking better lives for themselves and their children. Like their predecessors of the late-19th and early-20th centuries, they often come with no documentation. The only difference is that the laws have become much harsher and the number of grounds for exclusion and removal has greatly increased.

Lawyers who go into immigration court to diligently defend immigrants, even with the deck stacked against them, share a kindred spirit and gain a sense of respect among practitioners. Although there is very little in immigration—or any other area of law, for that matter—that is more difficult than, for example, gaining asylum in immigration court for an immigrant before a tough IJ, there is also very little in the practice of law that is more rewarding or makes more of a difference than saving someone's freedom, well-being, or life.

The following chapters are meant to be a primer, a helpful guide to new lawyers, pro bono lawyers, law students, or experienced veterans who may need a reminder on representing immigrants facing removal from the United States. Chapter 1 summarizes a history and background of U.S. immigration law. Chapters 2 and 3 analyze grounds of deportability/removability and inadmissibility, respectively. Chapter 4 is a discussion of DHS and DOJ procedures, starting with the government arrest powers, through DHS "processing" of an alien, and finally detailing immigration court procedures. Chapter 5 covers asylum, withholding of removal, and Convention Against Torture relief. Chapter 6 examines other forms of relief from removal. Finally, Chapter 7 considers post–immigration court hearing procedures including motions and administrative and judicial appeals. Tips for practitioners are included throughout the book to aide those representing immigrants and refugees before the immigration courts and DHS.

CHAPTER 1

IMMIGRATION LAW HISTORY AND BACKGROUND INFORMATION

History

The First Hundred Years: 1776 to 1875

During the 100 years after the Declaration of Independence and the establishment of an independent nation, there was very little restriction on immigration. Because there was such a need for immigrants to settle the land and expand, the United States had an open door policy. The Constitution mentions nothing about restrictions on immigration, grounds of inadmissibility, or grounds of deportability. The only outright mention of immigration has to do with the power to pass laws relating to naturalization. The first and only restriction on immigration during this initial period after the birth of the country was the Aliens Act of June 1798.[1] This law allowed the President to deport aliens who were considered to be a threat to the nation. However, the Aliens Act was allowed to expire after two years.

Exclusion of Poor People, Criminals, the Sick, and Other Undesirables: 1875 to 1900

The Immigration Act of 1875[2] was the beginning of the exclusion of various classes of individuals. This Act provided for the exclusion of convicts, prostitutes, the destitute, and the physically handicapped. Several years later, two acts in 1882 provided for the exclusion of lunatics, idiots, and persons likely to become public charges.[3] The Chinese Exclusion Act of 1882[4] began the exclusion of Chinese immigrants, and it suspended the entry of Chinese individuals for a period of 10 years. It also barred the Chinese from obtaining citizenship.

In 1885, the "Foran Act"[5] prohibited the recruitment of unskilled laborers from abroad. In 1888, Congress passed a law banning the return of Chinese immigrants who had departed. In addition, this law provided for the deportation of contract

---

[1] 1 Statutes-at-Large 570.

[2] Act of March 3, 1875, 18 Statutes-at-Large 477.

[3] Immigration Act of Aug. 3, 1882, 22 Statutes-at-Large 214.

[4] Chinese Exclusion Act of May 6, 1882, 22 Statutes-at-Large 58.

[5] Act of Feb. 26, 1885, 23 Statutes-at-Large 332.

laborers apprehended in the United States.[6] Polygamists, paupers, and those with contagious diseases were declared to be inadmissible by Congress in 1891.[7]

Expansion and Codification of Inadmissible Classes: 1900 to 1920

The later years of the 19th century and the early years of the 20th century saw an expansion in the number and nationalities of immigrants to the United States. In addition to the Northern Europeans who had migrated during the 19th century, there was a major increase in the number of immigrants from Southern Europe, including Greeks, Jews, and Italians. Additionally, Eastern Europeans were coming to the United States in increasing numbers, resulting in an expansion of the grounds of excludability.

In 1903, epileptics, professional beggars, and those who imported prostitutes or made profits from prostitution were added to the classes of those found to be inadmissible. That same year, after the assassination of President McKinley (by a U.S. citizen), anarchists and those advocating the overthrow of the U.S. government were declared to be inadmissible.[8] The 1907 law barred the entry of Japanese entering from Mexico or Canada; moreover, it raised the "head tax" from 50 cents to $4 (A head tax is a fee to be paid by each arriving alien).[9] In addition, the 1907 law excluded imbeciles, those suffering from tuberculosis, and those who had committed crimes involving moral turpitude.

The Immigration Act of 1917[10] was the first major expansion and codification of the grounds of inadmissibility. Individuals convicted of crimes after proper entry were declared deportable. To those classes previously named, Congress added chronic alcoholics; individuals suffering from tuberculosis; vagrants; persons with psychopathic personalities; those teaching opposition to organized governments; prior deportees; and individuals from the "Asiatic Barred Zone."[11] After several failed attempts, this law enabled restrictionists to set a literacy test for those seeking admission to the United States. In 1918, anarchists were found to be inadmissible through the Anarchist Act.[12]

The Quota Laws: 1920s

The first quota law was passed in 1921 as a result of a rise in anti-immigrant sentiment after World War I.[13] The quota for immigration from any non–western hemisphere country was set at 3 percent of the population of that country present in the

---

[6] Act of Oct. 19, 1888, 25 Statutes-at-Large 566.

[7] Immigration Act of Mar. 3, 1891, 26 Statutes-at-Large 1084.

[8] Immigration Act of Mar. 3, 1903, 32 Statutes-at-Large 1213.

[9] Act of Feb. 20, 1907.

[10] Immigration Act of Feb. 5, 1917, 39 Statutes-at-Large 874.

[11] This virtually included all Asians.

[12] Act of May 22, 1918, 40 Statutes-at-Large 559.

[13] Quota Law of May 19, 1921, 42 Statutes-at-Large 5.

United States in 1910. This quota law also capped an annual total of immigrants from European countries at 350,000.

The quota was tightened in 1924. The national quota for each non–western hemisphere country was decreased to 2 percent of the 1890 population from the given country present in the United States.[14] This limited Southern and Eastern European waves of migration; large numbers of immigrants from countries such as Greece, Italy and Turkey, did not begin coming until after 1890. The 1924 law banned all immigration from Asia with the exception of the Philippines.

In addition to exclusion grounds, the 1924 law provided, for the first time, the legal necessity of obtaining visas at American consulates abroad prior to entering the United States. Indicative of even more growing complexity in immigration law, it also distinguished nonimmigrants from immigrants (see discussion on differences between immigrants and nonimmigrants, *infra*).

The Depression Years: 1930s

The Great Depression of the 1930s resulted in a drop in the level of migration to the United States. It was during this period that there was a repatriation/deportation of approximately 400,000 Mexican nationals and Mexican Americans, justified on economic grounds.

Braceros and Refugees: 1940s

The Registration Act of 1940[15] provided for the registration of aliens. It also created the Board of Immigration Appeals (BIA). During World War II, in 1943, the underpinnings of the "Bracero" Program began.[16] This program, which lasted until 1947, permitted the entry of temporary workers from Mexico and other countries (the Bracero Program itself lasted until 1964). These workers were mainly meant to fill labor gaps that resulted from U.S. citizens serving in the military during World War II. Much of this work was in the area of agriculture in the southwest.

Also, the end of World War II brought the "War Brides Act."[17] This was liberalization on the admission of spouses and children of U.S. servicemen overseas. Almost 120,000 individuals entered under this program.

In 1948, the first law providing for the admission of refugees was passed.[18] The "Displaced Persons Act" ultimately provided for the admission of approximately 400,000 refugees who had been victims of persecution at the hands of the Nazi government.

---

[14] Immigration Act of May 26, 1924, 43 Statutes-at-Large 153.

[15] Alien Registration Act of June 28, 1940, 54 Statutes-at-Large 670.

[16] Act of April 29, 1943, 57 Statutes-at-Large 70.

[17] War Brides Act of Dec. 28, 1945, 59 Statutes-at-Large 659.

[18] Displaced Persons Act of June 25, 1948, 62 Statutes-at-Large 1009.

Immigration and Nationality Act: 1950s

The Internal Security Act of 1950 provided for the exclusion and deportation of persons deemed to be a risk to national security, including communists.[19] Two years later, Congress passed the McCarran-Walter Act—the basis of today's Immigration and Nationality Act (INA).[20] This law created preferences based on family- and employment-based immigration categories. Also, it created visa issuance and inspection procedures. On the enforcement side, it expanded the quota system; codified, under INA §212, the exclusion grounds; and added new security grounds. Additionally, this law expanded the deportation grounds and created deportation procedures as well as procedures for relief from deportation. The grounds of inadmissibility and deportability in the McCarran-Walter Act were based on the same general grounds upon which today's laws are based: health grounds; crime; immigration violations; security risks; and public charge grounds.

In 1953, Congress passed the Refugee Relief Act providing for the admission of refugees and establishing a new category of persons persecuted because of their political beliefs.[21] This law was used in 1956 by President Dwight D. Eisenhower to admit approximately 5,000 refugees fleeing Hungary after the failed revolution. He later brought in approximately 30,000 more refugees via parole procedures.[22] President Eisenhower used his parole power in the late 1950s to admit Cuban refugees fleeing the Castro government after the revolution.

The Immigration Act of 1965: 1960s

In the early 1960s, President John F. Kennedy indicated his desire to reform the immigration laws; he was open to a less restrictionist immigration policy. After President Kennedy's assassination, President Lyndon B. Johnson continued this reform, passing the 1965 Immigration Act.[23] The 1965 law finally abolished national origins quotas. It established overall quotas of 120,000 immigrants for the western hemisphere and 160,000 immigrants for the rest of the world with a 20,000 per country visa limit for those outside of the western hemisphere. The 1965 law continued the grounds of exclusion for individuals based on crime, health, security, public charge, and immigration violation grounds. Last, it established the labor certification requirement for workers to obtain employment-based visas in the United States.

---

[19] Internal Security Act of Sept. 22, 1950, 64 Statutes-at-Large 987.

[20] Immigration and Nationality Act of 1952, Pub. L. No. 82-414, 66 Stat. 163 (codified as amended at 8 USC §§1101 *et seq.*).

[21] Refugee Relief Act of 1953, Pub. L. No. 83-203, 67 Stat. 400 (1953), amended by Act of Aug. 1954, Pub. L. No. 83-751, 68 Stat. 1044 (1954).

[22] Parole is a procedure whereby an individual is physically permitted by immigration officials to enter the country but is not admitted (as that term is defined in INA §101(a)(13)) in any immigrant or nonimmigrant status. It is an action generally taken for humanitarian or public interest reasons where the individual does not have a proper visa or entry document, or is otherwise inadmissible, but where there are urgent reasons for permitting the person to enter. *See* INA §212(d)(5).

[23] Immigration and Nationality Act Amendments of Oct. 3, 1965, 79 Statutes-at-Large 911.

One year later, in 1966, the Cuban Adjustment Act[24] was passed to provide for the legalization of Cubans fleeing Cuba one year after their arrival to the United States.

Abolition of Hemisphere Distinctions: 1970s

There was no major restrictive legislation passed during the 1970s. The significant changes in the law had to do with the visa issuance policies of the United States. In 1970, the nonimmigrant classifications were expanded to include fiancé(e)s and intra-company transferees.[25] In 1975, Congress approved the Indo-Chinese Refugee Resettlement Program, which provided for the parole and adjustment of status of refugees from Indo-China.[26]

The following year, Congress abolished the distinction between the hemispheres and applied the preference system as well as the 20,000 per country visa limit to the western hemisphere.[27] The word "preference" refers to categories of family members and employment-based applicants eligible to seek immigrant status.[28] The quota for the eastern and western hemispheres was combined for a total world-wide quota of 290,000 in 1978.[29]

The Refugee Act: 1980

The Refugee Act of 1980[30] was the first major piece of legislation establishing a procedure for asylees and refugees to legalize their status within the United States. Congress adopted as part of U.S. law the international definition of refugee found in the 1951 Convention Relating to the Status of Refugees.[31] The statute provides for the legalization of refugees overseas as well as the processing of asylum applicants within the United States or at the border of the United States. Ultimately, the law provided for adjustment of status to lawful permanent resident (LPR) for asylees and refugees. This statute added to the overall worldwide visa quota an additional 50,000 visas for refugees. Five thousand of these visas were reserved for asylum applicants.[32]

---

[24] Act of Nov. 2, 1966, 80 Statutes-at-Large 1161.

[25] Act of Apr. 7, 1970, 84 Statutes-at-Large 116.

[26] Indochina Migration and Refugee Assistance Act of May 23, 1975, 89 Statutes-at-Large 87.

[27] Immigration and Nationality Act Amendments of Oct. 20, 1976, 90 Statutes-at-Large 2703.

[28] *See* INA §§203(a) and (b) for family- and employment-based preferences.

[29] Act of Oct. 5, 1978, 92 Statutes-at-Large 907.

[30] Refugee Act of Mar. 17, 1980, 94 Statutes-at-Large 102.

[31] The 1951 Convention Relating to the Status of Refugees, July 28, 1951, 189 U.N.T.S. 150 (entered into force Apr. 22, 1954).

[32] T. David Parish, "Membership in a Particular Social Group Under the Refugee Act of 1980, Social Identity and the Legal Concept of the Refugee," 92 *Columbia Law Review* 923, 935 (May 1992).

ADAA, IRCA, and IMFA: 1986

1986 saw massive chances in the immigration laws. The most extensive of these changes was the Immigration Reform and Control Act (IRCA).[33] This law provided for a general legalization of individuals who had been present in the United States since prior to 1982. In addition, the law set out a process of legalization for "special agricultural workers" who had worked for brief periods of time in agriculture during 1985 and 1986. Approximately 3 million people legalized status under this law. However, IRCA also provided for "employer sanctions," whereby employers could be sanctioned with civil penalties for the unlawful employment of aliens as well as the failure to properly complete the necessary paperwork for verification of employment authorization status. This law established a visa waiver program (which allows nationals of certain countries to enter without a visa for short timeframes) and changed the date of "registry" from January 1, 1948, to January 1, 1972.[34] Registry is a program whereby individuals who have lived in the United States for long periods of time may adjust status to lawful permanent residence provided they are not inadmissible as criminals, subversives, smugglers, procurers, immoral persons, for lack of good moral character, or because they have violated the narcotics laws.[35]

The Anti-Drug Abuse Act (ADAA) of 1986[36] defined drug offenses as grounds of excludability and deportability. This law also provided that grounds of removability based on controlled substances would be given retroactive effect. Two years later, the omnibus Anti-Drug Abuse Act of 1988 provided for the first definition of "aggravated felony."[37] This included drug trafficking crimes as well as trafficking in weapons and murder. A new ground of deportability was added based on convictions for aggravated felonies.

For a last immigration law change in 1986, Congress passed the Immigration and Marriage Fraud Amendments (IMFA).[38] IMFA established conditional residence for individuals who had been married less than two years at the time of their adjustment of status or their consulate appointment for their immigrant visa. The law also created waivers for the removal of conditional residence. Additionally, IMFA contains bars to adjustment of status for those who entered into marriage seeking lawful status during deportation proceedings.

Liberalization Followed by Later Restrictions—IMMACT, AEDPA, IIRAIRA: 1990s

The 1990s started with the liberalization of immigration laws. The Lautenberg Amendment of 1990 granted the opportunity for nationals of the former Soviet Union

---

[33] Immigration Reform and Control Act of 1986, Pub. L. No. 99-603, 100 Stat. 3359 (partially codified in scattered sections of the INA).

[34] For more information on the Visa Waiver Program, see INA §217(a) *et seq.*

[35] INA §249.

[36] Pub. L. No. 99-570.

[37] Pub. L. No. 100-690.

[38] Immigration Marriage Fraud Act of 1986, Pub. L. No. 99-639, 100 Stat. 3537 (IMFA).

to adjust status in the United States.[39] The Immigration Act of 1990 (IMMACT90)[40] increased the number of immigrant visas for both family- and employment-based categories. Congress also enacted a diversity, or "lottery," visa system creating 55,000 new visas for immigrants from under-represented countries. The law further contained family unity provisions for children and spouses of principal aliens granted permanent residence through the legalization program. It also made available 10,000 immigrant visas for investors and provided for temporary protected status (TPS) for individuals victimized by civil unrest or natural disasters. On the enforcement end, IMMACT90 created two new grounds of aggravated felonies for "crimes of violence" (as defined pursuant to 18 USC §16) and money laundering offenses.

The Chinese Student Protection Act enabled Chinese persons who had entered the country before April 11, 1990, to adjust status.[41] The North American Free Trade Agreement of 1993 provided for the admission of Mexican and Canadian citizens along with their spouses and children under a Trade NAFTA (TN) visa.[42]

The Violence Against Women Act (VAWA) was enacted in 1994 to provide both protection to and a means to legalize status for battered spouses and children of U.S. citizens and LPRs.[43] This law allows victims of abuse at the hands of U.S. citizens or LPR spouses or parents to self petition and obtain lawful status.

The same year, Congress enacted the first of several pieces of legislation that tighten immigration laws. The Immigration and Nationality Technical Corrections Act of 1994 expanded the aggravated felony definition and provided for expedited removal of aggravated felons ineligible for release.[44]

In 1996, Congress enacted the Antiterrorism and Effective Death Penalty Act (AEDPA),[45] which created strict limitations on relief for criminal aliens. Specifically, it removed eligibility for relief under (former) INA §212(c) for most aliens convicted of crimes. The then-Attorney General (AG) interpreted AEDPA retroactively so that convictions prior to the April 24, 1996, enactment date also barred §212(c) relief. The U.S. Supreme Court later found that AEDPA only barred relief for those who pleaded guilty to the offense after AEDPA's date of enactment, or had been convicted in a trial prior to, or subsequent to, the date of enactment.[46]

---

[39] Section 599E of the Foreign Operations, Export Financing, and Related Programs Appropriations Act, 1990, Pub. L. No. 101-167.

[40] Immigration Act of 1990, Pub. L. No. 101-649, 104 Stat. 4978.

[41] Chinese Student Protection Act of Oct. 9, 1992, 106 Statutes-at-Large 1969.

[42] Pub. L. No. 103-182.

[43] Violence Against Women Act of 1994, Pub. L. No. 103-322, 108 Stat. 1902-1955 (codified as 8 USC §§1151, 1154, 1186a note, 1254, 2245).

[44] Immigration and Nationality Technical Corrections Act of 1994, Pub. L. No. 103-416, 108 Stat. 4305 (INTCA).

[45] Antiterrorism and Effective Death Penalty Act of 1996, Pub. L. No. 104-132, 110 Stat. 1214 (AEDPA).

[46] *INS v. St. Cyr*, 533 U.S. 289 (2001).

That same year, Congress enacted the Personal Responsibility and Work Opportunity Reconciliation Act, which limited eligibility for federal public benefits for LPRs.[47]

By far the most restrictive piece of legislation passed was the Illegal Immigrant Reform and Immigrant Responsibility Act of 1996 (IIRAIRA).[48] This law greatly expanded the definition of aggravated felonies to include most crimes. Also, Congress created a much broader definition of the term "conviction" for immigration purposes. IIRAIRA created new procedures for removal, whereby immigrants could be removed without hearings before an immigration judge (IJ). These expedited removal provisions provided for the immediate detention and return of individuals attempting to enter the United States who were not LPRs, asylees, or refugees, and it provided for "administrative" removal without a hearing of non–LPRs who had aggravated felony convictions.

IIRAIRA eliminated many forms of relief for individuals convicted of aggravated felonies, including the elimination of cancellation of removal, asylum, and certain waivers for LPRs. It created new bars for immigrants seeking to legalize their status, including a new unlawful presence bar for individuals who had been illegally present in the United States for 180 days or more. IIRAIRA limited judicial review for appeals of deportation orders based on criminal convictions and petition denials based on discretionary relief. It created mandatory detention provisions for most aliens convicted of crimes. The law added new grounds of removability for domestic violence crimes and crimes against children. And, it made those with false claims to citizenship ineligible for relief.

The USA PATRIOT Act of 2001: New Millennium USA

After the bombing of the World Trade Center on September 11, 2001, Congress immediately enacted the USA PATRIOT Act.[49] This law, in addition to greatly increasing the number of border patrol agents and Immigration and Naturalization Service (INS) personnel on the northern border, requires INS (now the Department of Homeland Security (DHS)) to develop a system for the identification of persons applying for visas or entering the country. It created new security-based grounds for exclusion and deportation. Individuals who solicit funds or support organizations that have a terrorist nature, or that they should know are terrorist organizations, are to be declared inadmissible under this statute. The law also allows the AG to detain an individual for seven days before deciding whether to charge him or her as a terrorist if there is reason to believe that the person has engaged in terrorist activity. Once charged as a terrorist, the person can be detained indefinitely. The USA PATRIOT Act provides for the sharing

---

[47] Personal Responsibility and Work Opportunity Reconciliation Act of Aug. 22, 1996, 110 Statutes-at-Large 2105 (part of Welfare Reform Act of 1996).

[48] Illegal Immigration Reform and Immigrant Responsibility Act of 1996, Division C of the Omnibus Appropriations Act of 1996 (H.R. 3610), Pub. L. No. 104-208, 110 Stat. 3009.

[49] Uniting and Strengthening America by Providing Appropriate Tools Required to Intercept and Obstruct Terrorism Act of 2001, Pub. L. No. 107-56, 115 Stat. 272.

of information between the U.S. government and foreign governments. Last, the definition of terrorism is expanded to include groups whose public endorsement of terrorism impedes U.S. efforts to reduce or eliminate terrorism.

Departments and Agencies

Department of Homeland Security (DHS)

Since 2003, DHS has helmed the responsibilities of the former INS in administering the immigration laws. The enforcement and services functions of INS are divided among three different agencies within DHS: U.S. Citizenship and Immigration Services (USCIS), U.S. Immigrations and Customs Enforcement (ICE), and U.S. Customs and Border Patrol (CBP).

USCIS handles all applications for benefits (immigrant and nonimmigrant), including: family- and employment-based petitions; changes of nonimmigrant status; asylum and refugee processing; citizenship; special status programs; document issuance; and renewal.

ICE is responsible for investigation (primarily in the interior United States) and enforcement of the immigration laws. It coordinates with other departments and agencies to combat smuggling; human trafficking; drug trafficking; crimes against children; immigration fraud; weapons trafficking; and other immigration and criminal violations. This agency also handles the detention and removal of aliens. In addition, immigration litigation falls within ICE's jurisdiction.

The function of CBP is to handle enforcement at the border; the agency consists of U.S. Customs; the Animal, Plant, and Health Inspection Service; Border Patrol; and other elements of the former INS. CBP is responsible for determining the admissibility of arriving aliens at border and interior inspection points, such as airports and seaports.

Department of Justice (DOJ)

DOJ maintains jurisdiction over several facets of immigration law enforcement. The immigration court system is directed by the AG through the Executive Office for Immigration Review (EOIR). EOIR was created in 1983, and although both it and former INS were overseen by DOJ, EOIR was its own separate unit. EOIR contains the Office of the Chief Immigration Judge, the Office of the Chief Administrative Hearing Officer, and the BIA.

Office of the Chief Immigration Judge

This office supervises more than 200 IJs at the immigration courts throughout the country. These courts are charged with the responsibility of adjudicating immigration cases involving individuals charged with removability. The courts determine issues of removability as well as relief from removal.

Board of Immigration Appeals (BIA)

This is an 11-member body that adjudicates appeals of decisions made by IJs and certain directors of DHS offices. In addition, the BIA determines whether organizations and individuals will be accredited to represent clients before the BIA, the immigration courts, or DHS.[50] The powers of the BIA are outlined in the regulations.[51]

Office of Chief Administrative Hearing Officer (OCAHO)

This office was created in 1986 at the time of the implementation of the employer sanctions laws. These judges hear cases involving charges against employers for violations of the employer sanctions laws (employment of unauthorized aliens) or failure to follow the employment verification requirements. The office also handles document fraud charges.

Office of Special Counsel (OSC)

The Office of Special Counsel for immigration-related unfair employment practices (OSC) is responsible for addressing charges of immigration-related unfair employment practices. It is part of DOJ.

Office of Immigration Litigation (OIL)

The OIL has jurisdiction over litigation of civil immigration matters before the federal district courts and circuit courts of appeal on behalf of the government. Also, it provides legal support to federal agencies that are involved in the admission, regulation, or removal of aliens under the immigration laws.

Department of State (DOS)

DOS has several agencies and bureaus that are responsible for immigration issues. The Bureau of Consular Affairs adjudicates temporary and permanent visa applications for individuals outside the United States seeking admission. The consular officers review visa applications and determine if the individual qualifies for the visa or is barred based on one of the INA §212(a) grounds of inadmissibility. The consular office issues the monthly "Visa Bulletin" showing immigrant visa availability.

DOS, through the Passport Services Office, provides information on passports and adjudicates first-time applications and renewal of passports. The National Visa Center, located in New Hampshire, processes all immigrant visa petitions that are to be sent overseas to the DOS consular officers for adjudication of the immigrant visa. USCIS adjudicates visa applications then sends them to the National Visa Center, which then forwards the visa packet to the consulate when the immigrant visa priority date is about to become current.

Finally, the Bureau of Democracy, Human Rights and Labor prepares the yearly *State Department County Reports on Human Rights Practices*. These reports are ex-

---

[50] 8 CFR §§292.2, 1292.2.

[51] 8 CFR §1003.1(d).

tremely important to the asylum officers and IJs in their adjudication of asylum claims. Additionally, all applications for asylum are forwarded to DOS, which may provide an opinion letter or general information on country conditions that can impact the strength or validity of the asylum application.

Department of Health and Human Services (HHS)

The Center for Disease Control (CDC) provides DOS and USCIS with guidelines for the use of all government-certified physicians and clinics in the screening of aliens for communicable diseases and verification of compliance with the vaccination requirements. A medical examination is required of all immigrants and refugees applying for an immigrant visa or adjustment of status. These guidelines are developed in accordance with the ground of inadmissibility for health-related reasons of INA §212(a)(1). CDC also adjudicates waivers of this ground of inadmissibility.

Department of Labor (DOL)

DOL's Employment Training Administration (ETA) is responsible for overseeing the alien labor certification process. In short, this agency is charged with the responsibility of working with the state employment offices to verify that aliens seeking skilled or unskilled labor in the United States are certified by DOL and are not negatively impacting job opportunities for U.S. workers (which include LPRs). In addition, ETA is responsible for the labor condition application (LCA)—a verification from an employer seeking a temporary work visa for an alien worker that the worker will be paid the prevailing wage, and that the employment of this alien will not negatively impact job opportunities for U.S. workers or be used for purposes of a lockout or to break a strike.

Basic Terminology Used in Removal Cases

The enforcement sections of the INA have become over the years an entangled jumble of poorly drafted laws. In order to even attempt to understand the enforcement portions of the INA, there are a few basic concepts that must be comprehended; they are the concepts of excludability (a/k/a inadmissibility), deportability, removability, and admission.

Immigrant and Nonimmigrant

The term "immigrant" means every alien except an alien who is within one of the nonimmigrant categories found at INA §101(a)(15).[52] It generally refers to individuals who are coming to the United States to stay on a permanent basis. The classes of those eligible to seek "immigrant" visas are defined at INA §§101(b)[53] and 203.[54] The

---

52 INA §101(a)(15).

53 Defining immediate relatives, special immigrants, and other groups not subject to numerical limitations.

54 Defining family, employment, and diversity visa classifications that are restricted by numerical limitations.

term "nonimmigrant" means an individual entering the United States (generally with a visa with an exception for those coming on the Visa Waiver Program) for a temporary period and entering for a specific activity that is in accord with the purpose of the visa, *e.g.*, tourists and students. The INA lists all of the various classes of nonimmigrant visa classifications.[55]

Inadmissibility/Excludability

In order for an individual to be admitted to the United States or granted LPR status once within the United States (*i.e.*, adjustment of status), the individual must be admissible. In other words, he or she must not be excludable. The grounds of inadmissibility are found at INA §212(a). These grounds of inadmissibility apply to individuals seeking to be granted a visa at a consulate; admitted at a port of inspection or airport; or legally admitted to LPR status if they already have entered the United States. There are 10 separate grounds of inadmissibility listed under §212(a); they fall within five general categories: health grounds; crimes; security; immigration; and economic grounds. An individual can be denied admission if he or she is barred under any one of these grounds of inadmissibility and does not qualify for a waiver. That is, he or she can be stopped at the border or the airport and refused admission or denied a visa at the American consulate overseas. The individual also can be denied adjustment of status at the interview with DHS if he or she is barred under one of these grounds of inadmissibility.

Deportability and Removability

Prior to 1996 and the implementation of IIRAIRA, individuals who already had entered the United States and were sought to be removed by INS, were charged with grounds of deportability. These grounds of deportability were separate and apart from the grounds of inadmissibility found in INA §212(a). Prior to 1996, the grounds of deportability were found under former INA §241, "General Classes of Deportable Aliens."

In 1996, Congress passed IIRAIRA and dropped the term deportability. In its place, Congress established grounds of "removability," which are found at INA §237. While Congress dropped the term "deportability" for all individuals placed into proceedings after the enactment of IIRAIRA, it forgot to change the title of that section; thus, §237 is still listed as "Classes of Deportable Aliens." These classifications are generally broken down into the following categories: immigration violations (including overstays, individuals present without lawful inspection, and smugglers); criminal grounds (including crimes involving moral turpitude, aggravated felonies, controlled substance violations, weapon offenses, domestic violence, and crimes against children); security grounds; false claims to citizenship and unlawful voting charges; public charge grounds; and charges relating to failure to register or falsification of documents.

---

[55] INA §101(a)(15).

Under INA §237, an individual can be removed from the United States even if he or she has been previously "admitted" if at the time of his or her admission, the individual was not authorized to be admitted. Thus, for individuals who were inspected and admitted by DHS, the government can later remove that person if at the time of the admission the individual committed fraud or was otherwise not authorized to be admitted.[56]

Deeming all proceedings (whether based on inadmissibility grounds or deportability/removability grounds) "removal proceedings" results in confusion. Individuals who have been "admitted," as that term is defined in INA §101(a)(13), are charged with grounds of removability under §237(a). Individuals who have never been admitted are charged with grounds of inadmissibility under §212(a). The determinative factor in whether an individual is charged with grounds of inadmissibility or grounds of removability is whether that individual has been "admitted" per INA §212.

Admission

Removal proceedings revolve around the issue of admission. The section of the INA under which an individual is charged (§212(a) or §237(a)) depends on whether one has been admitted. Certain grounds of removability depend on the date of "admission" (*e.g.*, crimes involving moral turpitude (CIMT) under INA §237(a)(2)(A)(i)). For instance, a CIMT committed "within five years after the date of "admission" may make one removable. In addition, certain forms of relief are dependent on the date of admission as an LPR (*e.g.*, cancellation of removal under INA §240A(a)).

"Admission" is defined at INA §101(a)(13)(A). It is "the lawful entry of an alien into the United States after inspection and authorization by an immigration officer." The LPR who returns to the United States after a temporary departure is not seeking new admission unless he or she:

- has abandoned or relinquished LPR status;
- has been absent from the United States for a continuous period of over 180 days;
- has engaged in illegal activity after departing the United States;
- departs during removal proceedings;
- committed an offense making him or her inadmissible under §212(a);
- is attempting to enter at a place other than a point of entry; or
- has entered without inspection.[57]

The BIA has found that the term "admission" also includes "adjustment of status" under INA §245.[58]

---

[56] INA §237(a)(1).

[57] *See* INA §101(a)(13)(C).

[58] *Matter of Shanu*, 23 I&N Dec. 754 (BIA 2005).

Notice to Appear (NTA)

The NTA is the charging document that commences removal proceedings.[59] The contents of this document and the manner of service will be discussed in Chapter 4. However, at a minimum, this document does the following:

- states the factual allegations for which the person is charged with removability;
- indicates the section of law allegedly violated;
- gives the date and time of the hearing;
- advises the individual of certain rights, including the right to counsel at no expense to the government;
- notifies the alien of his or her obligation regarding change of address and the consequences for failing to appear for a hearing.

There are numerous other terms considered terms of art in the immigration context. They will be explained as they appear in the chapters that follow.

---

[59] INA §239(a).

CHAPTER 2

GROUNDS OF DEPORTABILITY

***Note*: This chapter deals with grounds of removability/deportability. Prior to IIRAIRA, the procedure for expelling an alien who was already admitted to the United States was termed "deportability." With IIRAIRA, the term changed to "removability." However, "removability" also is the name of any proceeding whereby the Department of Homeland Security (DHS) petitions an immigration court to oust an individual based on either inadmissibility or "deportability" grounds. Moreover, the INA maintains the term "deportability" instead of "removability." Thus, to remain consistent with the INA and to avoid confusion between the two uses of "removability," this chapter refers to grounds on which the government can expel an individual already admitted as grounds of *deportability*.

Immigration Violations

Introduction

The grounds of deportability based on immigration violations are outlined at Immigration and Nationality Act (INA)[1] §237(a)(1) ("Inadmissible at time of entry or of adjustment of status or violates status"). These differ from the grounds of inadmissibility under INA §212(a)(6) in that there has been an "admission." In order for an individual to be charged with a ground of deportability under §237(a), there must be an admission of the individual to the United States as defined in INA §101(a)(13). Those who have not been admitted and are alleged to have violated the immigration laws are charged under INA §§212(a)(6) or (7). Following is a summary of the various grounds of deportability related to violations of immigration laws.

[1] Immigration and Nationality Act of 1952 (INA), Pub. L. No. 82-414, 66 Stat. 163 (codified as amended at 8 USC §§1101 *et seq.*).

Inadmissible Aliens

Any individual who falls within any ground of inadmissibility under INA §212(a) is deportable. This section of the law both incorporates all of the grounds of inadmissibility and makes an individual deportable if at the time of admission or adjustment of status, he or she was in fact inadmissible based on any of the grounds of inadmissibility under §212(a).

For example, if an individual is admitted to the United States or is granted adjustment of status based on a fraudulent statement or willful misrepresentation of material fact, that individual can be found deportable based on the fact that he or she was actually inadmissible at the time of admission or adjustment but for the fraud or misrepresentation.[2] The statute makes no distinction between grounds of inadmissibility. It states merely that an individual is deportable if he or she was "within one or more of the classes of aliens inadmissible" at the time of entry or adjustment.[3] Thus, individuals who gained admission through fraud under INA §212(a)(6)(C), or were admitted without proper documentation under INA §212(a)(7) and no fraud was involved, are inadmissible under the strict wording of the statute in that both are "within one or more of the classes of aliens inadmissible" at the time of entry or adjustment of status. The government can reach back to the point in time at which the individual was admitted, or granted adjustment of status, and find that person to be deportable based on the mistake or the fraud committed at the time the individual was given the benefit, no matter how much time has passed.[4]

The misrepresentation scenario has appeared in cases where the individual was inadmissible due to a medical condition. Those who are medically inadmissible but succeed in being admitted by hiding or misrepresenting the medical ground of inadmissibility are deportable as individuals who were inadmissible at the time of entry.[5]

In a similar situation, an alien has been found deportable as an individual inadmissible at the time of entry after he entered the United Status seeking to perform skilled or unskilled labor without a valid labor certification, although he had a labor certification for a different job at which he never worked.[6] In that case, the government was not required to prove fraud or misrepresentation—it needed only to prove the fact that the alien was admitted to perform certain work with a valid labor certification but worked at different labor for which he had no certification, thus making him inadmissible by violating INA §212(a)(5).[7]

---

[2] *See* INA §212(a)(6)(C)—an individual who has gained admission "by fraud or willfully misrepresenting a material fact."

[3] *See* INA §237(a)(1)(A).

[4] *Matter of Y*, 8 I&N Dec. 143 (BIA 1958) (an individual who gains admission by fraud is deportable).

[5] *In re La Rochelle*, 11 I&N Dec. 436 (BIA 1965); *Matter of Longstaff*, 716 F. 2d 1439 (5th Cir. 1983) (an individual who gains lawful permanent resident status by hiding a medical ground of inadmissibility is not a "lawful" permanent resident).

[6] *Spyropoulos v. INS*, 591 F.2d 1 (1st Cir. 1978).

[7] *Id.* at 4.

Present in Violation of Law

INA §237(a)(1)(B) makes an individual deportable if that person is present in the United States in violation of the immigration laws "or any other law of the United States."[8] This is a very broad statute making an individual subject to deportation if he or she is present in violation of virtually any of the immigration statutes. For example, an individual is present in violation of law where his or her authorized stay under a nonimmigrant visa has expired even where there is an extension request pending, unless and until that extension request is approved. The fact that an extension request is pending before U.S. Citizenship and Immigration Services (USCIS) does not legalize one's status before the immigration court.[9] For the government to meet its burden, it need only prove that the individual was admitted for a temporary period and that the period has expired.[10] Due to §237(a)(1)(B)'s breadth, a nonimmigrant is *present in violation of law* upon the expiration of his or her temporary stay unless that stay has been timely extended.[11] Also, INA §237(a)(1)(B) specifically renders deportable an individual whose originally-granted visa has been revoked under INA §221(i).[12]

Violation of Nonimmigrant Status or Conditions of Entry

An individual is deportable even if lawfully admitted as a nonimmigrant "temporary visitor" if that person fails to maintain lawful nonimmigrant status. Noncompliance with the conditions of nonimmigrant status makes an individual deportable under INA §237(a)(1)(C)(i). Often, this involves individuals whose temporary status has expired or individuals who have taken some action that violates the conditions of their temporary status, *e.g.*, working without authorization. Also, as a student, failure to attend school as required after admission is a deportable offense.[13]

The second part of this statute[14] makes an individual deportable if he or she has failed to comply with conditions of a previous waiver under INA §212(g) regarding conditions of admission for persons with communicable diseases or physical or mental disorders.[15] An individual may be admitted even if inadmissible under the health-related grounds of INA §212(a)(1)(A) if a waiver is granted under INA §212(g). However, if the individual fails to comply with the conditions as stated in the waiver, that individual may become deportable pursuant to INA §237(a)(1)(C)(ii).

---

[8] INA §237(a)(1)(B).

[9] *Matter of Teberen*, 15 I&N Dec. 689 (BIA 1976).

[10] *Id.*

[11] *Detroit Free Press v. Ashcroft*, 303 F.3d 689 (6th Cir. 2002).

[12] INA §221(i) allows a consular officer in his or her discretion to revoke a visa or other documentation.

[13] *Farroki v. INS*, 900 F. 2d 697 (4th Cir. 1990).

[14] INA §237(a)(1)(C)(ii).

[15] *Id.*

Termination of Conditional Permanent Residence

Conditional permanent residence is granted in two situations. First, under INA §216(a), an individual who has gained lawful permanent resident (LPR) status based on a marriage that was entered into "less than 24 months before the date the alien obtains such status by virtue of such marriage" is granted "conditional permanent resident" status.[16] The son or daughter of a conditional permanent resident who is given lawful status in the United States also is subject to the same "conditional" status.[17]

Second, INA §216A provides for a two-year conditional permanent resident status for "alien entrepreneurs."[18] These are individuals, along with their spouses and children, who obtain LPR status under the investor provisions of INA §203(b)(5). In both the marriage and entrepreneur situations, the alien must petition for removal or waiver of the conditional status.[19]

Conditional Residence—Marriage

Individuals who have been granted "conditional" permanent residence under INA §216(a) (via marriage) are deportable upon the termination of the conditional permanent residence. "Termination" of conditional resident status under INA §212(b) is distinguished from "removal" of conditional residence under INA §216(c). "Removal" of conditional resident status means that the alien has fulfilled the requirement of the law by filing the proper application (Form I-751) and supporting documentation with USCIS and appeared for any scheduled interviews, showing that either: (a) he or she has remained married in a bona fide marriage for the required two-year period,[20] or (b) he or she qualifies for a waiver of this requirement on the basis of extreme hardship, battery or extreme cruelty, or a good faith marriage that was terminated through no fault of the alien.[21] The Form I-751 and supporting documentation for removal of conditional resident status are to be filed with USCIS during the 90-day period preceding the second anniversary of the grant of conditional resident status.[22] The regulations state that the "Service should notify the alien" of the requirement to file the request for removal of the conditional basis for residence and that this notice "should" be given "approximately 90 days before the second anniversary of the date on which the alien obtained conditional resident status."[23] After filing the petition for removal of conditional basis of permanent residence, an interview may be scheduled; however, the interview may be waived by the government if it is satisfied that the marriage was not

---

[16] INA §§216(a) and 216(g)(1).

[17] INA §216(g)(2).

[18] INA §216A(c).

[19] *See* INA §§216(c)(1) and (4). *See also* INA §216A(c).

[20] INA §216(c)(3)(B).

[21] INA §216(c)(4).

[22] 8 CFR §§216.4(a)(1), 1216.4(a)(1).

[23] 8 CFR §§216.2(b), 1216.2(b).

entered into for purposes of evading the immigration laws.[24] With or without an interview, the applicant must show that the marriage was not entered into to evade the immigration laws and documentation must be submitted as proof.[25]

The application for "waiver" of the conditional basis for permanent residence is also filed on Form I-751 and documentation should be submitted to prove that the alien falls within one of the three protected groups—extreme hardship, domestic abuse, or good faith marriage. Neither the INA nor the regulations specifically mentions the 90-day filing window for applications to waive the conditional basis for permanent residence (as is mentioned in the application for removal of the conditional basis). However, the waiver should be filed as soon as the alien realizes that the requirements for removing the conditional basis for permanent residence cannot be met and the alien meets the qualifications for the waiver. The regulations state that an individual in deportation, exclusion, or removal proceedings may apply for the waiver in proceedings "only until such time as there is a final order of exclusion, deportation or removal."[26] Upon filing the waiver of conditional basis for permanent resident status with the USCIS service center, the director of the service center "may refer the application to the appropriate local office and require that the alien appear for an interview in connection with the application for a waiver."[27]

Upon proof of eligibility for the removal or waiver of the conditional basis for lawful resident status, the two-year condition is removed and lawful resident status is made permanent without conditions (unless the alien takes some action that makes him or her deportable, *e.g.*, crime). A denial of the application for waiver or removal of conditional basis for permanent resident status results in the issuance of a Notice to Appear (NTA) and the commencement of removal proceedings where the charge under INA §237(a)(1)(D) is made.[28]

"Termination" of conditional resident status means the "Attorney General (AG)" (now referring also to USCIS, which handles conditional resident applications) may terminate such status upon a determination prior to the second anniversary of obtaining such status that the marriage was (a) entered into for the purpose of securing admission into the United States; (b) judicially annulled or terminated other than through the death of the spouse; or (c) a fee or other consideration was given for the filing of the petition (other than for legal services to an attorney for assisting in preparing the application).[29]

The termination process involves notice to the alien that such status is to be terminated if the USCIS "director" determines that any of these conditions are true during the two-year period of conditional resident status.[30] Likewise, the failure to timely file

---

[24] 8 CFR §§216.4(b), 1216.4(b).

[25] 8 CFR §§216.4(a)(5), 1216.4(a)(5).

[26] 8 CFR §§216.5(a)(2), 1216.5(a)(2).

[27] 8 CFR §§216.5(d), 1216.5(d).

[28] 8 CFR §§216.4(d)(2) and 216.5(f), 1216.4(d)(2) and 1216.5(f).

[29] INA §216(b)(1).

[30] 8 CFR §§216.3(a), 1216.3(a).

the application for removal or waiver of conditional permanent resident status will result in a termination of the status.[31] The alien has the right to request review of the termination of conditional resident status before an immigration judge (IJ) in a removal proceeding.[32] In such proceeding, the government has to prove by a preponderance of the evidence that the status should be terminated.[33] If a determination is made after the removal of the conditional basis for permanent residence that it was obtained by fraud, rescission proceedings under INA §246 may be commenced.[34]

Conditional Residence—Entrepreneurs

Entrepreneurs under INA §216A (relating to those individuals who acquire lawful resident status under INA §203(b)(5) based on investments in new commercial enterprises) also are subject to the two-year conditional resident requirement. The removal and termination issues are similar, in that that the conditional resident must file the application form (I-829) with the appropriate fee and supporting documentation during the 90-day period immediately preceding the second anniversary of the grant of conditional resident status.[35]

Failure to do so results in termination of the conditional resident status unless the applicant can show that the failure was for "good cause and due to extenuating circumstances."[36] If the documentation is sufficient, the interview may be waived, the petition approved, and the condition removed.[37] The decision must be made on the petition within 90 days of the filing. If the removal petition is denied, USCIS provides a written notice to the alien and resident status is terminated.[38] The alien may seek review of the decision in removal proceedings.[39] There is no waiver in the statute or regulations of the conditional basis (for hardship, good faith, etc.) in the entrepreneur situation as there is in marriage cases.

Smuggling

An alien who has knowingly encouraged, induced, assisted, abetted, or aided any alien to enter or try to enter the United States is deportable. An individual is deportable if he or she has taken such action prior to the date of his or her own entry, at the time of his or her own entry, or within five years of the date of any entry into the United States.[40] Other smuggling-related offenses such as transporting aliens or har-

---

[31] 8 CFR §§216.4(a)(6), 1216.4(a)(6).

[32] INA §216(b)(2).

[33] *Id.*

[34] 8 CFR §§216.3(b), 1216.3(b).

[35] 8 CFR §§216.6(a)(1), 1216.6(a)(1). See 8 CFR §§216.6(a)(4), 1216.6(a)(4) for required documentation.

[36] 8 CFR §§216.6(a)(5), 1216.6(a)(5).

[37] 8 CFR §§216.6(b)(1), 1216.6(b)(1).

[38] 8 CFR §§216.6(c), 1216.6(c).

[39] 8 CFR §§216.6(d), 1216.6(d).

[40] INA §237(a)(1)(E)(i).

boring aliens under INA §274(a) are not deportable offenses pursuant to this section of the INA.[41]

The §237(a)(1)(E) ground of deportability does not apply in certain family reunification situations. The following are not deportable under this ground:

- spouses or unmarried children of principal aliens who were granted legalization under the Immigration Reform and Control Act of 1986 (IRCA);[42] and
- who were physically present in the United States as of May 5, 1988; and
- who are seeking: (1) admission as immediate relatives or second preference beneficiaries of the petition filed by the principal alien; or (2) family unity benefits under Section 301 of the Immigration Act of 1990 (IMMACT90);[43] and
- who have attempted to smuggle a spouse, parent, son, or daughter, and no other individual prior to May 5, 1988.[44]

In addition, there is a waiver of this ground of deportation for LPRs under the following conditions: (a) the LPR has encouraged, induced, assisted, abetted, or aided only an individual who was a spouse, parent, son, or daughter to enter the United States; and (b) that relationship existed at the time of the smuggling offense.[45] This waiver may be sought in cases where an LPR is deportable under this ground for smuggling the family members cited above on *or after* May 5, 1988.

Marriage Fraud

An individual is deportable for having procured a visa or other documentation by fraud under INA §212(a)(6)(C)(i) when the following conditions are met:

(1) the individual obtains any admission into the United States with an immigrant visa or other documentation procured on the basis of a marriage; and

(2) that marriage was entered into less than two years prior to the date of such admission of the alien; and

(3) within two years subsequent to the date of the admission, the alien has the marriage annulled or terminated, unless the alien establishes that such marriage was not contracted for the purpose of evading the immigration laws.[46]

---

[41] However, under INA §101(a)(43)(N), other crimes related to smuggling, such as transporting aliens, have been found to be aggravated felonies and therefore a basis for deportability under INA §237(a)(2)(A)(iii). *See Matter of Ruiz-Romero*, 22 I&N Dec. 486 (BIA 1999).

[42] Immigration Reform and Control Act of 1986, Pub. L. No. 99-603, 100 Stat. 3359 (partially codified in scattered sections of the INA).

[43] Immigration Act of 1990, Pub. L. No. 101-649, 104 Stat. 4978.

[44] INA §237(a)(1)(E)(ii).

[45] *See* INA §237(a)(1)(E)(iii); prior to IIRAIRA's amendments, the Board of Immigration Appeals (BIA) interpreted the waiver to include spouses, sons, and daughters even if that relationship arose after the incident. *Matter of Farias-Mendoza*, 21 I&N Dec. 269 (BIA 1996).

[46] INA §237(a)(1)(G)(i).

Further, INA §237(a)(1)(G)(ii) makes an individual deportable under its marriage fraud provisions if it appears to the satisfaction of the AG that the individual has failed or refused to fulfill the marital agreement, which in the opinion of the AG was made for the purpose of gaining immigrant admission.

Other Noncriminal Grounds of Deportability

Failure to Register and Falsification of Documents—INA §237(a)(3)

This ground of deportation is based on four violations of the documentary and registration requirements to which aliens are subject: (1) failure to file change of address reports; (2) failure to register or falsification of documents; (3) document fraud; and (4) falsely claiming citizenship.

Change of address—INA §237(a)(3)(A)

INA §265 requires that each alien subject to mandatory registration "who is within the United States shall notify the Attorney General in writing of each change of address and new address within ten days from the date of such change and furnish with such notice such additional information as the Attorney General may require by regulation."[47] Registration regulations are found at 8 CFR §264.1, and the "AG" may discretionarily require the citizens of any foreign state, or any class or group from that state who are required to register, to notify the AG of their current address as well as any additional information the AG may require.

For example, the NSEERS[48] program (effective Aug. 12, 2002) required males 16 years and older from several countries (mainly from the Middle East, South Asia, and North Africa) to be fingerprinted and photographed at the time of entry into the United States. Individuals of "elevated national security concern" who remained in the country for more than 30 days had to register with the former Immigration and Naturalization Service (INS).

The program permits the Secretary of the Department of Homeland Security (DHS) to designate countries as special registration countries and require nationals of those countries to register with DHS upon entry into the United States and also after entry.[49] They may also be required to register upon departure from the United States.

The DHS Secretary, in consultation with the Secretary of State, may designate classes of nonimmigrants seeking admission as subject to special registration, finger-

---

[47] INA §265(a).

[48] NSEERS is the National Security Entry-Exit Registration System, 67 Fed. Reg. 52584–93 (effective Aug. 12, 2002). As part of the Uniting and Strengthening America by Providing Appropriate Tools Required to Intercept and Obstruct Terrorism Act of 2001, Pub. L. No. 107-56, 115 Stat. 272 (USA PATRIOT Act), certain foreign nationals from specific countries were required to be fingerprinted upon admission, photographed, and registered with INS.

[49] 8 CFR §§264.1(f)(2)(iii) and 264.1(f)(4)

printing, and photographing.[50] The DHS Secretary also may impose special registration, photographing, and fingerprinting requirements on individuals already present in the United States or individuals who are nationals, citizens, or residents (as compared to classes of individuals) of certain countries.[51] Under the regulations, those who fail to register without good cause face a presumption of inadmissibility under INA §212(a)(3)(A)(ii).[52] This may be overcome by a showing that there was good cause for the failure to register.[53]

Where a child or an incompetent must register, the obligation falls to the parent or legal guardian to provide notice of change of address and/or receive any notice to register from the AG.[54]

Failure to register or falsification of documents—INA §237(a)(3)(B)

An individual who has been convicted at any time of any of the following is deportable pursuant to INA §237(a)(3)(B):

Violation of INA §266(c)

Any alien who files a registration application with statements known to be false, or who procures, or attempts to procure, registration of him- or herself or another person by fraud is deportable. Any parent or legal guardian of an alien who takes any of the above actions on behalf of an alien child or others under his or her charge is liable under this statute (fine and/or imprisonment). In addition, anyone convicted under §36(c) of the Alien Registration Act[55] is deportable. Willful failure to file a change of address card[56] and/or comply with the alien regulation laws[57] is a deportable offense.

Violation of Foreign Agents Registration Act—22 USC §611

Conviction for violating, attempting, or conspiring to violate any section of this statute is a basis for deportability under INA §237(a)(3)(B)(ii). The purpose of 22 USC §611 is to identify foreign principals who might engage in subversive acts or in spreading foreign propaganda, and to require them to make public record of the nature of their employment.[58]

Visa fraud—18 USC §1546

Knowingly forging, counterfeiting, altering, or falsely making any temporary or permanent visa, permit, border crossing card, or other document prescribed for lawful

---

[50] 8 CFR §264.1(f)(1).

[51] 8 CFR §264.1(f)(4)(i).

[52] 8 CFR §264.1(f)(8)(ii).

[53] 8 CFR §264.1(f)(8)(iii).

[54] INA §265(c).

[55] Alien Registration Act of June 28, 1940, 54 Statutes-at-Large 670.

[56] *Patsis v. INS*, 337 F.2d 733 (8th Cir. 1964).

[57] *Matter of V–R–*, 9 I&N Dec. 340 (BIA 1961).

[58] *Viereck v. U.S.*, 318 U.S. 236 (1943).

entry into the country, or used as evidence of lawful stay or employment is a crime. In addition, uttering, using, possessing, obtaining, accepting, receiving, or attempting to use such documents with knowledge that the document is forged, counterfeited, altered, falsely made, or procured by fraud violates 18 USC §1546.[59]

Also, 18 USC §1546 makes it a crime to possess, use, engrave, or sell any plate in the likeness of a plate designed for printing permits, or to make any likeness of a visa or other document required for entry into the United States. Section 1546 of 18 USC criminalizes impersonating another, using the identity of a deceased person, and using a fictitious name. Selling a visa or other document to one not authorized to use it is a crime.[60]

The making of any false statement under oath or under penalty of perjury (under 28 USC §1746) with respect to a material fact in any application, affidavit, or other document required by the immigration laws or regulations is a crime under 18 USC §1546. Finally, use of a false or unlawful identity document or attestation for employment verification purposes under INA §274A(b) is another type of visa fraud crime.

Document fraud—INA §237(a)(3)(C)

INA §274C makes it a violation of law to forge, counterfeit, alter, or falsely make any document for the purpose of gaining a benefit under the immigration laws.[61] In addition, using or attempting to use, possessing, obtaining, accepting, receiving, or providing any such document to gain a benefit under the immigration laws is a violation.[62] An alien who is the subject of a final order for violation of the document fraud provisions of INA §274C is deportable.

The statute furthermore lists a series of actions relating to the usage, acceptance, preparation, filing, presentation, or attempts to do any of these, with relation to forged, counterfeited, false, or altered documentation. All such actions are violations of law.[63] The statute sets out a hearing procedure, separate and apart from INA §240's removal proceedings.[64] A final order by an administrative law judge that an individual has violated any of the document fraud provisions of INA §274C(a) makes that person deportable.[65] The regulations regarding procedures for document fraud hearings are at 28 CFR §68.1 *et seq*. The definition of the term "final order" and the contents of such an order are found at 28 CFR §68.52.

---

[59] 18 USC §1546(a).

[60] *Id.*

[61] INA §274C(a)(1).

[62] INA §274C(a)(2).

[63] INA §§274C(a)(3)–(6).

[64] INA §274C(d)(2).

[65] INA §237(a)(3)(C).

Waiver

Document fraud can be waived under the following conditions:

- the alien responsible for the offense is an LPR;
- no previous civil money penalty has been imposed; and
- the offense was incurred solely to assist and/or support the alien's spouse or child (and no other person).

Falsely claiming citizenship—INA §237(a)(3)(D)

Any alien who falsely represents, or has falsely represented, him- or herself to be a U.S. citizen for any benefit under the INA (including employment authorization) or any federal or state law is deportable. This section applies to false U.S. citizenship claims made on or after the date of enactment of IIRAIRA,[66] Sept. 30, 1996.[67]

Waiver

An individual making a false claim to citizenship is not deportable under INA §237(a)(3)(D) if:

- each parent (natural or adoptive) of the alien is or was a U.S. citizen whether by birth or naturalization;
- the alien permanently resided in the United States prior to turning the age of 16; and
- at the time of making the misrepresentation, the alien reasonably believed he or she was a U.S. citizen.[68]

Public Charge—INA §237(a)(5)

Any alien who within five years after the date of "entry" becomes a public charge from causes not affirmatively shown to have arisen since "entry" is deportable.[69] The public charge ground of inadmissibility under INA §212(a)(4) differs from this ground of deportability in that it is prospective in nature, *i.e.*, makes inadmissible individuals "likely" to become public charges, while the ground of deportability makes past receipt of public assistance a possible basis for removal.[70] However, the meaning of "public charge" is the same both for the ground of inadmissibility and the ground

---

[66] Illegal Immigration Reform and Immigrant Responsibility Act of 1996, Division C of the Omnibus Appropriations Act of 1996 (H.R. 3610), Pub. L. No. 104-208, 110 Stat. 3009 (IIRAIRA).

[67] *See* IIRAIRA §344(c).

[68] INA §237(a)(3)(C)(ii).

[69] This removal ground uses the term "entry," while most of the other grounds of removability are based on actions taken before, on , or after "admission," as defined at INA §101(a)(13).

[70] Receipt of Supplemental Security Income (SSI) constitutes receipt of public assistance and is sufficient to cause a breach of a public charge bond. *Matter of Viado*, 19 I&N Dec. 252 (BIA 1985).

of deportability.[71] The Board of Immigration Appeals (BIA) has defined the term "public charge" as involving the following elements:

- the state, by law, imposes a charge for the services, thereby creating a debt to be paid by the alien or other designated persons;
- the authorities have made a demand for payment; and
- there was a failure to pay.[72]

Hospitalization for a contagious disease at state expense, where medical care was financed by the state, is a basis for finding an individual deportable as a public charge.[73] However, an individual hospitalized in a state hospital who makes minimal payments, even if less than the cost to the taxpayer for the care, is not a public charge *if* payments are made as scheduled.[74]

In addition, INA §250 states that the AG may remove any alien "who falls into distress or who needs public aid from causes arising subsequent to entry, and is desirous of being so removed." Any such removal makes the individual ineligible to apply for a visa or admission without the prior approval of the AG.[75]

Unlawful Voters—INA §237(a)(6)

Voting in violation of any federal, state, or local constitutional provision, statute, ordinance, or regulation is a deportable offense. This applies to actions taken in violation of this provision after September 30, 1996, the date of enactment of IIRAIRA.[76] An individual is not deportable for voting unlawfully under this provision where the following conditions are present:

- each parent (natural or adoptive) is or was a U.S. citizen;
- the alien permanently resided in the United States prior to the age of 16; and
- the alien reasonably believed at the time of the violation that he or she was a U.S. citizen.[77]

Criminal Grounds—Determining Deportability

Introduction

The following section outlines the key issues affecting aliens charged with criminal violations. In determining what impact criminal activity will have on an alien,

---

[71] *Matter of Harutunian*, 14 I&N Dec. 583 (BIA 1964).

[72] *Id.* at 588; *see also Matter of B*, 3 I&N Dec. 323 (A.G. 1948).

[73] *Matter of Vallejos*, 14 I&N Dec. 68 (BIA 1972).

[74] *Matter of Kowalski*, 10 I&N Dec. 159 (BIA 1963).

[75] INA §250.

[76] *See* IIRAIRA §347(c).

[77] INA §237(a)(6)(A).

counsel must first determine the person's immigration situation. There are a few general rules (with exceptions, of course) for various classes of immigrants.

- *Individuals seeking lawful status, admission to the country, or some other benefit*—Such individuals may be denied if there is an admission or proof of criminal behavior (crimes relating to drugs, violence, moral turpitude, security, or immigration violations). An admission of criminal conduct or other evidence short of a conviction can be enough to deny an individual a visa or citizenship.
- *Individuals who are already here and facing deportation/removal*—In most cases, there must be a conviction to deport or remove an individual already in the United States. Most (but not all) criminal grounds of deportability require that DHS prove that a conviction exists. The exceptions are outlined below.

In assessing a case, the practitioner should first investigate the client's entire criminal history. Even incidents that took place many years ago are relevant. An immigration law practitioner's worst nightmare is to file for lawful status (a Green Card) or naturalization with DHS on behalf of a client, only to discover a 20-year-old conviction that negates eligibility for the benefit sought, and causes DHS to arrest, detain, and place the client in removal proceedings. The following questions should be addressed:

- *Conviction*—What is a "conviction" for immigration purposes? Is a "conviction" required in order to find the individual deportable, inadmissible, or ineligible for the benefit sought? Has the individual been "convicted" as that term is defined at INA §101(a)(48)?
- *Sentence/term of imprisonment*—If a conviction is required to prove deportability or inadmissibility, must there be a "sentence" or "term of imprisonment" for a certain period of time to sustain such a finding? For example, deportability for a crime of violence or an aggravated felony requires not only a conviction but also a "term of imprisonment" of "at least one year."
- *Nature of the offense*—Is the type of criminal conduct for which the individual has been charged actually a deportable offense or a basis for a finding of inadmissibility? Not every crime supports a ground of deportability or inadmissibility.
- *Time of the offense*—Must the criminal offense or conviction take place within a certain time span to make the individual deportable, inadmissible, or ineligible for the benefits sought? For example, deportability for a crime involving moral turpitude (a single conviction) must take place within five years of the date of admission. If this criterion is not met, the individual is not deportable.
- *Effective date*—Does the statute cover the period of time when the criminal offense took place or the conviction rendered? Was the crime a deportable offense at the time it took place? If not, can the present law be applied retroactively?
- *Relief or waiver*—If the criminal action makes the individual deportable, inadmissible, or ineligible for the benefit sought, is there a waiver or other relief under the immigration laws? For example, even if an individual is convicted for a crime involving moral turpitude, there may be a wavier available under INA §212(h).

Conviction—INA §101(a)(48)

Definition

Most grounds of deportability require proof by DHS of a "conviction." However, smuggling, drug addiction or abuse, violation of protective orders issued by a civil or criminal court, immigration fraud, terrorism, unlawful voting, or persecutions of others do not require a "conviction" to sustain a finding of deportability.[78]

In 1996, Congress enacted a new definition of the term "conviction" as part of IIRAIRA, found at INA §101(a)(48). The term "conviction" means, with respect to an alien, a formal judgment of guilt entered by the court or, if adjudication of guilt has been withheld, where—

> (i) the judge or jury has found the alien guilty, or the alien has entered the plea of guilty or *nolo contendere*, or has admitted sufficient facts to warrant a finding of guilt, and
>
> (ii) the judge has ordered some form of punishment, penalty, or restraint to be imposed on the alien's liberty.[79]

Finality of the conviction

Prior to the changes resulting from IIRAIRA, some criminal court judgments (*e.g.*, deferred adjudication in certain states) were not considered to be final convictions.[80] The possibility of future proceedings to determine guilt or innocence upon a finding of a violation of the terms of the court's deferral order prevented a deferred adjudication from being a "final" conviction for immigration purposes. However, Congress's 1996 definition of "conviction" makes a deferred adjudication a "conviction" for immigration purposes in that there is at least a plea of *nolo contendere* and some restraint on the alien's liberty.[81]

Post-conviction relief—impact on deportability[82]

The BIA has ruled that it is the basis on which a conviction is vacated that determines its effect on immigration proceedings. A conviction that is vacated by the trial court after completion of a state rehabilitative scheme, or merely for immigration

---

[78] The grounds of removability for crimes are found at INA §237(a)(2); terrorism and security grounds are at INA §237(a)(4).

[79] INA §101(a)(48)(A).

[80] *Martinez-Montoya v. INS*, 904 F.2d 1025 (5th Cir. 1990).

[81] *Moosa v. INS*, 171 F.3d 994 (5th Cir. 1999); *Madriz-Alvarado v. Ashcroft*, 383 F.3d 321 (5th Cir. 2004); *see also Matter of Punu*, 22 I&N Dec. 224 (BIA 1998).

[82] For a detailed analysis of expungements, rehabilitative statutes, and first offender provisions, see Mary E. Kramer, *Immigration Consequences of Criminal Activity: A Guide to Representing Foreign-Born Defendants*, 2d Ed., 48–60 (AILA 2005) (hereinafter Kramer), available through *www.ailapubs.org*.

purposes, can still be the basis for a finding of deportability.[83] However, a conviction that is vacated by the trial court for substantive defects, *e.g.*, failure to give admonishment on the immigration consequences of a guilty plea, is not valid basis for a finding of deportability.[84]

Most circuit courts have found that where a conviction is vacated by the trial court for procedural or other substantive defects, it cannot form the basis for a charge of deportability.[85] The Fifth Circuit has indicated that even where a conviction is vacated for substantive reasons, it may be used to form the basis for a charge of deportability. The court stated, "When a court vacates an otherwise final and valid conviction on equitable grounds merely to avoid the immigration-law consequences of the conviction, it usurps Congress's plenary power to set the terms and conditions of American citizenship and the executive's discretion to administer the immigration laws."[86] The Fifth Circuit made no distinction in the decision between convictions expunged under a state rehabilitative scheme (or for immigration purposes) and those vacated for procedural or other substantive reasons. The BIA has stated that it will follow the reasoning of the other circuits and decline to follow the Fifth Circuit in this respect, so that when a conviction is vacated for procedural or other substantive defects, the conviction is not valid for immigration purposes.[87]

Contrary to the majority of circuits, the Ninth Circuit ruled that an expungement of certain first-time drug offenses under a state rehabilitative scheme that removes the conviction upon completion of probation is not a basis for deportation if it would not be a basis for deportation under the Federal First Offender Act.[88] Reasoning similar to the majority of circuits is applied to foreign expungements.

However, a vacation of a *sentence* that makes an alien deportable and substitution of a new, lesser sentence will be honored by the government.[89]

Pardons

An individual is not deportable based on a conviction for a crime involving moral turpitude or an aggravated felony if he or she is granted a full and uncondi-

---

[83] *Matter of Pickering*, 23 I&N Dec. 621 (BIA 2003); *Matter of Roldan-Santoyo*, 22 I&N Dec. 512 (BIA 1999); *see also Matter of Marroquin-Garcia*, 23 I&N Dec. 705 (A.G. 2005); *Matter of Luviano-Rodriguez*, 23 I&N Dec. 718 (A.G. 2005).

[84] *Matter of Adamiak*, 23 I&N Dec. 878 (BIA 2006); *Matter of Rodriguez-Ruiz*, 22 I&N Dec. 1378 (BIA 2000) (*Matter of Rodriguez-Ruiz* appears to indicate that convictions vacated for reasons other than state rehabilitative schemes would not form the basis for deportability; however, the BIA in *Matter of Pickering* found that convictions vacated for immigration hardships would still serve as a basis for deportability).

[85] *Pinho v. Gonzales*, 432 F.3d 193, 195 (6th Cir. 2005); *Herrera-Inirio v. INS*, 208 F.3d 299, 305 (1st Cir. 2000); *Sandoval v. INS*, 240 F.3d 577, 583, 584 (7th Cir. 2001).

[86] *Renteria-Gonzalez v. INS*, 322 F.3d 804 (5th Cir. 2002).

[87] *Adamiak*, 23 I&N Dec. 878.

[88] *Lujan-Armendariz v. INS*, 22 F.3d 728 (9th Cir. 2000). The Federal First Offender Act is at 18 USC §3607.

[89] *Matter of Song*, 23 I&N Dec. 173 (BIA 2001).

tional pardon subsequent to the conviction by the President of the United States or by the governor of any of the several states.[90] Foreign pardons or expungements are not effective to prevent a finding of deportability.[91] The pardon is only applicable to the specific crime that was pardoned and an alien may still be found deportable on another charge if that other charge was not specifically included in the pardon.[92]

Sentence/Term of Imprisonment

Several of the grounds of deportability require not only a conviction but a "sentence" or "term of imprisonment" for a certain amount of time. For example, the deportability charge relating to a single crime of moral turpitude, INA §237(a)(2)(A), and certain aggravated felony charges in INA §101(a)(43) require a conviction coupled with a sentence or term of imprisonment of at least one year to sustain a finding of deportability. Therefore, DHS, in these cases, must prove not only that a conviction exists, but that there has been a sentence or term of imprisonment imposed for the required period of time. The definition of the term "conviction" under IIRAIRA indicates that even where there has been a suspension of imprisonment or sentence, the sentence is still considered to have been imposed for purposes of the immigration statutes. INA §101(a)(48)(B) states:

> Any reference to a term of imprisonment or a sentence with respect to an offense is deemed to include the period of incarceration or confinement ordered by a court of law regardless of any suspension of the imposition or execution of that imprisonment or sentence in whole or in part.

An indeterminate sentence (*i.e.*, "not to exceed five years)" is interpreted as the "maximum potential term" for immigration purposes, even though the individual does not necessarily serve the full sentence.[93] Probation as opposed to a sentence that is suspended means there is no "term of imprisonment" for immigration purposes.[94] Where an individual is given concurrent sentences for two separate crimes, the aggregate term of imprisonment is the length of the longer of the two concurrent sentences, not the sum of the two sentences.[95]

Nature of the Offense

Once DHS establishes that there is a conviction and that there has been a sentence or term of imprisonment for the period required by the statute, counsel must next consider whether the type of criminal activity makes the individual deportable under the charge stated in the NTA. The following sections analyze and define the most common criminal grounds of deportability including: (a) crimes involving moral tur-

---

[90] INA §237(a)(2)(A)(v).

[91] *Matter of Dillingham*, 21 I&N Dec. 1001 (BIA 1997).

[92] *In re Suh*, 23 I&N Dec. 626 (BIA 2003).

[93] *In re S– S–*, 21 I&N Dec. 900 (BIA 1997).

[94] *United States v. Banda-Zamora*, 178 F.3d 728 (5th Cir. 1999).

[95] *Matter of Aldabesheh*, 22 I&N Dec. 983 (BIA 1999).

pitude; (b) aggravated felonies; (c) controlled substance violations; (d) firearms convictions; and (e) crimes of domestic violence.

Criminal Grounds—Crimes Involving Moral Turpitude

Introduction

The INA has several grounds of deportability based on criminal activity; this section will survey what is required for a crime to be one involving "moral turpitude."

Crimes Involving Moral Turpitude—INA §237(a)(2)(A)(i)

INA §237(a)(2)(A)(i) makes an individual deportable for a conviction of a crime involving moral turpitude (a/k/a CIMT) committed within five years of the date of admission, or 10 years in the case of an individual who adjusts under INA §245(j) (relating to individuals who were initially admitted as a witness under INA §101(a)(15)(S)(i)). The term "admission" refers not only to lawful entry after inspection under INA §101(a)(13), but also adjustment of status to LPR status per INA §101(a)(20).[96]

The crime must carry a possible sentence of one year or longer. In addition, individuals who have been convicted of multiple crimes involving moral turpitude not arising out of a single scheme of criminal misconduct are deportable regardless of the date of the commission or conviction for the offenses.[97]

Definition of a crime involving moral turpitude

A crime of moral turpitude has been defined as a crime that is inherently base, vile, or depraved, and contrary to the excepted rules of morality[98]—a crime that is *malum in se*.[99] The BIA has been conflicted on the issue of whether "evil or malicious intent" is required in order to establish moral turpitude.[100] Generally, crimes involving moral turpitude require evil intent;[101] however, in a recent case, the BIA found that specific evil intent is not always required to find that a crime involves moral turpitude.[102] In *Torres-Varela*, the BIA stated that "although crimes involving moral turpitude often involve an evil intent, such specific intent is not a prerequisite to finding that a crime involves moral turpitude."[103] Among the criteria to determine if a crime involves moral turpitude is whether the act is accompanied

---

96 *Matter of Shanu*, 23 I&N Dec. 754 (BIA 2005).

97 INA §237(a)(2)(A)(ii).

98 *Matter of Danesh*, 19 I&N Dec. 669, 670 (BIA 1988); *In re L–V–C–*, 22 I&N Dec. 594 (BIA 1999).

99 *Matter of Franklin*, 20 I&N Dec. 867 (BIA 1994), *aff'd, Franklin v. INS*, 72 F.3d 571 (8th Cir. 1995).

100 *Cf. Matter of Khourn*, 21 I&N Dec. 1041, 1046 (BIA 1997) (where the BIA held that evil intent is a requisite element for a CIMT); *Matter of Medina*, 15 I&N Dec. 611 (BIA 1976), *aff'd sub nom. Medina-Luna v. INS*, 547 F.2d 1171 (9th Cir. 1977) (BIA held that criminally reckless behavior without evil intent may be a basis for a finding of moral turpitude). *See also Matter of Flores*, 17 I&N Dec. 225 (BIA 1980).

101 *Matter of Flores*, 17 I&N Dec. 225.

102 *Matter of Torres-Varela*, 23 I&N Dec. 78 (BIA 2001).

103 *Id.* at 83.

by "a vicious or corrupt mind."[104] However, in *Matter of Medina*, the BIA stated "the presence or absence of a corrupt or vicious mind is not controlling";[105] rather, criminally reckless behavior may be a basis for a finding of moral turpitude.[106]

Generally, courts have found that actions that are basically offensive to American ethics and accepted moral standards are morally turpitudinous.[107] The issue of moral turpitude is judged by the nature of the act when measured by contemporary moral or ethical standards. Thus, as community standards change, so does the definition of what is morally turpitudinous.[108] The standard by which an offense is to be judged is that prevailing in the United States as a whole regarding the "common view of our people concerning its vile character."[109] Certain crimes have been regularly categorized as crimes involving moral turpitude—murder, rape, robbery, aggravated assault, fraud, theft, spousal or child abuse, incest, voluntary manslaughter, and statutory rape. Most, if not all, of these cases contained an underlying criminal statute that had some type of intent requirement in order to prove guilt. (Statutory rape, however, carries no intent or knowledge requirement).

Crimes that are "*malum in se*" are generally considered to involve moral turpitude, while crimes that are not evil in and of themselves ("*malum prohibitum*") are not considered to be morally turpitudinous.[110]

Reviewing the elements of the crime under the criminal statute

Moral turpitude always has been determined by the elements of the underlying criminal statute—not the definition of a crime, the seriousness of an offense, or the severity of the sentence imposed.[111] The first step, therefore, is to look at the statutory elements of the crime to see whether evil intent is one of the elements.[112] If the statute is plain on its face that evil intent is an element—*e.g.*, when the criminal statute by its terms includes a specific intent to harm another individual or knowledge that harm will be done—the crime is morally turpitudinous.[113]

The BIA has further held that criminal recklessness and a conscious disregard of the possible harm to others is morally turpitudinous. An offense defined by the term

---

104 *Matter of Wojtkow*, 18 I&N Dec. 111 (BIA 1981).

105 *Matter of Medina*, 15 I&N Dec., at 614.

106 *Id.*

107 *See, e.g.*, *Castle v. INS*, 541 F.2d 1064, 1066 (4th Cir. 1976).

108 *United States v. Francioso*, 164 F.2d 163 (2d Cir. 1947).

109 *Matter of G–*, 1 I&N Dec. 59, 60 (BIA 1941).

110 *Kempe v. United States*, 151 F.2d 680, 688 (8th Cir. 1945); *see also Matter of Torres-Varela*, 23 I&N Dec. 78 (BIA 2001).

111 *Matter of Serna*, 20 I&N Dec. 579, 581 (BIA 1992).

112 *Matter of Short*, 20 I&N Dec. 136 (BIA 1989).

113 *McNaughton v. INS*, 612 F.2d 457, 459 (9th Cir. 1980).

"reckless" also may be morally turpitudinous.[114] The BIA has stated that it is the "inherent nature of the crime as defined by statute and interpreted by the courts, as limited and described by, the record of conviction" that is determinative as to whether the crime is morally turpitudinous.[115] It is not the specific facts or circumstances of the individual case that determines whether a crime is one of moral turpitude.[116]

Divisible statutes

More complicated are situations where the underlying statute proscribes conduct that is both morally turpitudinous and conduct that is not—a "divisible" statute. In this situation, the record of conviction will determine whether the crime involves moral turpitude.[117] The practitioner will have to analyze the record of conviction to determine if the crime for which the individual was actually charged and convicted involved evil intent or, for certain statutes, recklessness. The record of conviction is limited to the indictment, plea, verdict, and sentence.[118] It does not include other documents such as police reports or presentencing reports.[119] However, the police report or presentencing investigation report may be considered in determining relief issues (this will be discussed in a later section).[120]

If, after reviewing the elements of the statute and the record of conviction, it is still unclear whether the violated section of the divisible statute involved moral turpitude, the individual is not deportable under INA §237(a)(2)(A)(i). The evidence on the issue of deportability must be clear and convincing.

Classification of Crimes Involving Moral Turpitude

Crimes Against the Person

Involving Moral Turpitude	Not Involving Moral Turpitude
Accessory after the Fact (Murder)[121] Aggravated Assault[122] Aggravated Battery[123] Aggravated Child Abuse[124]	Aggravated Assault[145] Aggravated Assault (third degree, New Jersey)[146] *continued*

[114] *Matter of Torres-Varela*, 23 I&N Dec. 78. *See also Matter of Perez-Contreras*, 20 I&N Dec. 615 (BIA 1992).

[115] *Matter of Short*, 20 I&N Dec. 136.

[116] *Id.*; *see also Matter of Esfandiary*, 16 I&N Dec. 659 (BIA 1979).

[117] *Matter of V–Z–S–*, 22 I&N Dec. 1338 (BIA 2000).

[118] *Matter of Pichardo-Sufren*, 22 I&N Dec. 330 (BIA 1996).

[119] *Id.; see also Matter of Teixeira*, 21 I&N Dec. 316 (BIA 1996).

[120] *See Matter of Sweetser*, 22 I&N Dec. 709 (BIA 1999).

[121] *Cabral v. INS*, 15 F.3d 193 (BIA 1964);

[122] *Matter of Medina*, 15 I&N Dec. 611 (BIA 1970); *Pichardo v. INS*, 104 F.3d 756 (5th Cir. 1997).

[123] *Sosa-Martinez v. U.S. Att'y Gen.*, 420 F.3d 1338 (11th Cir. 2005).

[124] *Garcia v. Att'y Gen.*, 329 F.3d 1217 (11th Cir. 2003).

Involving Moral Turpitude	Not Involving Moral Turpitude
Aggravated Stalking[125] Assault (third degree)[126] Assault by Means to Produce Great Bodily Harm[127] Assault (Knife) (second degree)[128] Assault with a Dangerous Weapon[129] Assault with a Deadly Weapon[130] Assault/Intent to Cause Serious Injury[131]	Assault (third degree, Hawaii)[147] Assault (second degree)[148] Assault and Battery[149] Attempted Reckless Assault (New York)[150] Attempted Reckless Endangerment (New York)[151] Battery[152] *continued*

[125] *Matter of Ajami*, 22 I&N Dec. 949 (BIA 1999).

[126] *Matter of Baker*, 15 I&N Dec. 50 (BIA 1970).

[127] *Matter of R*, 1 I&N Dec. 352 (BIA 1942).

[128] Matter *of Goodalle*, 12 I&N Dec. 106 (BIA 1967).

[129] *Matter of J*, 4 I&N Dec. 512 (BIA 1951).

[130] *Matter of G–R–*, 2 I&N Dec. 733 (BIA 1988).

[131] *Nguyen v. Reno*, 211 F.3d 692 (1st Cir. 2000).

[132] *Matter of C–*, 5 I&N Dec. 370 (BIA 1953).

[133] *Matter of Quedara*, 11 I&N Dec. 457 (BIA 1966).

[134] *Mohsoudi v. INS*, 181 F.3d 8 (1st Cir. 1999).

[135] *Matter of Beato*, 10 I&N Dec. 730 (BIA 1964).

[136] *In re Yeung*, 21 I&N Dec. 610 (BIA 1997).

[137] *Matter of Awaijane*, 14 I&N Dec. 117 (BIA 1972).

[138] *Matter of S–*, 9 I&N Dec. 370 (BIA 1962).

[139] *Matter of Tran*, 21 I&N Dec. 291 (BIA 1996).

[140] *Cabral v. INS*, 15 F.3d 193 (1st Cir. 1994).

[141] *Knapik v. Ashcroft*, 384 F.3d 84 (3d Cir. 2004).

[142] *Matter of Pataki*, 15 I&N Dec. 324 (BIA 1975).

[143] *Matter of Lopez-Amaro*, 20 I&N Dec. 668 (BIA 1993); *Matter of Rodriquez-Vera*, 17 I&N Dec. 105 (BIA 1979).

[144] *Matter of Rodriguez-Palma*, 17 I&N Dec. 465 (BIA 1980).

[145] *Matter of Z*, 1 I&N Dec. 446 (BIA 1973).

[146] *Partijka v. Att'y Gen.*, 417 F.3d 408 (3d Cir. 2005); *see also Zaitona v. INS*, 9 F.3d 432 (6th Cir. 1993).

[147] *Matter of Fualaau*, 21 I&N Dec. 475 (BIA 1996); *see also Matter of Perez-Contreras*, 20 I&N Dec. 615 (BIA 1992) (statute did not require intentional or reckless conduct); *Matter of S*, 9 I&N Dec. 688 (BIA 1962); *Matter of E*, 1 I&N Dec. 505 (BIA 1943); *Matter of Baker*, 15 I&N Dec. 50 (BIA 1974).

[148] *Matter of Z*, 5 I&N Dec. 383 (BIA 1953).

[149] *Matter of S*, 9 I&N Dec. 688 (BIA 1960).

[150] *Gill v. INS*, 420 F.3d 82 (2d Cir. 2005).

[151] *Knapik v. Ashcroft*, 384 F.3d 84 (3d Cir. 2004).

[152] *Matter of Garcia-Hernandez*, 23 I&N Dec. 590 (BIA 2003).

[153] *Matter of Szegedi*, 10 I&N Dec. 28 (BIA 1962).

Involving Moral Turpitude	Not Involving Moral Turpitude
Assault with Intent to Commit Murder[132] Assault with Intent to Commit Robbery[133] Assault and Robbery[134] Attempted Assault/Intent to Commit Rape[135] Attempted Manslaughter[136] Attempted Murder[137] Atrocious Assault and Battery[138] Domestic Violence[139] Manslaughter[140] Reckless Endangerment[141] Manslaughter (Voluntary)[142] Murder[143] Robbery[144]	Homicide by Reckless Conduct[153]

Property Crimes

Involving Moral Turpitude	Not Involving Moral Turpitude
Burglary with Intent to Commit Theft[154] Grand Larceny[155] Grand Theft[156] Petty Larceny[157] Petty Theft[158] Receiving Stolen Property[159] Robbery[160] Theft (Canada)[161]	Possession of Burglary Tools[162]

---

[154] *Matter of Z*, 5 I&N Dec. 383 (BIA 1953).

[155] *United States ex rel. Meyer v. Day*, 54 F.2d 336 (2d Cir. 1931).

[156] *Nwobue v. INS*, 907 F.2d 155 (9th Cir. 1990).

[157] *Brett v. INS*, 386 F.2d 439 (2d Cir. 1967); *Matter of N*, 3 I&N Dec. 723 (BIA 1945).

[158] *Matter of R–*, 1 I&N Dec. 540 (BIA 1940).

[159] *U.S. ex rel. Ventura v. Shaughnessy*, 219 F.2d 266 (2d Cir. 1955); *see also Smriko v. Ashcroft*, 387 F.3d 279 (3d Cir. 2004).

[160] *Matter of Pineda-Castellanos*, 21 I&N Dec. 1017 (BIA 1997).

[161] *Matter of F*, 2 I&N Dec. 517 (BIA 1946).

[162] *Matter of S*, 6 I&N Dec. 769 (BIA 1955).

Crimes Related to Fraud

Involving Moral Turpitude	Not Involving Moral Turpitude
Attempted Bribery[163] Bad Checks[164] Conspiracy to Defraud the United States by Making False Statements[165] Conspiracy to Evade Federal Taxes[166] Counterfeiting/Conspiracy to Counterfeit[167] Forgery/Altering a False Document[168] Illegal Possession/Fraudulent Use of Credit Cards and Forgery (Alabama)[169] Mail Fraud[170] Money Laundering[171] Obtaining Pell Grant by Fraud[172] Offering to Bribe Immigration Officer[173] Publishing/Passing Counterfeit Federal Reserve Notes with Intent to Defraud[174] Purchase of Food Stamps for Cash[175] Tax Evasion[176]	Fraudulent Taking (nonpermanent)[177]

[163] *Matter of V*, 4 I&N Dec. 100 (BIA 1950).

[164] *Matter of Bart*, 20 I&N Dec. 436 (BIA 1992).

[165] *Matter of Arevalo*, 22 I&N Dec. 398 (BIA 1998).

[166] *Jordan v. DeGeorge*, 341 U.S. 223 (1951).

[167] *Matter of K*, 7 I&N Dec. 178 (BIA 1956).

[168] *Matter of S–C–*, 3 I&N Dec. 350 (BIA 1948).

[169] *Balogun v. Ashcroft*, 270 F.3d 274 (5th Cir. 2001).

[170] *Matter of G–N–C–*, 22 I&N Dec. 281 (BIA 1998).

[171] *Smalley v. Ashcroft*, 354 F.3d 332 (5th Cir. 2003).

[172] *Izedonmwen v. INS*, 37 F.3d 416 (8th Cir. 1994).

[173] *Okabe v. INS*, 671 F.2d 863 (5th Cir. 1982).

[174] *Matter of P*, 6 I&N Dec. 795 (BIA 1955).

[175] *Abdelqadar v. Gonzales*, 413 F.3d 668 (7th Cir. 2005).

[176] *Carty v. Ashcroft*, 395 F.3d 1081 (9th Cir. 2005).

[177] *Matter of T*, 2 I&N Dec. 22 (BIA 1944).

Sexual Crimes

Involving Moral Turpitude	Not Involving Moral Turpitude
Assault/Intent to Commit Abortion[178] Assault and Battery/Intent to Ravish[179] Attempted Compulsory Prostitution of Women[180] Disorderly Conduct (involving soliciting for lewd conduct)[181] Disorderly Conduct (loitering in a public place to solicit men)[182] Incest[183] Indecent Assault (Canada)[184] Indecent Liberties with a Female Child (nine years)[185] Lewdness[186] Sodomy[187] Soliciting Sexual Activity with Child[188] Statutory Rape[189]	Fornication[190]

[178] *Matter of M*, 2 I&N Dec. 525 (BIA 1940).

[179] *Matter of M*, 2 I&N Dec. 629 (BIA 1946).

[180] *Matter of E*, 1 I&N Dec. 505 (BIA 1943).

[181] *Matter of Alfonso-Bermudez*, 12 I&N Dec. 225 (BIA 1967).

[182] *Wyngaard v. Kennedy*, 295 F.2d 184 (D.C. Cir. 1961).

[183] *Matter of Y*, 3 I&N Dec. 546 (BIA 1949).

[184] *Matter of S*, 5 I&N Dec. 686 (BIA 1954); *Matter of Z*, 7 I&N Dec. 253 (BIA 1956).

[185] *Matter of Garcia*, 11 I&N Dec. 521 (BIA 1966).

[186] *Matter of M*, 7 I&N Dec. 144 (BIA 1956).

[187] *Velez-Lozano v. INS*, 463 F.3d 1305 (D.C. Cir 1972).

[188] *Taylor v. America*, 396 F.3d 1322 (11th Cir. 2005).

[189] *Castle v. INS*, 541 F.2d 1064 (4th Cir. 1976); *Matter of S*, 2 I&N Dec. 553 (BIA 1946).

[190] *Matter of R*, 6 I&N Dec. 444 (BIA 1954).

Crimes Related to Operating a Motor Vehicle

Involving Moral Turpitude	Not Involving Moral Turpitude
Aggravated Driving Under the Influence[191] Reckless Endangerment[192]	Aggravated Driving Under the Influence[193] Attempted Reckless Endangerment[194] Unauthorized Use of a Motor Vehicle[195]

Weapons Offenses

Involving Moral Turpitude	Not Involving Moral Turpitude
Assault with a Firearm (California)[196]	Possession of a Concealed Sawed-off Shotgun[197] Possession of a Sawed-off Shotgun[198]

Drug Crimes

Involving Moral Turpitude	Not Involving Moral Turpitude
Concealing Drug Money[199] Distribution of Cocaine[200] Unlawful Sale of Narcotics[201]	Importation of Narcotics[202] Unlawful Sale and Possession of LSD[203]

---

[191] *Hernandez-Martinez v. Ashcroft*, 343 F.3d 1075 (9th Cir. 2003); *Matter of Lopez-Mesa*, 22 I&N Dec. 1188 (BIA 1999).

[192] *Knapik v. Ashcroft*, 384 F.3d 84 (3d Cir. 2004).

[193] *Matter of Torres-Varela*, 23 I&N Dec. 78 (BIA 1999).

[194] *Knapik v. Ashcroft*, 384 F.3d 84 (3d Cir. 2004).

[195] *Matter of Brieva-Perez*, 23 I&N Dec. 766 (BIA 2005); *Matter of D*, 1 I&N Dec. 143 (BIA 1941).

[196] *Membreno v. Ashcroft*, 385 F.3d 1245 (9th Cir. 2004).

[197] *Matter of G–R–*, 2 I&N Dec. 733 (BIA 1946).

[198] *U.S. v. Quintana*, 914 F.2d 1409 (10th Cir. 1990).

[199] *Smalley v. Ashcroft*, 354 F.3d 332 (5th Cir. 2003).

[200] *Matter of Khourn,* 21 I&N Dec. 1041 (BIA 1997).

[201] *Matter of Y*, 2 I&N Dec. 600 (BIA 1948).

[202] *Matter of V–*, 1 I&N Dec. 293 (BIA 1942).

[203] *Matter of Abreu-Semino*, 12 I&N Dec. 77 (BIA 1968).

Other Crimes

Involving Moral Turpitude	Not Involving Moral Turpitude
Accessory Before the Fact (if underlying crime is a CIMT)[204]	Aiding One to Escape from Jail[214]
Accessory after the Fact (Manslaughter)[205]	Attempt to Escape from Prison[215]
Accessory after the Fact (Murder)[206]	Bastardy[216]
Aggravated Fleeing from a Police Officer[207]	Contributing to Delinquency of a Minor[217]
Bigamy[208]	Disorderly Conduct[218]
Impersonating a Federal Officer[209]	Failure to Prevent Commission of Crime[219]
Mayhem (Involving Mutilation of Another)[210]	Failure to Support Wife and Child[220]
Obstruction of Justice (Illinois)[211]	Gambling[221]
Perjury[212]	Loan-sharking[222]
Possession of Stolen Bus Transfers[213]	Mailing an Obscene Letter[223]
	Malicious Mischief[224]
	Obstruction of Justice[225]
	Smuggling aliens[226]
	Vagrancy[227]

204 *Matter of Short*, 20 I&N Dec. 136 (BIA 1989).

205 *Matter of Sanchez*, 11 I&N Dec. 264 (BIA 1965).

206 *Cabral v. INS*, 15 F.3d 193 (1st Cir. 1994).

207 *Mei v. Ashcroft*, 393 F.3d 737 (7th Cir. 2004).

208 *Matter of S–*, 2 I&N Dec. 328 (BIA 1945).

209 *Matter of H*, 1 I&N Dec. 509 (BIA 1943).

210 *Matter of Santoro*, 12 I&N Dec. 840 (BIA 1966).

211 *Padilla v. Gonzales*, 397 F.3d 1016 (7th Cir. 2005).

212 *Matter of Martinez-Recinos*, 23 I&N Dec. 175 (BIA 2001); *U.S. ex rel. Alvarez-Flores v. Savoretti*, 205 F.2d 544 (5th Cir. 1953).

213 *Michel v. INS*, 206 F.3d 253 (2d Cir. 2000).

214 *Matter of Sloan*, 12 I&N Dec. 840 (BIA 1976).

215 *Matter of B*, 5 I&N Dec. 538 (BIA 1953).

216 *Matter of D–*, 1 I&N Dec. 186 (BIA 1941).

217 *Matter of C*, 2 I&N Dec. 220 (BIA 1944).

218 *Matter of E*, 2 I&N Dec. 134 (BIA 1944).

219 *Matter of S–C–*, 3 I&N Dec. 350 (BIA 1948).

220 *Matter of E*, 2 I&N Dec. 134 (BIA 1946).

221 *Matter of G,* 1 I&N Dec. 59 (BIA 1941).

222 *Matter of B*, 6 I&N Dec. 98 (BIA 1954).

223 *Matter of D*, 1 I&N Dec. 190 (BIA 1942).

224 *Rodriguez-Herrera v. INS*, 52 F.3d 238 (9th Cir. 1995).

225 *Padilla v. Gonzalez*, 397 F.3d 1016 (7th Cir. 2005).

226 *Matter of Tiwari*, 19 I&N Dec. 875 (BIA 1989).

227 *Matter of G–R–*, 5 I&N Dec. 18 (BIA 1952).

Regulatory or licensing violations not involving moral turpitude

Most regulatory crimes are not crimes involving moral turpitude because there is no evil intent or knowledge requirement.

- Conspiracy to Illegally Transfer Gasoline Ration Stamps[228]
- Failure to File Invoices[229]
- Failure to Timely File a Tax Return[230]
- Possession of Alcoholic Beverages in a Dry County[231]
- Removal of Distilled Spirits Without Payment of Taxes (under 26 USC §404)[232]
- Sale of Narcotics[233]
- Tax Evasion (without intent to defraud IRS)[234]

Multiple Crimes Involving Moral Turpitude—INA §237(a)(2)(A)(ii)

An alien is deportable if he or she is convicted of two or more crimes involving moral turpitude not arising out of a single scheme of criminal misconduct at any time after admission. "Moral turpitude" is defined above. The meaning of the term "not arising out of a single scheme" has changed over time. In recent years, the BIA has been stricter in its interpretation of this term. The phrase "single scheme of criminal misconduct" means that the crimes are performed in furtherance of a "single criminal episode" or where two crimes flow from and are the natural consequences of a single act of criminal misconduct.[235]

The government bears the burden of proving that the two crimes are crimes involving moral turpitude and that they are not part of a single scheme.[236] The issue of what constitutes a single scheme is determined by several factors: the nature of the crimes; timing of the commission of the crimes; similarity of the crimes in terms of object or purpose; methods or techniques; identity of participants; similarity of victims; and whether the acts or transactions that constitute the crimes are connected.[237]

When there is a substantial period of time separating crimes, there can be no single scheme.[238] However, the fact that the crimes follow almost immediately in se-

---

228 *Matter of P*, 5 I&N Dec. 582 (BIA 1953).

229 *Matter of D–*, 9 I&N Dec. 605 (BIA 1962).

230 *Matter of S*, 9 I&N Dec. 688 (BIA 1962); *Cortes v. Ashcroft*, 395 F.3d 1081 (9th Cir. 2005).

231 *U.S. v. Smith*, 420 F.2d 428 (5th Cir. 1970).

232 *Matter of A*, 6 I&N Dec. 242 (BIA 1954).

233 *Matter of Abreu-Semino*, 12 I&N Dec. 775 (BIA 1968).

234 *Matter of R*, 4 I&N Dec. 176 (BIA 1950).

235 *Matter of Adetiba*, 20 I&N Dec. 506 (BIA 1992).

236 *Hamdan v. INS*, 98 F.3d 183 (5th Cir. 1996); *Wood v. Hay*, 266 F.2d 825 (9th Cir. 1959).

237 *Pacheco v. INS*, 546 F.2d 448 (1st Cir. 1976).

238 *Nason v. INS*, 394 F.2d 223 (2d Cir. 1968).

quence and are similar in nature is not automatically determinative of a single scheme.[239] Following are case examples of single schemes of criminal misconduct and crime sequences that do not comprise single schemes.

Crimes not part of a single scheme

- Separate offenses of purchasing food stamps from welfare recipients two days apart did not arise out of a single scheme of criminal conduct.[240]
- Convictions for lewdness committed over a period of three months and indecent assault during that three-month period were not part of a single scheme.[241]
- Forgery of two checks on two different accounts one year apart is not a single scheme.[242]
- Two separate convictions for mail fraud during two separate periods 11 months apart was not a single scheme even though convictions were issued by the same court on the same day.[243]
- Use of several credit cards in names of different people with intent to defraud did not arise out of a single scheme.[244]
- There was no single scheme where there were two separate fraudulent check convictions by two separate courts in two different states regarding criminal acts committed three weeks apart.[245]

Crimes forming a single scheme

- Separate crimes of assault with intent to kill and voluntary manslaughter arose out of a single scheme where respondent pushed his mother-in-law down the stairs and stabbed his wife within a few minutes.[246]
- Conviction for bribery, grand larceny, and conspiracy were part of a single scheme to unlawfully obtain money from a city.[247]
- Convictions on August 2, 1977, and June 30, 1978, for passing counterfeit Federal Reserve notes arose out of a single scheme.[248]

---

[239] *Matter of M*, 7 I&N Dec. 144 (BIA 1956).

[240] *Abdelqadar v. Gonzales*, 413 F.3d 668 (7th Cir. 2005).

[241] *Matter of M*, 7 I&N Dec. 144.

[242] *Matter of O'Gorman*, 11 I&N Dec. 6 (BIA 1965).

[243] *Matter of Nason*, 12 I&N Dec. 452 (BIA 1967).

[244] *Matter of Adetiba*, 20 I&N Dec. 506 (BIA 1992).

[245] *Matter of McLean*, 12 I&N Dec. 551 (BIA 1967).

[246] *Matter of Pataki*, 15 I&N Dec. 324 (BIA 2002).

[247] *Jeronimo v. Murff*, 157 F. Supp. 808 (S.D.N.Y. 1957).

[248] *Matter of Paradi*, 17 I&N Dec. 608 (BIA 1980).

- Convictions for failing to pay federal occupational tax in two successive years for sale of liquor were a single scheme.[249]

Criminal Grounds—Aggravated Felonies

Introduction

"Aggravated felony" is a term of art defined by INA §101(a)(43). What crimes constitute an aggravated felony is an area of law in flux. Several federal court and BIA precedent decisions have addressed the issue; most of these cases involve "crimes of violence" under INA §101(a)(43)(F) and "drug trafficking" crimes under INA §101(a)(43)(B). There are, however, more than 20 different types of aggravated felonies defined at INA §101(a)(43). To further complicate matters, an aggravated felony need not be "aggravated" and often is not a "felony."[250]

Pursuant to INA §237(a)(2)(A)(iii), an alien is deportable if convicted of an aggravated felony at any time after admission. INA §101(a)(13) defines "admission" as a lawful entry after inspection and authorization by an immigration officer.

Consequences

Conviction of a crime classified as an aggravated felony has far reaching consequences for aliens. An aggravated felony conviction precludes various relief applications, including applications for bond (INA §236(c)(1)(B)); asylum (INA §208(b)(2)(B)(ii)); withholding of removal (if the sentence is five years or more) (INA §241(b)(3)(B)(ii)); cancellation of removal for permanent residents (INA §240A(a)(3)); cancellation of removal for non–permanent residents (INA §240A(b)(1)(C)); voluntary departure (INA §§240B(a)(1) and (b)(1)(C)); and, for LPRs only, the waiver of inadmissibility at INA §212(h).

Moreover, if the alien is not an LPR or conditional resident, then conviction of an aggravated felony can lead to expedited removal proceedings per INA §238(b), instead of INA §240 removal proceedings. In these expedited proceedings, the only relief available is withholding of removal.[251]

When an alien convicted of an aggravated felony has been physically removed, he or she becomes permanently inadmissible[252] (in contrast to the standard 10-year bar to admissibility resulting from removal at the end of INA §240 removal proceedings). A waiver is available for this particular inadmissibility ground at INA §212(a)(9)(A)(iii).

---

[249] *Barrese v. Ryan*, 203 F. Supp. 880 (D.C. Conn. 1962).

[250] The definition of "aggravated felony" will be further analyzed, *infra*.

[251] INA §238(b). Withholding of removal will be further discussed in Chapter 5.

[252] INA §§212(a)(9)(A)(i), (a)(9)(A)(ii)(II).

Because aggravated felony is not listed as a ground of inadmissibility at INA §212(a)(2), a conviction of an aggravated felony *technically* does not render an alien inadmissible.[253] However, many crimes that are deemed aggravated felonies also will be captured under a §212(a)(2) inadmissibility ground (crimes involving moral turpitude, controlled substance violations, money laundering, etc.) and can make the alien permanently inadmissible as an immigrant without the possibility of a waiver.

Thus, conviction of an aggravated felony as defined in INA §101(a)(43) results in significant, sometimes permanent, procedural and substantive consequences for immigrants.

Expansion of the Aggravated Felony Definition

The aggravated felony ground of deportation was first enacted in the Anti-Drug Abuse Act (ADAA) of 1988.[254] The ADAA defined aggravated felony to include murder, drug trafficking and weapons trafficking, and it only applied to aliens charged as deportable for conviction of an aggravated felony after its date of enactment—November 18, 1988.

Next, the Immigration Act of 1990 (IMMACT90)[255] added new crimes to the list of aggravated felonies under INA §101(a)(43), including crimes of violence (as defined by 18 USC §16) and money laundering (as described in 18 USC §1956) where the conviction occurred after the date of enactment—November 29, 1990.[256] In addition, IMMACT90 barred aliens who had "served" a sentence of five or more years for an aggravated felony from applying for a waiver of inadmissibility or deportability under former INA §212(c). The BIA has held that IMMACT90's bar to former §212(c) relief applies to aggravated felony convictions entered prior to the enactment of the ADAA.[257]

The Immigration and Nationality Technical Corrections Act of 1994 (INTCA)[258] broadened the definition again to include, among other crimes, theft or burglary with a term of imprisonment of at least five years; child pornography; racketeering; offenses related to treason or disclosure of classified information; fraud offenses where the loss was at least $200,000; certain alien smuggling offenses; document fraud; and conspiracy or attempt to commit an aggravated felony.[259]

The Antiterrorism and Effective Death Penalty Act of 1986 (AEDPA)[260] expanded the aggravated felony definition further. AEDPA made aggravated felonies of gam-

---

[253] *Matter of Kanga*, 22 I&N Dec. 1206 (BIA 2000).

[254] Pub. L. No. 100-690 (Nov. 18, 1988).

[255] Immigration Act of 1990, *supra* note 43.

[256] *Id.*, §501.

[257] *See Matter of Gomez Giraldo*, 20 I&N Dec. 957 (BIA 1995).

[258] Immigration and Nationality Technical Corrections Act of 1994, Pub. L. No. 103-416, 108 Stat. 4305 (Oct. 25, 1994).

[259] *Id.*, §222.

[260] Pub. L. No. 104-132, §440(e), 110 Stat. 1277 (Apr. 24, 1996).

bling offenses; forging or counterfeiting a passport (if the term of imprisonment was at least 18 months); commercial bribery; counterfeiting; forgery; perjury; bribery of a witness; and trafficking in vehicles with altered vehicle identification numbers. Many of the above-listed crimes require a minimum sentence of five years' imprisonment.

AEDPA also made ineligible for relief under former INA §212(c) individuals deportable for aggravated felonies, controlled substance violations, firearms offenses, and certain crimes involving moral turpitude.[261] However, the Supreme Court held that this bar was not retroactive and did not to apply to those who had pleaded guilty to these crimes before AEDPA's April 24, 1996, enactment.[262] The Court found that where an individual pleads to a crime and prosecutors have received the benefit of the plea, facilitated by the alien's belief in his or her continued eligibility for §212(c) relief, it would be contrary to considerations of fair notice, reasonable reliance, and settled expectations to hold that a later change in the law under AEDPA and IIRAIRA deprives the person of eligibility for relief.[263]

Congress last revised the aggravated felony definition in IIRAIRA.[264] The current definition at INA §101(a)(43) now includes the following crimes:

(a) Murder, rape, or sexual abuse of a minor;

(b) Controlled substance trafficking, including drug trafficking under 18 USC §924(c);

(c) Firearms or destructive device trafficking under 18 USC §§921 or 841(c);

(d) Money laundering or certain other specified financial transactions under 18 USC §§1956 or 1957 involving more than $10,000;

(e) Offenses related to explosive materials and firearms under 18 USC §§842, 844, 922, or 924, or 26 USC §5861;

(f) Crimes of violence as defined by 18 USC §16 with a one (or more) year term of imprisonment;

(g) Theft or burglary offenses with a one (or more) year term of imprisonment;

(h) Ransom offenses described in 18 USC §§875, 876, 877, or 1202;

(i) Child pornography offenses described in 18 USC §§2251, 2251A, or 2252;

(j) Racketeering as described in 18 USC §§1962 or 1084, or gambling offenses under 18 USC §1955 for which a sentence of one (or more) year of imprisonment may be imposed;

(k) Prostitution management, transportation, or offenses relating to involuntary servitude, slavery, or trafficking in persons as described in 18 USC §§2421–2423, 1581–1585, or 1588–1591;

---

[261] *Id.*, §440(d).

[262] *INS v. St. Cyr*, 533 U.S. 289 (2001).

[263] *Id.* at 291. *St. Cyr* will be discussed further in Chapter 6 in the section on INA §212(c) relief.

[264] IIRAIRA, *supra* note 66.

(l) Gathering, disclosing, or transmitting classified information as described in 18 USC §§793 or 798; sabotage under 18 USC §2153; treason under 18 USC §§2381 or 2382; disclosing the identity of undercover agents under 50 USC §421;

(m) Offenses involving fraud or deceit if loss to victim exceeds $10,000, or tax evasion if revenue loss to the government exceeds $10,000;

(n) Smuggling under 8 USC §1324(a) (except for a first time offense involving only the alien's spouse, child, or parent);

(o) Unlawful entry or re-entry into the United States under 8 USC §§1325 or 1326 after prior deportation for an aggravated felony;

(p) Counterfeiting, forgery, or altering passports or other instruments under 18 USC §1543, or document fraud under 18 USC §1546(a) for which the term of imprisonment is 12 or more months (except where the offense involved assisting only the alien's spouse, parent, or child);

(q) Failure to appear to serve a sentence if the offense is punishable by imprisonment for five or more years;

(r) Commercial bribery, forgery, counterfeiting, or trafficking in vehicles with altered vehicle identification numbers if term of imprisonment is at least one year;

(s) Perjury or subornation of perjury, obstruction of justice, or bribery of a witness if the term of imprisonment is at least one year;

(t) Failure to appear before court after a court order to respond to felony charge if a two- (or more) year sentence may be imposed;

(u) Any attempt or conspiracy to commit an aggravated felony.

The definition of the term aggravated felony as amended by IIRAIRA applies to convictions "entered before, on or after the date of enactment" of IIRAIRA.[265]

Analysis of an Aggravated Felony Charge

Sufficient notice of the charge

Be sure that the NTA does not merely charge that your client is deportable under INA §237(a)(2)(A)(iii) for conviction of an aggravated felony. DHS also must charge the specific aggravated felony subsection at issue under INA §101(a)(43)(A)–(U); it must do so because aliens have the right to notice of the exact removal charge being lodged against them.[266]

---

[265] INA §101(a)(43) (final paragraph).

[266] *Matter of Siffre*, 14 I&N Dec. 444, 445 (BIA 1973); *Chew v. Colding*, 344 U.S. 590, 597 (1953); *See also Chowdhury v. INS*, 249 F.3d 970, 975 (9th Cir. 2001); *Matter of Lopez-Barrios*, 20 I&N Dec. 203 (BIA 1990).

Conviction required

Next, make sure that the misconduct alleged is a "conviction" under the INA; the aggravated felony ground of deportability applies to convictions only—not to mere admissions of criminal conduct, or admission of the elements of a crime.[267]

Aggravated felony convictions can be based on either federal or state law.[268] Convictions under foreign law can satisfy the aggravated felony definition if 15 years have not passed since the term of imprisonment ended.[269] An adjudication of delinquency for a juvenile, however, is not a conviction for immigration purposes.[270]

Pursuant to INA §101(a)(43)(U), a conviction for attempt or conspiracy to commit an aggravated felony is defined as an aggravated felony. The BIA has interpreted "attempt" broadly, and even upheld deportation based on an aggravated felony attempt when the alien had been convicted not of attempt, but of a completed crime that itself was not an aggravated felony.[271]

The complexity and extensiveness of the aggravated felony definition has led to splits in the circuits as to which crimes are aggravated felonies. The circuit courts' decisions are binding on the BIA and IJs in cases arising in their respective jurisdictions.[272]

"Described in" a federal criminal statute

Check the definition of the crime at INA §101(a)(43) to see if the relevant aggravated felony subsection cross-references a specific federal criminal statute. Certain aggravated felony subsections state that the offense is one "*defined in*" a federal statute, *e.g.*, INA §101(a)(43)(F) refers to a crime of violence as defined at 18 USC §16, while others only require that the offense be one "*described in*" a federal statute, *e.g.*, INA §101(a)(43)(E).

When the aggravated felony must be "defined in" a federal statute, there must be more than just a similarity between the state statute and that specified federal statute. The state statute under which the alien was convicted must be analogous to the federal statute cross-referenced in INA §101(a)(43), which means it must contain all of the elements of the federal statute[273] (except, necessarily, the jurisdictional element of the federal statute[274]). If the state criminal statute does not track the federal statute in

---

267 INA §237(a)(2)(A)(iii); *see also Matter of Barrett*, 20 I&N Dec. 171, 177 (BIA 1990) (deportation proceedings). For more analysis of convictions, see "Conviction—INA §101(a)(48)," *supra*.

268 INA §101(a)(43) (final paragraph).

269 *Id.*

270 *Matter of Devison*, 22 I&N Dec. 1362 (BIA 2000).

271 *Matter of Onyido*, 22 I&N Dec. 552, 556–57 (BIA 1999) (Board Member Heilman dissenting).

272 *Matter of Yanez*, 23 I&N Dec. 390, 391 (BIA 2002). For more on the circuit splits regarding aggravated felonies, see Kramer, *supra* note 82, at 144–64.

273 *Matter of Barret*, 20 I&N Dec. 171, 178 (BIA 1990).

274 *Matter of Vasquez-Muniz*, 23 I&N Dec. 207 (BIA 2002).

all respects, then the crime articulated in the state statute is not an aggravated felony.[275]

The BIA has stated that if the aggravated felony subsection charged does not define the crime in INA §101(a)(43) or cross-reference another statute's definition (*e.g.*, INA §101(a)(43)(G) (theft)), then the BIA looks to analogous provisions of federal and state statutes and case law as well as "authoritative compendiums," such as the Model Penal Code, in order to determine if the crime meets the definition of an aggravated felony under the Act.[276]

Ambiguous or divisible criminal statute

When the criminal statute includes conduct that would and conduct that would not constitute an aggravated felony, it is necessary to go beyond the statute and review the record of conviction, including the charging document and judgment to determine if the offense constitutes an aggravated felony.[277] If the indictment or information does not clearly indicate which section of a divisible criminal statute was violated, then a charge that the individual is deportable as an aggravated felon cannot be sustained.

Classification as a felony or misdemeanor

A state misdemeanor can be an aggravated felony notwithstanding its classification as a misdemeanor if it contains all the elements required in INA §101(a)(43).[278] Whether a crime is classified as a misdemeanor by the convicting jurisdiction or would be a misdemeanor under federal law, may be relevant to whether the crime is an aggravated felony; the definition at INA §101(a)(43) controls.

For instance, in some circuits, for certain drug crimes, the labeling of the crime as a misdemeanor or felony by the convicting jurisdiction is determinative of whether the crime is an aggravated felony, while in other circuits a state's classification of a drug crime as a misdemeanor is irrelevant to the analysis.[279] This is the result of the circuit courts' differing definitions of a "felony punishable under the Controlled Substances Act," which is a term from the cross-referenced definition at 18 USC §924(c), not from INA §101(a)(43)(B) itself.

In other instances (*e.g.*, crimes of violence or burglary), the aggravated felony subsection at INA §101(a)(43) is so specific as to the requirements regarding the na-

---

[275] *United States v. Valansi*, 278 F. 3d 203, 215–17 (3d Cir. 2002) (holding that embezzlement under the federal criminal statute was not an aggravated felony for fraud because the crime as defined did not track all of the elements necessary for fraud).

[276] *Matter of V–Z–S–*, 22 I&N Dec. 1338 (BIA 2000).

[277] *Matter of Sweetser*, 22 I&N Dec. 709 (BIA 1999).

[278] *Matter of Small*, 23 I&N Dec. 448, 450 (BIA 2002) (citing *United States v. Robles-Rodriguez*, 281 F.3d 900, 903 (9th Cir. 2002)).

[279] Compare *United States v. Ibarra-Galindo*, 206 F.3d 1337 (9th Cir. 2000) (convicting jurisdiction's classification is determinative for drug crimes) with *Gerbier v. Holmes*, 280 F.3d 297 (3d Cir. 2002) (federal classification is determinative for drug crimes).

ture of the crime and the length of the sentence that whether the convicting jurisdiction classifies the crime as a misdemeanor or as a felony is irrelevant to whether the crime is an aggravated felony.[280]

Term of imprisonment

Does the aggravated felony definition's relevant subsection require a "term of imprisonment"? Certain aggravated felonies—including crimes of violence, theft, racketeering, gambling offenses, bribery, counterfeiting, forgery, obstruction of justice, perjury or subornation of perjury, trafficking in vehicles with altered vehicle identification numbers, and forging or altering a passport—require a term of imprisonment of at least one year.[281] If the client's term of imprisonment for one of these crimes is less than one year, then the crime is not an aggravated felony.

A "term of imprisonment" includes the period of confinement ordered by the court regardless of whether there has been any suspension of imposition or execution of a sentence.[282] However, a direct sentence of probation—not a period of incarceration suspended—is not a sentence to a "term of imprisonment."[283] The term of imprisonment for an indeterminate sentence is considered to be for the maximum term possible.[284]

Additionally, the term of imprisonment is determined by the most recent sentence imposed.[285] Thus, if a criminal court vacates a one-year sentence and imposes a new sentence of less than 365 days, that new term of imprisonment governs, and the crime—although it remains a "conviction"—will not be an aggravated felony.[286]

Effective dates and retroactivity

The aggravated felony definition applies to convictions entered before, on, or after IIRAIRA's enactment—September 30, 1996.[287] The aggravated felony ground of removability/deportability applies to all individuals placed into proceedings after March 1, 1991.[288]

---

[280] INA §§101(a)(43)(F) (under 8 USC §16(b)) and (G).

[281] INA §§101(a)(43)(F), (G), and (J) (may be imposed); (P) and (Q) (punishable by five or more years); and (R), (S), and (T) (may be imposed).

[282] INA §101(a)(48)(B).

[283] *United States v. Banda-Zamora*, 178 F.3d 728, 730 (5th Cir. 1999).

[284] *Matter of S–S–*, 21 I&N Dec. 900, 903 (BIA 1997).

[285] *Matter of Song*, 23 I&N Dec. 173, 174 (BIA 2001).

[286] *Id.*

[287] INA §101(a)(43) (final paragraph).

[288] *Matter of Lettman*, 22 I&N Dec. 365 (BIA 1999), *aff'd Lettman v. Reno,* 207 F.3d 1368 (11th Cir. 2000).

Aggravated Felony Charges

The most common aggravated felony charges are those involving controlled substances and crimes of violence. Other common aggravated felony charges include theft and burglary offenses, fraud, smuggling, and sexual abuse of a minor.

Drug trafficking crimes—INA §101(a)(43)(B)

A drug trafficking crime is an aggravated felony if it involves illicit trafficking in a "controlled substance" and/or any "drug trafficking crime."[289] Illicit trafficking is unlawful trading or dealing.[290] Under this prong of the definition, the offense must be classified as a felony by the prosecuting jurisdiction to be an aggravated felony.[291] Simple possession offenses may not satisfy this definition.

A "controlled substance" is a drug or other substance listed in the statutory and regulatory schedules at 21 USC §812 and 8 CFR §1308.01 *et seq.*[292] Distilled spirits, wine, malt beverages, and tobacco (as defined at 26 USC §5001 *et seq.*) are not controlled substances.

Alternatively, any "drug trafficking crime" defined at 18 USC §924(c) is an aggravated felony.[293] Section 924(c)(2) of 18 USC defines a "drug trafficking crime" as "any felony" "punishable" under three different laws: the Controlled Substances Act (21 USC §801 *et seq.*); the Controlled Substances Import and Export Act (21 USC §951 *et seq.*); and the Maritime Drug Law Enforcement Act (46 USC App. 1901 *et seq.*). The most common drug trafficking aggravated felonies are sale, distribution, or possession under the Controlled Substances Act.[294] Under this prong of the definition, simple possession may be an aggravated felony.

The BIA has stated that state felony drug convictions meet the definition of "any felony" at 18 USC §924(c) because they are felonies under state law.[295] There has been some conflict among the circuits on the meaning of "any felony." In the Second and Third Circuits, to be an aggravated felony, a crime must be a felony *under the Controlled Substances Act itself* (or one of the other defining statutes).[296] These decisions adopted the BIA's own position.[297] In other circuits, the crime must be punishable under the Controlled Substances Act (or one of the other defining statutes) *and be classified as a felony by the prosecuting jurisdiction.*[298]

---

[289] INA §101(a)(43)(B).

[290] *Matter of Davis*, 20 I&N Dec. 536 (BIA 1992) (modified on other grounds at 23 I&N Dec. 390).

[291] *Id.*

[292] 21 USC §802(6).

[293] INA §101(a)(43)(B).

[294] 21 USC §§841–44.

[295] *Matter of Yanez-Garcia*, 23 I&N Dec. 390 (BIA 2002).

[296] *Gerbier v. Holmes*, 280 F.3d 297 (3d Cir. 2002); *Aguirre v. INS*, 79 F.3d 315 (2d Cir. 1996).

[297] *See Matter of K–V–D–*, 22 I&N Dec. 1163 (BIA 1999).

[298] *United States v. Hernandez-Avalos*, 251 F.3d 505 (5th Cir. 2001).

Gerbier and *Aguirre* were direct appeals of immigration court orders and the Second and Third Circuits distinguished immigration interpretations from sentencing guideline interpretations as the BIA had done in *K–V–D–*. Other courts that were considering the criminal sentencing context have rejected this distinction and indicated that a circuit court's interpretation of the aggravated felony definition for sentencing guidelines purposes is binding on the BIA.[299]

The BIA now follows the circuit courts in cases arising in their respective jurisdictions, and follows the majority approach in cases where the circuit court has not decided the issue.[300] Thus, a state or foreign felony controlled substance crime that would be punishable as a misdemeanor under federal law and that contains no trafficking element is not an aggravated felony in the Second and Third Circuits' jurisdictions, but it is an aggravated felony in the majority's jurisdictions.

Crimes of violence—INA §101(a)(43)(F)

A crime is an aggravated felony if the offense meets the definition of "crime of violence" at 18 USC §16, and a "term of imprisonment" of at least one year has been imposed.[301] Purely political offenses, however, are not crimes of violence.[302]

18 USC §16 defines "crime of violence" as:

> (a) an offense that has as an element the use, attempted use, or threatened use of physical force against the person or property of another; or
>
> (b) any other offense that is a felony and that, by its nature, involves a substantial risk that physical force against the person or property of another may be used in the course of committing the offense.

In defining whether a crime fits this definition, the particular facts of the crime are not the focus. Rather, the proper inquiry is whether a particular offense, as defined in the abstract, is a crime of violence looking to the crime's elements and, if necessary, its nature in general—a categorical approach.[303]

Under 18 USC §16(a), it is irrelevant whether a crime is a misdemeanor or felony. An offense will be an aggravated felony so long as it has as an element the use (or attempt or threat of use) of physical force and is punished with a term of imprisonment of one year or longer.[304] In contrast, 18 USC §16(b) applies only to felony convictions.

---

[299] *See, e.g., id.* at 509.

[300] *Matter of Yanez*, 23 I&N Dec. 390, 397 (BIA 2002); *Matter of Santos-Lopez*, 23 I&N Dec. 419 (BIA 2002).

[301] INA §101(a)(43)(F).

[302] *Id.*

[303] *Leocal v. Ashcroft*, 543 U.S. 1 (2004). *See also United States v. Chapa-Garza*, 243 F.3d 921 (5th Cir. 2001); *U.S. v. Taylor*, 495 U.S. 575 (1990).

[304] *Matter of Martin*, 23 I&N Dec. 491 (BIA 2002).

"Use" of force under 18 USC §16(a) requires active employment of force and therefore a *mens rea* higher than negligent or merely accidental conduct.[305]

The language of §16(b) is broader than that of §16(a) because it requires only a *risk* of force, not an element of force.[306] 18 USC §16(b)'s requirement of a "substantial risk that physical force be used" relates not to the possibility that harm will result, but to the risk that the use of physical force will be required in order to commit the crime.[307]

In spite of the difference, "use" of force under §16(b), like "use" under §16(a), requires active employment of force and therefore a *mens rea* higher than negligent or accidental conduct.[308]

When a crime of violence is implicated in removal proceedings, first review the charge on the NTA. Make certain that this charging document specifies the exact aggravated felony subsection, *e.g.*, INA §101(a)(43)(F). Review 18 USC §16 and determine precisely those subsections that DHS charges as applicable.

It is DHS's burden to prove deportability under INA §237 by "clear and convincing" evidence in removal proceedings.[309] Therefore, require DHS to produce the conviction record. Only specific documents will suffice as proof of a conviction, including an official record of judgment and conviction; an official record of plea, verdict, and sentence; a docket entry from court records indicating existence of conviction; official minutes of a court proceeding or transcript of court hearing where the court takes notice of the existence of conviction; an abstract of record of conviction; document or record prepared by, or under the direction of, the court indicating the existence of the conviction; or document or record maintained by a penal institution indicating existence of conviction.[310]

Generally, DHS provides a certified copy instead of the official record itself.[311] Conviction records sent from a state or court to DHS via electronic means are admissible in removal proceedings if the state or court certifies that the record is from its official repository of criminal justice records, and a DHS official also certifies the record as having been received electronically from the state or court's official repository. Police reports or arrest records are *not* sufficient to establish a conviction in removal proceedings.[312]

---

[305] *Leocal*, 543 U.S. 1.

[306] *Id.* at 383.

[307] *Id.*; *Matter of Sweetser*, 22 I&N Dec. 709, 716 (BIA 1999).

[308] *Leocal*, 543 U.S. at 383; *see also United States v. Chapa-Garza*, 243 F.3d 921 (5th Cir. 2001) ("use" requires at least recklessness towards a substantial likelihood that *intentional* force will be applied against person or property); *Matter of Ramos*, 23 I&N Dec. 336 (BIA 2002).

[309] INA §240(c)(3)(A).

[310] INA §240(c)(3)(B).

[311] *Id.*

[312] *Matter of Teixeira*, 21 I&N Dec. 316, 319–20 (BIA 1996).

Review the elements of the criminal statute. If the criminal statute is divisible and describes both offenses that are aggravated felonies and offenses that are not, then the IJ may look to the record of conviction including the charging document to determine under which section the individual was convicted.[313]

It is the elements of the specific statute under which the client was convicted that control.[314] Make certain that the elements in the offense for which the individual was convicted correspond to the elements in INA §101(a)(43).[315] The criminal statute must have as an element the "use of physical force," or be a felony with a "substantial risk" that physical force may be used against persons or property under 18 USC §16.

Finally, even if the crime is one defined under 18 USC §16, the crime is not an aggravated felony under INA §101(a)(43)(F) unless the criminal court has imposed a "term of imprisonment" of at least one year.

Classification of Crimes That Might Be Crimes of Violence

Are Crimes of Violence	Are Not Crimes of Violence
Arson[316] Assault (third degree under Connecticut law)[317] Burglary[318] Burglary of a Habitation[319] Burglary of a Vehicle[320] Criminal Contempt[321] Criminal Trespass[322] Indecency with a Child[323] Indecent Assault and Battery[324] Manslaughter[325]	Burglary of automobile[332] Criminally Negligent Child Abuse[333] Driving While Intoxicated[334] Injury to a Child[335]

---

[313] *Matter of Sweetser*, 22 I&N Dec. 709 (BIA 1999).

[314] *Matter of Short*, 20 I&N Dec. 136 (BIA 1989).

[315] *Matter of Espinoza*, 22 I&N Dec. 889 (BIA 1999).

[316] *Matter of Palacios*, 22 I&N Dec. 434 (BIA 1998).

[317] *Matter of Martin*, 23 I&N Dec.491 (BIA 2002).

[318] *Matter of Truong*, 22 I&N Dec. 1090 (BIA 1999).

[319] *U.S. v. Guadardo*, 40 F.3d 102 (5th Cir. 1994).

[320] *Lopez-Elias v. Reno*, 209 F.3d 788 (5th Cir. 2000).

[321] *U.S. v. Delgado- Enriquez*, 188 F.3d 592 (5th Cir. 1999).

[322] *Matter of Aldebesheh*, 22 I&N Dec. 983 (BIA 1999).

[323] *U.S. v. Velasquez-Olvera*, 100 F.3d 418 (5th Cir. 1996).

[324] *Sutherland v. Reno*, 228 F.3d 171 (2d Cir. 2000).

[325] *Matter of Jean*, 23 I&N Dec. 373, 385 (A.G. 2002).

Unlawful Possession of Firearm[326] Statutory Rape[327] Terrorism[328] Terroristic Threats[329] Unauthorized Use of Motor Vehicle[330] Vehicular Homicide[331]	

Theft—INA §101(a)(43)(G)

Theft may be an aggravated felony depending on the elements of the state offense and sentence. The necessary elements include a conviction for theft offense and a term of imprisonment[336] of one year or longer. Theft is defined as the taking of property with the intent to deprive the owner of the rights and benefits of ownership; this may be even for a temporary period.[337] Even a state-labeled misdemeanor theft offense is considered an aggravated felony for immigration law purposes if the sentence is one or more years.[338]

Attempted possession of stolen property under INA §§101(a)(43)(G) and (U) is an aggravated felony for attempted theft.[339] Conviction for possession of stolen mail is a theft offense and an aggravated felony.[340] Conviction for possession of a stolen vehicle is an aggravated felony as a theft offense.[341] Attempted robbery is an aggravated felony.[342]

---

[326] *U.S. v. Rivas-Palacios*, 244 F.3d 396 (5th Cir. 2001).

[327] *Matter of B–*, 21 I&N Dec. 287 (BIA 1996).

[328] *Matter of S–S–*, 21 I&N Dec. 900 (BIA 1997).

[329] *U.S. v. Bovkun*, 283 F.3d 166 (3d Cir. 2002).

[330] *U.S. v. Galvan-Rodriguez*, 169 F.3d 217 (5th Cir. 1999).

[331] *Omar v. INS*, 298 F.3d 710 (8th Cir. 2002).

[332] *U.S. v. Solorzano-Patlan*, 207 F.3d 869 (7th Cir. 2000); *but see Santos v. Reno*, 228 F.3d 591 (5th Cir. 2000).

[333] *Matter of Sweetser*, 22 I&N Dec. 709 (BIA 1999).

[334] *Leocal v. Ashcroft*, 543 U.S. 1 (2004).

[335] *U.S. v. Gracia-Cantu*, 302 F.3d 308 (5th Cir. 2002).

[336] INA §101(a)(48)(B).

[337] *Matter of V–Z–S–*, 22 I&N Dec. 1338 (BIA 2000) (holding unauthorized use of a motor vehicle to be theft).

[338] *U.S. V. Graham*, 169 F.3d 787 (3d. Cir. 1999).

[339] *Matter of Bahta*, 22 I&N Dec. 1381 (BIA 2000).

[340] *Randhawa v. Ashcroft*, 298 F.3d 1148 (9th Cir. 2002).

[341] *Hernandez-Mancilla v. INS*, 246 F.3d 1002 (4th Cir. 2001).

[342] *U.S. v. Fernandez-Antonia*, 278 F.3d 150, 162 (2d Cir. 2002) (interpreting sentencing guidelines).

Burglary—INA §101(a)(43)(G)

Burglary under INA §101(a)(43)(G) is an aggravated felony where there is a conviction for burglary and sentencing to a minimum one-year term of imprisonment. Burglary is the unlawful or unprivileged entry into, or remaining in, a building or structure with intent to commit a crime.[343]

Burglary of a motor vehicle is not an aggravated felony since the definition specifically refers to entry into a building or structure.[344]

Fraud—INA §101(a)(43)(M)

Conviction for fraud is an aggravated felony. However, it is not the length of the term of imprisonment that is determinative, but, rather, the elements of the offense combined with the dollar amount of the fraud. Conviction for an offense involving fraud or deceit in which the loss to the victim exceeds $10,000, or conviction for tax evasion in which the revenue loss to the government exceeds $10,000 is an aggravated felony.

While fraud involving actual loss of less than $10,000 is not an aggravated felony under INA §101(a)(43)(M), it may be an aggravated felony under INA §101(a)(43)(U), as a crime involving attempts or conspiracy to commit an aggravated felony.[345]

Tax evasion by subscribing to a false tax return where the loss to the government was more than $10,000 is an aggravated felony.[346]

Embezzlement is not an aggravated felony as a fraud offense where the statute and record of conviction were not clear that intent to defraud was an element of the offense.[347]

Smuggling, transporting, and harboring—INA §101(a)(43)(N)

Conviction of an "offense described in" INA §§274(a)(1)(A) or (a)(2) is an aggravated felony regardless of the term of imprisonment. Such convictions include (1) bringing an alien, or attempting to bring, an alien to the United States at a place other than a designated port of entry; (2) transporting an alien within the United States, knowing or in reckless disregard of the fact that the alien is present in violation of law; [348] (3) harboring an alien, knowing or in reckless disregard of the fact that the alien is present in violation of law; [349] (4) encouraging or inducing an alien to enter

---

[343] *Matter of Perez*, 22 I&N Dec. 1325 (BIA 2000).

[344] *Id.*

[345] *Matter of Onyido*, 22 I&N Dec. 552 (BIA 1999).

[346] *Abreu-Reyes v. INS*, 292 F.3d 1029 (9th Cir. 2002).

[347] *Valansi v. INS*, 278 F.3d 203 (3d Cir. 2002).

[348] *Ruiz-Romero v. Reno*, 205 F.3d. 837 (5th Cir. 2000).

[349] *Rivera Sanchez v. Reno*, 198 F.3d 545, 547 (5th Cir. 1999); *Patel v. Ashcroft*, 294 F.3d. 465 (3d Cir. 2002).

into, or reside in, the United States, knowing or in reckless disregard of the fact that the entry or residence will be in violation of law; or (5) conspiring, aiding, or abetting in any of the above.[350]

A conviction for illegal entry under INA §275—"Improper Entry by Alien"—is not an aggravated felony; INA §101(a)(43)(N) is limited only to offenses "described in" INA §§274(a)(1)(A) or (2).

Obstruction of justice—INA §101(a)(43)(S)

A conviction for any of the offenses listed under INA §101(a)(43)(S)—perjury, subornation of perjury, obstruction of justice, or bribery of a witness—is an aggravated felony if the term of imprisonment[351] is at least one year.

- Misprision of a felony is not obstruction of justice and, therefore, not an aggravated felony.[352]
- Accessory after the fact is obstruction of justice and an aggravated felony.[353]
- Perjury is an aggravated felony.[354]

Sexual abuse of a minor—INA §101(a)(43)(A)

A state misdemeanor conviction for sexual abuse of a minor is an aggravated felony.[355] This is true regardless of the sentence. Sexual abuse of a minor is one of the aggravated felonies, like drug trafficking and murder, that is an aggravated felony based on the conviction alone.[356] A conviction for indecency with a child "by exposure" is an aggravated felony under INA §101(a)(43)(A).[357]

Conclusion

If nothing else, three things are imperative in analyzing an aggravated felony charge. First, make certain that DHS states the charge exactly. Second, obtain the entire record of conviction (the charging document also), not just the judgment. Third, thoroughly analyze the wording in the underlying criminal statute to make certain that it is directly on point with the charge made by DHS in the NTA. If the battle is lost on the aggravated felony issue at the removability stage, then the opportunity to apply for most forms of relief also will be lost to the client.

---

[350] INA §274(a)(1)(A).

[351] INA §101(a)(48)(B).

[352] *Matter of Espinoza*, 22 I&N Dec. 889 (BIA 1999).

[353] *Matter of Batista-Hernandez*, 21 I&N Dec. 955 (BIA 1997).

[354] *Matter of Martinez-Recinos*, 23 I&N Dec. 175 (BIA 2001).

[355] *Matter of Small*, 23 I&N Dec. 448 (BIA 2002).

[356] INA §101(a)(43)(A).

[357] *Matter of Rodriguez-Rodriguez*, 22 I&N Dec. 991 (BIA 1999).

Criminal Grounds—Controlled Substances, Firearms, and Domestic Violence Offenses

Introduction

In addition to the grounds of deportability based on convictions for crimes involving moral turpitude and aggravated felonies, three other grounds of deportability based on crimes exist in the INA—controlled substance violations, firearms convictions, and crimes of domestic violence.

Controlled Substance Violations—INA §237(a)(2)(B)

This ground of deportability makes removable an alien who meets the following elements:

- has been convicted;
- of a violation of any law or regulation under U.S. or foreign law;
- relating to a controlled substance (as defined in 21 USC §802);
- at any time after admission.

The only exception to this rule involves crimes relating to a single offense for possession of marijuana of 30 grams or less for personal use. This ground of deportability is separate and apart from the aggravated felony ground of deportability relating to "illicit trafficking in a controlled substance."[358] In addition, anyone who is a drug abuser or addict at any time after admission is removable.[359]

Controlled substance violations that are deportable offenses

The BIA has found that an offense relating to "being under the influence of a controlled substance" can be the basis for a finding of deportability on the grounds that it is "related to a controlled substance."[360] In the same case, the BIA also held that there is no requirement of guilty knowledge or *mens rea* in order to find an individual deportable for being under the influence of a controlled substance.[361] Furthermore, a conviction for attempted possession of a controlled substance is a deportable offense,[362] as is facilitating the sale or use of a controlled substance as a crime "relating to a controlled substance."[363]

The meaning of the term "relating to a controlled substance" has been broadened in several decisions. For instance, possession of drug paraphernalia under Arizona law has been defined as a conviction relating to a controlled substance.[364] A conviction for so-

---

[358] INA §101(a)(43)(B).

[359] INA §237(a)(2)(B)(ii).

[360] *Matter of Hernandez-Ponce*, 19 I&N Dec. 613 (BIA 1988).

[361] *See Matter of Esqueda*, 20 I&N Dec. 850 (BIA 1994).

[362] *Bronsztejn v. INS*, 526 F.2d 1290 (2d Cir. 1975).

[363] *Matter of Del Risco*, 20 I&N Dec. 109 (BIA 1989).

[364] *Luu-Le v. INS*, 224 F.3d 911 (9th Cir. 2000).

liciting to commit a crime relating to a controlled substance also makes an individual removable.[365] Furthermore, foreign convictions make an individual removable.[366]

Crimes not related to controlled substance offenses

The BIA has found that the offense of "accessory after the fact" to a drug trafficking crime under 18 USC §3 is not a crime "relating to a controlled substance" sufficient for a finding of deportability.[367] However, in that same case, the BIA did find that being an accessory after the fact was an aggravated felony under INA §101(a)(43)(S), making the alien removable under INA §241(a)(2)(A)(iii), in that it was "obstruction of justice."[368] A conviction for conspiracy to commit money laundering (when that money was related to the drug trade) was not considered to be a conviction for a crime relating to a controlled substance.[369]

Limited defenses

There are limited defenses to a conviction for a crime relating to controlled substances. An individual is not removable if he or she has been convicted for a single offense involving possession for his or her own use of 30 grams or less of marijuana.[370] In addition, a presidential or gubernatorial pardon will waive a ground of deportability even if it relates to a controlled substance.[371] However, note that in that case, the BIA found that a presidential or gubernatorial pardon will waive deportability only for that conviction that is pardoned. If there are other grounds of deportability, the individual may be found deportable and ordered removed based on those crimes that were not pardoned by the President or state governor.

An individual who is convicted of a crime, including one relating to controlled substance, is still deportable even if he or she has been accorded first offender treatment under a state rehabilitative statute and the conviction has been expunged.[372] The BIA has found that first offender rehabilitative treatment that expunged a conviction for immigration purposes under its prior decision in *Matter of Manrique*,[373] no longer precludes such a conviction from supporting removability.

It is the government's burden to prove that an individual has been convicted of a crime that makes a person deportable under INA §237(a)(2)(B). If the case involves a conviction for a single offense of possession of marijuana, the government has the

---

[365] *Matter of Beltran*, 20 I&N Dec. 521 (BIA 1992).

[366] *Matter of Dellingham*, 21 I&N Dec. 1001 (BIA 1997).

[367] *Matter of Batitsa-Hernandez*, 21 I&N Dec. 955 (BIA 1997).

[368] *Id.*

[369] *Lara-Chacon v. Ashcroft*, 345 F.3d 1148 (9th Cir. 2003).

[370] INA §237(a)(2)(B)(i).

[371] *Matter Suh*, 23 I&N Dec. 626 (BIA 2003).

[372] *Matter of Roldan-Santoyo*, 22 I&N Dec. 512 (BIA 1999).

[373] 21 I&N Dec. 58 (BIA 1995).

burden to prove the amount involved was more than 30 grams in order to establish deportability.

In summary, an individual who has been convicted for almost any crime relating to a controlled substance is, in most cases, deportable, unless that crime is for one single offense relating to possession for one's own use of 30 grams or less of marijuana.

Firearms Offenses—INA §237(a)(2)(C)

An alien is removable for conviction of certain crimes relating to firearms or destructive devices. A firearms offense is one of the few crimes that is not also a ground of inadmissibility, *i.e.*, it is not listed in the grounds at INA §212(a)(2). Following are the elements of this ground of deportability:

- purchasing, selling, offering for sale, exchanging, using, owning, possessing, or carrying any weapon, part, or accessory that is a firearm or destructive device as defined under 18 USC §921(a);
- at any time after admission;
- in violation of any law; or
- any attempt or conspiracy to do any of the above.

In order for an offense to serve as a basis for deportability under INA §237(a)(2)(C), the use, possession, sale (or other actions relating to a weapon as stated in the statute) "must be an essential element within the definition of the offense."[374]

The firearms offense ground of deportability also encompasses convictions of crimes for which possession of or carrying of firearms is an element of the offense.[375] For example, a crime of violence with a deadly weapon under a Colorado statute was found to be a firearms offense under INA §237(a)(2)(C).[376]

In *Vue v. INS*,[377] the court found that a conviction under Minnesota law for aggravated robbery was a firearms offense. An alien convicted of the first degree felonies of armed burglary and robbery with a firearm was convicted of firearms offenses for the purpose of deportability under INA §237(a)(2)(C).[378] Conviction for first degree murder with a firearm under Florida law has been found to be a firearms offense.[379] An individual convicted of aggravated murder in the second degree whose sentence was enhanced because a codefendant was armed with a firearm during the attempted

---

[374] *Vue v. INS*, 92 F.3d 696 (8th Cir. 1996).

[375] *Kuhali v. Reno*, 266 F.3d 93 (2d Cir. 2001).

[376] *See Bereag v. INS*, 114 F.3d 159 (10th Cir. 1997).

[377] *Vue*, 92 F.3d 696.

[378] *See Matter of P–F–*, 20 I&N Dec. 661 (BIA 1993).

[379] *Matter of Lopez-Amaro*, 20 I&N Dec. 668 (BIA 1993).

commission of the felony was deemed to not have been convicted of a firearms offense under INA §241(a)(2)(C) (now INA §237(a)(2)(C)).[380]

A conviction for attempted purchase, sale, use, etc., of a firearm or destructive device is also a ground of removability.[381] The BIA has found that this ground of deportability, amended under IMMACT90, is applicable to convictions entered before, on, or after the date of enactment.[382] Therefore, the BIA's prior decision under *Matter of Hue*,[383] which stated that a conviction for an attempted firearms offense would not support a ground of deportability under the INA, has been superseded.

Note: A conviction for a firearms offense is not a ground of inadmissibility under INA §212(a) and, therefore, a waiver under former INA §212(c) (repealed 1996) is not available to waive this ground.[384] In addition, because firearms offenses do not trigger grounds of inadmissibility under INA §212(a), the clock-stopping provisions of INA §240A(d), which limits the availability of cancellation of removal under INA §240A(b), do not come into play.

Crimes of Domestic Violence—INA §237(a)(2)(E)

An individual convicted of a crime of domestic violence "at any time after entry" (not admission) or a crime of child abuse, neglect, or abandonment is "deportable." A crime of domestic violence is defined as a crime of violence (18 USC §16) committed against any of the following:

- current or former spouse;
- parent of child shared in common;
- person cohabiting or formerly cohabiting as spouse;
- a person similarly situated to a spouse under the domestic violence laws of the jurisdiction where the offense occurs; or
- any individual protected against such abuse under the domestic or family violence laws of the federal, state, or local government.[385]

The court may not look beyond the record of conviction in order to determine if the crime was one of domestic violence, *i.e.*, to shore-up the spousal-like relationship between the assailant and the victim.[386] The record of conviction is limited to the charge, plea, verdict, and sentence.[387]

---

[380] *Matter of Rodriguez-Cortes*, 20 I&N Dec. 587 (BIA 1992).

[381] INA §237(a)(2)(C). *See also Matter of Saint John*, 21 I&N Dec. 593 (BIA 1996).

[382] *Matter of Chow*, 20 I&N Dec. 647 (BIA 1993).

[383] 20 I&N Dec. 513 (BIA 1992).

[384] *Cf. Matter of Aruzin*, 23 I&N Dec. 695 (BIA 2005) (firearms offense needs no waiver in context of application to readjust status).

[385] INA §237(a)(2)(E)(i).

[386] *Tokatly v. Ashcroft*, 371 F.3d 613 (9th Cir. 2004).

[387] *Matter of Pichardo-Sufren*, 21 I&N Dec. 330 (BIA 1996).

A crime of violence under 18 USC §16 is one that has as an essential element the use of force, or one that, by its nature, entails a substantial risk that force will be used against persons or property.[388]

The INA §237(a)(2)(E) ground of deportability also makes a violation of a protection order a deportable offense when the court determines that the offense involves a violation of the part of the order that protects against threats of violence, harassment, or bodily injury.[389] In addition, a conviction for the willful infliction of corporal injury on a spouse, cohabitant, or parent of the perpetrator's child is a crime involving moral turpitude, even if the offense is a misdemeanor.[390]

Conclusion

Deportability based on any of the criminal grounds outlined above should never be conceded without requiring DHS to present a conviction record that conforms to the requirements at INA §§240(c)(3)(B) and (C). Doing so without clear and convincing proof on the part of the government is to jeopardize a client's status without forcing DHS to meet its burden. Your client may be left without relief.

Security, Terrorism, and Related Grounds of Deportability

The security grounds of deportability under INA §237(a)(4) are similar in many ways to the security grounds of inadmissibility under INA §212(a)(3). There are five separate security-related grounds of deportability.

General Security-Related Grounds

A non–American citizen may be deported where he or she has engaged, is engaged, or at any time after admission engages in:

- any activity relating to sabotage; espionage; or a violation or evasion of any law prohibiting the export of technology, sensitive information, or goods;
- any activity a purpose of which is the overthrow of the government by force or unlawful means; or
- any other criminal activity that endangers public safety or national security.[391]

An alien need not be engaged in an act of espionage or have been convicted of violating a law relating to espionage to be deportable. If the alien has knowledge of, or has received instruction in, the espionage or counter-espionage service or tactics of a foreign government in violation of 50 USC §851, he or she is deportable as a security threat.[392]

---

[388] *Leocal v. Ashcroft*, 543 U.S. 1 (2004).

[389] INA §237(a)(2)(E)(ii).

[390] *Matter of Tran*, 21 I&N Dec. 291 (BIA 1996).

[391] INA §237(a)(4)(A).

[392] *Matter of Luis-Rodriguez*, 22 I&N Dec. 747 (BIA 1999)

Terrorism

An alien who has engaged, is engaged, or at any time after admission engages in any terrorist activity (as defined in INA §212(a)(3)(B)(iv)) is deportable. Terrorist activity is defined as action that is unlawful under the laws of the place where it is committed (including overseas actions that would have been unlawful under U.S. federal or state law) and that involves any of the following:

- hijacking or sabotage of any conveyance;
- seizing or detaining and threatening to kill another individual in order to compel a person or entity to do, or refrain from doing, something to obtain the person's release;
- violent attack on an internationally protected person or upon the person's liberty;[393]
- assassination;
- use of biological or chemical agent, nuclear device, firearm, explosive, or other weapon with intent to endanger directly or indirectly the safety of one or more individuals or cause substantial damage to property; or
- threat, attempt, or conspiracy to do any of the foregoing.[394]

The USA PATRIOT Act[395] added fundraising, solicitation of members, and material support to terrorist organizations as terrorist activities.[396] See section on USA PATRIOT Act, below.

USA PATRIOT Act

On October 26, 2001, six weeks after the 9/11 attacks on the World Trade Center and the Pentagon, President Bush signed into law the "Uniting and Strengthening America by Providing Appropriate Tools Required to Intercept and Obstruct Terrorism Act" of 2001 (USA PATRIOT Act).[397] The USA PATRIOT Act greatly expands law enforcement's authority in various ways, including over electronic intelligence; foreign intelligence; surveillance; criminal law and procedure; and especially in the area of detention and removal of immigrants suspected of terrorist activity. The USA PATRIOT Act's definition of terrorist activity adds the use of "any weapon or dangerous device" as a ground of inadmissibility and deportability.[398]

---

[393] *See* 18 USC §1116(b)(4).

[394] INA §237(a)(4)(B).

[395] USA PATRIOT Act, *supra* note 48.

[396] INA §212(a)(3)(B)(iv).

[397] USA PATRIOT Act, *supra* note 48.

[398] INA §212(a)(3)(B)(iii)(V)(b).

Definition relating to terrorism

The USA PATRIOT Act also added several new grounds of inadmissibility for representatives of foreign terrorist organizations or groups that endorse acts of terrorism. It authorizes the Secretary of State the power to designate any group, foreign or domestic, as a terrorist organization through publication in the *Federal Register*.[399] In addition, fundraising, solicitation for membership, or material support of any group designated as a terrorist organization by the Secretary of State is a deportable offense.[400] It does not matter whether the activities are in furtherance of humanitarian, educational, or other nonmilitant endeavors if the group itself has been designated as a terrorist organization. In addition, solicitation of funds or support for groups that are not officially designated as terrorist organizations also can be a removable offense if the individual knew or should have known that such solicitation might further an organization's terrorist activities.[401]

Detention of foreign nationals

Under the USA PATRIOT Act, the AG or the deputy AG may certify an individual as a terrorist if there are reasonable grounds to believe that the individual is a terrorist or has committed a terrorist activity.[402] Such a designation requires mandatory detention of an individual so certified. Once an individual is certified by the AG as a terrorist, that individual remains detained even if he or she is found eligible for, or granted, some form of relief by the IJ.[403] On October 29, 2001, an executive regulation was issued stating that the government has the power to detain an alien even after an IJ has ordered that person's release.[404] Where DHS has designated an individual as security risk under INA §237(a)(4) and subjected that individual to detention, the IJ may not redetermine the custody status of that person.[405]

DHS is permitted to detain a suspected terrorist for seven days before bringing any charges against the individual.[406] The individual has the right to file a petition for writ of habeas corpus to challenge the detention and/or the basis for the AG's certification as a terrorist. This may be filed in any federal district court having jurisdiction to hear such a case. Appeal of the decision of the federal district court goes to the U.S. Court of Appeals for the District of Columbia Circuit.[407]

---

[399] INA §212(a)(2)(A)(ii).

[400] INA §237(a)(4)(B).

[401] *Id*; *see also* INA §212(a)(3)(B)(iv)(IV).

[402] INA §236A(a)(3).

[403] INA §236A(a)(2).

[404] 8 CFR §1003.19(i)(2).

[405] 8 CFR §1003.19(h)(2)(i).

[406] INA §236A(a)(5).

[407] INA §236A(b)(1)–(3).

Sharing of information with foreign governments

Department of State (DOS) records pertaining to the issuance or denial of visas are confidential and can be used only for enforcement of U.S. law.[408] The USA PATRIOT Act, however, provides for the release of these records to a foreign government on an individual basis for the purpose of preventing, investigating, or punishing acts of terrorism.[409]

The immigration regulations provide that information contained in an asylum application shall not be disclosed without the written consent of the applicant except as permitted under certain limited conditions at the discretion of the AG.[410] Such asylum records, however, can be released to other government agencies, such as DOS or other branches of the Department of Justice (DOJ) in certain instances including the investigation of any criminal or civil matter.[411] The government has been required to ensure that the confidentiality of this information is maintained if it is transmitted to DOS offices in other countries.

The USA PATRIOT Act provides that these confidentiality provisions will not apply if such disclosure is made during the investigation of an individual to determine if the applicant is a terrorist, and if the AG has reasonable grounds to believe that the individual is a terrorist.[412] The USA PATRIOT Act also mandates that DOJ provide access to criminal history record information contained in the National Crimes Information Center Interstate Identification Index for DOS and DHS.[413]

Antiterrorism and Effective Death Penalty Act (AEDPA)

After the 1995 bombing of the federal building in Oklahoma City, public awareness of the possibility of domestic terrorism was heightened and there was strong sentiment to toughen laws relating to national security. Partially as a result of the bombing, AEDPA passed on April 24, 1996.[414] The following is a summary of some of the major aspects relating to detention, inadmissibility, and deportation of those believed to be non–American citizen terrorists.

Establishment of a removal court

The Chief Justice of the Supreme Court appoints five district court judges from different circuits to conduct removal proceedings under INA §502(a) involving those persons claimed by the AG to be "alien terrorists."

---

[408] INA §222(f)(1).

[409] INA §222(f)(2).

[410] 8 CFR §§208.6, 1208.6.

[411] 8 CFR §§208.6(b), 1208.6(b).

[412] USA PATRIOT Act, *supra* note 48, at §205.

[413] *Id.* at §207.

[414] AEDPA, *supra* note 260.

Application for removal

In any case in which the AG has reason to believe based on classified information that an individual is an alien terrorist, he may seek deportation by filing an application with the removal court.[415] The application must contain the facts and circumstances upon which the AG relies to establish: (1) the alien is a terrorist; (2) the alien is physically present within the United States; and (3) regular removal procedures would pose a risk to the national security of the United States.[416] The application is submitted "ex parte" and "in camera" to the court.[417] The decision on whether to grant the application is taken by a single judge on the court who may consider also classified information. If the judge finds that there is probable cause to believe that the individual is a terrorist, the application shall be granted.[418] If not, the application is denied in a written order.[419]

Removal hearing

The removal hearing is conducted as expeditiously as possible and is open to the public.[420]

An alien in these proceedings is accorded certain rights including the following:

- notice of charges;
- notice of place and time of hearing;
- right to counsel (to be appointed if unable to afford counsel);
- reasonable opportunity to present evidence; and
- reasonable opportunity to examine evidence against him or her and cross-examine opposing witnesses (subject to the special rules stated below).[421]

The government may introduce evidence obtained by electronic or other surveillance techniques including "unconsented physical searches."[422] Discovery of this evidence is not authorized if disclosure would present a risk to the national security of the United States or threaten the integrity of a pending investigation.[423] There is no requirement of notice if such evidence is to be used. There is no right to suppress evidence alleged to be unlawfully obtained.[424] The federal rules of evidence do not apply. The judge examines ex parte and in camera the evidence that the AG claims

---

[415] *Id.*

[416] INA §503(a)(1).

[417] INA §503(a)(2).

[418] INA §503(c)(2).

[419] INA §503(c)(3).

[420] INA §§504(a)(1) and (2).

[421] INA §§504(b)–(c).

[422] INA §504(e)(1)(A).

[423] INA §§504(e)(1)(A) and (C).

[424] INA §504(e)(1)(B).

would pose a national security risk if disclosed. The government submits an unclassified summary of this evidence that the judge reviews and then approves if it is sufficient to permit the individual to prepare a defense. A copy is served on the individual.[425]

Burden of proof

The government must prove by a preponderance of the evidence that the individual is an "alien terrorist" and is subject to removal.[426] If the government, after notice from the judge, fails to correct deficiencies in its charges and proof, the removal hearing is terminated. The definition of an "alien terrorist" is stated above and is found in the INA.[427]

Decision of removal

If the judge finds that the government has met its burden, a removal order is issued with a written statement of the facts and conclusion that the individual is an alien terrorist and a removal order is entered.[428] There is no right to various forms of relief (except, possibly, Convention Against Torture relief).[429] Either side may appeal, and the appeal must be filed within 20 days to the U.S. Court of Appeals for the District of Columbia Circuit.[430] The AG may take into custody any individual on whom an application is filed.[431] However, during the pendency of proceedings, an LPR may seek release if he or she can prove that the release will not endanger national security or the safety of any person or the community.[432] If a removal order is issued, the individual is taken back into custody during the appeal.[433]

Foreign Policy

An alien is deportable whose presence or activities in the United States the Secretary of State reasonably believes would have potentially serious adverse foreign policy consequences for the United States.[434] This ground of deportability does not apply to an official of a foreign government or candidate for foreign office during the period immediately preceding the election solely because of beliefs or statements (past or present) that would be lawful in the United States unless the Secretary of State determines that the alien's admission would compromise a compelling U.S. foreign pol-

---

[425] INA §504(e)(3)(B)–(C).

[426] INA §504(g).

[427] INA §§212(a)(3)(B)(iv), 237(a)(4)(B).

[428] INA §504(i).

[429] INA §504(k).

[430] INA §505(c)(1).

[431] INA §506(a)(1).

[432] INA §506(a)(2).

[433] INA §507(b)(1).

[434] INA §237(a)(4)(C)(i).

icy interest.[435] In order to establish removability under INA §237(a)(4), DHS must establish by clear and convincing evidence that the Secretary of State has made a facially reasonable and bona fide determination that an alien's presence or activities in the United States would have potentially serious adverse foreign policy consequences for the United States.[436]

Nazi Persecution, Genocide, or Acts of Torture

Any alien who incited, ordered, assisted, or participated in the persecution of any person on account of race, religion, national origin, or political opinion by the Nazis (between 1933 and 1945) is deportable.[437] Any alien who has engaged in genocide (as defined in 18 USC §1091(a)) also is deportable.[438] Finally, any alien who ordered, incited, assisted, or otherwise participated in the commission of any act of torture, as defined in 18 USC §2340, or any judicial killing as defined in §3(a) of the Torture Protection Act, 28 USC §1350,[439] is subject to deportation.

Recipient of Military-Style Training

An alien who has received military-type training from, or on behalf of, any "terrorist organization" as that term is defined in INA §212(a)(3)(B)(vi), is deportable pursuant to INA §237(a)(4)(E). A terrorist organization is a foreign organization found by the Secretary of State to engage in terrorist activity, or that retains the capability and intent to engage in this activity, and the terrorist activity threatens the security of the United States.[440]

Conclusion

While the security ground of deportability is not frequently charged against an individual, if alleged and proven, the consequences are permanent and serious. With the changes made by the USA PATRIOT Act, it is not necessary to do harm or have other evil intent in order to be found deportable under this section. Even sending money to an individual or organization for a humanitarian reason may be a basis for deportability if that organization or person is one that the donor should have known was involved in terrorist activity. INA §237(a)(4) incorporates all of the activities outlined at INA §212(a)(3)(B) as bases for deportability. In addition, it is important to remember that no conviction or judicial finding of guilt is necessary for the IJ to find an individual deportable under this section.

---

[435] INA §237(a)(4)(C)(ii); *see also* INA §§212(a)(3)(C)(ii) and (iii).

[436] *Matter of Ruiz-Massieu*, 22 I&N Dec. 833 (BIA 1999).

[437] INA §237(a)(4)(D); *see also* INA §212(a)(3)(E)(i).

[438] INA §237(a)(4)(D); *see also* INA §212(a)(3)(E)(ii).

[439] INA §237(a)(4)(D); *see also* INA §212(a)(3)(E)(iii).

[440] INA §219(a).

CHAPTER 3

GROUNDS OF INADMISSIBILITY

Introduction

All individuals unlawfully present within the United States are subject to the same type of proceedings—removal proceedings. The central difference is that those who have not yet been "admitted" lawfully are charged under the Immigration and Nationality Act[1] (INA) §212(a), while those who have been admitted to the United States and have then taken some action (or failed to take some action) that makes them unlawfully present in the United States, are charged under INA §237(a).

The grounds of inadmissibility, which are found at INA §212(a), affect individuals who:

- seek admission to the United States;
- are present in the United States unlawfully without having been inspected and admitted; or
- seek adjustment of status or other possible benefits under the INA.

Many of the grounds of inadmissibility, especially in the criminal and security areas, overlap with the grounds of deportation found at INA §237(a). In the sections of this chapter where such overlap occurs, those sections will summarize only the differences between the grounds of inadmissibility and grounds of deportation, rather than restate what has previously been written in Chapter 2.

---

[1] Immigration and Nationality Act of 1952 (INA), Pub. L. No. 82-414, 66 Stat. 163 (codified as amended at 8 USC §§1101 *et seq.*).

Individuals Seeking Admission from Outside the United States

Applicants for visas seeking entry into the United States are not eligible for the visa if it appears to the consular officer that the individual is ineligible under INA §212.[2] Where the consular officer knows or has reason to believe that an alien is inadmissible under INA §212, no visa will be issued.[3] There are certain exceptions when an individual inadmissible under one of the grounds of inadmissibility (*e.g.*, public charge) may be admitted by posting a bond.[4] Individuals seeking entry who are not in possession of the valid entry documentation not only are inadmissible but may be subject to detention and expedited removal.[5]

Arriving Aliens

The term "arriving alien" means an applicant for admission coming or attempting to come into the United States at a port of entry; an alien seeking transit through the United States at a port of entry; or an alien interdicted in international or U.S. waters and brought into the United States by any means.[6] An arriving alien who is paroled into the United States remains an arriving alien (unless granted parole prior to April 1, 1997). This includes, therefore, not only those individuals stopped at the border but those paroled into the United States.[7] An alien who arrives in the United States pursuant to a grant of advance parole is an arriving alien[8] (parole and advance parole will be discussed, *infra*).

Any alien present in the United States who has not been admitted or who arrives at the border is deemed to be an applicant for admission.[9] All applicants for admission "shall be inspected" by immigration officers.[10] An applicant for admission bears the burden of establishing "clearly and beyond doubt" that he or she is entitled to be admitted and is not inadmissible under INA §212(a).[11] An applicant for admission must present the necessary documentation and establish that he or she is not subject to removal.[12] If the officer determines that the alien is not admissible because of lack of proper documentation or because of fraud, the alien is ordered removed from the United States without a hearing or review by an immigration judge (IJ), unless that person applies for asylum.[13] This process of removal without further review is called

---

[2] INA §221(g).

[3] *Id.*

[4] *Id. See also* 8 CFR §221.1

[5] INA §235(b)(1)(A).

[6] 8 CFR §§1.1(q), 1101.1(q).

[7] *Zheng v. Gonzales*, 422 F.2d 98 (3d Cir. 2005).

[8] *Matter of Oseiwusu*, 22 I&N Dec. 19 (BIA 1998).

[9] INA §235(a)(1).

[10] INA §235(a)(3).

[11] INA §240(c)(2). *See also Altamarino v. Gonzales*, 427 F.3d 586 (9th Cir. 2005).

[12] 8 CFR §§235.1(d), 1235.1(d).

[13] INA §235(b)(1)(A)(i).

expedited removal. Lawful permanent residents (LPRs), asylees, and refugees are not subject to expedited removal.[14] If the alien is not "clearly and beyond doubt" entitled to be admitted, the alien "shall be detained," and may be placed into removal proceedings.[15] Even those applicants for admission seeking asylum are subject to detention.[16]

Parole and Advance Parole

If an inspector at an airport or border checkpoint is not certain as to whether the person should be admitted or refused admission, he or she may parole that person for deferred inspection.[17] An individual may be paroled into the country at the discretion of the Department of Homeland Security (DHS) and under such conditions as DHS may prescribe when it is not certain that he or she is entitled to be admitted.[18] The individual may be paroled for urgent humanitarian reasons or reasons of significant public benefit, rather than be turned away or detained. Examples of individuals who might fall into the humanitarian or public benefit categories outlined at 8 CFR §212.5(b) include individuals with serious medical conditions; pregnant women; juveniles; witnesses in administrative, judicial, or legislative proceedings; or others whose detention is not in the public interest.[19]

However, parole is not considered to be an "admission" as that term is defined at INA §101(a)(13), even if the person is not detained and permitted to physically enter the United States.[20] The person may be required to post a bond during this process.[21] Parole may be terminated at the discretion of DHS when its purpose has been completed; such termination of parole must be by "written notice."[22] The service of a charging document on an individual is considered written notice.[23]

The regulations provide also for "advance parole" at 8 CFR §212.5(f), where an individual is given advance authorization while in the United States that he or she will be permitted to return via parole (not admission) to the United States to continue his or her prior status or application (*e.g.*, pending adjustment of status application or Temporary Protected Status under INA §244).[24] The advance parole regulation is based on the statutory parole provision found at INA §212(d)(5)(A).

---

[14] 8 CFR §235.3(b)(5), 1235.3(b)(5).

[15] INA §235(a)(2)(A).

[16] 8 CFR §§235.3(b)(4)(ii), 1235.3(b)(4)(ii).

[17] *See* 8 CFR §§235.2, 1235.2.

[18] 8 CFR §212.5(c).

[19] 8 CFR §212.5(b)(1)–(5).

[20] *See* INA §212(d)(5)(A).

[21] 8 CFR §212.5(d)(1).

[22] 8 CFR §212.5(e)(1).

[23] 8 CFR §212.5(e)(2).

[24] 8 CFR §212.5(f).

Any departure of a non–American citizen from the country often involves some level of risk, even with the guarantee of "advance parole" upon return. No matter what the status of the individual is upon departure (*e.g.*, valid nonimmigrant status) he or she is treated as an arriving alien upon return. Thus, if DHS charges that he or she is not admissible upon return, the individual is placed in removal proceedings and the burden falls on the individual to prove that he or she is entitled to enter the country. He or she may be charged as inadmissible even if prior to the departure under advance parole, he or she was not "inadmissible" under one of the grounds listed at INA 212(a).[25] DHS reserves the right to detain the individual, even if paroled into the country, as an arriving alien.[26] Any individual seeking advance parole should apply prior to departure by filing an I-131.

Individuals Present without "Admission"

Any individual who is unlawfully present in the United States without having been "admitted" may be placed into removal proceedings.[27] During removal proceedings, the individual would be charged with a ground of inadmissibility under INA §212(a), as opposed to a ground of deportation under INA §237(a) because he or she had not yet been admitted.

Individuals Seeking Adjustment of Status

Any individual who seeks adjustment of status, *i.e.*, to change from unlawful or temporary status to LPR/Green Card status, under INA §245 must prove that he or she is not "inadmissible" under any of the provisions found at INA §212(a). The Board of Immigration Appeals (BIA) has stated that an adjustment of status is an "admission."[28] Therefore, any individual who is present in the United States, whether having entered legally or illegally, and who seeks adjustment of status under INA §245 is subject to INA §212(a) scrutiny and must prove he or she is not barred from admission under any of those provisions before being granted LPR status. There are exceptions for certain groups for whom some grounds of inadmissibility are waived.[29]

---

[25] *Matter of G–A–C–*, 22 I&N Dec. 83 (BIA 1998).

[26] 8 CFR §212.5(e)(2).

[27] INA §101(a)(13) defines "admission" as the lawful entry of an alien after inspection and authorization.

[28] *Matter Shanu*, 23 I&N Dec. 754 (BIA 2005).

[29] For example, Cuban Adjustment Act,, Pub. L. No. 89-732 (1966); Immigration Reform and Control Act of 1986 (IRCA), Pub. L. No 99-603 (1986) (codified at INA §245A); Nicaraguan Adjustment and Central American Relief Act (NACARA), Pub. L. No. 105-100, 111 Stat. 2160, 2193. There also are several other adjustment statutes for specific groups in which certain grounds of inadmissibility are waived. None waives the criminal or security grounds; however, several waive the public charge grounds (INA §212(a)(4)), labor certification grounds (INA §212(a)(5)), and certain of the immigration violation grounds found at INA §212(a)(6)–(9).

Lawful Permanent Residents

Under changes made in 1996, via IIRAIRA,[30] there are occasions when an LPR who is attempting to enter the United States is considered to be seeking an admission and the grounds of inadmissibility apply. Prior to 1996, LPRs who departed and returned to the United States were generally not considered to be seeking "admission" upon return. The Supreme Court decided in 1963 that an LPR who was returning from a "brief, casual, and innocent" trip overseas was not considered to be seeking admission upon return and, therefore, did not have to deal with the inadmissibility grounds at INA §212(a) each time he or she departed and returned to the country.[31] Under pre-IIRAIRA law, the only time that a returning LPR was considered to be seeking an "admission" was if he or she departed the country with intention to commit a crime or intended to abandon a U.S. residence, or remained outside of the country for a lengthy period of time that equated to abandonment.[32] This was called the "*Fleuti*" doctrine.[33]

Congress amended the "*Fleuti*" doctrine in 1996, and provided that LPRs were considered to be seeking a new admission and would have to prove admissibility under INA §212(a) in the following situations:

- abandonment or relinquishment of LPR status;
- absence for a continuous period in excess of 180 days;
- illegal activity after departure from the United States and prior to return;
- departure while under removal or extradition proceedings;
- commission of an offense identified in INA §212(a)(2) (relating to crimes of moral turpitude or controlled substances), where that offense has not been waived under INA §212(h) or INA §240A(a);[34] or
- an attempt to enter without inspection and authorization, or at a time and place that has not been designated by immigration officers as a port of entry.[35]

The major change made by Congress through IIRAIRA is that an individual with any type of past criminal record that might be a ground of inadmissibility can be found inadmissible upon return, even if that person is an LPR who is returning from a

---

[30] Illegal Immigration Reform and Immigrant Responsibility Act, Pub. L. No. 104-208, 110 Stat. 3009 (Sept. 30, 1996).

[31] *Rosenberg v. Fleuti*, 374 U.S. 449 (1963) (the Court found that a returning LPR who was a homosexual, and might have been barred because of his homosexuality as inadmissible, was not seeking a new admission since he was a returning resident and, therefore, did not have to prove admissibility under the inadmissibility grounds at INA §212(a)).

[32] *See Carbajal-Gonzalez v. INS*, 78 F.3d 194 (5th Cir. 1996).

[33] *See Fleuti*, 374 U.S. 449, at n.5.

[34] Although it is not mentioned in this part of the statute, INA §101(a)(13)(C)(v), a waiver under INA §212(c), will also remove crimes involving moral turpitude and drug crimes as grounds of inadmissibility for a returning LPR.

[35] INA §101(a)(13)(C).

brief, casual, and innocent departure abroad. In sum, the LPR's entire history may come into play upon each departure and return to the United States, and any past criminal action that might be a crime of moral turpitude or other ground of inadmissibility under INA §212(a) may bar that individual from being admitted into the country.[36] The only exception is when that offense has been previously waived by an IJ or DHS.

Immigration Violation Grounds of Inadmissibility—INA §§212(a)(6), (7), and (9)

There are several immigration-related grounds of inadmissibility. Some of these are pure administrative violations (such as student visa abusers under INA §212(a)(6)(G)), while others are not only administrative violations of the law but also criminal violations (such as smuggling under INA §212(a)(6)(E)). Following is a breakdown of the immigration violations that make one inadmissible:

Lack of Inspection or Admission—INA §212(a)(6)(A)(i)

Lack of inspection or admission pursuant to INA §212(a)(6)(A)(i) is the most common charge of all removal proceedings. Any alien who is present in the United States without having been "admitted" or "paroled" is present illegally.[37] In addition, an individual who has entered the United States at any time or place other than that designated by the Attorney General (AG) is inadmissible. He or she is considered to be an applicant for admission and is subject to the inadmissibility grounds at INA §212(a).[38] DHS may place that individual into removal proceedings and charge him or her under INA §212(a)(6)(A)(i).[39] The relevant concept is "admission," which requires a lawful entry. The only exception to this rule involves battered spouses and children under INA §204(a)(1) if it can be shown that there is a substantial connection between the battery and the individual's unlawful entry into the United States.[40]

Stowaways—INA §212(a)(6)(D)

An arriving alien who is a stowaway is not eligible to apply for admission nor to be admitted and "shall be ordered removed" upon inspection by an immigration officer, unless he or she intends to apply for asylum.[41] The term "stowaway" is defined at INA §101(a)(49) as a person who obtains transportation without consent and through concealment. This does not include a person who boards a transport with a valid ticket. Stowaways are consistently treated differently than other aliens detained by

---

[36] *Matter of Collado-Munoz*, 21 I&N Dec. 1061 (BIA 1997).

[37] INA §212(a)(6)(A)(i).

[38] INA §235(a)(1).

[39] Previously this was called "entry without inspection" and charged under the former INA §241(a)(2).

[40] *See* INA §212(a)(6)(A)(ii).

[41] INA §235(a)(1).

DHS. They are not entitled to removal proceedings under INA §240 even if found to have a credible fear of persecution in their country of nationality.[42] If found to have a credible fear of persecution, the asylum claim of a stowaway is heard by an IJ in an "asylum only" hearing where a claim to withholding of removal also may be heard in accordance with 8 CFR §§208.4(b)(3)(iii), 1208.4(b)(3)(iii).[43] There is no right to a removal hearing or any right to seek further relief. However, a stowaway may appeal the denial of an asylum claim to the BIA.[44]

Failure to Attend Removal Proceeding—INA §212(a)(6)(B)

Any individual who fails to attend a removal/deportation hearing without reasonable cause, and seeks admission into the United States within five years of his or her departure or removal is inadmissible.

Fraud or Willful Misrepresentation—INA §212(a)(6)(C)

An individual is inadmissible and removable under this section if he or she has done the following:

- seeks to procure a visa, other documentation, admission to the United States, or other immigration benefit;
- by fraud or willful misrepresentation;
- of a material fact.

This ground of inadmissibility most often involves individuals who make a false claim to lawful status, present false documentation to the immigration inspector, or make a false claim to U.S. citizenship. An individual does not commit fraud, even if traveling with false documents, if immediately upon encountering the immigration inspector, the individual turns over false documents, gives his or her true identity, and seeks asylum.[45] However, where an inspector discovers the fraud prior to such admission by the alien, the alien is inadmissible based on willful misrepresentation.[46] Those who arrive in the United States in transit without visa (TWOV) by using fraudulent passports in order to gain access to the United States to seek asylum commit fraud by using the fraudulent nationality documents, since TWOV status is considered to be an immigration benefit.[47] A finding of a lack of credibility by an IJ in an asylum hearing may be the basis for a finding of fraud in a later application for relief by the former asylum applicant.[48]

---

[42] *In re X–K–*, 23 I&N Dec. 731 (BIA 2005). *See also* 8 CFR §§208.2(c)(1)(i), 1208.2(c)(1)(i).

[43] *See* 8 CFR §§208.30(g)(2)(iv)(B), 1208.30(g)(2)(iv)(B).

[44] *Id.*

[45] *Matter of D–L– & A–M–*, 20 I&N Dec. 409 (BIA 1991).

[46] *Ymeri v. Ashcroft*, 387 F.3d 12 (1st Cir. 2004).

[47] *Id.*; *Matter of Shirdel*, 19 I&N Dec. 33 (BIA 1984).

[48] *Singh v. Gonzales*, 413 F.3d 156 (1st Cir. 2005).

A material fact is one that, had it been known by the government official, was predictably capable of affecting the official decision.[49] In determining whether a misrepresentation or concealment is material, the misrepresentation must be shown by "clear, unequivocal and convincing evidence to be predictably capable of affecting, i.e., to have had a natural tendency to affect the Immigration and Naturalization Service's decisions."[50] The test for materiality is whether the false statement has a tendency to influence, or is capable of influencing, a federal agency.[51]

It should be noted that anyone found removable based on a false claim to U.S. citizenship may be denied any type of relief under the immigration laws at any time in the future since there are no waivers for this ground of inadmissibility.

Smugglers—INA §212(a)(6)(E)

Any alien who knowingly encourages, induces, assists, abets, or aids any other alien to enter, or to try to enter, the United States is inadmissible. This ground of inadmissibility does not apply to certain spouses, parents, and children of individuals who legalized through the IRCA,[52] if that person was here as of May 5, 1998; seeks admission as an immediate relative or second preference beneficiary or benefits under the Family Unity Program; or if that person has assisted only a spouse, parent, son, or daughter to enter the United States "and no other individuals" prior to May 5, 1998. There is a waiver for this ground of inadmissibility under INA §212(d)(11).

The smuggling ground of inadmissibility "requires am affirmative and illicit act of assistance in shepherding someone across the border."[53] One may not be classified as a smuggler without a single affirmative act.[54] Mere presence at the border with knowledge that a person is being smuggled into the country in the same vehicle in which one is riding does not make one a smuggler without action or encouragement by the individual.[55] There is a waiver of this ground of inadmissibility for certain LPRs and others seeking admission as immediate relatives of U.S. citizens or preference immigrants if they are smuggling only their spouse, parent, or child[56] (see waiver section in Chapter 6).

Document Fraud—INA §212(a)(6)(F)

Any individual who is subject to a final order for violation of the document fraud provisions of INA §274C is inadmissible. INA §274C makes it unlawful to forge, counterfeit, alter, falsely make, use, possess, obtain, accept, or provide to another a

---

[49] *Kungys v. United States*, 485 U.S. 759 (1988).

[50] *Id.* at 760.

[51] *Matter of Sparrow*, 20 I&N Dec. 920 (BIA 1984).

[52] IRCA, *supra* note 29.

[53] *Tapucu v. Gonzales*, 399 F.3d 736 (6th Cir. 2005).

[54] *Id.* at 741.

[55] *Altimorano v. Gonzales*, 427 F.3d 586 (9th Cir. 2005).

[56] INA §212(d)(11).

forged, altered, or counterfeit document in order to satisfy the immigration laws or obtain an immigration benefit.[57] In addition, INA §274C makes it a crime to use a lawful document belonging to another in order to gain an immigration benefit, or to prepare or assist in preparing an application for benefits with knowledge of, or in reckless disregard of, the fact that the application or document prepared was falsely made.[58] Presentation of an altered U.S. birth certificate belonging to a relative for employment purposes is document fraud under INA§274C.[59] There is no waiver under INA §212(i) (waiver for fraud) specifically for document fraud under INA §274C.[60] However, there is a possible waiver of this ground of inadmissibility for humanitarian purposes or to assure family unity. It is available only to returning LPRs, and those seeking admission or adjustment of status under INA as immediate relatives or within one of the family preferences who have smuggled or assisted in smuggling only a spouse or child (and no other person) and have had no other civil monetary penalties imposed for this offense.[61]

Foreign Residency Requirements—INA §212(a)(6)(G)

An individual who obtains student status under INA §101(a)(15)(F), and who fails to fulfill the two-year foreign residency requirement after completion of studies in the United States, is ineligible to return for a period of five years. There is a waiver of the two-year foreign residence requirement outlined under INA §212(e). The waiver must be based on one of the following: (1) a request of an interested U.S. government agency; (2) exceptional hardship to the alien's U.S. citizen or LPR spouse or child; (3) inability to return because of persecution "on account of race, religion or political opinion"; (4) admission of the alien is in the public interest; or (5) the favorable exercise of discretion where the foreign government has furnished a written "no objection" letter on granting the waiver for medical graduates.

Lack of Proper Documentation—INA §212(a)(7)

An individual who does not possess a proper visa, re-entry permit, or valid entry document and a valid passport or other suitable travel document, or identification document at the time of his or her application for admission if such a document is required under the immigration laws, is inadmissible and thus, removable.

INA §212(a)(7) does not involve any charge of fraud; it merely makes an individual inadmissible if he or she lacks the proper entry documentation or identification documentation. This also includes individuals who have obtained documentation without any misrepresentation, but where the documentation was improperly or in-

---

[57] INA §§274C(a)(1) and (2).

[58] INA §§274C(a)(3) and (4).

[59] *Remileh v. INS*, 101 F.3d 66 (8th Cir. 1999).

[60] *Matter of Lazarte*, 21 I&N Dec. 214 (BIA 1996).

[61] INA §212(d)(12).

correctly issued by a U.S. official.[62] A valid advance parole document is considered a valid entry document for purposes of this section.[63] However, when the parole is later terminated or revoked, the individual may be charged as inadmissible under INA §212(a)(7).

Additionally, individuals who are not in possession of a passport that is valid for a minimum of six months after the expiration of the date of the permitted stay in the United States may be denied admission.[64]

Immigrants with Prior Immigration Violations

Immigrants previously removed—INA §212(a)(9)(A)

Those individuals who are ordered removed from the United States are barred from admission for a certain period of time—sometimes permanently—depending on the reason for which they were removed.

Expedited removal—INA §235(b)

Those individuals who are ordered removed under the expedited removal provisions of INA §235(b)(1) are barred from admission to the United States for a period of five years. This group includes individuals who are seeking admission to the United States and are found inadmissible because of fraud or willful misrepresentation under INA §212(a)(6)(C) or for lack of valid documentation under INA §212(a)(7). These individuals are ordered removed without a hearing before an IJ (unless the individual seeks asylum under INA §208). Expedited removal was enacted as part of IIRAIRA, and provides for the immediate expulsion of individuals stopped at airports or border checkpoints, as well as those who are illegally present in the United States for a period of less than two years, without a hearing before an IJ. If an individual stopped by the immigration inspector while seeking admission is permitted by the immigration official to withdraw the application for admission, there is no five-year bar.[65] It is only those who are ordered removed under INA §235(b) who are subject to the five-year bar. A second expedited removal order will render an individual subject to a 20-year bar.[66]

Aliens ordered removed by IJ under INA §240

Individuals who are ordered removed by an IJ after removal proceedings are barred for a period of 10 years from seeking readmission into the United States.[67] In

---

[62] *See* INA §212(a)(7)(A)(ii).

[63] *Sissoko v. Rocha*, 412 F.3d 1021 (9th Cir. 2005) (the court found that the individual was not an inadmissible arriving alien when in possession of an advance parole document).

[64] INA§212(a)(7)(A)(ii). There is a waiver of the documentary requirements at INA §§212(a)(7)(B)(ii) and 212(k).

[65] INA §235(a)(4).

[66] INA §212(a)(9)(A)(i).

[67] INA §212(a)(9)(A)(ii).

addition, any individual who departs the United States while an order of removal is outstanding is considered to be a self-deportee and the same bar goes into effect. There is a waiver of this bar (discussed in Chapter 6).

Aliens unlawfully present (3- and 10-Year Bars)—INA §212(a)(9)(B)

Another bar to admissibility is the unlawful presence bar that was enacted via IIRAIRA. There are two separate bars. The first bar is a three-year bar for individuals who have been unlawfully present in the United States for a period of "more than 180 days but less than 1 year." If the individual has been unlawfully present for periods of more than six months but less than one year and has voluntarily departed the United States prior to commencement of proceedings, he or she is barred from seeking readmission for a period of only three years.[68]

The second bar is the 10-year bar. An individual who has been unlawfully present for a period of one year or more and seeks admission within 10 years of his or her removal from the United States, after accumulating one year or more unlawful presence, is inadmissible.[69]

Definition of unlawful presence—INA §212(a)(9)(B)(ii)

The INA defines unlawful presence as the period where an individual is present in the United States after the expiration of the period of lawful stay authorized by the government, or is present in the United States without having been admitted or paroled.

Exceptions to unlawful presence rule

Following are classes of individuals who do not accumulate unlawful presence.

- Minors: A juvenile does not accumulate unlawful presence while under the age of 18.[70]
- Asylees: An individual with a pending bona fide application for asylum does not accumulate unlawful presence while the application is being adjudicated unless the individual has worked without authorization during that period.[71]
- Family unity: Those individuals who are granted family unity status under §301 of IMMACT90[72] do not accumulate unlawful presence.[73] See 8 CFR §236.10–18 for regulations relating to family unity benefits.

---

[68] INA §212(a)(9)(B)(i)(I).

[69] INA §212(a)(9)(B)(i)(II).

[70] INA §212(a)(9)(B)(iii)(I).

[71] INA §212(a)(9)(B)(iii)(II).

[72] Immigration Act of 1990, Pub. L. No. 101-649, 104 Stat. 4978.

[73] INA §212(a)(9)(B)(iii)(III).

- Battered women and children: Battered spouses and children who may qualify for benefits under the Violence Against Women Act (VAWA)[74] do not accumulate unlawful presence where there is a substantial connection between the battery or cruelty suffered by the spouse or child and the unlawful presence.[75]

Tolling of unlawful presence

The accumulation of unlawful presence can be "tolled" for good cause. The following do not accumulate unlawful presence:

- an alien who has been lawfully admitted or paroled into the United States; and
- has filed a non-frivolous application for a change or extension of stay before the expiration of period of authorized stay date; and
- has not been employed without authorization.

The period of unlawful stay is tolled during the pendency of the application, but may not exceed 120 days.[76]

Waiver of unlawful presence

The AG and DHS have discretion to waive the unlawful presence bar for individuals who meet the following requirements:

- individuals who are spouses, sons, or daughters of U.S. citizens or LPRs; and
- whose removal or refusal of admission would result in extreme hardship to the U.S. citizen or LPR spouse or parent.[77]

Aliens unlawfully present after previous immigration violations—INA §212(a)(9)(C)

This ground of inadmissibility makes an individual inadmissible if he or she falls into either of the following categories:

- he or she has been unlawfully present in the United States for an aggregate period of more than one year; or
- he or she has been ordered removed under the expedited removal provisions of INA §235 or the removal hearing provisions of INA §240.

An individual meeting either INA §§212(a)(9)(C)(i)(I) or (II) who enters or attempts to enter the United States without being admitted is inadmissible. Such an individual is barred from readmission for a period of 10 years.[78]

---

[74] Violence Against Women Act of 1994, Pub. L. No. 103-322, 108 Stat. 1902-1955 (codified as 8 USC §§1151, 1154, 1186a note, 1254, 2245).

[75] INA §212(a)(9)(B)(iii)(IV).

[76] INA §212(a)(9)(B)(iv).

[77] INA §212(a)(9)(B)(v).

[78] INA §212(a)(9)(C)(ii) states that this bar "shall not apply to an alien seeking admission more than 10 years after the date of the alien's last departure from the United States if, prior to the alien's re-

continued

This is an especially strict provision because there is no waiver of this provision under INA §212(a)(9)(C). In addition, at least one circuit court has found that this provision also eliminates eligibility for those seeking adjustment of status under INA §245(i), which allows adjustment to LPR status to certain individuals who are unlawfully present in the United States. The Fifth Circuit Court of Appeals has found that while adjustment of status is permitted for individuals seeking this relief under §245(i) after one unlawful entry into the United States, such relief is not available to individuals unlawfully present who depart and then return to the United States.[79] However, in a later decision, the Tenth Circuit Court of Appeals went the other way and found that an individual who normally would be barred under INA §212(a)(9)(C) for having re-entered after one year of unlawful presence was eligible to adjust status under INA §245(i).[80]

Health-Related Grounds of Inadmissibility—INA §212(a)(1)

Introduction

There are several health-related grounds of inadmissibility including: (1) communicable diseases; (2) lack of proof of vaccinations; (3) physical or mental disorders and associated behavior that may pose or has posed a threat to the property, safety, or welfare of the alien or others, including where such behavior is likely to recur or lead to other harmful behavior; and (4) drug addiction or abuse.[81] Except for drug addiction and abuse, none of the health-related grounds of inadmissibility is a ground of removability.[82]

Communicable Diseases—INA §212(a)(1)(A)

The statute specifically names only one communicable disease as a ground of inadmissibility—HIV.[83] However, there are numerous communicable diseases (though not specifically named) that make one inadmissible under this subsection including active tuberculosis, active leprosy, hepatitis, and sexually transmitted diseases (syphilis, gonorrhea).[84] The regulations regarding communicable diseases are prescribed by the Department of Health and Human Services (HHS).[85]

---

embarkation at a place outside the United States or attempt to be readmitted from a foreign contiguous territory," the AG consents to the alien's reapplying for admission.

[79] *Mortera-Cruz v. Gonzales*, 409 F.3d 246 (5th Cir. 2005).

[80] *See Padilla-Caldera v. Gonzales*, 426 F.3d 1294 (10th Cir. 2005).

[81] INA §212(a)(1).

[82] INA §237(a)(2)(B)(ii).

[83] INA §212(a)(1)(A)(i).

[84] 42 CFR §34.2(b).

[85] INA §212(a)(1)(A)(i); *see also* 42 CFR §34.1 *et seq.*

These regulations apply to aliens who are: (1) seeking visas at the consulate overseas; (2) arriving in the United States; (3) applying for adjustment of status; or (4) required by DHS to have a medical examination in connection with their admissibility. Not all aliens seeking to come to the United States are required to obtain a medical examination in order to prove that they have no communicable disease. Those classes of aliens required to do so by law are: (1) applicants for immigrant visas (*i.e.*, Green Cards); (2) students, exchange visitors, and any nonimmigrant (*i.e.*, temporary) visa applicants who are required by a consular office to have a medical examination; (3) refugee applicants outside the United States; and (4) applicants for adjustment of status.[86] The medical examination is performed by a DHS-certified physician.[87] In a removal hearing, the issue of inadmissibility based on a communicable disease would most likely arise only in the relief phase of proceedings where an individual is seeking adjustment of status.[88]

Proof of Vaccinations—INA §212(a)(1)(A)(ii)

INA §212(a)(1)(A)(ii) makes inadmissible any alien seeking admission as an immigrant or seeking adjustment of status without proof of vaccination against "vaccine preventable" diseases—mumps, measles, rubella, polio, tetanus and diphtheria toxoids, pertussis, influenza type B, and hepatitis type B, as well as other vaccinations recommended by the Advisory Committee for Immigration Practices.[89] The vaccination requirement applies only to those seeking LPR status through an application for an immigrant visa or adjustment of status. The vaccination requirement does not apply to orphan children (as defined in INA §101(b)(1)(F)) who are under the age of 10 and seek an immigrant visa as an immediate relative of a U.S. citizen, if prior to the admission of the child, the adoptive (or prospective) parent of the child has executed an affidavit stating that he or she is aware of the vaccination requirement and will ensure that the child is vaccinated within 30 days of the child's admission or at the earliest medically appropriate time.[90]

Physical or Mental Disorder—INA §212(a)(1)(A)(iii)

An individual is inadmissible if it is determined that he or she has a physical or mental disorder and behavior associated with the disorder that may pose, or has posed, a threat to the property, safety, or welfare of that person or others; or has had in the past such a physical or mental disorder, and associated behavior, posing such a threat, and there is a likelihood of a recurrence of such behavior, or that it will lead to other harmful behavior.[91] The HHS regulations have defined the terms mental disor-

---

[86] 42 CFR §34.3(b).

[87] 42 CFR §34.2(j).

[88] *See* INA §245 (to be discussed, *infra*, in Chapter 5).

[89] INA §212(a)(1)(A)(ii).

[90] INA §212(a)(1)(C).

[91] INA §212(a)(1)(A)(iii).

der[92] and physical disorder.[93] Mental shortcomings due to ignorance or suffering from a condition attributable to remedial physical causes, or of a temporary nature caused by toxins, medically prescribed drugs, or diseases, shall not be a basis for a finding of a physical or mental disorder.[94]

Drug Abusers and Addicts—INA §212(a)(1)(A)(iv)

The statute also makes inadmissible anyone who *is* determined to be a drug abuser or addict in accordance with HHS regulations.[95] The ground of inadmissibility is written in the *present tense* and does not make one inadmissible for past drug use or addiction. Drug abuse is defined as the nonmedical use of a substance listed in §202 of the Controlled Substance Act,[96] which has not necessarily resulted in physical or psychological dependence.[97] Drug addiction is defined as the nonmedical use of a controlled substance listed in the Controlled Substance Act that has resulted in physical or psychological dependence.[98]

Waivers of Health-Related Grounds of Inadmissibility—INA §212(g)

Communicable diseases—waiver requirements

- Alien is the spouse, unmarried son or daughter of a U.S. citizen, LPR, or alien issued an immigrant visa; or alien is the parent of a U.S. citizen, LPR, or individual granted an immigrant visa;

  or

- the alien is the victim of domestic violence as defined in INA §§204(a)(1)(A)(iii) or (iv), or (a)(1)(B)(ii) or (iii); and
- in accordance with the terms, conditions, and controls as prescribed by the AG in consultation with the director of HHS.[99]

Proof of vaccinations—waiver requirements

The requirement of proof of vaccinations under INA §212(a)(1)(A)(ii) may be waived in the following situations:

- alien receives the vaccination required for which he or she previously lacked proof;

---

[92] 42 CFR §34.2(n).

[93] 42 CFR §34.2(p).

[94] 42 CFR §§34.4(b) and 42.4(c)(1).

[95] 42 CFR §34.1 *et seq.*

[96] 21 USC §802.

[97] 42 CFR §34.2(g).

[98] 42 CFR §34.2(h).

[99] INA §212(g)(1).

- a civil surgeon defined under 42 CFR §34.2 certifies that the vaccination is not medically appropriate according to HHS regulations; or
- the AG approves a waiver based on a finding that the vaccination would be contrary to the alien's religious beliefs/moral convictions.[100]

Physical or mental disorder—waiver requirements

The AG may waive the physical or mental disorder grounds of inadmissibility under INA §212(a)(1)(A)(iii) at his discretion under the terms, conditions, and controls he chooses including posting a bond after consultation with the Secretary of HHS, and in accordance with regulations prescribed by the AG.[101]

Criminal Grounds of Inadmissibility—INA §212(a)(2)

Introduction

The major difference between the criminal grounds of inadmissibility and the criminal grounds of deportability is that there is no "conviction" required in order to find an individual inadmissible under INA §212(a)(2); admission to the crime, or the elements thereof, suffices for a finding of inadmissibility. An individual can be denied admission or adjustment of status for the commission of, or the conviction of, various types of crimes, including crimes involving moral turpitude (a/ka/ CIMT), controlled substance violations, or drug trafficking. In addition, if the government finds that someone is coming to engage in prostitution, is procuring prostitutes, or has engaged in prostitution in the last 10 years, he or she is inadmissible without a conviction for the offense. Human traffickers, money launderers, government officials who violate human rights or escape prosecution in the United States for crimes are also inadmissible under INA §212(a) without a conviction.

Remember, there is no "aggravated felony" ground of inadmissibility. An individual can be *deported* as an aggravated felon under INA §237(a)(2)(A)(iii); but he or she cannot be found inadmissible as an aggravated felon. However, many of the crimes that are aggravated felonies will fall under one of the inadmissibility grounds. Thus, individuals who commit aggravated felonies do not necessarily have an inadmissibility loophole, as that same crime can fit into one of the four specified criminal inadmissibility grounds. An individual may be denied admission or adjustment of status as an individual who has been convicted of, *or admitted to the commission of*, a crime, or the elements of an offense, that falls under INA §212(a)(2)(A)–(D).

Crimes Involving Moral Turpitude—INA §212(a)(2)(A)(i)(I)

This ground of inadmissibility requires either the conviction for a crime involving moral turpitude, or the admission of the commission of such an offense, or its ele-

---

[100] INA §212(g)(2).

[101] INA §212(g)(3).

ments. A crime involving moral turpitude is defined as a crime that is "inherently base, evil, or depraved, and contrary to the accepted rules of morality and the duties owed between persons or to society in general."[102] Generally, a crime involving moral turpitude requires evil intent.[103] The same definition applies in the interpretation of this term whether the individual is charged as deportable under INA §237(a)(2) or inadmissible under INA §212(a)(2) (for more information about crimes involving moral turpitude, see Chapter 2).

In seeking entry/admission into the United States, or adjusting one's status from temporary resident to LPR, the mere admission of the commission of the elements of a crime involving moral turpitude is a basis for denial under INA §212(a)(2). However, such an admission must be voluntary and complete; the individual must have admitted all of the facts necessary to constitute the crime.[104]

Waivers

INA §212(a)(2)(A)(ii) provides for certain waivers of this ground of inadmissibility.

- Minors: This ground of inadmissibility can be waived where the following elements are met:
  - the applicant for a visa or adjustment of status is a minor under the age of 18; *and*
  - the crime was committed more than five years before the date of application for visa or date of application for admission to the United States.[105]
- Petty Offense Exception: This ground of inadmissibility also does not apply in the following circumstances:
  - only one offense has been committed;
  - the maximum penalty for the crime does not exceed imprisonment for one year; and
  - if there is a conviction, the term of imprisonment does not exceed six months.[106]

This "petty offense" exception may be raised where there has been one offense involving moral turpitude committed; it does not apply to other criminal grounds of inadmissibility such as controlled substances.[107]

---

[102] *Matter of Franklin*, 20 I&N Dec. 867, 868 (BIA 1994).

[103] *Matter of Flores*, 17 I&N Dec. 225 (BIA 1980).

[104] *See Matter of E–N–*, 7 I&N Dec. 153 (BIA 1956).

[105] INA §212(a)(2)(A)(ii)(I).

[106] INA §212(a)(2)(A)(ii)(II).

[107] See Chapter 2 for a detailed list of crimes involving moral turpitude.

Controlled Substances Violations—INA §212(a)(2)(A)(i)(II)

An individual is inadmissible based on controlled substance violations for the following:

- conviction for an offense, or admission to the commission of the offense or the elements of;
- a violation or conspiracy or attempt to violate;
- any law or regulation of a state, the United States, or foreign country;
- relating to a controlled substance.[108]

This ground of inadmissibility may be established by a conviction for a controlled substance violation, the admission of the commission of such an offense, or the admission of the commission of the elements of a controlled substance violation.[109] The phrase "relating to" has been interpreted broadly to mean "in connection with", "associated with", with respect to", and "with reference to."[110] The BIA has found that Congress intended to give inclusive meaning to the phrase "relating to" in the immigration laws.[111]

An alien is inadmissible under this ground based on a foreign controlled substance violation even if the conviction is expunged.[112]

Multiple Criminal Convictions—INA §212(a)(2)(B)

An individual is inadmissible where he or she has been convicted of the following:

- two or more offenses, regardless of whether they are in a single scheme or single trial; and
- regardless of whether the crimes involve moral turpitude;
- for which the aggregate sentences to confinement are five or more years.

This is a criminal ground of inadmissibility that is based on actual convictions—not just admissions to the crimes or the elements thereof.

Not only is there a requirement of two or more convictions, but the aggregate sentences must be five or more years. "Five or more years" means the amount of time that has been sentenced, not "time served." It should be noted that this ground involves any type of crime regardless of whether the crimes are related to moral turpitude or controlled substances; the statute does not distinguish based on the type of crime.[113]

---

[108] Controlled substance definition is found at 21 USC §802.

[109] *Matter of Perez*, 22 I&N Dec. 689 (BIA 1999).

[110] *Coregis Ins. Co. v. Am. Health Found., Inc.*, 241 F.3d 123, 128–29 (2d Cir. 2001).

[111] *In re Beltran*, 20 I&N Dec. 521, 525–26 (BIA 2001).

[112] *Matter of Dillingham*, 21 I&N Dec. 1001(BIA 1997); *Elkins v. Comfort*, 392 F.3d 1159 (10th Cir. 2004); *Kent v. INS* 28 F.3d 113 (10th Cir. 1994).

[113] INA §212(a)(2)(B).

Controlled Substance Traffickers—INA §212(a)(2)(C)

This ground of inadmissibility defines groups of individuals who may be denied admission based on various forms of involvement in trafficking of controlled substances. The elements of this ground of inadmissibility are:

- the individual is *or has been* an illicit trafficker in any controlled substance or listed chemical in Controlled Substance Act;[114] or
- is or has been a knowing aider, abettor, assister, conspirator, or colluder with those involved in the illicit tracking of control substances; or
- is the spouse, son, or daughter of an alien inadmissible under the above sections who has obtained any financial or other benefit within five years of the illicit activity of the alien and knew or should have known that the financial benefit was the product of illicit drug trafficking.

It is important to note also that this section of law provides only that the consular officer or the immigration officer (under the AG) has "reason to believe" that the individual is involved in any such activity, or has received any such benefit and should have known better.[115] Additionally, the wording of the statute makes an individual inadmissible whether he or she currently is, or in the past "has been," an illicit trafficker in a controlled substance.[116]

The BIA has found that where the consular officer or immigration officer fails to detect a controlled substance in the possession of the alien at the time of inspection and admission, the individual may not later be deported as an individual inadmissible under INA §212(a)(2)(C)'s inadmissibility ground. The officer had no "reason to believe" where he failed to detect that the individual possessed controlled substances at the time of inspection and admission.[117] The BIA further found that the examining officer who inspected the alien must in fact have known or suspected that the alien was a trafficker at the time of application for admission.[118]

No conviction is required in order for an officer to have a "reason to believe" that the individual is a trafficker in controlled substances; however, drug trafficking does have an element of intent. In order for an officer to have a "reasonable belief" that an individual is a drug trafficker, there must be reason to believe that the individual knows the drugs were in his or her possession, or in the possession of another whom he or she is assisting.[119]

---

[114] 21 USC §802.

[115] INA §212(a)(2)(C).

[116] INA §212(a)(2)(C)(i).

[117] *Matter of Rocha*, 20 I&N Dec. 944 (BIA 1995).

[118] *Id.* at 946.

[119] *Pichardo v. INS*, 188 F.3d 1079, 1081–82 (9th Cir. 1999).

An individual who acts as a conduit between a dealer and his or her customer is inadmissible under this ground.[120] A Department of Public Safety (DPS) report coupled with a guilty plea at the criminal proceeding provides sufficient "reason to believe" that the individual is a drug trafficker.[121] Attempted escape from police and driving a car with more than 100 pounds of marijuana is sufficient "reason to believe" that an individual is a drug trafficker.[122] Traveling across the border in a vehicle with a large amount of marijuana concealed in the vehicle is sufficient basis for a finding of inadmissibility based on a reason to believe that the individual is a drug trafficker.[123]

Prostitution and Commercialized Vice—INA §212(a)(2)(D)

This ground of inadmissibility makes an individual inadmissible under the following elements:

- the individual is coming to the United States principally or incidentally to engage in prostitution; or
- has engaged in prostitution within 10 years of the date of application for admission or adjustment of status; or
- attempts to procure, or has within the 10 years prior to application for admission, procured or attempted to import prostitutes or persons for the purpose of prostitution, or receives the proceeds from prostitution; or
- is coming to the United States to engage in any unlawful commercialized vice whether or not related to prostitution.

A single act of solicitation for immoral purposes may be a ground of inadmissibility under INA §212(a)(2)(D).[124]

Security Grounds of Inadmissibility—INA §212(a)(3)

Introduction

The security grounds of inadmissibility at INA §212(a)(3) (although not commonly used) are the longest and most detailed of any of the grounds of inadmissibility found at INA §212(a). The security section contains six different subsections of classes of individuals who are inadmissible: (1) general class of security threats (espionage, sabotage); (2) terrorist threats; (3) those whose admission might have adverse foreign policy consequences; (4) members in totalitarian parties; (5) Nazis and others who have participated in torture or genocide; and (6) those associating with

---

[120] *Nunez-Payan v. INS*, 811 F.2d 264, 267 (5th Cir. 1987); *see also Matter of Favela*, 16 I&N Dec. 753 (BIA 1979); *Matter of Rico*, 16 I& N Dec. 181 (BIA 1977).

[121] *Lopez-Molina v. Ashcroft*, 368 F.3d 1206 (9th Cir. 2004).

[122] *Id.*

[123] *Alarcon-Serrano v. INS*, 220 F.3d. 1116 (9th Cir. 2000).

[124] *Amador-Palomares v. Ashcroft*, 382 F.3d 864 (8th Cir. 2004) .

terrorist organizations. The following discusses the elements of each class of individual inadmissible as a security risk:

In General—INA §212(a)(3)(A)

A non–American citizen may be denied admission for security reasons where the consular officer has knowledge or a reasonable ground to believe[125] that he or she seeks to enter the United States to engage solely, principally, or incidentally in:

- any activity to violate any law of the United States relating to sabotage or espionage, or to violate or evade any law prohibiting the export of technology, sensitive information, or goods;
- any activity a purpose of which is the overthrow of the government by force or unlawful means; or
- "any other unlawful activity."[126]

Although the statutory ground of inadmissibility is written broadly, and was expanded in the USA PATRIOT Act of 2001,[127] the government has been required to prove that there is knowledge, or reason to believe, that the alien seeks to engage in activities that would be prejudicial to the public interest or endanger the welfare, safety, and security of the United States.[128]

Espionage is terrorism even if done for political reasons.[129] An alien who has knowledge of, or has received instruction in, the espionage or counterespionage service or tactics of a foreign government is guilty of an offense "relating to espionage."[130] Books, magazines, and printed articles may form the basis for a reasonable belief that one was, is, or may be, engaged in terrorist activities.[131]

Terrorism—INA §212(a)(3)(B)

Definition of terrorist activity

An individual is inadmissible based on actual or suspected terrorist activity for any of the following:

- engaging in terrorist activity;[132]

---

[125] Reasonable grounds means that a reasonable person would believe that there is a danger. It is equated with "probable cause" as a standard. *Matter of A–H–*, 23 I&N Dec. 774, 788–89 (BIA 2005).

[126] INA §212(a)(3)(A).

[127] Uniting and Strengthening America by Providing Appropriate Tools Required to Intercept and Obstruct Terrorism Act of 2001, Pub. L. No. 107-56, 115 Stat. 272.

[128] *Allende v Shultz*, 845 F.2d 1111 (1st Cir. 1988).

[129] *Matter of V–T–S–*, 21 I&N Dec. 792, 808 (BIA 1997); *see also Matter of D–V–*, 21 I&N Dec. 77 (BIA 1993).

[130] *Matter of Luis-Rodriguez*, 22 I&N Dec. 747 (BIA 1999).

[131] *Adams v. Baker*, 909 F.2d 643, 649 (1st Cir. 1990).

[132] INA §212(a)(3)(B)(iii)—defining terrorism as any activity that is unlawful under the laws of the place where it is committed (or which, if it had been committed in the United States, would be unlawful

continued

- reason to believe that he or she has engaged, or is likely to engage, in terrorist activity;
- incited terrorist activity, indicating an intention to cause death or serious bodily injury;
- is a representative of a terrorist organization (designated under INA §219) or other organization that espouses terrorism;
- is a member of a foreign terrorist organization (designated at INA §219) that he or she knows or should have known is a terrorist organization;[133]
- endorses or espouses terrorist activity or persuades others to do so;
- has received military-type training[134] from, or on behalf of, an organization that was a terrorist organization[135] at the time of the training;
- is the spouse or child of an alien who is inadmissible under this section if the alien family member's activity occurred in the last five years.[136]

To *engage* in terrorist activity includes not only the commission of the above acts but also assisting in preparing or planning a terrorist attack, inciting someone to commit such an attack, or gathering information on potential targets for terrorist activity.[137] Furthermore, engaging in terrorist activity includes soliciting people for membership in, or funds for support of, a terrorist organization.[138] It includes providing material support such as a "safe house, transportation, communications, funds, transfer of funds or other material benefit, false documentation or identification, weapons, explosives or training" to a terrorist organization, or any member thereof, or any individual, for the commission of a terrorist activity, "unless the actor can

---

under the law of the United States or any state) and which involves hijacking or sabotage of any conveyance vessel or vehicle; seizing, detaining, and threatening to kill, harm, or continue in detention in order to compel a third person or governmental organization to do or abstain from doing any act, as a condition for the release of the seized person; violently attacking an internationally protected person as defined in 18 USC §1116(b)(4); assassination; use of biological or chemical agent or nuclear device, or firearm, explosive, weapon, or other dangerous device (other than for mere monetary gain) with intent to endanger, directly or indirectly, individual(s) safety or cause substantial property damage; or threat, attempt, or conspiracy of any of these.

[133] For example, membership in the Armed Islamic Group (GIA) of Algeria, a group designated by the Secretary of State as a terrorist group, is sufficient basis for a finding of inadmissibility as a terrorist and that the individual is a danger to the security of the United States under INA §212(a)(3)(B). *Bellout v. Ashcroft*, 363 F.2d 975 (9th Cir. 2004).

[134] Defined in 18 USC §2339D(c)(1).

[135] Terrorist organization is defined at INA §212(a)(3)(B)(vi).

[136] Officers, officials, representatives, or spokespersons for the Palestinian Liberation Organization (PLO) are considered for the purposes of this subsection to be engaged in terrorist activity. INA §212(a)(3)(B)(i).

[137] INA §212(a)(3)(B)(iv).

[138] INA §212(a)(3)(B)(iv)(IV)–(V).

show by clear and convincing evidence that the actor did not know and should not reasonably have known that the organization was a terrorist organization."[139]

Furnishing food and shelter at meetings for Sikh militants who had committed, or planned to commit, terrorist activities against the Indian government was a basis for a finding of inadmissibility under INA §212(a)(3)(B) in that the alien had provided "material support" to terrorists.[140] In determining whether a person is inadmissible on terrorist grounds, a court must consider the alien's state of mind, including the age of the individual and awareness of the organization's activities.[141] An alien who engages in terrorist activity against a foreign country is not necessarily a danger to the security of the United States.[142]

Terrorism and the USA PATRIOT Act

The USA PATRIOT Act added several new grounds of inadmissibility for representatives of foreign terrorist organizations or groups that endorse acts of terrorism. It authorizes the Secretary of State to designate any group, foreign or domestic, as a terrorist organization through publication in the *Federal Register*.[143] In addition, fundraising,[144] solicitation for membership,[145] or material support[146] of any group designated as a terrorist organization by the Secretary of State makes an individual inadmissible. It does not matter whether the activities are in furtherance of humanitarian, educational, or other nonmilitant endeavors if the group itself has been designated as a terrorist organization. The only defense to this charge under the USA PATRIOT Act is if the alien can prove "by clear and convincing evidence" that he or she did not know and should not have known that the organization was a terrorist organization.[147]

Solicitation of funds or support for groups that are not officially designated as terrorist organizations also are inadmissible offenses if the individual knew or should have known that such solicitation might further an organization's terrorist activities.[148] In addition, either the Secretary of State or the AG, after consultation with each other, may in their "unreviewable discretion" determine that these grounds of inadmissibility do not apply.[149]

---

[139] INA§212(a)(3)(B)(iv)(VI).

[140] *Singh-Kaur v. Ashcroft*, 385 F.3d. 293 (3d Cir. 2004).

[141] *Daneshvar v. Ashcroft*, 355 F.3d 615 (6th Cir. 2004).

[142] *Cheema v. INS*, 350 F.3d 1035 (9th Cir. 2003).

[143] INA §212(a)(3)(B)(vi)(II).

[144] INA §212(a)(3)(B)(iv)(IV).

[145] INA §212(a)(3)(B)(iv)(V).

[146] INA §212(a)(3)(B)(iv)(VI).

[147] INA §§212(a)(3)(B)(iv)(IV)(cc); 212(a)(3)(B)(iv)(V)(cc); 212(a)(3)(B)(iv)(VI)(dd).

[148] INA §212(a)(3)(B)(iv)(IV).

[149] INA §212(a)(3)(B)(iv)(VI).

Under the USA PATRIOT Act, the AG or the deputy AG may certify that there are reasonable grounds to believe that the individual is a terrorist, has engaged in terrorist activity, or is likely to engage in terrorist activity.[150] Such a designation requires mandatory detention of an individual so certified.[151] Once an individual is certified by the AG as a terrorist, that individual remains detained and the IJ may not redetermine the conditions of release for that alien if DHS decides to hold that person in custody.[152] This is so regardless of any relief for which the alien might be eligible or which might have been granted until the AG determines that the alien is no longer a threat.[153]

When an immigration officer or IJ suspects that an arriving alien appears to be inadmissible under INA §212(a)(3)(A),(B), or (C) (unless the security ground is for "other unlawful activity"), the immigration officer or judge "shall order the alien removed."[154]

Foreign Policy—INA §212(a)(3)(C)

An individual is inadmissible if there is a reasonable ground to believe his or her entry or proposed activities would have potentially adverse foreign policy consequences for the United States.[155] A letter from the Secretary of State conveying the Secretary's determination that an alien's presence in the country would have potentially serious adverse foreign policy consequences for the United States is presumptive and sufficient proof.[156]

An individual is not inadmissible for past or present beliefs, statements, or associations if such statements, beliefs, or associations would be lawful within the United States "unless the Secretary of State personally determines that the alien's admission would compromise a compelling United States foreign policy interest."[157] An official of a foreign government, or a candidate for election to a foreign government, during the period immediately preceding the election is not inadmissible based on beliefs, statements, or associations if such would be lawful within the United States.[158]

Membership in a Totalitarian Party—INA §212(a)(3)(D)

An individual who is or has been a member of the Communist Party or another totalitarian party is inadmissible except in the following circumstances:

---

[150] INA §212(a)(3)(B)(i)(II).

[151] INA §236A(a)(1)–(3).

[152] 8 CFR §1003.19(h)(1)(i)(C).

[153] INA §236A(a)(2).

[154] 8 CFR §§235.8(a), 1235.8(a).

[155] INA §212(a)(3)(C)(i).

[156] *Matter of Ruiz-Massieu*, 22 I&N Dec. 833 (BIA 1999).

[157] INA §212(a)(3)(C)(iii).

[158] INA §212(a)(3)(C)(ii),

- that the membership in the party is or was involuntary; was only while under the age of 16; was by operation of law; or where necessary to obtain employment or some basic "essential of living" (*e.g.*, food rations);[159] or
- the membership in the party ended at least two years before applying for the visa (five years where the party of which he or she was a member controlled the government at the time of the application for a visa);[160] and
- the alien is not a threat to the security of the United States.[161]

Nazi Persecution, Genocide, or Commission of Acts of Torture—INA §212(a)(3)(E)

The following groups of individuals are inadmissible for reasons of persecution, genocide, torture, or extrajudicial killings.

- Any alien who incited, ordered, assisted, or participated in the persecution of any person on account of race, religion, national origin, or political opinion by the Nazis (between 1933 and 1945).[162]
- Any alien who has engaged in genocide (as defined in the International Convention on the Prevention and Punishment of Genocide[163]) is inadmissible.[164]
- Any alien who outside the United States has committed any act of torture,[165] or ordered, incited, assisted, or participated in the commission of torture,[166] or any act of extrajudicial killing.[167]

Association with Terrorist Organizations—INA §212(a)(3)(F)

Any alien who has been determined by the Secretary of State or AG after mutual consultation to be associated with a terrorist organization and intending to engage in any way in activities that could endanger the welfare, safety, or security of the United States is inadmissible.[168]

Detention of Foreign Nationals

DHS is permitted to detain a suspected terrorist for seven days before bringing any charges against the individual.[169] The individual does have the right to file a petition

---

[159] INA §212(a)(3)(D)(ii).

[160] INA §212(a)(3)(D)(iii)(I).

[161] INA §212(a)(3)(D)(iii)(II).

[162] INA §212(a)(3)(E)(i).

[163] Defined at 18 USC §1091(a).

[164] INA §212(a)(3)(E)(ii).

[165] Defined at 18 USC §2340.

[166] INA §212(a)(3)(E)(iii).

[167] Defined at 28 USC §1350; *see also* §3(a) of the Torture Victim Protection Act.

[168] INA §212(a)(3)(F).

[169] INA §236A(a)(5).

for writ of habeas corpus to challenge the detention and/or the basis for the AG's certification as a terrorist.[170] This may be filed in any federal district court having the jurisdiction to hear such a case.[171] Appeal of the decision of the federal district court goes to the U.S. Court of Appeals for the District of Columbia Circuit.[172]

Registration of Foreign Nationals at Ports of Entry (NSEERS)

On June 6, 2002, the AG announced a new program—the "National Security Entry-Exit Registration System" (NSEERS).[173] Certain nonimmigrants may be required to be fingerprinted, photographed, and registered by DHS at a port of entry. The proposal requires the fingerprinting and photographing of applicants for admission "at the port of entry at such time the non-immigrant alien applies for admission."[174] The regulations also state that aliens subject to special registration who remain in the United States for more than 30 days may be required to report to DHS by mail or other means of any change in status (address, employment, education, etc). Special registration, as outlined under the regulations for those seeking admission to the United States, includes being fingerprinted and photographed by DHS upon admission. It also may include reporting to the U.S. Immigration and Customs Enforcement (ICE) office upon 10 days notice.[175] For those present in the United States who are from countries designated for special registration, the obligations include also reporting for fingerprinting and photographs and being interviewed by DHS officials.[176] Those who may be required include nonimmigrant aliens who: (1) are nationals or citizens of any country designated by the DHS Secretary; (2) whom a consular officer or inspections officer has reason to believe are citizens or nationals of a country designated as a special registration country by the DHS Secretary; or (3) who meet pre-existing criteria, or whom the inspecting officer has reason to believe meet pre-existing criteria, that such alien's presence in the United States warrants monitoring.[177]

Only males over the age of 17 have been required to register. Of those, LPRs, asylum applicants, and asylees have not been required to register. There have been four separate groups of countries whose citizens or nationals have been required to register during 2002 and 2003. The first group was from the following countries: Iran, Iraq, Syria, Sudan, and Libya. Group two included individuals from Afghanistan, Algeria, Bahrain, Lebanon, Morocco, North Korea, Oman, Qatar, Somalia, Tunisia, United Arab Emirates, and Yemen. The third group covered individuals from Pakistan and Saudi Arabia. The fourth included individuals from Bangladesh, Egypt, Indonesian,

---

[170] INA §236A(b)(1).

[171] INA §236A(b)(2).

[172] INA §236A(b)(3).

[173] The guidelines are found at 8 CFR §264.1.

[174] 8 CFR §264.1(f)(3).

[175] 8 CFR §264.1(f)(3)(i).

[176] 8 CFR §264.1(f)(4)(i).

[177] 8 CFR §264.1(f)(2).

Jordan, and Kuwait. The registration period for all groups has ended. Those who failed to register may be found removable from the United States or may be subject to criminal charges.[178]

Public Charge Ground of Inadmissibility—INA §212(a)(4)

Introduction

The public charge ground of inadmissibility makes an individual inadmissible for a visa or adjustment of status if, in the opinion of the consular officer or the immigration official, the individual is "likely at any time to become a public charge."[179] This ground of inadmissibility is prospective in nature, *i.e.*, the officer must look at the applicant's financial situation and make a determination as to whether it is likely in the future at any time that the alien will become public charge. This ground of inadmissibility covers both nonimmigrants and immigrants. There are certain groups of immigrants who do not have to meet this ground of inadmissibility. For example, the public charge ground of inadmissibility is waived for the following groups: refugees seeking adjustment;[180] asylees seeking adjustment;[181] those seeking benefits under the Nicaraguan Adjustment and Central American Relief Act (NACARA);[182] applicants under the Haitian Refugee Immigrant Fairness Act (HRIFA);[183] applicants under the Cuban Adjustment Act of 1966;[184] and special immigrant juveniles (SIJ)[185] seeking adjustment. There are other groups of individuals from specific countries who need not meet the public charge ground of inadmissibility in order to adjust status.[186]

Factors to Be Considered in Determining Public Charge

In determining whether an individual may be subject to the public charge ground of inadmissibility, the consular or immigration officer may consider the following factors: age; health; family status; assets; resources and financial status; education; and skills.[187]

---

[178] INA §237(a)(3).

[179] INA §212(a)(4)(A).

[180] INA §209(c).

[181] 8 CFR §§209.2(a)(1)(v), 1209.2(a)(1)(v).

[182] 8 CFR §§245.13(c), 1245.13(c). *See also* NACARA, *supra* note 29.

[183] 8 CFR §§245.15(e)(1), 1245.15(e)(1). *See also* Haitian Refugee Immigration Fairness Act of 1998, Pub. L. No. 105-277, 112 Stat. 2681 (div. A, title IX) (HRIFA).

[184] Pub. L. No. 89-732 (1966); *Matter of Mesa*, 12 I&N Dec. 4432 (BIA 1967).

[185] 8 CFR §§245.1(e)(2)(vi), 1245.1(e)(2)(vi).

[186] 8 CFR §§245.12, 1245.12; 245.20, 1245.20; and 245.21, 1245.21.

[187] INA §212(a)(4)(B)(i); *Matter of Harutunian*, 14 I&N Dec. 583 (BIA 1974).

To determine whether one is likely to become a public charge in the future, the totality of the factors must be considered.[188] Aliens who are likely to be, or who are, supported at public expense because of poverty or physical handicaps are within the proscribed groups.[189] Lack of a valid work offer does not mean an individual is likely to become a public charge.[190] Past receipt of welfare does not necessarily mean that one is likely to become a public charge in the future.[191] A 33-year-old mother of three children, employed and physically capable of earning a living, is not likely to become a public charge, notwithstanding the fact that her children received public cash assistance for four years.[192] A 70-year-old person with no means of support and no one responsible for supporting her, and who expects to be dependent on "old-age assistance" is inadmissible as a public charge.[193]

A demand for repayment of the public costs is not necessary for such a finding to be made.[194] Receipt of Supplemental Security Income (SSI) benefits constitutes receipt of public assistance and can be the basis for the breach of a public charge bond.[195] IJs have a right to waive this ground of inadmissibility.[196] Where a waiver is available, DHS must advise the visa applicant of this possibility.[197]

Affidavit of Support—INA §213A

In family-based petitions for immigrant (permanent) visa status under INA §§201(b)(2) or 203(a), the U.S. citizen or LPR petitioner must file an affidavit of support as required under INA §213A. The regulations state that an intending immigrant is inadmissible unless a sponsor executes an affidavit of support on Form I-864.[198] The purpose of the form is to show that the immigrant has adequate means of support and is not likely to become a public charge; it is submitted in consideration of the sponsored immigrant(s) not being found inadmissible as a public charge.[199] The person who filed the family-based petition must execute the affidavit of support.[200] If that person does not earn sufficient income to demonstrate an ability to support the beneficiary at 125 percent of the poverty guidelines, then the sponsor and intending

188 *Matter of A–*, 19 I&N Dec. 867 (BIA 1988).

189 *Matter of Mesa*, 12 I&N Dec. 432 (BIA 1967).

190 *Matter of Martinez-Lopez*, 10 I&N Dec. 409 (BIA 1962).

191 *Matter of Perez*, 15 I&N Dec. 136 (BIA 1974).

192 *Matter of A–*, 19 I&N Dec. 867 (BIA 1988).

193 *Matter of Harutunian*, 14 I&N Dec. 583 (BIA 1974).

194 *Id.*

195 *Matter of Viado*, 19 I&N Dec. 252 (BIA 1985).

196 *Matter of Ulloa*, 22 I&N Dec. 725 (BIA 1999).

197 *Matter of A–*, 19 I&N Dec. 867 (BIA 1988).

198 8 CFR §212a.2(a)(1).

199 *U.S. v. Wu*, 419 F.3d 142 (5th Cir 2005).

200 8 CFR §213a.2(b)(1).

immigrant must show "significant assets"[201] or obtain a joint sponsor, *i.e.*, another sponsor with significant assets.[202]

The exceptions to this rule are self-petitioners who are listed at INA §§204(a)(1)(A)(ii) and (iii) or §§204(a)(1)(B)(ii), (iii), or (iv), widow(er)s and those spouses and children who have been the victims of domestic violence under VAWA,[203] as well as those accompanying or following to join the self-petitioners.[204] Although they are still subject to INA §212(a)(4), these applicants need no affidavit of support to meet the public charge ground of inadmissibility. The officer may consider any affidavit submitted as support in determining public charge.[205]

In addition to the family-based immigrants listed above, family members of employment-based immigrants under INA §203(b) seeking an immigrant visa who either filed the immigrant visa on behalf of the intending immigrant or own a significant interest in the entity that filed the immigrant visa must also submit an affidavit if support.[206] The affiant must be a citizen or LPR, 18 years of age, domiciled in the United States, and must demonstrate an ability to maintain an annual income of at least 125 percent of the federal poverty guidelines.[207]

Labor Certification Ground of Inadmissibility—INA §212(a)(5)

Introduction

The labor certification ground of inadmissibility is meant, at least in part, to protect the U.S. labor market. This ground of inadmissibility, in summary, states that aliens coming to the United States to perform skilled or unskilled labor are inadmissible unless they first obtain from the Department of Labor (DOL) a "labor certification," *i.e.*, a finding that there are not sufficient qualified U.S. workers available at that time, in a particular area of employment, and that the employment of the alien will not adversely affect the wages and working conditions of U.S. workers.[208] It is a long, tedious, and bureaucratic process involving generally at least three different state and federal government agencies or departments (state employment agency, DOL, DHS, and, in some cases, the Department of State). It is a more complicated and lengthy process for those workers seeking an immigrant visa under INA §203(b) than it is for those seeking a temporary work visa under INA §§101(a)(15)(H)(ii)(a) and (b).

---

[201] 8 CFR §213a.2(c)(2)(iv)(A).

[202] 8 CFR §213a.2(c)(2)(iv)(B)

[203] VAWA, *supra* note 74.

[204] INA §212(a)(4)(C); 8 CFR §213a.2(a)(2)(ii)(A).

[205] INA §212(a)(4)(B)(ii).

[206] 8 CFR §213a.2(b)(2).

[207] 8 CFR §§213a.2(c)(1) and (2).

[208] INA §212(a)(5)(A)(i).

The purpose of this process ultimately is to make certain that a job that might go to a qualified U.S. worker is not given to an immigrant worker, unless it is shown that no qualified U.S. worker is available at the place where the work is to be employed. In making certain that the working conditions of similarly employed U.S. workers are not affected, U.S. employers are required to pay the "prevailing wage" within the industry to the alien worker for the job.[209] The statute states that "priority workers" under the first employment-based preference[210] are not subject to the labor certification requirement, while those who are in the second and third employment-based preference categories[211] are subject to the labor certification requirement. In the second and third preference categories there may be ways to avoid the lengthy and extensive labor certification process for immigrant visa applicants. The DOL regulations should be consulted.[212]

Miscellaneous Grounds of Inadmissibility

Ineligible for Citizenship—INA §212(a)(8)

An immigrant permanently ineligible for citizenship is inadmissible. The statute specifically refers to "draft evaders," *i.e.*, those who departed the United States or remained outside the United States in time of war or during a period declared as a national emergency by the President.[213] This statute does not apply to an alien who was in nonimmigrant status at the time of departure and is returning as a nonimmigrant.[214] The phrase "ineligible for citizenship" refers only to those who are barred from naturalization by virtue of their evasion of military service.

Delaying or postponing induction is not a basis for a finding of this ground of inadmissibility.[215] An LPR ordered to report for induction who departs the country in order to return as a "draft free" immigrant is "ineligible for citizenship."[216] For INA §212(a)(8) to apply, however, the primary purpose of leaving the country must be to avoid training or military service. The mere fact of leaving the military alone does not trigger this ground of inadmissibility.[217] An individual who seeks an exemption from

---

[209] 20 CFR §656.40.

[210] INA §203(b)(1) includes: aliens with extraordinary ability in the sciences, arts, education, business, or athletics; outstanding professors and researchers; and certain multinational executives and managers.

[211] INA §§203(b)(2) and (3) include members of the professions holding advanced degrees, professionals, skilled workers, and other workers.

[212] 20 CFR §§655 and 656.

[213] INA §212(a)(8)(B).

[214] *Matter of Kanga*, 22 I&N Dec. 1206 (BIA 2000).

[215] *Matter of Mincheff*, 13 I&N Dec. 715 (BIA 1971).

[216] *Matter of Riva*, 13 I&N Dec. 268 (BIA 1969).

[217] *Matter of Nunez-Toro*, 11 I&N Dec. 501 (BIA 1966).

military service is not inadmissible unless he or she knowingly and voluntarily waives his or her right to U.S. citizenship.[218]

Practicing Polygamists—INA §212(a)(10)(A)

An immigrant coming to the United States to practice polygamy is inadmissible. Under former INA §212(a)(11), anyone who had been guilty of polygamy was inadmissible.[219] The statute has been amended to require that the alien must currently be a "practicing" polygamist to be inadmissible.

International Child Abductors—INA §212(a)(10)(C)

Any alien who after entry of an order by a U.S. court granting custody of a U.S. citizen child detains that child or withholds custody of that child, outside the United States from the person granted custody by the court, is inadmissible until the child is surrendered to the person granted custody under the court's order. Moreover, any alien who is known by the Secretary of State to have intentionally assisted another individual in detaining or withholding of custody of the child, or providing material support or safe haven to such individual, also is inadmissible until the child is surrendered.[220] The spouse, children, parents, siblings, or agents of the alien detaining or withholding the child are inadmissible until the child is surrendered (unless the spouse is the parent of the abducted child, or the child is the child being detained).[221] This ground of inadmissibility does not apply to a government official detaining or withholding the child as part of his or her official duties;[222] nor does this ground apply to a government official of any foreign government if the official has been designated by the Secretary of State at his or her sole discretion.[223]

Last, the ground of inadmissibility at INA §212(a)(10)(C) does not apply if the child is found in a state that is a signatory to the Hague Convention on the Civil Aspects of International Child Abduction.[224]

Unlawful Voters—INA §212(a)(10)(D)

Any alien who has voted in violation of any federal, state, or local law, statute, ordinance, or regulation is inadmissible. The statute makes this action a ground of inadmissibility without regard to intent or knowledge, and the BIA has indicated in at least one (nonprecedent) case dealing with unlawful voting that intent or knowledge is not required.[225]

---

[218] *Matter of R–E–*, 9 I&N Dec. 720 (BIA 1962).

[219] *Nemetz v. INS*, 647 F.2d 432, 437 (4th Cir. 1981).

[220] INA §§212(a)(10)(C)(ii)(I) and (II).

[221] INA §212(a)(10)(C)(ii)(III).

[222] INA §212(a)(10)(C)(iii)(I).

[223] INA §212(a)(10)(C)(iii)(II).

[224] INA §212(a)(10)(C)(iii)(III).

[225] *In re Simone Angela Long*, 2004 WL 2952185 (BIA Nov. 4, 2004).

The only exception to this ground of inadmissibility is for an individual who meets the following criteria:

- each natural or adoptive parent is or was a citizen (by birth or naturalization);
- the alien permanently resided in the United States prior to his or her 16th birthday; and
- the alien reasonably believed he or she was a citizen at the time of the violation.[226]

Former Citizens Who Renounced Citizenship to Avoid Taxation—INA §212(a)(10)(E)

Any alien who is a former citizen of the United States who officially renounces U.S. citizenship, and who is determined by the AG to have renounced citizenship for the purpose of avoiding taxation by the United States is inadmissible.

Guardians Required to Help Helpless Aliens—INA §212(a)(10)(B)

An alien is inadmissible who is accompanying another alien who is inadmissible and certified to be helpless from sickness, mental or physical disability, or infancy;[227] and whose protection or guardianship is determined to be required by the alien.

---

[226] INA §212(a)(10)(D)(ii).

[227] INA §232(c). This section provides that once an examining officer determines that an alien is inadmissible due to sickness, mental or physical disability, or infancy, the officer may certify this fact for purposes of applying this ground of inadmissibility to the guardian.

CHAPTER 4

ENFORCEMENT AND ADJUDICATORY POWERS OF DHS AND EOIR

Introduction

While government officials have certain powers to stop, question, and detain an individual where there is probable cause to suspect criminal activity, there are constitutional and statutory limitations on those powers to ensure that individuals are not subjected to unreasonable searches and seizures. In the immigration arena, there has been substantial litigation on the issue of due process for immigrants. In most cases, the issue involves the government's right to control immigration versus the Fourth and Fifth Amendments' rights of "persons"[1] inside the United States. The power of the political branches of government to control who gets admitted into the country is quite extensive, as Congress has "plenary power," over immigration.[2] The Supreme Court confirmed that "whatever the procedure authorized by Congress is, it is due process as far as an alien denied entry is concerned."[3] The Court also stated, "The exclusion of aliens is a fundamental act of sovereignty. The right to do so stems not alone from legislative power but is inherent in the executive power to control the foreign affairs of the nation."[4]

Conversely, the power to remove an alien who already has been admitted is not as extensive as the power over entry, and there are limits on what the political branches of government may do. Lawful permanent resident (LPR) aliens have a right to due process—a "fair hearing."[5] Since "due process" applies to all "persons" within the United States[6] regardless of immigration status, the right to a fair opportunity to be

---

1 *Accardi v. Shaughnessy*, 347 U.S. 260 (1954).

2 *Harisiades v. Shaughnessy*, 342 U.S. 580 (1952).

3 *United States ex rel. Knauff v. Shaughnessy*, 338 U.S. 537 (1950).

4 *Id.*

5 *Landon v. Placencia*, 459 U.S. 21 (1982); *Chew v. Colding*, 344 U.S. 590, 598 (1953).

6 *Plyler v. Doe*, 457 U.S. 202 (1982).

heard is given not only to LPRs but also to aliens in unlawful status within the United States.

The following section first discusses the powers of the government to exclude and remove aliens from the United States and the due process rights of aliens to be protected from unlawful arrests, detention, and removal. Second, this chapter covers the manners in which Department of Homeland Security (DHS) officials exercise that power under the Immigration and Nationality Act (INA).[7] Finally, procedures in representing someone before the immigration court are covered.

DHS Powers to Stop, Seize, Arrest, and Search

DHS officers have the power to stop, seize, arrest, and search individuals as outlined at INA §287. These powers are exercised in nondetentive stops; seizures; arrests; and searches at the border or functional equivalent and the interior of the country.

Nondetentive Stops—Individual Stops and Fixed Checkpoints

Government officers have the right to stop a person in a nondetentive manner to determine whether the person has a right to be in the country. An immigration agent may question an individual regarding his or her right to be in the country, and unless the questioning is so intimidating as to make the person believe he or she is not free to leave, no seizure has taken place and there is no requirement for a reasonable suspicion or probable cause of illegal activity.[8] Also, a nondetentive stop on the street by state or local law enforcement to question a person about identity, or request that a person present identification, does not constitute an arrest or seizure under the Fourth Amendment.[9] As long as the person to whom questions are directed by any law enforcement officer feels free to walk away and disregard the questions, there has been no intrusion by the government upon the person's liberty that would require some particularized and objective justification under the Constitution.[10]

The immigration regulations state that an immigration officer has a right to ask questions of anyone as long as the officer does not restrain the individual's ability to walk away.[11] In a situation where there has been no intrusion or restriction on the person's liberty, an immigration agent may ask questions of an individual. If the individual refuses to answer questions and the authorities take further action, including detaining the person, there must be at least some "minimal level" of objective justifica-

---

[7] Immigration and Nationality Act of 1952 (INA), Pub. L. No. 82-414, 66 Stat. 163 (codified as amended at 8 USC §§1101 *et seq.*).

[8] *INS v. Delgado*, 466 U.S. 210 (1984).

[9] *Florida v. Royer*, 460 U.S. 491 (1983).

[10] *U.S. v. Mendenhall*, 446 U.S. 544, 554 (1980).

[11] 8 CFR §287.8(b)(1).

tion to validate the arrest or detention of the person. At the point of arrest and/or detention, the seizure of the person must be based on specific objective facts.[12]

Border patrol stops of vehicles at a fixed checkpoint on roads leading away from the border are justified under the Fourth Amendment without a reasonable suspicion of illegal activity.[13] In this sense, stops of individuals at the border or fixed checkpoints near the border to question their right to enter the country do not require a showing of reasonable suspicion of illegal activity. The expectation of privacy is less at the border than in the interior and the balance of the interests between the government and the privacy rights of the individual leans more favorably toward the government at the border.[14]

Seizures

Where the questioning of the person includes physical detention so that the person reasonably concludes that he or she is not free to leave, the encounter rises to the level of a seizure. The U.S. Supreme Court has stated that an investigatory stop of a vehicle by a border patrol officer is justified where there is a reasonable suspicion that criminal activity may be afoot.[15] This concept of reasonable suspicion as a sufficient standard to justify an investigatory stop short of an actual arrest is "somewhat abstract" and the Supreme Court has deliberately avoided reducing it to a neat set of rules.[16] Although an officer's mere "hunch" that someone is here illegally is not sufficient to justify an investigatory stop, "the likelihood of criminal activity need not rise to the level required for probable cause, and it falls considerably short of satisfying a preponderance of the evidence standard."[17] The Court stated that an investigatory stop, short of an arrest, must still be justified by "some objective manifestation that the person stopped is about to be engaged in criminal behavior."[18]

An immigration officer may "briefly detain" an individual upon reasonable suspicion that the person being questioned is engaged or is attempting to be engaged in an offense against the United States or is an alien illegally in the United States.[19] The reasonableness of the investigatory stop depends on a balance between the public interest and the individual's right to personal security free from arbitrary interference by law enforcement officers.[20] Normally, such a seizure would demand probable cause under the Fourth Amendment. In *Brignoni-Ponce*, the Court stated that "in the appropriate circumstances, the Fourth Amendment allows a properly limited search or seizure on

---

[12] *Delaware v. Prouse*, 440 U.S. 648, 663 (1979).

[13] *United States v. Martinez-Fuerte*, 428 U.S. 543 (1976)

[14] *United States v. Montoya de Hernandez*, 473 U.S. 531, 540 (1985)

[15] *United States v. Arvizu*, 534 U.S. 266, 273 (2002).

[16] *Id.* at 274.

[17] *Id.; see also U.S. v. Cortez*, 449 U.S. 411, 418 (1981).

[18] *U.S. v. Cortez*, 449 U.S. at 417.

[19] 8 CFR §287.8(b)(2).

[20] *United States v. Brignoni-Ponce*, 422 U.S. 873, 881 (1978).

facts that do not constitute probable cause to arrest."[21] A reasonable suspicion of criminal activity warrants a temporary seizure for the purpose of questioning an individual. The Court in *Brignoni-Ponce* continued, "We hold that when an officer's suspicions lead him reasonably to suspect that when a particular vehicle may contain aliens who are in the country illegally, he may stop the vehicle briefly and investigate the circumstances that provoke the suspicion."[22] A government agent may not detain to investigate the immigration status of any individual without reasonable suspicion of illegal alienage. In addition, government agents may not "frisk" any individual who has not been arrested unless the agent has a reasonable suspicion based on articulable facts that the individual is armed.[23]

Roving Patrols

A roving patrol involves the stopping of vehicles by immigration officers while on patrol at locations other than fixed checkpoints.[24] A vehicle stop by border patrol agents within the United States at places other than the border or fixed checkpoint near the border, in order to question the occupants, is a seizure where those inside the vehicle are not free to leave and would not reasonably feel that they are free to leave.[25] Stops of moving automobiles can be made without a warrant, but there must be reasonable suspicion for the stop[26] U.S. Customs and Border Patrol (CBP—a component of DHS) border patrol agents on roving patrol may stop a vehicle if they are aware of specific articulable facts (with reasonable inferences from these facts) that reasonably warrant suspicion that the vehicle being stopped is engaged in illegal activity.[27]

What facts may form the basis for the reasonable suspicion in a vehicle stop situation? In *Brignoni-Ponce*, the Supreme Court gave examples of what such articulable facts might be: characteristics of the area where the stop is made; proximity to the border; traffic patterns in that area; type of car and suitability for carrying aliens; erratic behavior or attempts to evade officers; and a heavily loaded car or unusual number of passengers.[28] The police consider the totality of the circumstances,[29] and the officer is entitled to assess these factors and others in light of his or her experience in

---

[21] *Id.*

[22] *Id.*

[23] *Murillo v. Musegades*, 809 F. Supp. 487 (W.D. TX 1992).

[24] *Almeida-Sanchez v. United States*, 413 U.S. 266, 268 (1973).

[25] *Brignoni-Ponce*, 422 U.S. at 878. *See also English v. Sava*, 571 F. Supp. 1029 (S.D.N.Y. 1983) (stopping a public bus and moving it to an isolated area of a bus terminal to question those inside the bus can be classified as a seizure, in that those inside the bus are closed in and the bus was moved to an isolated area; those on the bus could reasonably conclude that they were not free to leave).

[26] *Id.* at 882; *see also United States v. Baron-Cabrera*, 119 F.3d 1454 (10th Cir. 1997).

[27] *United States v. Villalobos*, 161 F.3d 285 (5th Cir. 1998).

[28] *Brignoni-Ponce*, 422 U.S. at 884–85.

[29] *United States v. Cortez*, 449 U.S. 411, 418 (1981).

detecting illegal entry.[30] However, experience alone does not give the officer unlimited discretion in making a stop.[31] Nor is location by itself a sufficient factor.[32] A tip that is specific and detailed may be the basis for reasonable suspicion.[33] The reactions of the driver and the passengers in a vehicle also may form the basis for reasonable suspicion.[34]

Must the illegal activity be related to a violation of the immigration laws? The Fifth Circuit has indicated that the suspicion upon which the stop is based need not be limited to immigration violations.[35] However, the statute granting border patrol agents the power to arrest individuals limits to immigration violations the authority to arrest without a warrant, unless the crime is being committed in the officer's presence, or there are reasonable grounds to believe the person has committed or is committing an offense.[36] The language of the Supreme Court in *Brignoni-Ponce* also indicates that the authority of immigration officials to seize is extended to nonimmigration matters only where they are performing duties relating to the enforcement of immigration laws at the time of arrest.[37] The border patrol may consider other violations of the law if an alien is stopped; however, the initial stop must be based on a reasonable suspicion of an immigration law violation.[38] If the immigration officers wish to go further and *search* the vehicle without a warrant, there must be probable cause of criminal activity.[39]

Arrests

Authority

INA §287(a) sets out the authority of immigration agents to interrogate and arrest individuals believed to be present in violation of immigration law. Among other powers, a DHS agent has the authority to arrest a person if there is reason to believe the person has committed an offense against the United States, or is present in the United States in violation of immigration law.[40] An immigration officer may arrest an individual for felonies that have been committed under the immigration laws, if he or she has reason to believe that the person arrested is guilty of the offense and there is a likelihood of the person escaping before a warrant can be obtained.[41] In addition, an

---

30 *Brignoni-Ponce*, 422 U.S. at 885.

31 *Nicacio v. INS*, 797 F.2d 700, 705 (9th Cir. 1986).

32 *Brown v. Texas*, 443 U.S. 47, 52 (1979).

33 *United States v. Garcia-Nunez*, 709 F.2d 559 (9th Cir. 1983).

34 *United States v. Arvizu*, 534 U.S. 266 (2002).

35 *United States v. Nicholls*, 142 F.3d 857, 865 (5th Cir. 1998).

36 INA §§287(a)(8) and (9).

37 *United States v. Brignoni-Ponce*, 422 U.S. 873, 883 (1978).

38 *U.S. v. Garza*, 514 F.2d 222, 225 (5th Cir. 1976).

39 *Almeida-Sanchez v. U.S.*, 413 U.S. 266, 269–70 (1973).

40 8 CFR §287.8(c)(2).

41 INA §287(a)(4).

immigration officer may arrest any individual who in his or her presence or view is entering or attempting to enter the United States in violation of immigration law.[42]

Power of border patrol officers to arrest for nonimmigration violations

An immigration officer has the authority to arrest without warrant individuals for *any offense* against the United States if the offense is committed in the officer's presence and "if the officer or employee is performing duties relating to the enforcement of the immigration laws at the time of the arrest and if there is a likelihood of the person escaping before a warrant can be obtained for his arrest."[43] In addition, an immigration officer may make an arrest for any felony committed against the United States where there are reasonable grounds to believe that the person has committed, or is committing, such a felony "if the officer or employee is performing duties relating to the enforcement of the immigration laws at the time of the arrest and if there is a likelihood of the person escaping before a warrant can be obtained for his arrest."[44]

Immigration officers may not make arrests for nonimmigration offenses where the officers are not performing duties relating to the enforcement of immigration laws at the time of the arrest.[45] The Supreme Court in *Brignoni-Ponce* stated that border patrol officers may stop vehicles where they are "aware of specific articulable facts, together with reasonable inferences from these facts, that reasonably warrant suspicion that the vehicles contain aliens who may be illegally in the country."[46] Border patrol agents do not have authority to stop vehicles based only on a suspicion that a person is violating a state traffic law.[47] If an initial stop is based on a reasonable suspicion of an immigration law violation, the border patrol may consider other violations of the law.[48]

Searches

The authority for DHS officials to stop and search vehicles without a warrant depends on a number of circumstances. One of the major factors is the location of the search—*i.e.*, whether it is at the border, a fixed checkpoint close to the border, or away from the border.

---

[42] INA §287(a)(2).

[43] INA §287(a)(5).

[44] *Id.*

[45] *U.S. v. Perkins*, 166 F. Supp. 2d 1116 (W.D. Tex. 2001). *But see U.S. v. Villalobos*, 161 F.3d 289 (5th Cir. 1998) (which states that border patrol officers may make stops upon reasonable suspicion of "illegal activity").

[46] *United States v. Brignoni-Ponce*, 422 U.S. 873, 884 (1978).

[47] *U.S. v. Rubio-Hernandez*, 39 F. Supp. 2d 808, 830 (W.D. Tex. 1999); *U.S. v. Garza*, 544 F.2d 222, 225 (5th Cir. 1976).

[48] *Garza*, 544 F.2d at 225.

Fixed checkpoints

DHS can require vehicles to stop temporarily at fixed checkpoints away from the border as long as such checkpoints are clearly marked.[49] DHS has the power to search travelers at the border or the functional equivalent without probable cause.[50] However, when a search is away from the border, that power is limited to ensure a traveler's right to free passage is only minimally affected.[51] Away from the border, there must be probable cause for a search.[52] There is no violation of the Fourth Amendment where vehicles are briefly stopped at fixed checkpoints near the border and individuals are questioned about their right to be in the United States.[53] As an individual's privacy interest increases, so does the government's burden to justify a search or seizure.[54]

Whether a fixed checkpoint is the functional equivalent of the border (therefore, probable cause is not needed for a search) depends on whether almost all of the traffic is international in character.[55] If the search is made at a location that is not the functional equivalent of the border, probable cause must be established.[56] In *Almeida-Sanchez*, the Supreme Court ruled that a warrantless search conducted at a point on a road 25 miles from the border by a roving Immigration and Naturalization Service (INS) patrol was not the functional equivalent of the border. The Fifth Circuit has outlined three characteristics to be measured in determining whether the search is made at the border: (1) proximity to the border; (2) permanent nature of the checkpoint; and (3) hours of operation.[57] In addition, the court stated that a fixed checkpoint must intercept primarily international travelers.

Border searches

Border patrol agents are authorized to stop motorists without any individualized suspicion for the limited purpose of checking citizenship. They may ask questions, demand proof of citizenship, and conduct a "plain view" inspection of the vehicle to check for concealed aliens.[58] Where there is a reasonable certainty that the person has just crossed the border and the search is conducted at the earliest point after the border is crossed, there is no need for a warrant, individualized suspicion, or exigent circumstances. The government's need to police the border at the earliest possible point clearly outweighs the individual's interest in privacy.

---

[49] *United States v. Martinez-Fuerte*, 428 U.S. 543 (1976).

[50] *United States v. Montoya-Hernandez*, 473 U.S. 531 (1985).

[51] *Martinez-Fuerte*, 428 U.S. 543.

[52] *Almeida-Sanchez v. United States*, 413 U.S. 266, 269 (1973).

[53] *United States v. Blanford*, 566 F.2d 470 (5th Cir. 1978).

[54] *United States v. Ramsey*, 431 U.S. 606 (1977), *United States v. Garcia*, 672 F.2d 1349, 1364 (5th Cir. 1982).

[55] *Almeida-Sanchez*, 413 U.S. 266 (1973).

[56] *United States v. Morgan*, 501 F.2d 1351 (9th Cir. 1974); *Almeida-Sanchez*, 413 U.S. at 273.

[57] *United States v. Jackson*, 825 F.2d 853 (5th Cir. 1987).

[58] *Jasinski v. Adams*, 781 F.2d 843 (11th Cir. 1986).

The courts have also allowed warrantless searches in broader border areas—not at the first instance at the border but at a later point near the border. These "extended border searches"[59] have been permitted where there was "reasonable suspicion" of illegal activity.

Searches away from the border

Any search of an alien away from the border or the functional equivalent must be based on probable cause.[60]

Searches at places of employment

In order to conduct warrantless searches of factories, agents must have a valid search warrant, consent of the owner, or exigent circumstances establishing that the person may flee before a warrant can be obtained.[61] In *Pearl Meadows Mushroom Farm, Inc. v. Nelson*, the court stated that the former INS entry into the workplace without a warrant, consent, or exigent circumstances would violate the Fourth Amendment. Former INS/DHS may not detain an entire work force.[62] The Supreme Court has found that a sweep of a factory was constitutional where immigration agents with search warrants entered the factory premises and positioned agents at the exits to question individuals leaving the building.[63] The Court, in determining that there was no Fourth Amendment violation, found that the agents at the exits were merely questioning individuals leaving the building and that no unlawful search or seizure had occurred; mere questioning is not a seizure.[64]

Under the immigration regulations, a DHS officer may enter into any area of business or other activity to which the public has access or onto open fields that are not farms or agricultural operations. The officer may do so without consent or particularized suspicion in order to question any person whom the officer believes to be an alien regarding his or her right to be in the United States.[65] The officer may not enter into the nonpublic areas of a business, farm, or dwelling to question the occupants or employees regarding their right to be present or remain in the United States unless the officer has a warrant or the consent of the owner or other person in control of the site to be inspected.[66] A warrant to enter work premises to search for undocumented workers is sufficient if it narrows down the field of vulnerable persons to those rea-

[59] *United States v. Garcia*, 672 F.2d 1349, 1364 (5th Cir. 1982).

[60] *Almeida-Sanchez v. United States*, 413 U.S. 266 (1973).

[61] *Pearl Meadows Mushroom Farm, Inc. v. Nelson*, 723 F. Supp. 432, 439 (N.D. Cal. 1989).

[62] *Id.* at 445–50.

[63] *INS v. Delgado*, 466 U.S. 210 (1984).

[64] *Id.*

[65] 8 CFR §287.8(f)(4).

[66] 8 CFR §287.8(f)(2).

sonably believed to be illegally present, even if the warrant does not specifically name the persons being sought.[67]

Searches of dwellings

A DHS agent may not enter a dwelling without a warrant to conduct a search based on anything less than probable cause of an immigration violation.[68] Immigration agents are not permitted to enter dwellings without a warrant.[69]

Searches of the person

Persons and property may be searched at the border[70] without the requirement of reasonable suspicion or a warrant. These searches include the contents of one's "purse, wallet or pockets."[71] However, where a search becomes increasingly intrusive (*e.g.*, strip search), there must be "real suspicion" of the individual searched.[72] Customs officers may conduct a "pat-down" search at the border without probable cause or "real suspicion."[73] The INA states that authorized DHS officers have the power to conduct a search of the person "and of the personal effects in the possession of any person" without warrant of any person who is seeking admission to the United States where the officer may have reasonable cause to suspect that grounds exist for the denial of admission to the United States.[74]

Seizure of Documents

DHS officers are authorized to take a state driver's license away from an alien believed to be present in violation of immigration law. Even though federal law does not specifically authorize DHS officials to take driver's licenses, at least one court has found that such authority was inferred under federal law.[75]

State or Local Police Inquiry into Immigration Matters

Police stopping a vehicle briefly based on suspicion of criminal activity (*e.g.*, suspicion of driving intoxicated) have general investigative authority to inquire into possible immigration violations. Questioning an alien about his or her "Green Card" is

---

[67] *International Workers and Allied Local Workers Local Union No. 164 v. Nelson*, 799 F.2d 547 (9th Cir. 1986).

[68] *Illinois Migrant Council v. Pilliod*, 531 F. Supp. 1011 (N.D. Ill. 1982).

[69] *Duke v. Nelson*, 762 F.2d 1318 (9th Cir. 1985).

[70] *United States v. Ramsey*, 431 U.S. 606, 616 (1977).

[71] *United States v. Wilmot*, 563 F.2d 1298, 1300 (9th Cir. 1977).

[72] *United States v. Leverette*, 503 F.2d 269, 270 (9th Cir. 1974).

[73] *Wilmot*, 563 F.2d at 1300. *See also United States v. Grayson*, 597 F.2d 1225 (9th Cir. 1979).

[74] INA §287(c).

[75] *Pinon-Lopez v. INS*, 758 F.2d 1390 (10th Cir. 1985).

reasonable under such circumstances.[76] Whether there is reasonable suspicion of criminal activity depends on the totality of the circumstances.[77]

Where a state or local official stops an individual for a nonimmigration offense and then discovers that there may be an immigration violation, the official may contact DHS, which may then place a 48-hour detainer on the individual.[78] However, an extended detention of an individual by state or local police only for the purpose of enforcing immigration laws is not permitted.[79]

The INA contains both criminal and civil provisions. State and local police generally have been recognized as having authority over criminal violations. However, the civil area (arrest and detention of aliens for immigration violations) generally has been understood to be a DHS responsibility. In recent years, there has been controversy involving whether state and local police officers can, or should, be permitted to stop or arrest individuals solely for immigration violations. The issue is the extent to which state and local police may enforce these laws—specifically civil immigration laws relating to illegal presence in the country (as opposed to illegal entry which is a criminal as well as a civil violation).[80]

In 1996, the Department of Justice (DOJ), under Attorney General Janet Reno published a memorandum stating that state and local police were without authority to enforce the civil provisions of the INA.[81] However, in 2002, under Attorney General John Ashcroft, DOJ issued an opinion indicating that state and local police have "inherent" authority to arrest for civil violations of the INA. In 1996, Congress, through IIRAIRA,[82] gave the attorney general (AG) the authority to enter into written agreements with state and local police giving them authority under certain conditions for the "investigation, apprehension or detention of aliens in the United States."[83] There must be a memorandum of understanding (MOU) between the AG and the local police. The local police must receive training in immigration law and work under the supervision of the AG.[84] In addition, IIRAIRA allows the AG to call upon state and local officials where there is an "actual and imminent influx of aliens" to exercise certain enforcement duties of immigration officers in the arrest and detention of aliens.[85] Also, the INA permits state and local police to arrest and detain individuals illegally present in the

---

[76] *Terry v. Ohio*, 392 U.S. 1, 19 (1968).

[77] *U.S. v. Cortez*, 449 U.S. 411, 417–18 (1981).

[78] 8 CFR §287.7(d).

[79] *U.S. v. Cruz*, 559 F.2d 30 (5th Cir. 1995).

[80] INA §275.

[81] *See Assistance by State and Local Police in Apprehending Illegal Aliens*, Department of Justice Office of Legal Counsel (1996).

[82] Illegal Immigration Reform and Immigrant Responsibility Act of 1996, Division C of the Omnibus Appropriations Act of 1996 (H.R. 3610), Pub. L. No. 104-208, 110 Stat. 3009.

[83] INA §287(g).

[84] INA §§287(g)(2) and (3).

[85] INA §103(a)(10).

country who have previously been convicted of felonies and have left or been deported from the United States after the conviction.[86] Under the statute, local police must first confirm with DHS that the individual's status and detention is permitted only for the period needed for DHS to take the person into custody.[87]

Apart from these statutory amendments, the issue is still not settled as to the extent of state and local police power to enforce immigration laws.[88] Courts have rendered somewhat conflicting opinions.[89]

Detention Procedures Under the INA

"Processing" Detained Aliens—8 CFR §287.3

The procedures for "processing" non–American citizens arrested without a warrant are outlined in the regulations at 8 CFR §287.3. The officer who interviews the individual should not be the arresting officer unless no other officer is available.[90] The officer must advise the individual of the following:[91]

- reasons for the arrest;
- right to be represented at no expense to the government;
- availability of free legal services (a list of those agencies should be given); and
- that any statement made may be used against him or her in subsequent proceedings.

The officer also must advise the individual that a decision on custody status will be made within 48 hours, *i.e.*, whether the individual will be detained or released on bond and whether a Notice to Appear (NTA) or warrant of arrest will be issued.[92] Unfortunately, the regulations do not mandate that these advisals be given before the interrogation of the individual. They are often given *after* the questioning of the

---

[86] 8 USC §1252c; *see also* Antiterrorism and Effective Death Penalty Act of 1996, Pub. L. No. 104-132, Title IV, §439, 110 Stat. 1214, 1276 (Apr. 24, 1996) (AEDPA).

[87] *Id.*

[88] *Gonzalez v. City of Peoria*, 722 F.2d 468 (9th Cir. 1983) The court indicated that local authorities may enforce the criminal provisions of the INA, but enforcement of the civil provisions rests with the federal government. However, another circuit has found that state and local police have implicit authority to arrest for violations of immigration laws. *United States v. Santana-Garcia*, 264 F.2d 1188 (10th Cir. 2001).

[89] For a full discussion of this issue see "Enforcing Immigration Law: the Role of State and Local Enforcement," Congressional Research Service, Mar. 11, 2004.

[90] 8 CFR §287.3(a).

[91] 8 CFR §287.3(c).

[92] 8 CFR §287.3(d). Section 412 of the USA PATRIOT Act, Uniting and Strengthening America by Providing Appropriate Tools Required to Intercept and Obstruct Terrorism Act of 2001, Pub. L. No. 107-56, 115 Stat. 272, allows DHS to detain aliens suspected of being terrorists for seven days without charging them with immigration or criminal violations. If the alien is not charged within seven days, he or she shall be released.

alien and are therefore of limited value to an individual who may wish to remain silent, but is unaware he or she is able to do so.

The failure by DHS to notify individuals of these rights does not render a voluntary statement inadmissible.[93] Miranda warnings are not applicable in a deportation setting.[94] However, an voluntary statement taken in violation of an individual's due process rights is inadmissible.[95] Violation of a regulatory requirement by a government officer can result in evidence being excluded or proceedings invalidated where the regulation in question serves a purpose of benefit to the alien and the violation prejudiced interests of the alien that were protected by the regulation.[96]

In addition, the regulations mandate that every detained alien be notified that he or she may communicate with the consular or diplomatic officer of his or her nationality.[97] Existing treaties with some countries require immediate notification of the consular or diplomatic officer whenever a citizen of that country is detained by DHS, regardless of whether the alien requests such notification.[98]

After interrogating the individual, serving the notice of rights, and deciding on custody status, the government can serve the individual the charging document (NTA) and transfer him or her to a detention facility or release the individual on personal recognizance.

Mandatory Detention—INA §§235 and 236

Previously, the general rule regarding the detention of non–American citizens was that individuals should not be detained or required to post bond unless the government could establish that the individual was a threat to the community or a risk to abscond.[99] IIRAIRA added several classes of individuals who are not entitled to release from custody on their own recognizance or under bond:[100]

- Arriving aliens.[101]
- Individuals subject to expedited removal who claim a credible fear of persecution in their native country "shall be detained" pending a final determination of the credible fear.[102] However, if it is determined that there is a "credible fear" and the

---

[93] *Navarro-Chalan v. Ashcroft*, 359 F.3d 19, 23 (1st Cir. 2004).

[94] *Navia-Duran v. INS*, 568 F.2d 803 (1st Cir. 1977).

[95] *Id.* at 810.

[96] *Matter of Garcia-Flores*, 17 I&N Dec. 325 (BIA 1980).

[97] 8 CFR §§236.1(e), 1236.1(e).

[98] *Id.*; 8 CFR §§208.6(b), 1208.6(b) (records of asylum applications and credible fear interviews are protected from disclosure to foreign governments).

[99] *Matter of Patel*, 15 I&N Dec. 666 (BIA 1976).

[100] INA §236(c). *See Demore v. Kim*, 538 U.S. 510 (2003) (holding that Congress may detain deportable criminal aliens "for the brief period necessary for their removal proceedings.").

[101] 8 CFR §§235.3(a), 1235.3(a).

[102] INA §235(b)(1)(B)(ii).

individual is placed into removal proceedings, he or she is eligible for a custody redetermination before an immigration judge (IJ).[103]

- Criminal aliens who are inadmissible for having committed any offense listed in INA §212(a)(2) (drugs, crimes involving moral turpitude, prostitution).[104]
- Criminal aliens who are deportable or removable based on convictions for:
  - A single crime involving moral turpitude committed within five years of the date of admission where the term of imprisonment is one year or more;[105]
  - Multiple crimes involving moral turpitude;[106]
  - Aggravated felonies;[107]
  - Controlled substances (unless it is for a single offense involving possession for one's own use of 30 grams or less of marijuana);[108]
  - Certain firearms offenses.[109]
- Terrorists—individuals reasonably believed to be entering to engage in (or presently or previously engaged in) terroristic activities or any activity the purpose of which is a threat to the national security of the United States under INA §§212(a)(3) and 237(a)(4).[110]

Note: The IIRAIRA mandatory detention rules apply to those "released" on or after October 9, 1998.[111] Those released from detention, parole, probation, or supervised release *prior* to October 9, 1998, are *not* subject to mandatory detention. The mandatory detention provisions apply even where the person is not taken into custody upon release from criminal detention.[112]

The AG may release an individual subject to mandatory detention if it is necessary to protect a witness, potential witness, person cooperating with an investigation, or family member or close associate of any such person.[113]

An individual has a right to ask for a "*Joseph*" hearing to determine whether he or she should be subject to mandatory detention. The alien can avoid mandatory detention by proving citizenship, lack of predicate conviction, or that DHS is substantially unlikely to prove in its case.

---

[103] *Matter of X–K–*, 23 I&N Dec. 731 (BIA 2005).

[104] INA §236(c)(1)(A).

[105] INA §237(a)(2)(A)(i).

[106] INA §237(a)(2)(A)(ii).

[107] INA §237(a)(2)(A)(iii).

[108] INA §237(a)(2)(B).

[109] INA §237(a)(2)(C).

[110] INA §236A(a)(1).

[111] *Matter of Adeniji*, 22 I&N Dec. 1102, 1109–13 (BIA 1999).

[112] *Matter of Rojas*, 23 I&N Dec. 117 (BIA 2001).

[113] INA §236(c)(2).

Custody/Bond Hearings—8 CFR §1003.19

Authority of the court to redetermine custody/bond status—INA §236

After DHS's initial determination of the bond, a detained individual not subject to mandatory detention may, at any time before an administratively final order of removal, request a review of the DHS decision by the IJ.[114] The IJ may continue to detain the individual, release him or her, or redetermine the amount of bond.[115] In determining this amount, an IJ may release the alien on personal recognizance, or under bond of at least $1,500 or conditional parole.[116] Custody/bond hearings are informal in nature and there is usually no written or transcribed record of these proceedings. Requests for these hearings are made to the court having jurisdiction over the place where the individual is detained.[117] If there is no judge available at this location, the request is made to the court having administrative control over the case.[118] If that is not possible, the request is made directly to the Office of the Chief Immigration Judge for designation of an appropriate immigration court.[119] Request for a custody/bond hearing may be made verbally or in writing. A custody/bond hearing may not take place while the alien is still in local, state, or federal custody.[120]

The IJ has no authority to redetermine custody decisions made by DHS regarding the following classes of persons:[121]

- detainees in exclusion proceedings;
- arriving aliens, including those paroled into the country under INA §212(d)(5);
- aliens detained for criminal or security grounds described in INA §§237(a)(4) and 236(c)(1); and
- aggravated felons in deportation proceedings under the former INA §242(a)(2).

Custody/bond hearings should be held promptly. Since the issue involved is the liberty of the individual, these cases are supposed to be given top priority by the court. Unreasonable delays in setting a bond hearing should be challenged. Custody/bond hearings may be held even if the charging document has not been filed with the court.[122] The hearing may be held telephonically at the discretion of the IJ;[123] this usually occurs when the alien is detained at some distance. If an individual has

---

[114] 8 CFR §§236.1(d), 1236.1(d).

[115] *Id.*

[116] INA §236(a)(2).

[117] 8 CFR §1003.19(c)(1).

[118] 8 CFR §1003.19(c)(2).

[119] 8 CFR §1003.19(c)(3).

[120] *Matter of Sanchez*, 20 I&N Dec. 233 (BIA 1990).

[121] 8 CFR §1003.19(h)(2)(i).

[122] 8 CFR §1003.14(a).

[123] 8 CFR §1003.19(b).

managed to obtain his or her release, an application for amelioration of the terms of release must be made within seven days.[124]

Factors to be considered in determining custody/bond status

In *Matter of Daryoush*[125] and *Matter of Patel*,[126] the Board of Immigration Appeals (BIA) established the following factors to be considered in a custody/bond hearing:

- family ties;
- employment history;
- community ties;
- manner of entry and length of residence in the United States;
- prior criminal record (including nature and recency of any criminal activity);
- record of appearance at prior court proceedings;
- prior immoral acts or participation in subversive activities; and
- ability to post bond.

The IJ has wide latitude in deciding what factors to consider in setting bond and determining custody, including other factors that bear on the central issue of whether the individual is a risk to abscond or a threat to the community. The alien has the burden of showing that he or she is not a threat to the community or a risk to abscond.[127] Other possible relevant factors include:

- property ownership (home, personal, or business);
- health of the individual or immediate family members dependent on him or her;
- record of payment of taxes;
- stability of residence (has the individual lived at the address for a long period);
- prior immigration history;
- possible relief from removal available to the individual;
- other evidence relating to moral character;
- any existing criminal bonds, probation, parole, or court orders to monitor and insure the individual's presence in another court.

The AG has stated that national security interests and the "encouragement of further unlawful mass migrations" are factors to be weighed.[128]

---

[124] 8 CFR §§236.1(d)(1), 1236.1(d)(1).

[125] 18 I&N Dec. 352 (BIA 1982) (the BIA held that district director must state the reasons for his or her decision).

[126] 15 I&N Dec. 666 (BIA 1976).

[127] *Matter of Ellis*, 20 I&N Dec. 641 (BIA 1993).

[128] *Matter of D–J–*, 23 I&N Dec. 572 (A.G. 2003).

Evidence

In preparing for the hearing, it is wise to prepare the client to testify and to bring witnesses (although some courts do not allow witnesses to be present at a detention facility to testify). The presence of witnesses alone is evidence of family and/or community ties. In most cases, the court will ask the attorneys for both sides to summarize the factors each wishes to present. However, the court may ask the detainee about certain facts relating to the reason for his or her detention or other factors relating to the risk of absconding or possible threats to the community. In addition, DHS may bring witnesses in cases where it believes that there has been a serious violation of criminal or immigration laws.

Documentation should be submitted to support the detainee's request for reduction of bond. Although not mandated by the regulations, IJs do find it helpful to have some documentary record. This not only substantiates the claims made by the detainee, but is evidence that the individual takes the case seriously and is therefore likely to appear for later scheduled hearings. Items like birth certificates, property ownership papers, tax records, letters from community members (churches, etc.), employment records, character references, children's school records, medical records, or other documentation to show the person's character and ties should be submitted to the court. All documentation should be indexed and tabbed with a copy for DHS.

Appeal

Custody/bond redetermination hearings are relatively brief, lasting between 10 and 30 minutes. At the end of the hearing, the IJ renders a decision that is given to each side on a one-page form. There is a right to appeal.[129] The Notice of Appeal (form EOIR-26) must be filed directly with the BIA and *received by the BIA* within 30 days.[130] It should include the appropriate fee (presently $110) or an "Appeal Fee Waiver Request" (Form EOIR-26A) for indigent aliens.[131] An IJ maintains continuing jurisdiction to entertain custody/bond redetermination requests even while the appeal of an original bond decision is before the BIA.[132]

The filing of the custody/bond redetermination appeal does not stay the removal hearing.[133]

Stay of IJ's custody/bond order

In cases where DHS has originally set a bond of $10,000 or more, or has denied bond altogether, it may obtain an automatic stay of any order made by the IJ by filing a "Notice of Intent to Appeal Custody Re-determination" (Form EOIR-43) with the

---

[129] 8 CFR §1003.1(b)(7); *see also* 8 CFR §§236.1(d)(3), 1236.1(d)(3).

[130] 8 CFR §1003.38(b).

[131] 8 CFR §1003.38(d).

[132] *Matter of Valle-Perez*, 21 I&N Dec. 769 (BIA 1997).

[133] 8 CFR §§236.1(d)(4), 1236.1(d)(4).

court within one business day of the judge's order.[134] DHS has 10 days to file the appeal of the bond. If the appeal is not filed, the stay dissolves. The automatic stay is dissolved by the BIA's decision on the bond appeal.[135] However, if the BIA dismisses the appeal, the stay remains in effect for five business days while the AG reviews the decision.[136]

Several federal district courts have found the automatic stay regulation unconstitutional.[137] In *Zavala v. Ridge*, the court found a due process violation in the unilateral ability of DHS to detain an individual without a case-by-case determination after a finding by the IJ that the individual was not a threat to safety or a flight risk.

Post–custody/bond hearing issues

Revocation of bond

DHS has the authority to revoke a decision to release someone from custody and have the individual taken back into custody.[138] However, the alien can then seek a new redetermination by the court. The IJ does not have the power to determine that there has been a breach or that the bond should be revoked. [139]

Individuals with final removal orders

The IJ loses authority to review a bond when proceedings have become administratively final.[140] For those individuals ordered released under the Supreme Court's decision in *Zadvydas v. Davis*[141] (where there is no reasonably foreseeable possibility of removal), bond may be required as a condition of release and supervision.[142] The BIA has jurisdiction over an appeal from a district director's custody/bond determination made after the entry of a final order of deportation or removal.[143] An individual subject to a final order of removal based on an aggravated felony conviction may be detained after the expiration of the removal period pursuant to INA §241(a)(6).[144]

Federal court review

Where administrative remedies have been exhausted in seeking an individual's release, the appropriate remedy in federal court is a petition for writ of habeas corpus.

---

[134] 8 CFR §1003.19(i)(2).

[135] *Matter of Joseph*, 22 I&N Dec. 799 (BIA 1999).

[136] 8 CFR §1003.19(i)(2).

[137] *Zavala v Ridge*, 310 F. Supp. 2d 1071 (N.D. Cal. 2004); *Ashley v Ridge*, 288 F. Supp. 2d 662 (D.N.J. 2003); *Bezmen v Ashcroft*, 245 F. Supp. 2d 446 (D. Conn. 2003).

[138] 8 CFR §§236.1(c)(9), 1236.1(c)(9).

[139] 8 CFR §§236.1(b)(1), 1236.1(b)(1).

[140] 8 CFR §1236.1(c)(11).

[141] 5 U.S. 678 (2001).

[142] *See* 8 CFR §§236.1(c)(6), 1236.1(c)(6).

[143] *Matter of Saelee*, 22 I&N Dec. 1258 (2000).

[144] *Id.*

Although INA §236(e) bars "judicial review" of DHS decisions on custody status, the Supreme Court has found that habeas corpus is distinct from judicial review.[145] The REAL ID Act of 2005[146] eliminated habeas as a means of challenging a removal order; however, habeas still is available to challenge the wrongful detention of an alien.[147]

Removal Proceedings

There are five types of proceedings by which individuals may be removed from the United States—judicial removal; administrative removal; expedited removal proceedings; removal pursuant to entry under the Visa Waiver Program (VWP); and INA §240(a) proceedings (*i.e.*, those under the authority of IJs). For those attempting admission under the VWP, proceedings are commenced under 8 CFR §217.4 with the issuance of an I-863. Administrative removal begins with the issuance of a "Notice of Intent" (8 CFR §§238.1(b)(2), 1238.1(b)(2)). Expedited removal proceedings begin with Form I-860, and regular INA §240 proceedings begin with an NTA (Form I-862). Prior to September 30, 1996, the charging document was called an Order to Show Cause (OSC). The majority of this section explicates the IJ removal proceedings; however, the section will briefly cover judicial removal, administrative removal, expedited removal proceedings, and VWP removal (full detail on these proceedings is beyond the scope of this chapter).

Judicial Removal

A district court judge has jurisdiction to enter a judicial order of removal at the time of sentencing against an alien who is deportable if the order is requested by the U.S. Attorney with the concurrence of the (former INS) Commissioner (now DHS).[148] The U.S. Attorney must file with the court, and serve upon the defendant, a notice of intent to request judicial removal.[149] If the court determines that the defendant has provided substantial evidence to establish prima facie eligibility for relief from removal under the INA, DHS shall provide the court with a recommendation and report regarding the alien's eligibility for relief. The alien must be given an opportunity to present evidence on his or her behalf, review evidence against him or her, and cross-examine any opposing witnesses.[150] The court shall either grant or deny the relief,[151] order the defendant removed,[152] or merely deny the request for a judicial re-

---

145 *INS v. St. Cyr*, 533 U.S. 289 (2001).

146 Emergency Supplemental Appropriations Act for Defense, the Global War on Terror, and Tsunami Relief, 2005, Division B, Pub. L. No. 109-13, 119 Stat. 231.

147 *Sissoko v. Rocha*, 412 F.3d 1021, 1033 (9th Cir. 2005).

148 INA §238(c)(1).

149 INA §238(c)(2)(A).

150 INA §238(c)(2)(D)(i).

151 INA §238(c)(2)(C).

152 INA §238(c)(2)(D)(iv).

moval order. If the court denies the request for a judicial order of removal, DHS may initiate removal proceedings.[153]

Administrative Removal

The AG may issue an order of removal without placing an individual into removal proceedings before the immigration court under INA §240 if DHS determines that the individual has been convicted of an aggravated felony and is not an LPR.[154] This is commonly known as an order of administrative removal since there is no court proceeding, only the issuance of the order by DHS. This order may not be executed until 14 days have passed after the issuance of the order.[155] The alien must be given reasonable notice of the charges and the privilege of being represented by counsel (at no expense to the government). In addition, he or she has the right to inspect evidence and rebut charges against him or her.[156] An alien convicted of an aggravated felony is "conclusively presumed" to be deportable from the United States.[157]

There is judicial review of this order.[158]

Expedited Removal Proceedings

One of the major changes to the law as a result of IIRAIRA is the procedure for expedited or summary removal. If an alien attempts admission into the country and an immigration inspector determines that the person is inadmissible, "the officer shall order the alien removed from the United States without further hearing or review" unless the individual indicates an intent to apply for asylum or a fear of persecution.[159] This section does not apply to Cubans who land by aircraft at a port of entry as described in INA §235(b)(1)(F).[160]

The expedited removal provisions apply to arriving aliens (individuals who have not yet been admitted or paroled into the country)—applicants for admission coming or attempting to come into the United States at a port of entry; aliens seeking transit through the United States; and those granted parole.[161] In addition, expedited removal procedures apply to those who have entered illegally and cannot establish two years presence prior to the determination of inadmissibility.[162] Upon the determination of the DHS inspector, these individuals are immediately removed with no review process.

---

[153] INA §238(c)(4).

[154] INA §§238(b)(1) and (2).

[155] INA §238(b)(3).

[156] INA §238(b)(4).

[157] INA §238(c).

[158] INA §238(b)(3).

[159] INA §235(b)(1)(A)(i).

[160] INA §235(b)(1)(A)(iii)(II), 8 CFR §§235.3(b)(1)(i), 1235.3(b)(1)(i).

[161] Arriving aliens are defined at 8 CFR §§1.1(q), 1001.1(q).

[162] INA §235(b)(1)(A)(iii)(II); 8 CFR §§235.3(b)(1)(ii), 1235.3(b)(1)(ii).

In the expedited removal process, DHS may not charge an individual with any other ground of inadmissibility beyond INA §§212(a)(6)(C) or 212(a)(7) (fraud or lack of proper documentation). If DHS wishes to pursue charges beyond either of these, the individual is to be detained and referred to an IJ for a removal hearing under INA §§235(b) or 240.[163] If an individual subject to expedited removal proceedings indicates an intention to apply for asylum in any manner, the inspecting officer "shall not proceed" further with removal of the alien until the alien has been referred to an asylum officer.[164]

An arriving alien who is a stowaway is not eligible to apply for admission and "shall be ordered" removed upon inspection by an immigration officer."[165] He or she, however, may seek asylum if he or she is found to have a credible fear of persecution.

All aliens seeking admission, readmission, or transit through the United States are subject to inspection.[166] If not admissible, an alien may seek to withdraw his or her application for admission.[167] An applicant for admission may be required to give a sworn statement regarding the purpose and details of the intended visit.[168] An alien who is an applicant for admission and subject to expedited removal is also subject to mandatory detention.[169]

Those claiming to be LPRs must present evidentiary documents.[170] Those seeking admission on nonimmigrant visas may be required to provide fingerprints, photographs, and other "biometric identifiers" during the inspection process.[171]

Individuals who indicate an intent to apply for asylum or a fear of persecution are referred to an asylum officer who conducts a "credible fear" interview. The individual, based on his or her credibility and other facts known to the asylum officer, must show that there is a significant possibility that he or she can establish eligibility for asylum under INA §208.[172] If the officer determines that the individual does not have a credible fear, he or she orders the individual removed.[173] However, the individual does have a right to a "prompt" review of this finding by the immigration court

---

[163] 8 CFR §§235.3(b)(3), 1235.3(b)(3).

[164] 8 CFR §§235.3(b)(4), 1235.3(b)(4).

[165] INA §235(a)(2).

[166] INA §235(a)(3).

[167] INA §235(a)(4).

[168] INA §235(a)(5).

[169] INA §235(b)(1)(B)(iii)(IV).

[170] 8 CFR §235.1(d)(1)(i).

[171] 8 CFR §235.1(d)(1)(iii).

[172] INA §235(b)(1)(B)(v).

[173] INA §235(b)(1)(B)(iii)(I).

within seven days.[174] The credible fear interview is conducted in a nonadversarial manner.[175] If the person cannot speak English, an interpreter is arranged.[176]

The asylum officer must create a summary of the interview including the factual findings and the basis for his or her finding as to why there is (or is not) a credible fear.[177] The individual may consult with an attorney before or after the interview.[178] The asylum officer gives the individual a written notice of a negative decision, that is, if it was found that the alien did not have a credible fear of persecution or torture, and asks if the individual wishes to have the IJ review this decision.[179] Upon review by the IJ, the court will return the detainee to DHS for removal if the asylum officer's finding is upheld.[180]

If the asylum officer determines that the individual does have a credible fear of persecution, the officer informs the individual of this finding and refers the case to the immigration court for a hearing on the claim to asylum.[181] The putative asylee is issued Form I-863 for a hearing on the issues of asylum, withholding of removal, and any possible claim under the Convention Against Torture (CAT). The hearing is limited to the issue of the asylum application.[182] At the end of the asylum hearing, the IJ renders a decision on asylum (only) and both sides have a right to appeal that decision to the BIA.[183] Separate provisions are described for alien stowaways in 8 CFR §§208.30(e), (f), and (g).

The credible fear applicant is subject to mandatory detention pending a final determination on the credible fear issue, and if it is determined that he or she does not have a credible fear, the person is detained until removed from the country. Without the authorization of DHS, an individual subject to mandatory detention under INA §236(c)(1) may not be released from custody or paroled.[184] However, where it is determined that the person has a credible fear and is referred to an IJ, he or she is eligible for custody/bond redetermination.[185]

---

[174] INA §235(b)(1)(B)(iii)(III).

[175] 8 CFR §208.30.

[176] 8 CFR §208.30(d)(5).

[177] 8 CFR §208.30(e)(1).

[178] 8 CFR §208.30(d)(4).

[179] 8 CFR §208.30(g)(1).

[180] 8 CFR §208.30(g)(2)(iv)(A).

[181] 8 CFR §208.30(f).

[182] 8 CFR §208.30(g)(2)(iv)(C).

[183] *Id.*

[184] 8 CFR §236.1(c)(1) .

[185] *Matter of X–K–*, 23 I&N Dec. 731 (BIA 2005).

Visa Waiver Program

Under the provisions of 8 CFR §217.4(a)(1), where an individual is refused admission under the Visa Waiver Program (INA §217) and he or she has sought asylum, proceedings are commenced with a notice of referral to the IJ for an asylum hearing. Expedited removal proceedings do not apply to those seeking admission under the Visa Waiver Program.

Removal Proceedings Before the IJ Under INA §240

Service of NTA—INA §239

Every removal proceeding commences with the issuance of an NTA, which is issued by DHS (for individuals who were placed into deportation proceedings prior to September 30, 1996, the charging document was the OSC).[186] It is served on the immigration court, and proceedings do not commence until it is actually filed with the court.[187] The NTA may be canceled by DHS prior to jurisdiction vesting with the court for a variety of reasons, including the fact that the NTA was incorrectly or "improvidently" issued.[188] After jurisdiction vests with the court, DHS may make a motion to the court for dismissal of the charges.[189]

Additionally, DHS serves the NTA on the individual in person.[190] If personal service is "not practicable," it may be served by regular mail at the alien's last known address, or on alien's counsel of record.[191] The NTA must include the location of the court where it is filed and proof of service.[192] If a person is confined in a penal or mental institution or hospital and is competent to understand the nature of the proceedings against him or her, service is made on him or her and the person in charge of the institution.[193] In cases of incompetents and minors under the age of 14, service is made upon the person with whom the incompetent or minor resides.[194]

Contents of NTA—INA §239(a)(1)

The NTA is in English and contains the following information:

- nature of proceedings;
- legal authority under which proceedings are conducted;
- acts alleged to be violations of law;

---

[186] 8 CFR §§239.1(a), 1239.1(a).

[187] 8 CFR §1003.14(a).

[188] *See* 8 CFR §§239.2(a) and (b), 1239.2(a) and (b).

[189] 8 CFR §§239.2(c), 1239.2(c). *See also In re G–N–C–*, 22 I&N Dec. 281 (BIA 1998).

[190] INA §239(a)(1).

[191] 8 CFR §1003.13.

[192] 8 CFR §1003.14(a).

[193] 8 CFR §103.5a(c)(2)(i).

[194] 8 CFR §103.5a(c)(2)(ii).

- section of INA allegedly violated;
- notice of right to representation (at no expense to the government);
- notice that the individual will be given a list of legal service organizations;
- notice of change of address requirement (failure to give correct address or change of address alleviates notice requirement);
- time and place of the hearing;
- consequences for failing to appear for hearing—removal in absentia under INA §240(b)(5) (note: an individual is ineligible for future forms of relief for a period of 10 years under §240(b)(7) if the individual was given oral notice of the time and place of the hearing and fails to appear);
- name, alias, address, telephone number, and "A" number of individual.[195]

Who can issue the NTA—8 CFR §§239.1(a), 1239.1(a)

The regulations outline the immigration officials who are authorized to issue the charging document. They include:

- any immigration officer or supervisor performing inspections at the point of entry;
- district directors and deputy district directors;
- patrol agents and their supervisors;
- field operation supervisors;
- border patrol agents;
- service center directors;
- supervisory adjudication and asylum officers;
- certain special investigative agents;
- supervisory deportation and detention officers;
- directors of detention facilities; and
- port directors and deputy port directors.[196]

Venue—8 CFR §1003.20

Venue lies in the jurisdiction where the charging document is served on the court.[197] Venue may be changed upon a motion of either party for good cause; however, upon motion for change of venue, the other side must be given an opportunity to respond.[198] In addition, no change of venue may be granted without a complete street address (including zip code) where the individual may be notified for future proceedings.[199]

---

[195] INA §239(a)(1).

[196] 8 CFR §§239.1(a), 1239.1(a).

[197] 8 CFR §1003.20(a).

[198] 8 CFR §1003.20(b).

[199] 8 CFR §1003.20(c).

Relevant factors in determining venue include:[200]

- location of witnesses;
- cost of transporting witnesses or evidence to the changed venue site;
- importance of this evidence to the case;
- administrative convenience;
- unnecessary delay in completing case.
- residence of the individual;
- location of counsel; and
- relative harm to both sides in granting or denying the motion for change of venue.

As a practical matter, the issue of removability is often the decisive factor in determining venue. DHS generally opposes a change of venue unless removability has been conceded. Its argument is that it is costly to transport government witnesses to a new jurisdiction if removability is contested. This may be a valid point if the arresting and processing officers from DHS are located in the jurisdiction where the NTA was originally served. It is not a valid argument where there are no DHS witnesses located in that jurisdiction, and the individual is only in that location because DHS has detention space available in that locale, *e.g.*, Oakdale, Louisiana. In that case, there is no prejudice to the government and a concession of removability should not be required to transfer venue to the location where it is convenient to the respondent—his or her place of residence. However, it is common practice for DHS to contest the change of venue without this concession.

Time of hearing/continuances—8 CFR §§1003.29 and 1240.6

The hearing shall not be scheduled earlier than 10 days after the service of the NTA, in order for the individual to have reasonable time to secure counsel.[201] This 10-day period may be waived by the individual; that is, "the individual can request an earlier hearing date in writing."[202] A motion for continuance of a scheduled hearing may be granted for good cause upon request of either party or by the court.[203] The continuance shall be for a reasonable period of time.[204] The IJ has broad discretion in granting continuances.[205]

---

[200] *See Matter of Rahman*, 20 I&N Dec. 480 (BIA 1992). *See also Chlomos v. Dep't of Justice*, 516 F.2d 310 (3d Cir. 1975); *Garcia-Guzman v. Reno*, 65 F. Supp. 2d 1077 (N.D. Cal. 1999).

[201] INA §239(b)(1).

[202] *Id.*

[203] 8 CFR §§1003.29 and 1240.6.

[204] 8 CFR §1240.6.

[205] *Molina v. INS*, 981 F.2d 14, 16 (1st Cir. 1992).

Alien's rights in proceedings—INA §240(a)(4)

An individual in proceedings has certain rights. These include:[206]

- right to counsel at no expense to the government;
- right to present evidence on his or her own behalf;
- reasonable opportunity to examine evidence against him or her;
- right to cross-examine opposing witnesses;
- a complete record of all testimony and evidence produced at the hearing; and
- right to appeal decision of the IJ (except in absentia orders).[207]

The IJ should advise the individual of the above-mentioned rights at the commencement of proceedings[208] (except the notice of the right to appeal is given at the end of proceedings[209]). In addition, the IJ must advise the individual of the availability of free legal services located in the district where the case is heard and provide the individual with a list of such legal services.[210] A detained alien is to be notified that he or she may communicate with the consular or the diplomatic officer of the country of his or her nationality in the United States.[211]

The right to counsel at one's own expense is a fundamental right, [212] the denial of this right violates due process.[213] The right to examine evidence against an individual does not include the right to examine information related to national security proffered by the government in opposition to an application for admission or discretionary relief.[214] However, in exercising his or her power to adjudicate a relief application, where he or she can safeguard the information and its source, the IJ should inform the individual of the nature of the information so that the latter may have an opportunity to offer opposing evidence in support of an application for LPRs.[215] In an asylum hearing where DHS provides classified information to the judge, the alien must be informed and the agency that provides the classified information "may" provide a summary of the information for release to the alien if it determines that it can do so consistently with safeguarding the classified nature of the information.[216]

---

[206] INA §240(b)(4)(A)–(C).

[207] 8 CFR §1240.15.

[208] 8 CFR §1240.10(a).

[209] INA §240(b)(4).

[210] 8 CFR §1240.10(a)(2).

[211] 8 CFR §§236.1(e), 1236.1(e).

[212] *Orantes-Hernandez v. Thornburgh*, 919 F.2d 549 (9th Cir. 1990).

[213] *United States v Campos-Asencio*, 822 F.2d 506 (5th Cir. 1987).

[214] 8 CFR §1240.10(a)(4).

[215] 8 CFR §1240.11(a)(3).

[216] 8 CFR §1240.11(c)(3)(iv).

During the hearing, the IJ "shall inform" the individual of apparent eligibility to apply for certain benefits including cancellation of removal, adjustment of status, registry, asylum and withholding of removal where the individual expresses a fear of return to the native country, and voluntary departure.[217]

Interpretation of Hearing—8 CFR §1240.5

Proceedings are conducted in English or the language in which the individual is proficient. There is an absolute right to competent interpretation.[218] The right to present evidence and cross-examine witnesses includes the right to a translation of the evidence.[219] There is no right to simultaneous translation of the entire proceeding.[220]

The court provides an interpreter in the language of the respondent, if necessary. The interpreter must be sworn in by the judge;[221] he or she swears to interpret and translate correctly, unless the interpreter is an employee of the U.S. government, in which case no oath is required.[222] Many immigration courts have "in house" interpreters who are employees of DOJ and the court. For example, all of the immigration courts in Texas have Spanish language interpreters on staff. Interpreters in other languages are contracted on an individual basis from private companies.

Discovery in Removal Proceedings

FOIA—8 CFR §103.8 to 103.10

There are very limited rules of evidence in removal proceedings. The Federal Rules of Evidence are not applicable in deportation proceedings and there is no requirement that a request for discovery be honored.[223] For discovery, there is little apart from the Freedom of Information Act (FOIA).[224] In addition, some immigration courts have local rules regarding the submission of evidence to the opposing party and to the court.

The respondent has a right to examine evidence against him or her and to cross-examine opposing witnesses (certain national security exceptions apply).[225] Most immigration courts in Texas, for example, have local rules requiring each side to submit to the opposing party and to the court in advance of the hearing any documentation to be relied on during the hearing. For example, some immigration courts re-

---

[217] 8 CFR §§1240.11(a)(2), (b), and (c).

[218] *Matter of Tomas*, 19 I&N Dec. 464 (BIA 1987).

[219] *Amadou v. INS*, 226 F.3d 724 (6th Cir. 2000).

[220] *Matter of Exilus*, 18 I&N Dec. 276 (BIA 1982).

[221] 8 CFR §1240.5.

[222] *Id.*

[223] *Matter of Benitez*, 19 I&N Dec. 173 (BIA 1984).

[224] *See* 8 CFR §§103.8–103.10.

[225] INA §240(b)(4)(B).

quire each side to submit evidence 10 business days in advance of the hearing.[226] Failure to abide by the court's time limits on the submission of applications or documents may result in the waiver of the opportunity to file the application or document.[227] However, this rule is not always followed. It is not uncommon for a DHS attorney to fail to submit a relevant document prior to the hearing, and then file the document on the respondent as "impeachment" evidence after the respondent has made a statement that is contradicted by the document (*e.g.*, a conviction record submitted after a denial of any prior criminal history). For this reason, it is imperative to file a FOIA request with DHS prior to the hearing.

The FOIA request is filed in writing on Form G-639, and there is no fee for filing this form; however, an applicant may be required to pay fees up to $25 under certain circumstances.[228] The request must describe as completely as possible the information that is being sought. For emergency cases before the immigration court, one should seek to expedite the process by contacting the FOIA officer and sending a copy of the hearing notice with an explanation of the need for the evidence prior to the hearing. This may be a fruitless effort in many DHS offices.

Although the regulations indicate a 10-day deadline for response,[229] DHS rarely complies with this deadline. Where DHS has not responded prior to the hearing, it may be necessary to request a continuance to give the agency time to respond. However, in *Matter of Benitez*,[230] the BIA affirmed an IJ's denial of a continuance while a FOIA response was pending.

Subpoenas—8 CFR §§1003.35(b) and 1287.4

In removal proceedings before the court, the IJ has exclusive jurisdiction to issue subpoenas requiring the attendance of witnesses or the production of documentary evidence.[231] A subpoena may be issued on the court's own motion or at the request of either party.[232] A party seeking a subpoena must state in writing to the court what is expected to be proven through the issuance of the subpoena, and to show that he or she has made diligent efforts without success to produce the witness or evidence.[233] The judge shall issue a subpoena if the court is satisfied that the evidence sought is necessary and that it will not be produced without the subpoena.[234] The subpoena must state the title of the proceeding and command the person to whom it is directed

---

[226] Houston, Tex., Immigration Court Rule 2(a).

[227] *See* 8 CFR §1003.31(c).

[228] 8 CFR §103.10(e). *See also* 8 CFR §§103.10(a)(2) (for manner of request) and 103.7.

[229] 8 CFR §103.10(c)(1).

[230] 19 I&N Dec. 173 (BIA 1984).

[231] 8 CFR §1003.35(b)(1).

[232] *Id.*

[233] 8 CFR §§1003.35(b)(2) and 1287.4(a)(2)(ii)(B).

[234] 8 CFR §§1003.35(b)(3) and 1287.4(a)(2)(ii)(C).

to appear at a time and place specified.[235] It also may order the person to produce any documentary evidence necessary.[236] The subpoena may be served by anyone over 18-years old who is not a party to the case.[237]

If the witness is at a distance of more than 100 miles from the location of the proceeding, the subpoena shall provide for the witness's appearance at the immigration court closest to him or her to answer oral or written interrogatories, unless all parties agree to have the witness present at the hearing.[238] If a witness fails to appear or comply with the subpoena, the IJ shall request the U.S. Attorney to report the failure to comply with the U.S. district court and ask the court to force compliance.[239]

Depositions—8 CFR §§1003.35(a) and 1240.7(c)

The IJ may order the taking of depositions pursuant to 8 CFR §1003.35(a) if he or she is satisfied that a witness is not reasonably available at the place of the hearing, and that the witness's testimony or other evidence is essential. The IJ may order the taking of the deposition upon his or her own motion or at the request of either party. The order must designate the official before whom the deposition is to be taken and may limit the content, scope, and manner of taking the deposition. The judge may also direct the production of documents.

Interrogatories—8 CFR §§1003.35(b)(4) and 1287.4(a)(2)(ii)(D).

For a witness located at a distance of more than 100 miles from the court, the judge may order his or her appearance at the nearest immigration court to answer oral or written interrogatories.

Burden of Proof—INA §§240(c) and 291

The burden of proof in a removal proceeding shifts between the government and the respondent. On certain issues, DHS carries the burden, while on other issues, the burden is on the respondent. The Supreme Court has stated that deportability must be proven by "clear, unequivocal and convincing evidence."[240] The INA now contains a section defining the respective burdens of proof on DHS and the respondent.[241]

Alienage

The threshold factual allegation on the NTA in any removal proceeding is that the individual is not a citizen of the United States. It is DHS's initial burden to prove alienage by clear and convincing evidence.[242] As a practical matter, this allegation is

---

[235] *Id.*

[236] *Id.*

[237] 8 CFR §1003.35(b)(5).

[238] 8 CFR §§1003.35(b)(4) and 1287.4(a)(2)(ii)(D).

[239] 8 CFR §1003.35(b)(6).

[240] *Woodby v. INS*, 385 U.S. 276, 277 (1966).

[241] INA §240(c)(2)–(3).

[242] INA §240(c)(3)(A).

often (too often) admitted and the government is generally not put to its burden. If DHS fails to prove alienage, proceedings should be terminated by the court. If DHS does prove alienage, or it is conceded, the burden then shifts to the respondent to prove date, place, and manner of entry.[243]

Often, DHS presents the respondent's passport or birth certificate as proof of alienage. Even more often, it is proven by submitting Form I-213, Record of Deportable Alien. This is a summary of the findings of the DHS officer after taking the respondent's statement. This summary is an admissible document.[244]

Admissibility

In any removal proceeding, it is the burden of the respondent to prove time, place, and manner of admission.[245] If the individual is an applicant for admission, he or she must prove "clearly and beyond doubt" that he or she is entitled to be admitted.[246] If he or she is already present in the country and alienage has been established or conceded, the alien must prove by "clear and convincing evidence" that he or she is lawfully present.[247] In meeting the burden, the respondent is entitled to production of his or her immigration documents—for example his or her visa if held by DHS.[248]

After lawful admission

In the case of an individual who has proven that he or she was lawfully admitted into the country, the burden is on DHS to prove by clear and convincing evidence that the respondent is deportable (*i.e.*, subject to removability).[249]

Evidentiary Issues in Removal Proceedings

Introduction

There are two major issues in a removal proceeding—removability and relief. The issue of relief is not reached until removability is proven. Removability may be contested in three ways:

- the factual allegations may be denied;
- the legal charge may be denied even though the facts are admitted; or
- the factual allegations and the legal charge(s) may be denied.

In removal proceedings, the rules of evidence are very limited. The general rule is that any evidence from either side is admissible as long as it is relevant and the ad-

---

[243] INA §291; *see also Matter of Benitez*, 19 I&N Dec. 173 (1984).

[244] *Bustos-Torres v. INS*, 898 F.2d 1053 (5th Cir. 1990).

[245] INA §291.

[246] INA §240(c)(2)(A).

[247] INA §240(c)(2)(B).

[248] *Id.*

[249] INA §240(c)(3)(A).

mission of such evidence is not fundamentally unfair.[250] This is especially true in the area of hearings on discretionary relief applications, where immigration courts are generally open to what is admissible from each side. Relief applications and their particular evidentiary issues will be discussed further in Chapters 5 and 6.

On the issue of removability, the rules are stricter, especially regarding the admissibility of conviction records, governmental documents, and other official records. Although the immigration regulations contain very few rules governing evidence, there are limits. In addition to regulations, the INA, and case law, each local court may have its own rules relating to the submission of documentary evidence.

Basic evidentiary rules

Hearsay

Hearsay is generally admissible, but if the use of hearsay would not be probative or would be fundamentally unfair, it may not be admissible or sufficient to prove removability.[251] Form I-213, Record of Deportable Alien, prepared by DHS, is a hearsay statement summarizing the interview or "processing" of the individual by the DHS officer. The BIA has found Form I-213 to be a reliable document sufficient to prove deportability when not contested.[252]

Criminal convictions

The regulations permit proof of a conviction via any of the following:[253]

- record of a judgment and conviction;
- record of a plea, verdict, and sentence;
- docket entry from court records indicating a conviction;
- minutes or transcript of a court proceeding indicating existence of a conviction;
- abstract of a record of conviction prepared by the court or by a state official "associated with the state's repository of criminal justice records"; or
- a document prepared by or under the direction of the court in which the conviction was entered.

Police reports are not sufficient to prove a conviction for removability purposes.[254] For proof of foreign convictions and other records, see 8 CFR §§287.6(b) and (c),

---

[250] *Bustos-Torres v. INS*, 898 F.2d 1053, 1055 (5th Cir. 1990) ("The test for admissibility of evidence in a deportation proceeding is whether the evidence is probative and whether its use is fundamentally fair so as not to deprive the alien of due process of law.") (citing *Calderon-Ontiveros v. INS*, 809 F.2d 1050 (5th Cir. 1986)).

[251] *Olabanji v. INS*, 973 F.2d 1232 (5th Cir. 1992); *see also Cunanan v. INS*, 856 F.2d 1373 (9th Cir. 1988).

[252] *Matter of Ponce-Hernandez*, 22 I&N Dec. 784 (BIA 1999); *see also Matter of Barcenas*, 19 I&N Dec. 609 (BIA 1988).

[253] 8 CFR §§1003.41(a)(1)–(6).

[254] *See In re Teixeira*, 21 I&N Dec. 316 (BIA 1996).

1287.6(b) and (c). An electronic record is admissible under the regulations if the appropriate state official and an DHS official certify that it was received electronically from the state's record repository.[255]

Authentication of documents

In order for any "official record or entry therein" to be admissible, it must contain an attestation from an official (or designate) having legal custody over the document, or by official publication of the document.[256]

Prior statements

An IJ may receive in evidence any oral or written statement that is material and relevant to any issue in the case previously made by the respondent or any other person during any investigation, examination, hearing, or trial.[257]

Right to cross-examination

The statute and regulations indicate that the respondent has the right to cross-examine witnesses presented by the government.[258] However, this "right" is limited and several decisions have upheld the admissibility of documents where the author of the document was not presented for cross-examination.[259] For example, the statute and regulations allow the admissibility of documents by the government without the right to cross-examination where such right might require examination by the individual of "national security" information.[260]

As mentioned above, the Record of Deportable Alien has been found admissible even where the DHS officer who prepared the document was not produced; such documents are considered "inherently trustworthy."[261] However, even this document has been found inadmissible in cases where its admission would be fundamentally unfair.[262] In any case where the government attempts to submit a statement from an individual who is adverse to the client, including Form I-213, Record of Deportable Alien, the attorney should object based on the right to cross-examine opposing witnesses inherent in the idea of due process, and spelled out in the statute and regulations.

Motions to suppress evidence

As mentioned above, it is the government's burden to prove alienage, and ultimately removability, through evidence submitted into the record by DHS. In order to

---

[255] 8 CFR §1003.41(c)(1) and (2).

[256] 8 CFR §§287.6(a), 1287.6(a).

[257] 8 CFR §1240.7(a).

[258] INA §240(b)(4)(B); 8 CFR §1240.10(a)(4).

[259] *See Bustos-Torres v. INS*, 898 F.2d 1053 (5th Cir. 1990) and *Matter of Ramirez-Sanchez*, 17 I&N Dec. 503 (BIA 1980).

[260] INA §240(b)(4)(B).

[261] *In re Gomez-Gomez*, 23 I&N Dec. 522, 524 (BIA 2002).

[262] *See Bustos-Torres*, 898 F.2d 1053; *see also Murphy v. INS*, 54 F.3d 605 (9th Cir. 1995).

be admissible, evidence must comport with due process requirements under the Fifth Amendment; it cannot be obtained through coercion or duress.[263] A DHS attorney cannot use the statement of an individual that was obtained unlawfully through force or coercion as proof of inadmissibility.[264] Any such statement may be suppressible.[265] This is most common where DHS counsel moves to submit into the record Form I-213 or a statement from the respondent that contains information allegedly obtained through a threat, show of force, or some other unlawful manner, *i.e.*, it was not given knowingly and/or voluntarily. Such a statement may be suppressed under the Fifth Amendment.[266] The BIA has held that evidence may be suppressed if obtained in violation of due process.[267]

Where DHS attempts to submit a statement containing evidence obtained through coercion, duress, or otherwise unlawfully, counsel should file a motion to suppress such a statement on the ground that the evidence was obtained in violation of the Due Process Clause of the Fifth Amendment.[268] The motion should contain an explanation of the unlawful manner in which the evidence was obtained; it must be specific and supported by a statement or testimony outlining the due process violation.[269]

The right to suppress evidence obtained in violation of the Fifth Amendment does not generally extend to the suppression of evidence based on violations of the Fourth Amendment, *i.e.*, illegal arrests or searches.[270] However, even though an individual generally cannot suppress evidence based on Fourth Amendment violations, the Supreme Court has stated that where such violations are widespread or "egregious" and transgress fundamental notions of due process, the evidence might be excluded.[271]

Although the motion must be heard and ruled upon by the IJ, there is no right to a separate suppression hearing.[272] If a motion to suppress evidence is granted, DHS will often attempt to find other nonsuppressible evidence to prove removability, such as the individual's own testimony. The individual may, and should, decline to testify. If the motion to suppress is granted and the government does not have sufficient evidence to prove removability, the proceedings should be terminated.

The Fifth Amendment privilege against self-incrimination may be invoked in immigration proceedings, as it may be in other civil or criminal proceedings. There is no

---

[263] *See Navia-Duran v. INS*, 568 F.2d 803 (1st Cir. 1977).

[264] *Id.*

[265] *Id.*

[266] *Matter of Garcia-Flores*, 17 I&N Dec. 325 (BIA 1980).

[267] *Matter of Toro*, 17 I&N Dec. 340 (BIA 1980).

[268] *Matter of Wong*, 13 I&N Dec. 820 (BIA 1971).

[269] *Id.*

[270] *INS v. Lopez-Mendoza*, 468 U.S. 1032 (1984)

[271] *Id.*

[272] *Matter of Benitez*, 19 I&N Dec. 173, 175 (BIA 1984); *see also Matter of Velasquez*, 19 I&N Dec. 377 (BIA 1986).

absolute duty on an individual to testify in a deportation/removal proceeding.[273] An adverse inference may be drawn from a refusal to testify; however, such an inference does not rise to the level of "clear and convincing" evidence in order to prove removability.[274] The government must show more than the inference created by such silence in order to meet its burden of proving alienage or removability.[275]

In Absentia Proceedings—INA §240(b)(5)

The notice of the time and place of the hearing is often given to the individual by the immigration court in a separate notice after DHS files the NTA with the court. Such notice is usually served by regular mail. Failure by the individual to attend the hearing may result in an "in absentia" order of removal if the individual was given both notice (personally or by regular mail) of the hearing[276] and oral notice of the consequences for failure to attend, and fails to attend other than because of "exceptional circumstances."[277]

"Exceptional circumstances" is defined as "serious illness of the alien or serious illness or death of the spouse, child or parent of the alien, *but not including less compelling circumstances* (emphasis added)."[278] The BIA has been strict in interpreting this section of the statute. In *Matter of J–P–*,[279] the BIA looked at the totality of the circumstances in determining whether exceptional circumstances were present. Where there are changed circumstances, a proceeding may be reopened without a showing of reasonable or exceptional circumstances for the failure to appear.[280]

The entry of an in absentia order means that the individual is ineligible for a period of 10 years from the date of the order for any of the following forms of relief:[281]

- cancellation of removal for permanent and non–permanent residents under INA §240A;
- voluntary departure under INA §240B;
- adjustment of status under INA §245;
- change of nonimmigrant status under INA §248; and
- registry under INA §249.

---

[273] *Matter of Guevara*, 20 I&N Dec. 238 (BIA 1991).

[274] *INS v. Lopez-Mendoza*, 468 U.S. 1032, 1043 (1984).

[275] *Id.*

[276] INA §240(b)(5).

[277] INA §240(b)(7).

[278] INA §240(e).

[279] *Matter of J–P–*, 22 I&N Dec. 33 (BIA 1998) (citing H.R. Conf. Rep. No. 101-955, at 119, 132 (1990), *reprinted in* 1990 U.S.C.C.A.N. 6784, 6797 (instructing the AG to look at the totality of the circumstances to determine whether an alien's failure to appear was justifiable)).

[280] *Matter of A–N– and R–M–N–*, 22 I&N Dec. 953 (BIA 1999) (changed political circumstances in the respondents' native country demonstrate a reasonable likelihood of success on an asylum application).

[281] INA §240(b)(7).

If the NTA was not served, the IJ may not order removal "in absentia."[282] However, the alien may be charged with receipt of the NTA and notice of the hearing where the notice is sent by certified mail to the alien's correct address but is returned by the post office marked "unclaimed."[283] The BIA also has found that an NTA served on the father of an eight-year old child, with notices of hearings sent to the address given by the father, was proper notice to the child, and an in absentia removal order was appropriate where the child did not appear for the hearing.[284] In a separate case, the BIA held that service of the NTA on the alleged uncle of a seven-year-old child was not proper service of the NTA. The BIA ruled that proceedings were properly terminated for improper service.[285]

The Hearing—What to Do in Court

Master Calendar Hearing—Introduction

Unless the person has been detained and has had a bond hearing, the master calendar hearing is usually the initial appearance before the court. The master calendar hearing is a setting in which the court has held aside a brief period of time to conduct some matter that it believes can be handled expeditiously, as opposed to a "merits hearing," which is generally set to conduct some contested matter requiring a longer period of time. That is, the master calendar hearings—there may be several—are brief hearings that set up the issues in contention on removability and relief that will come later at the merits hearing phase. The main purposes of the initial master calendar hearing follow:

- enter an attorney's notice of appearance;
- notify the court of the respondent's address or make any address changes;
- identify the language of the respondent;
- plead to the allegations;
- state the form of relief to be sought (if prepared to do so); possibly let the court know the amount of time needed to prepare and the basis for relief; or
- request a continuance for time to prepare for pleading if not prepared to do any of the above.

For an unrepresented respondent, the master calendar hearing also may be used as an opportunity to request more time to find an attorney and prepare the pleadings. Most courts will grant one continuance to an attorney for preparation, and/or one continuance to an unrepresented respondent to find an attorney.

---

282 *Matter of G–Y–R–*, 23 I&N Dec. 181 (BIA 2001).

283 *In re M–D–*, 23 I&N Dec. 540 (BIA 2002).

284 *In re Gomez-Gomez*, 23 I&N Dec. 522 (BIA 2002).

285 *Matter of Mejia-Andino*, 23 I&N Dec. 533 (BIA 2002).

Master Calendar Checklist

The following is a checklist of issues that are generally handled at the master calendar hearing. Each IJ and each court is different; thus, not all courts will cover all of the items listed below, and even where an IJ does cover all of the following, he or she will probably conduct the hearing in a different order. If counsel is aware of all of the possible issues listed on the checklist and is prepared to address them at the master calendar hearing, he or she should be able to represent the client capably.

- *Beginning of hearing:* The judge may wish to discuss the case off the record to determine whether counsel is ready to go forward (or needs a continuance) before turning on the tape and going on the record. (All removal proceedings are taped on cassette.)
- *Notices of Appearance:* File a Notice of Appearance with the court clerk (Form E-28), and a Notice of Appearance with DHS (Form G-28). Make certain the Notices of Appearance have the correct address for the client.
- *Identification of attorneys:* The court will go on the record (*i.e.*, turn on the tape) and ask attorneys for both sides to identify themselves. Some IJs will merely identify the attorneys without asking the attorneys to state their names.
- *Identification of client:* Make certain the name on the NTA is correctly spelled.
- *Address of client:* Make certain that the court has the correct address. If not, have the blue change of address form ready (Form EOIR-33). It can be obtained from the court clerk or the interpreter.
- *Client's language:* The court will ask in which language the client wishes to testify to see if an interpreter is needed. If one is needed, the case may be reset.
- *Advisal to client of his or her rights in proceedings:* The court will ask if the client understands his or her rights in immigration proceedings. See above for discussion of rights in removal proceedings.
- *Service of NTA:* Has there been proper service of the charging document (NTA) on the client or counsel? If so, the IJ will mark and admit the NTA as an exhibit into the record.
- *Continuances:* The court will ask if counsel is ready to plead to the factual allegations and the legal charge of removability. If not, request additional time. The court generally is reasonable in granting an attorney a first continuance for preparation. Further continuances will not be granted absent "good cause."[286]

  Note: The court has various ways of asking if one is ready to plead. All mean the same thing—for example: "Counsel, what are we doing today?" or "Counsel, how do you wish to proceed today?" Translation: "Are you ready to plead to the allegations and charges, as well as designate a country for removal and the type of relief sought?"

---

[286] 8 CFR §§1240.6 and 1003.29.

- *Manner of pleading:* The court may ask if counsel wishes to plead to the charges individually or collectively. If all the allegations are to be admitted, charges are generally pleaded in a collective manner. If one or more factual allegations are to be denied, it is best to plead individually to each factual allegation to avoid the possibility of confusion.
- *Pleadings:* There are two separate pleadings:
  - Factual allegations (admitted or denied) and
  - Legal charge(s) under INA §212(a) or 237(a) (conceded or denied)
- *Admission of charges/designation of country for removal:* If the charges are admitted, be ready to designate a country for removal should removal become necessary. If counsel is not certain, he or she may "decline to designate" a country for removal and the court will designate a country "in the alternative." The purpose of the designation is so that the court knows what country to designate in its order if the application(s) for relief is (are) denied. Designation is not a requirement. If the client is not certain where he or she wishes to go should his or her relief application be denied, it may be safest not to designate a country for removal. This is common where one will be seeking asylum, withholding, or CAT relief. Frequently, those who fear persecution or torture if returned to their native countries will decline to designate a country of removal should their applications be denied, rather than designate their native country where they fear persecution or harm. An individual cannot designate a contiguous country (Mexico or Canada) unless he or she is a national or citizen of the country.
- *Denial of charges:* If one or more of the allegations or charges is denied, the case is generally reset for a future date for a merits hearing on the contested allegations/charges. The court may ask the basis for the denial. If the issue is one where the burden is on the government, it is sufficient to state that it is the government's burden to prove the charge, *i.e.*, present the conviction record, affidavit, governmental record, or other document on which the allegations are based.
- *Burden of proof:* It is the government's burden to prove alienage. If alienage is not conceded or proven, the case should be terminated at that point because the remaining allegations become irrelevant. If alienage is proven, the burden then becomes the alien's to prove the date, place, and manner of entry, *i.e.*, the lawfulness of his or her entry/status. Once this is proven, if the government alleges that the alien has taken some action (criminal conviction or immigration violation) that should result in the loss of such status, it again becomes the government's burden to prove this action through criminal conviction records or other documentation that shows that the alien is now removable after having been lawfully admitted.
- *Relief sought:* If the charges are admitted or the court sustains the charges, be ready to identify the types of relief sought—*e.g.*, asylum, withholding of removal, cancellation of removal, adjustment of status, registry, voluntary departure, etc. If asylum is sought, the IJ gives advisals regarding frivolous asylum claims.
- *Prima facie eligibility:* Is the client prima facie eligible for relief? Be ready to explain the basis for the claim. Although the claim for relief is decided at the later

merits hearing, it is not uncommon for the IJ to ask for a summary of the claim at the master calendar hearing to show that the individual is prima facie eligible for the relief.

- *Time needed for relief hearing:* Be ready to give information on the following:
  - how much time is needed to prepare and file the application for relief;
  - number of witnesses foreseen for the merits hearing;
  - time needed to present client's case;
  - if an interpreter is needed for any of the witnesses.
- *Filing date(s):* The court gives both sides filing date(s) for applications, supporting documentation, briefs, and responses.
- *Notice of calendar date for future hearing:* Receipt of court notices calendaring the next hearing. The court gives notices to both sides with the date and time of next hearing.
- *Advisals for failure to appear:* The court gives oral advisals to the client regarding consequences of failure to appear at the next hearing. The master calendar hearing ends.

Termination or Moving to the Relief Phase

At the end of a contested removal hearing, the IJ will make a ruling on the issue of removability. If the IJ finds that the government has not carried its burden of proof—*i.e.*, there is no proof or at least not sufficient proof that the individual respondent is unlawfully present—proceedings should be terminated. The government may reserve the right to appeal at that point and will be given advisals by the court on the due date for the appeal notice.

However, if the IJ finds in favor of the government after a contested removal hearing, the respondent must be ready to designate the relief being sought and the amount of time he or she will need to prepare and submit such relief applications. The IJ generally will give the respondent or counsel two dates: (1) a date for filing the application for relief; and (2) a date for the hearing on the merits of the relief, *i.e.*, a trial date on the benefit being sought. Depending on the jurisdiction, the court will generally want the following submitted prior to the date of the merits hearing in accordance with the court's instructions or the local court rules:

- application(s) for relief;
- proof of payment for all filing fees;
- documentary evidence in support of the application;
- translation of any foreign document with certificate of translation;
- proof of biometrics (fingerprints completed);
- other supporting documentation (*e.g.*, police letter or medical exam);
- list of witnesses; and
- summary of issues to be covered.

If there are local court rules regarding submission of evidence, the court will want the application and supporting documentation filed in accordance with the local rules, *e.g.*, indexed, tabbed, paginated, highlighted, etc.

For most respondents, the relief phase is the central part of proceedings. At this phase, the burden of proof is on the respondent to prove eligibility for whatever relief is sought. There is little that the government must do except to review the application and monitor the evidence being presented by the respondent. The respondent, however, must prepare all applications and supporting documentation as well the testimony of any witness who will be presented before the court. The IJ generally gives the respondent a period of time to prepare the application and supporting documentation for submission to the court between the end of the removal phase and the beginning of the relief phase.

Most forms of relief before an IJ are based on one of the following: (1) persecution or harm in one's native country (asylum, withholding of removal, and relief under the Convention Against Torture); (2) length of physical presence or residence in the United States (cancellation of removal for non–permanent residents and registry); (3) relationships to family or employers (adjustment of status); or (4) prior lawful permanent resident (LPR) status or eligibility for this status (cancellation of removal for LPRs and waivers). In addition, there are certain forms of relief that can be directly sought from the Department of Homeland Security (DHS). These include exercise of prosecutorial discretion, deferred action, and stays of removal.

Chapters 5 and 6 will outline the statutory and regulatory requirements for each form of relief. Additionally, a series of practice tips for the preparation and presentation of given relief claims before the immigration court or the appropriate government agency is included in the appendix portion of this book.

CHAPTER FIVE

RELIEF FROM REMOVAL—ASYLUM, WITHHOLDING OF REMOVAL, AND CAT RELIEF

Asylum and Withholding of Removal

Introduction

There are three forms of relief based on an individual's fear of persecution, harm, or torture in the native country—asylum, withholding of removal, and relief under the Convention Against Torture (CAT).

Asylum is the most common form of relief. An individual must prove to the immigration court that he or she has a "well-founded" or "reasonable" fear of harm if returned to the native country. The individual must show either past harm or fear of future harm as well as some evidence as to the motivation of the persecutor. Moreover, the applicant must show that there is direct or circumstantial evidence that this fear of harm is based on one of five statutory grounds—race, religion, nationality, political opinion, or membership in a particular social group. The "well-founded" standard means that a reasonable person in a similar situation would have a fear of harm (this may be as little as a 10 percent chance).[1] A well-founded fear can be shown by proving past persecution or by showing that there is reason to believe that an individual will be harmed in the future even if he or she has not been harmed in the past.

Withholding of removal is similar to asylum in that an individual must prove that there is some type of threat to his or her life or freedom. In addition, like asylum, the applicant must show that this threat is connected to one of the five statutory grounds—race, religion, nationality, political opinion, or membership in a particular social group. However, there are substantial differences between asylum and withholding of removal. Withholding of removal carries a higher burden of proof. An individual must show that it is "more likely than not" that his or her life or freedom will be threatened if returned. Thus, there must be better than a 50 percent chance of threat to the individual's well-being.[2] The relief granted under a withholding of removal approval is much more limited than relief through asylum. Unlike asylum,

---

[1] *INS v. Cardoza-Fonseca*, 480 U.S. 421, 440 (1987).

[2] *INS. v. Stevic*, 467 U.S. 407 (1984).

which leads to LPR status (a Green Card), withholding of removal does not lead to LPR status. Withholding of removal does not give an individual the possibility of travel. There is no derivative benefit to family members of an individual granted withholding of removal, whereas those granted asylum can bring spouses and children under 21 years old to the United States. Finally, withholding of removal is country specific. Thus, the government will withhold removal to the individual's country of nationality. If the government can find another country to which the individual may be removed, then it may remove the individual to that country.

Withholding of removal is beneficial, however, because it is a mandatory form of relief, whereas asylum is discretionary. Article 33 (nonrefoulement or nonreturn of an individual who meets the refugee definition) of the 1951 Convention Relating to the Status of Refugees,[3] a document to which the United States acceded by signing the 1967 Protocol Relating to the Status of Refugees,[4] makes withholding of removal mandatory for all treaty signatories. Like asylum, however, there are certain statutory bars against receipt based on prior criminal activity or persecution of other individuals (discussed below).

Relief under CAT will be discussed separately from asylum and withholding of removal because it is a very different form of relief with far different standards and procedures. It requires a clear probability of torture by, or with the acquiescence of, the government or others affiliated with the government. There are no statutory bars to deferral of removal under CAT.

Basic History

The asylum law of the United States is built on the definition of the term "refugee" adopted by the international community in the Convention, where a refugee was defined as someone who, as a result of pre-1951 events "and owing to a well-founded fear of being persecuted for reasons of race, religion, nationality, membership in a particular social group or political opinion," was outside of his or her country of nationality and was "unable, or owing to such fear, unwilling to avail himself of the protection of that country."[5] By so defining a refugee, the Convention conferred refugee status only on persons displaced by pre-1951 events in Europe, thus, potentially limiting both the prospective obligations of the signatories and the number of prospective refugees that they would have to accept under the Convention. Second, it excluded people who were fleeing their countries for economic reasons, natural or man-made disasters, or war. This definition reflected the geopolitical climate at the time as it allowed Western countries to give refuge to dissidents (many of whom already had begun escaping because of violations of civil and political rights) from

---

[3] The 1951 Convention Relating to the Status of Refugees, July 28, 1951, 189 U.N.T.S. 150 (entered into force Apr. 22, 1954) (hereinafter Convention).

[4] The 1967 Protocol relating to the Status of Refugees, Jan. 31, 1967, 606 U.N.T.S. 267, art. I (entered into force Oct. 4, 1967) (hereinafter Protocol).

[5] Convention, *supra* note 3, chapter I, arts. 21–23; Immigration and Nationality Act of 1952 (INA), Pub. L. No. 82-414, §101(a)(42), 66 Stat. 163 (codified as amended at 8 USC §§1101 *et seq.*).

communist countries under Soviet control and focus world attention on the political failings of the Soviet bloc countries.[6]

Eventually, the need arose to address new refugee situations outside of the scope of the Convention and to make the provisions of the Convention applicable to such new refugees. The Protocol Relating to the Status of Refugees was prepared in 1967 to address this need. The Protocol retained the substantive provisions of the refugee definition of the Convention, but it removed the temporal and geographical limitations of the Convention.[7] Thus, it made the refugee definition more generic and refugee status available to a greater number of prospective refugees.

The United States acceded to the Protocol in 1968, thereby accepting the Convention as modified by the Protocol.[8] Twelve years later, Congress enacted the Refugee Act of 1980,[9] which was the first comprehensive refugee legislation in the history of the United States.[10] The 1980 Act provided a statutory definition of refugee modeled on the definition of "refugee" set out in the Convention.

Statutory Elements of an Asylum Claim: Legal Standards

An applicant for asylum must prove:

- that he or she is unable or unwilling to return to the country of nationality or, if homeless, of last habitual residence, and is unable or unwilling to avail him- or herself of the protection of that country;
- because of past persecution or a well-founded fear of future persecution;
- on account of race, religion, nationality, political opinion, or membership in a particular social group; and
- that the applicant is discretionarily deserving of asylum relief.[11]

The applicant must meet all of the elements above and be outside his or her country of nationality in order to qualify for *refugee* status. (However, as an exception to this rule, the President "may in such special circumstances as the President . . . may specify," permit individuals within their country of nationality to qualify as refugees.[12]) An asylee is an alien who meets all of the above criteria, but is physically present in the United States or is at a land border or port of entry when he or she applies for refugee status. Several of the elements listed above have been the subject of litigation between refugee advocates and the government.

---

[6] *See* Philip G. Schrag, *A Well-Founded Fear: The Congressional Battle to Save Political Asylum in America* 25 (2000); James C. Hathaway, *The Law of Refugee Status* 8 (1991).

[7] Protocol, *supra* note 4, art. I.

[8] Stephen H. Legomsky, *Immigration and Refugee Law and Policy* 861 (3rd ed. 2002).

[9] The Refugee Act of 1980, Pub. L. No. 96-212, 94 Stat. 102 (Mar. 17, 1980) (hereinafter 1980 Act).

[10] Legomsky, *supra* note 8, at 862.

[11] INA §101(a)(42).

[12] *See* INA §101(a)(42)(B).

Unable or unwilling to return and avail oneself of the protection of the country of nationality

The applicant for asylum must show that he or she is "unable or unwilling to return to his country and is unable or unwilling to avail himself of the protection of that country because of past persecution or a well-founded fear of future persecution on account of race, religion, national origin, political opinion, or membership in a particular social group."[13] Being "unable" to avail oneself of the protection of one's country implies that there are circumstances preventing protection that lie beyond the will of the person to change.[14] If the protection from perceived harm has been denied by the government of the country of nationality, the individual's claim to asylum is strengthened; the denial of protection itself may be an element of persecution, if such denial is based on one of the five statutory grounds.[15] The *UNHCR Handbook* states that if an individual has been denied services generally provided for other nationals of the country, this may constitute a refusal of protection.[16]

The term "unwilling" applies to individuals who choose not to avail themselves of the protection of their country.[17] If an individual refuses to avail him- or herself of the protection of his or her native country, that individual should be able to show that such unwillingness is based on persecution or a well-founded fear of future persecution.[18] If protection is available and there is not a reason based on a well-founded fear of persecution for refusing this protection, the claim for asylum will not be granted.[19]

Persecution

Definition

In order to qualify for asylum, the applicant must prove past persecution or a well-founded fear of future persecution; the *UNHCR Handbook* defines persecution as a "threat to life or freedom on account of race, religion, nationality, political opinion or membership of a particular social group."[20] The persecution may be inflicted by the established government of the country or other groups that the government is unable or unwilling to control.[21] A subjective, punitive, or malignant intent is not required in order for the harm inflicted to constitute persecution.[22] For example, forced psychiat-

---

[13] *Id.*

[14] *See United Nations High Commissioner for Refugees, Handbook on Procedures and Criteria for Determining Refugee Status* para. 98 (1979) (hereinafter *UNHCR Handbook*).

[15] *Id.*

[16] *Id.* para. 99.

[17] *Id.* para. 100.

[18] *Id.*

[19] *Id.* para. 100.

[20] *Id.* para. 51.

[21] *Matter of McMullen*, 17 I&N Dec. 542, 545 (BIA 1980).

[22] Proposed federal regulations, if passed, will codify the notion embraced by both the Board of Immigration Appeals (BIA) and the Ninth Circuit, and "impose an objective standard on the concept of per-

continued

ric "therapy by a government to force a woman to change her sexual orientation is persecution even if the government is not attempting to punish the person in the process, just change her."[23]

The *UNHCR Handbook* states that serious human rights violations would constitute persecution.[24] A combination of minor actions taken against an individual may amount to persecution even where each individual incident alone may not. A series of smaller incidents, if taken together, may produce an effect on the mind of the applicant that can reasonably justify a claim to a well-founded fear of persecution on cumulative grounds.[25] The *Basic Law Manual*, used as a training manual for asylum officers, lists a series of actions that may amount to an overall scheme of persecution especially if cumulative, including: arbitrary interference with one's privacy, family, home, or correspondence; relegation to substandard dwellings; exclusion from institutions of higher learning; enforced social inactivity; passport denial; constant surveillance; and pressure to become an informer.[26] The list above is not exhaustive and other acts may cumulatively amount to persecution even if each action individually would not.[27]

The Board of Immigration Appeals (BIA) has defined the term "persecution" as a "threat to the life or freedom of, or the infliction of suffering upon, those who differ in a way regarded as offensive."[28] It does not encompass all treatment that society regards as unfair, unjust, unlawful, or unconstitutional.[29] It is "only when there is a difference between the persecutor's view or status and that of the victim; it is oppression which is inflicted on groups or individuals because of a difference that the perse-

---

secution." Regulation Concerning Establishing Asylum Eligibility, 65 Fed. Reg. 76588, 76590 (proposed Dec. 7, 2000) (to be codified at 8 CFR §208.23(b)) (citing *Matter of Kasinga*, 21 I&N Dec. 357, 365 (BIA 1996) and *Pitcherskaia v. INS*, 118 F.3d 641 (9th Cir. 1997)).

[23] *Pitcherskaia*, 118 F.3d 641.

[24] *UNHCR Handbook*, *supra* note 14, para. 51.

[25] *Id.* para. 53; *see also Matter of O–Z and I–Z*, 22 I&N Dec. 23 (BIA 1998) (holding that a Russian citizen suffered persecution on account of his Jewish nationality where he was assaulted on three separate occasions by individuals who expressed anti-Semitic sentiments; received threats and anti-Semitic materials at home; and his son was harassed by schoolmates); *Baballah v. Ashcroft*, 335 F.3d 981 (9th Cir. 2003) (finding that persistent threatening behavior directed against an Israeli Muslim and members of his fishing crew when Israeli Marines circled the boat and caused it to fill with water, shot bullets overhead, sprayed pressurized water at boat in freezing temperatures, and purposefully destroyed his fishing nets and boats rose to the level of persecution).

[26] *See Asylum Division and Office of the General Counsel of the INS, Basic Law Manual: U.S. Law and INS Refugee/Asylum Adjudications* 25 (1994) (hereinafter *Basic Law Manual*).

[27] *See id.*

[28] *Matter of Sanchez and Escobar*, 19 I&N Dec. 276, 284 (BIA 1985) (citing *Cardoza-Fonseca v. INS*, 767 F.2d 1448, 1452 (9th Cir. 1985); *Bolanos-Hernandez v. INS*, 767 F.2d 1277, 1283 (9th Cir. 1984); *Matter of Acosta*, 19 I&N Dec. 211, 216 (BIA 1985).

[29] *Matter of V–T–S*, 21 I&N Dec. 792, 798 (BIA 1997) (citing *Fatin v. INS*, 12 F.3d 1233 (3d Cir. 1993)).

cutor will not tolerate."[30] For example, arrest, detention, interrogation, and six days' imprisonment because of a difference in political opinion constitutes persecution.[31] Persecution includes confinement and torture, but may also include mental suffering and severe economic deprivation constituting a threat to an individual's life or freedom.[32] Further, it is not necessary to show total deprivation of one's livelihood to establish persecution,[33] but economic deprivation stripping an individual of all means of earning a livelihood may amount to persecution.[34]

Rape and physical mistreatment have been classified as persecution.[35] A Chinese citizen whose spouse was forced to undergo an abortion or sterilization procedure established past persecution on account of political opinion.[36] The practice of female genital mutilation (FGM) in various countries is considered to be persecution even in the absence of any "punitive" or "malignant" intent.[37]

The definition of persecution includes, at a minimum, conduct that threatens life or freedom. Threats may, under certain circumstances, amount to persecution.[38] However, the identity of the persecutor, the setting, and the purpose of the threat should be shown in order to determine if there is a realistic threat to life or freedom.[39]

Discrimination is not generally classified as persecution,[40] although discriminatory practices, if persistent, may rise to the level of persecution.[41] Detention for brief periods of time without mistreatment is not persecution.[42] Punishment for violating Islamic dress and conduct codes for women in Iran is not persecution unless the law is selectively enforced, stemming from the government's desire to single out the applicant.[43] Harsh conditions shared by many, or general civil strife, anarchy, or criminal

---

[30] *Matter of Maldonado-Cruz*, 19 I&N Dec. 509, 513 (BIA 1988) (quoting *Hernandez-Ortiz v. INS*, 777 F.2d 509 (9th Cir. 1985)).

[31] *Singh v. Ilchert*, 69 F.3d 375, 377–81 (9th Cir. 1995).

[32] *Compare Dunat v. Hurney*, 297 F.2d 744, 746 (3d Cir. 1961), *Berdo v. INS*, 432 F.2d 824, 847 (6th Cir. 1970), and *Kovac v. INS*, 407 F.2d 102, 107 (9th Cir. 1969) with *Chen v. INS*, 195 F.3d 198, 204–05 (4th Cir. 1999), and *Raudez-Hurtada v. INS*, 37 F.3d 1506 (9th Cir. 1994). *See also Borca v. INS*, 77 F.3d 210, 215 (7th Cir. 1996) (adopting the decision in *Kovac v. INS*, 407 F.2d 102, 107 (9th Cir. 1969)).

[33] *Borca*, 77 F.3d at 215.

[34] *See Matter of Eusaph*, 10 I&N Dec. 453, 454 (BIA 1964).

[35] *Matter of D–V–*, 21 I&N Dec. 77 (BIA 1993).

[36] *Matter of C–Y–Z*, 21 I&N Dec. 915 (BIA 1997). *See also Matter of X–P–T*, 21 I&N Dec. 634 (BIA 1996).

[37] *Matter of Kasinga*, 21 I&N Dec. 357 (BIA 1996).

[38] *Compare Garrovillas v. INS*, 156 F.3d 1010, 1016 (9th Cir. 1998) and *Sangha v. INS*, 103 F.3d 1482, 1487 (9th Cir. 1997), *with Matter of A–E–M–*, 21 I&N Dec. 1157 (BIA 1998).

[39] *Mite v. INS*, 67 F.3d 1325, 1331 (7th Cir. 1995).

[40] *See De Souza v. INS*, 999 F.2d 1156, 1159 (7th Cir. 1993).

[41] *UNHCR Handbook*, *supra* note 14, paras. 54, 55.

[42] *Zalega v. INS*, 916 F.2d 1257 (7th Cir. 1990).

[43] *Fisher v. INS*, 79 F.3d 955 (9th Cir. 1996).

punishment for violating laws (such as exit laws or military conscription) are not considered persecution by the BIA.[44]

In 1992, the Immigration and Naturalization Service (INS)[45] General Counsel issued an opinion stating that the expulsion of Palestinians and seizure of their property by a nation during time of war or other national emergency did not constitute persecution. "It is the sovereign prerogative of each independent nation to determine whether and under what circumstances individuals may enter and remain in the nation's territory."[46]

Past persecution

An applicant for asylum may establish his or her claim by presenting evidence of past persecution in lieu of evidence of a well-founded fear of future persecution.[47] A showing of past persecution creates a presumption of a well-founded fear of future persecution.[48]

Under regulations effective January 5, 2001, this presumption may be overcome if the government can show by a preponderance of the evidence that a fundamental change in circumstances has occurred, such that there is no longer a well-founded fear or that the applicant could avoid persecution by relocating to another part of the country.[49] The regulations place the burden on the government to rebut the presumption of a well-founded fear after a showing of past persecution by a preponderance of the evidence.[50]

Finally, the regulations indicate that where past persecution has been shown, but the presumption of a well-founded fear is overcome by a showing of fundamentally changed conditions or a possibility of relocation, as stated above, the applicant may still be granted asylum if he or she demonstrates compelling reasons for being unwilling to return to his or her country arising out of the severity of his or her past persecution, or there is a showing of a reasonable possibility that serious harm may be suffered upon return to the country.[51]

---

[44] *Matter of Sanchez and Escobar*, 19 I&N Dec. 276, 284 (BIA 1985) (noting that "generally harsh conditions shared by many others in a country and the harm arising out of civil strife did not amount to 'persecution' within the meaning of our law"); *see also Rejaie v. INS*, 691 F.2d 139 (3d Cir. 1982); *Matter of Chang*, 20 I&N Dec. 38 (BIA 1989).

[45] The former INS is now part of DHS; within DHS, U.S. Citizenship and Immigration Services (USCIS) handles asylum.

[46] *See* Legal Opinion of Grover Joseph Rees III, General Counsel, *reproduced in* 69 *Interpreter Releases* 1631 (1992).

[47] 8 CFR §§208.13(b)(1), 1208.13(b)(1); *see also Matter of Chen*, 20 I&N Dec. 16 (BIA 1989).

[48] *See Matter of B*, 21 I&N Dec. 66 (BIA 1995); *Kotasz v. INS*, 132 F.3d 39 (9th Cir. 1997); *Mikhael v. INS*, 115 F.3d 299, 303 (5th Cir. 1997); 8 CFR §§208.13(b)(1), 1208.13(b)(1).

[49] 8 CFR §§208.16(b)(1)(i)(A),(B), 1208.16(b)(1)(i)(A),(B).

[50] 8 CFR §§208.16(b)(1)(ii), 1208.16(b)(1)(ii).

[51] 8 CFR §208.13(b)(1)(iii). *See also Matter of B*, 21 I&N Dec. 66.

Countrywide persecution—reasonableness of internal relocation

Prior BIA decisions have stated that the feared persecution generally must be countrywide.[52] However, where the persecution is by the government, there is a presumption that the danger extends countrywide.[53] When an applicant shows that a national government is the persecutor, the burden shifts to DHS to prove that the government's persecutory actions are confined to a clearly "delineated and limited locality and situation."[54] The possibility that an individual who fears persecution by a national government might be safe from persecution by that government in other areas of the country that are not under government control does not prove that the applicant lacks a well-founded fear.[55] Likewise, the regulations state that where the persecutor is the government or a government-inspired agent, "it shall be presumed that internal relocation would not be reasonable, unless the government establishes by a preponderance of the evidence that, under all the circumstances, it would be reasonable for the applicant to relocate."[56]

The BIA has held that an individual must show fear of persecution on a nationwide basis.[57] "An alien seeking to meet the definition of a refugee must do more than show a well-founded fear of persecution in a particular place or abode within a country – he must show that the threat of persecution exists for him countrywide."[58] The U.S. Supreme Court has reiterated this rule in a *per curiam* opinion issued November 4, 2002.[59] The Court interpreted the federal regulations to mean that "an individual who can relocate safely within his home country ordinarily cannot qualify for asylum" in the United States, and emphasized the 1997 State Department report on Guatemala, which stated that "party leaders ... would be vulnerable to ... harassment ...

---

[52] *Matter of Acosta*, 19 I&N Dec. 211 (BIA 1985); *see also Matter of R*, 20 I&N Dec. 621, 627 (BIA 1992).

[53] *Abdel-Masieh v. INS*, 73 F.3d 579, 587 (5th Cir. 1996); *see also Matter of C–A–L*, 21 I&N Dec. 754 (BIA 1997) (stating that the Fifth Circuit's decision in *Abdel-Masieh* does not address the issue of countrywide persecution by a nongovernmental actor).

[54] *Abdel-Masieh*, 73 F.3d at 587.

[55] *Id.* at 586; *see Singh v. Moschorak*, 53 F.3d 1031, 1034 (9th Cir. 1995) ("It has never been thought that there are safe places within a nation that have driven a victim to leave the country."); *see also Damaize-Job v. INS*, 787 F.2d 1332 (9th Cir. 1986).

[56] 8 CFR §§208.13(b)(3)(ii), 1208.13(b)(3)(ii).

[57] *Matter of R*, 20 I&N Dec. 621 (BIA 1992) (denying asylum to a Sikh from Punjab, who had suffered physical abuse by the Indian police, because he did not provide evidence demonstrating countrywide persecution); *Matter of C–A–L–*, 21 I&N Dec. 754 (BIA 1997) (denying asylum claim because the applicant did not provide sufficient evidence to prove persecution throughout Guatemala); *Matter of A–E–M–*, 21 I&N Dec. 1157 (BIA 1998) (finding that a Peruvian asylum applicant who feared persecution at the hands of the Shining Path guerillas did not qualify for asylum because the country reports showed that the Shining Path operated in only a few areas of Peru).

[58] *Matter of R*, 20 I&N Dec. 621, 625 (BIA 1992).

[59] *See INS v. Ventura*, 537 U.S. 12 (2002) (per curiam). *Cf. Melkonian v. Ashcroft*, 320 F.3d 1061 (9th Cir. 2003) (finding that internal relocation was not reasonable where the alien's immediate family members did not speak the language and there was a general lack of food in other areas of the country).

usually only in their home communities."[60] This finding appears to be at odds with the *UNHCR Handbook*, which states:

> The fear of being persecuted need not always extend to the *whole* territory of the refugee's country of nationality. Thus in ethnic clashes or in cases of grave disturbances involving civil war conditions, persecution of a specific ethnic or national group may occur in only one part of the country. In such situations, a person will not be excluded from refugee status merely because he could have sought refuge in another part of the same country, if under all the circumstances it would not have been reasonable to expect him to do so.[61]

The Eleventh and Fifth Circuits are in agreement that persecution by nongovernmental actors must be countrywide. Both circuits affirmed BIA decisions denying asylum claims where the petitioner could avoid persecution by moving to another part of the country.[62] The Fifth Circuit held that where the applicant for asylum has not shown that the government is the persecutor, an applicant bears the burden of proving that relocation within the applicant's country of origin would not be reasonable under the circumstances.

However, in the First Circuit, the court held that where the petitioner established past persecution in one region of the country with *possible* federal government involvement, INS had the burden to prove by a preponderance of the evidence that the threat was limited to a particular region of the country.[63] The court held that INS improperly placed this burden on the petitioner.[64]

Motivation of persecutor

An applicant for asylum is not required to provide direct proof of the persecutor's motivation.[65] The claim may be denied, however, where there is *no* showing of the possible motivation of the persecutor.[66] While the applicant need not establish the exact motivation of the persecutor, he or she must establish facts upon which a reasonable person would fear that the danger arises on account of one of the five grounds.[67]

The BIA has required that an individual prove the intent or motivation of the persecutor. The Ninth Circuit has ruled that this standard was too strict. The circuit court

---

[60] *Id.* (citing 8 CFR §§208.13(b)(1)(i), 1208.13(b)(1)(i) and emphasizing the 1997 State Department report on Guatemala).

[61] *UNHCR Handbook, supra*, note 14, para. 91.

[62] *Mazariegos v. Att'y Gen.*, 241 F.3d 1320 (11th Cir. 2001); *Lopez-Gomez v. Ashcroft*, 263 F.3d 442 (5th Cir. 2001).

[63] *Manzoor v. Dept. of Justice*, 254 F.3d 342, 344 (1st Cir. 2001).

[64] *Id.*

[65] *INS v. Elias-Zacarias*, 502 U.S. 478, 483 (1992).

[66] *Campos-Guardado v. INS*, 809 F.2d 285, 29 (5th Cir. 1987).

[67] *Matter of Fuentes*, 19 I&N Dec. 658, 660–62 (BIA 1988); *see also Matter of Canas*, 19 I&N Dec. 697, 700 (BIA 1988).

held that while a showing of the persecutor's intent or motive is a relevant factor, it is not an absolute requirement.[68] In *INS v. Elias-Zacarias*, the Supreme Court, addressing the issue of the motivation of the persecutor, stated that an applicant for asylum must "provide some evidence of it, direct or circumstantial."[69] In most cases, this must be done based on circumstantial evidence, as persecutors generally do not give direct statements or evidence of their motivation.[70] The Court also ruled in *Elias-Zacarias* that forced recruitment by a guerrilla organization was not per se persecution because such recruitment was not tied to the individual's political opinion.[71] The BIA has ruled that while there may be a number of reasons for a kidnapping, the respondent bears the burden of establishing that one motivation is to persecute him or her on account of an enumerated ground.[72] The Fifth Circuit recently upheld two denials where the BIA found that the applicant had not established that the motivation of the persecutor was related to one of the five enumerated grounds.[73] With the passage of the REAL ID Act of 2005,[74] Congress mandated that one of the five statutory grounds for asylum must be "a central factor" motivating the persecutor.

Persecution versus prosecution

Whether the harm inflicted is actually *persecution* or whether it is *prosecution* for some violation of a country's laws is frequently an issue in asylum cases. Those fleeing harm resulting from prosecution are not refugees.[75] This distinction is often difficult to make.

The most common example highlighting the difficulty involves individuals who are ordered to perform some type of military service on behalf of the government or some group opposed to the government. The BIA has stated that an individual who is harmed

---

68 *Canas-Segovia v. INS*, 902 F.2d 717 (9th Cir. 1990).

69 *Elias-Zacarias*, 502 U.S. at 483.

70 *Id.*

71 *Id.* at 482.

72 *Matter of V–T–S–*, 21 I&N Dec. 792, 798 (BIA 1997); *see also Lukwago v. Ashcroft*, 329 F.3d 157 (3rd Cir. 2003) (holding that the confinement and treatment by the Lord's Resistance Army (LRA) of a Ugandan child who had been abducted and enslaved may constitute past persecution under the INA, but it was not sufficient to make him eligible for asylum because the persecution was not on account of any of the five factors).

73 *Girma v. INS*, 283 F.3d 664 (5th Cir. 2002) (holding that an Ethiopian woman who had been assaulted and raped by several masked men in army fatigues failed to establish that their motivation was related to one of the five grounds as she was unable to identify her assailants as members of, or connected to, the government); *Ontunez-Tursios v. Ashcroft*, 303 F.3d 341 (5th Cir. 2002) (finding that although the applicant, a member of a land cooperative, was threatened and placed in danger after a fight with landlords over the ownership of farmland, there was no evidence that the landlords were motivated by one of the five statutory grounds in threatening him).

74 Pub. L. No. 109-13, 119, Stat. 231 (May 11, 2005), to be codified at 8 USC §1252 (a)(2)(D).

75 *Saleh v. Dept. of Justice*, 962 F.2d 234 (2nd Cir. 1992) (finding that an individual sentenced to death "in absentia" in his home country for the death of another was not the victim of persecution but prosecution).

by a government for assisting an opposition force is not a refugee, but the object of legitimate prosecution since the government "has a legitimate right to seek him out and determine whether he is indeed involved in such an organization."[76] Although the Ninth Circuit reversed this decision on appeal in *Maldonado-Cruz v. INS*,[77] the BIA has always applied its rationale in cases arising outside the Ninth Circuit.

In *Matter of Izatula*, the BIA held that the legitimacy of the government inflicting the harm may be a relevant issue and that the possibility of democratic change is a relevant factor in determining which government actions are persecution and which are prosecution.[78] The BIA stated that punishment of opponents of a "non-democratic" government may, in some situations, constitute persecution,[79] and that where there is no democratic method of changing the government, punishment of individuals who resort to force may be persecution.[80] As a result, what is found to be legitimate governmental prosecution in one case may be classified by the BIA as persecution in another depending on the type of government. To compare, the BIA stated that the Salvadoran government in *Maldonado-Cruz* did have the "legitimate right to seek out" and punish individuals suspected of aiding opposition forces while the Afghan government in *Izatula* did not have such a right. The BIA found that the Salvadoran government was a legitimate government while the Afghan government was not. The target of the governmental action in *Maldonado-Cruz* did not qualify for asylum while in *Izatula*, he did qualify. Practitioners may have to be prepared to present evidence on the legitimacy or illegitimacy of the government in the country where the persecution is claimed.

Punishment for refusal to serve in the military generally is considered prosecution, not persecution.[81] There are, however, examples where punishment for refusal to perform military service may amount to persecution. "Where … the type of military action, with which the individual does not wish to be associated, is condemned by the international community as contrary to the basic rules of human conduct, punishment for desertion or draft evasion could be regarded as persecution."[82]

---

[76] *Matter of Maldonado-Cruz*, 19 I&N Dec. 509, 518 (BIA 1988).

[77] *Maldonado-Cruz v. INS*, 883 F.2d 788 (9th Cir. 1989).

[78] *Matter of Izatula*, 20 I&N Dec. 149 (BIA 1990) (finding the actions taken by a government against an individual who assisted forces attempting to overthrow the government to be persecution, not prosecution).

[79] *Id.*

[80] *Id.*

[81] *See Matter of Lee*, 13 I&N Dec. 236 (BIA 1969); *Matter of Vigil*, 19 I&N Dec. 572 (BIA 1988).

[82] *UNHCR Handbook*, *supra* note 14, para. 171; *see also Barraza-Rivera v. INS*, 913 F.2d 1443 (9th Cir. 1990) ("[P]unishment based on objection to participation in inhuman acts as part of forced military service is 'persecution' within the meaning of 8 U.S.C. §1101(a)(42)(A)."); "INS Grants Asylum To South African Draft Resister," 67 No. 15 *Interpreter Releases* 436 (1990) (INS reversed its position in previously denying an application for political asylum filed by a South African draft resister based on his refusal to serve because of his opposition to apartheid, which the South African Defense Force (SADF) enforced).

Punishment for refusal to perform military service based on religious grounds also may be the basis for a claim to refugee status.[83] A deserter or draft evader may be considered a refugee if he or she would suffer disproportionately severe punishment for refusal to serve on account of his or her race, religion, national origin, political opinion, or membership in a particular social group.[84]

The line between what is persecution and what is not can be murky. Threats or actions against a deserter from a guerrilla organization during a civil war are not persecution since the guerrillas are a military organization and the threats are "a tool of discipline necessary to the continued functioning of the organization."[85] However, one circuit court held that nongovernmental groups lack legitimate authority to conscript individuals.[86] Their actions therefore "are tantamount to kidnapping and constitute persecution."[87]

In summary, prosecution may amount to persecution if punishment is disproportionately severe on account of one of the five enumerated grounds.[88] Alternatively, a claim under the CAT may be appropriate where the harm inflicted, *i.e.*, "prosecution," is not "on account of" any of the five grounds, but rises to the level of torture (CAT claims will be further discussed, *infra*).

Well-founded fear

The definition of the phrase "well-founded fear" was an area of controversy for many years after the 1980 Refugee Act[89] was passed. Several court decisions have clarified the issue. In *Guevara-Flores*, the Fifth Circuit gave the following definition of the term: "An alien possesses a well-founded fear of persecution if a reasonable person in her circumstances would fear persecution if she were to be returned to her native country."[90]

In addition, the court stated that the "well-founded fear standard is at least partially subjective, because fear is a state of apprehension or anxiety not normally subject to rational measurement."[91] However, the fear must "have some basis in reality."[92] Finally, the court stated that the "well-founded fear" standard is different from

---

[83] *UNHCR Handbook, supra* note 14, para. 172. *Cf. Canas-Segovia v. INS*, 970 F.2d 599, 601 (9th Cir. 1992) (holding that in claims involving religious persecution based on punishment threatened or imposed upon a conscientious objector for refusal to submit to conscription, the applicant must show that the motivation of authorities in imposing the punishment would be to persecute the applicant because of his or her beliefs).

[84] *See Matter of Vigil*, 19 I&N Dec. 572 (BIA 1988).

[85] *Matter of Maldonado-Cruz*, 19 I&N Dec. 509, 515 (BIA 1988).

[86] *Arteaga v. INS*, 836 F.2d 1227, 1232 (9th Cir. 1988).

[87] *Id.*

[88] *See Matter of R–R*, 20 I&N Dec. 547 (BIA 1992).

[89] 1980 Act, *supra* note 9.

[90] *Guevara-Flores v. INS*, 786 F.2d 1242, 1249 (5th Cir. 1986).

[91] *Id.*

[92] *Id.*

the "clear probability" standard, in that the evidentiary burden for establishing entitlement to withholding of removal (which is mandatory, not discretionary, should the requirements be met) should be greater than that imposed on aliens who seek asylum.[93] In a later decision, the Fifth Circuit reiterated the reasonableness standard and vacated the BIA's decision where the BIA applied a stricter standard.[94]

In *INS v. Cardoza-Fonseca*, the Supreme Court, in 1987, took up the issue and clarified the meaning of the term: "so long as an objective situation is established by the evidence, it is enough that persecution is a *reasonable possibility*."[95] The standard is "*reasonableness*" not "*definitiveness*."[96] A one-in-ten chance of harm may be considered the basis for a reasonable fear.[97] The Supreme Court reaffirmed the Fifth Circuit's finding that the "well-founded fear" standard under INA §208 carries a lesser burden of proof than the "clear probability" standard under §243(h) (now §241(b)(3)). There are subjective and objective components, *i.e.*, the individual must be subjectively fearful and there must be an objective basis for the fear.[98]

After the Court's decision in *Cardoza-Fonseca*, the BIA addressed the issue. The BIA adopted the "*reasonable person*" standard of *Guevara-Flores* in *Matter of Mogharrabi*, stating that the applicant has established a well-founded fear of persecution if he or she shows that a reasonable person in that situation would fear persecution.[99] In order to establish the reasonableness of the individual's fear, the BIA outlined the following four-point test:

1. The alien must possess a belief or characteristic a persecutor seeks to overcome in others by means of punishment of some sort.
2. The persecutor is already aware or could become aware that the alien possesses this belief or characteristic.
3. The persecutor has the capability of punishing the alien.
4. The persecutor has the inclination to punish the alien.[100]

The BIA also has stated that when the country at issue has a history of persecuting people in circumstances similar to those of the asylum applicant, careful consideration should be given to this fact in assessing the applicant's claim.[101] In other words, a well-founded fear can be based on what has happened to others who are similarly

---

[93] *Id.* at 1250.

[94] *Mikhael v. INS*, 115 F.3d 299 (5th Cir. 1997).

[95] *INS v. Cardoza-Fonseca*, 480 U.S. 421, 440 (1987) (citing *INS v. Stevic*, 467 U.S. 407, 424–25 (1984)).

[96] *Matter of A–E–M–*, 21 I&N Dec. 1157, 1167 (BIA 1998).

[97] *Cardoza-Fonseca*, 480 U.S. at 440.

[98] *Id.*

[99] *Matter of Mogharrabi*, 19 I&N Dec. 439 (BIA 1987).

[100] *Id.* at 446.

[101] *Id.*

situated.[102] The asylum regulations incorporate the "*reasonableness*" standard within the definition of "well-founded fear."[103] The BIA has found that the reasonableness of an individual's fear is reduced when his or her family remains in his or her native country unharmed for a long period of time after his or her departure.[104]

In determining whether a person has a well-founded fear of persecution, the IJ must evaluate current country conditions to see if they have changed. With the number and speed of the changes in governments throughout Central America, the Middle Eastern, Europe, the former Soviet Union, and other parts of the world during the past two decades, the issue of whether conditions have changed so as to lessen the reasonableness of one's fear is a major one. Frequently, the Department of Justice (DOJ) and DHS are finding that claims must be denied because of "democratic" changes in such countries as Nicaragua, Romania, Haiti, Guatemala, and others. DHS argues that even where past persecution has been shown, applications for asylum should be denied because of "changed conditions" in these countries.[105] The BIA, in the past, denied several applications for political asylum from Nicaragua by taking "administrative notice" of "changed conditions" within that country.[106] It denied asylum to an applicant from Haiti based in part on the finding of changed conditions in that country since the applicant's departure.[107]

Conversely, the Ninth Circuit has overturned the BIA's decisions in several cases holding that the BIA has improperly taken administrative notice of changed conditions in Nicaragua without affording the applicants the opportunity to show reasons why such notice should not be taken.[108] The BIA's past practice of taking administrative notice of changed conditions without offering the parties an opportunity to address the issue or a chance to respond has been criticized by several courts, even where the courts have upheld the BIA's decisions on other grounds.[109] The court in *Gutierrez-Roque v. INS* stated:

---

102 *Id. See also* 8 CFR §§208.13(b)(2)(i)(A), 1208.13(b)(2)(i)(A) (identifying country of nationality, race, religion, membership in a particular social group, or political opinion as the recognized grounds for persecution).

103 *See* 8 CFR §§208.13(b)(2)(i)(B), 1208.13(b)(2)(i)(B).

104 *Matter of A–E–M–*, 21 I&N Dec. 1157 (BIA 1998).

105 8 CFR §§208.13(b)(1)(i)(a), 1208.13(b)(1)(i)(a).

106 *See Matter of H–M–*, 20 I&N Dec. 683 (BIA 1993).

107 *Matter of E–P–*, 21 I&N Dec. 860 (BIA 1997); *see also Matter of A–E–M–*, 21 I&N Dec. 1157 (BIA 1998) (denying the claim based in part on the BIA's findings of changed conditions with regard to the Shining Path guerrillas in Peru since the applicant's departure).

108 *Castillo-Villagra v. INS*, 972 F.2d 1017, 1021 (9th Cir. 1992); *Sarria-Sibaja v. INS*, 990 F.2d 442, 443 (9th Cir. 1993); *Perez-Tan v. INS*, 992 F.2d 1219 (9th Cir. 1993). *But see Gonzales-Hernandez v. Ashcroft*, 336 F.3d 995 (9th Cir. 2003) (holding that the court of appeals is bound by the agency's determination of changed conditions).

109 *Castillo v. INS*, 951 F.2d 1117, 1123 (9th Cir. 1991); *see also Gutierrez-Roque v. INS*, 954 F.2d 769 (D.C. Cir. 1992).

> Neither the INA nor the INS regulation implementing it expressly provides the alien with an opportunity to challenge an officially noticed fact. Because a hearing is not truly meaningful if a critical issue is effectively omitted from consideration, Gutierrez appears to be correct in arguing that due process guarantees an asylum applicant the right to challenge an officially noticed fact with respect both to its truth and its significance.[110]

The Tenth Circuit reversed the BIA in *Kowalczyk v. INS*, finding that failure to allow petitioner an opportunity to respond to facts presented more than nine years after his defection was a violation of due process.[111]

Under regulations effective January 5, 2001, after a showing of past persecution, it will be the DHS's burden to show changed conditions.[112] Where no such evidence is introduced and DHS argues that the court should take administrative notice of these changed conditions, the Federal Rules of Evidence provide guidance as to when a court may take judicial notice of adjudicative acts.[113] While the Federal Rules of Evidence are not controlling in immigration courts, they are sometimes relied on where there are no immigration regulations or guidelines. At a minimum, the attorney should request the opportunity to respond to the court's proposed taking of administrative notice of changed conditions. Even where there is a showing of "changed conditions," the asylum claim still may be granted where there is proof of past persecution and "compelling reasons" to grant the claim in spite of changed conditions.[114]

In a 2002 decision, the Supreme Court overturned a circuit court decision in which the court addressed the factual issues relating to changed conditions "de novo," where the BIA did not consider the issue.[115] The Supreme Court found that the Ninth Circuit should have remanded the case to the BIA in order to address the issue of changed conditions rather than addressing it for the first time at the circuit court level.[116]

On account of

An alien who succeeds in establishing a well-founded fear of persecution will not necessarily be granted asylum.[117] For example, aliens fearing retribution over purely personal matters do not qualify.[118] In addition, those "fleeing general conditions of

---

[110] *Gutierrez-Roque*, 954 F.2d at 773.

[111] *Kowalczyk v. INS*, 245 F.3d 1143, 1148 (10th Cir. 2001).

[112] 8 CFR §§208.16(b)(1)(ii), 1208.16(b)(1)(ii).

[113] *See* F.R. Evid. 201.

[114] 8 CFR §§208.13(b)(1)(ii), 1208.13(b)(1)(ii); *see also* 63 Fed. Reg. 31945–50, June 11, 1998, *reproduced in Interpreter Releases* Appendix I (June 15, 1998).

[115] *INS v. Ventura*, 537 U.S. 12 (2002).

[116] *Id.* at 355–56.

[117] *See, e.g., Lukwago v. Ashcroft*, 329 F.3d 157 (3d Cir. 2003).

[118] *See Adebisi v. INS*, 952 F.2d 910 (5th Cir. 1992) (denying asylum to applicant when harm was found to be "on account of" a personal dispute).

violence and upheaval in their native countries would not qualify for asylum."[119] Such persons may have a well-founded fear of harm, but such harm would not be on account of their race, religion, nationality, membership in a particular social group, or political opinion.[120]

The Supreme Court has stated that an individual must present some evidence—"direct or circumstantial"—that the feared harm is "on account of" the *individual's* political opinion, not the *persecutor's* political opinion.[121] An asylum applicant need not express his or her political disagreement to the feared persecutor. It is enough if there is circumstantial evidence that the persecutor was aware or could become aware of the political differences.[122]

There may be certain situations where there are multiple reasons for the persecutor's actions. The BIA has stated that even where there are multiple motives, some protected and others not, an individual may qualify for asylum if at least one of the possible motives is reasonably one of the five statutory grounds.[123] In 2005, Congress passed the REAL ID Act, which mandated that one of the five statutory grounds be "a central reason" for the claim.[124]

The difficulty in gaining asylum absent a clear nexus between the harm and one of the five stated grounds is evidenced in several BIA decisions. For example, the BIA affirmed the denial of asylum to two Jehovah's Witnesses from El Salvador who refused military service because of their religious beliefs. The harm suffered was not "on account of" religion, but rather because of legitimate governmental interests in raising an army.[125] Similarly, the Seventh Circuit held that a Jehovah's Witness seeking to avoid serving in her country's military on the basis of her religious beliefs did not qualify for asylum even where she might be subject to punishment.[126] The court found that such punishment was not focused on Jehovah's Witnesses, and the government had not sought to draft only Jehovah's Witnesses or to punish only Jehovah's Witnesses for resisting conscription.[127] Likewise, threats by a guerrilla group against a student who terminated his association with the group did not establish past

---

[119] *Matter of Maldonado-Cruz*, 19 I&N Dec. 509, 512 (BIA 1988).

[120] *Id.*

[121] *INS v. Elias-Zacarias*, 502 U.S. 478, 483 (1992).

[122] *Compare Rivas-Martinez v. INS*, 997 F.2d 1143 (5th Cir. 1993) (remanding to the BIA to take into consideration any circumstantial evidence that the applicant's position was motivated by political opinion and that opinion was known to the persecutor), *with Ontunez-Tursios v. Ashcroft*, 303 F.3d 341 (5th Cir. 2002) (affirming the BIA's denial of asylum because the applicant failed to demonstrate *other evidence* connecting his persecution to a difference of political opinion between himself and the persecutor).

[123] *Matter of S–P–*, 21 I&N Dec. 486 (BIA 1996).

[124] REAL ID Act of 2005, *supra* note 74.

[125] *Matter of Canas*, 19 I&N Dec. 697 (BIA 1988).

[126] *Tesfu v. Ashcroft*, 322 F.3d 477 (7th Cir. 2003).

[127] *Id.*

persecution or a well-founded fear of future persecution on account of political opinion.[128] Nor did severe physical beatings of an individual by police seeking to obtain information about antigovernment militants constitute persecution on account of any of the five grounds.[129]

Several courts have taken a strict interpretation of the "on account of" language. In one case, the applicant was a woman who had been raped and had witnessed the killings of her uncle and cousin.[130] She claimed that she had been victimized partially because her uncle, a chairman in an agricultural cooperative, had disagreed with the Salvadoran guerrillas.[131] She claimed persecution on account of political opinion attributed to her by the guerrillas and membership in a particular social group (*i.e.*, her family) that was targeted by the guerrillas.[132] The court acknowledged the facts of the harm suffered by the applicant, but decided that the harm inflicted was not "on account of" her political opinion or membership in a particular social group, and affirmed the BIA's denial of the applicant's claim.[133]

In *Young v. INS*, the applicant, a native of Guatemala, alleged that his son had been arrested, detained, beaten, and interrogated by Guatemalan security officials because of his involvement with a student organization.[134] After securing his son's release, the applicant alleged that he was threatened and that armed individuals believed to be members of the Guatemalan police attempted to kidnap him. Also, his employment with the Guatemalan government as a civil engineer was terminated. The court denied the asylum claim finding that no showing had been made that these events were "on account of" the applicant's political opinion.[135]

In summary, there are three fundamental requirements that one must establish in order to fulfill the nexus between the persecution feared and one of the five grounds: (1) a real or imputed characteristic of the applicant (*e.g.*, an actual or imputed membership in a social group); (2) that there is at least some "circumstantial" evidence to show that the actions taken by the persecutor, or which are feared, are reasonably connected to this characteristic; and (3) this characteristic must be based on one of the five statutory grounds. This may be proven circumstantially or directly; that is, the persecutor can give some evidence (statement or otherwise) that the harm is related, or there is evidence of a pattern of harm to others with characteristics similar to the applicant.[136]

---

[128] *Matter of R–O–*, 20 I&N Dec. 455 (BIA 1992).

[129] *Matter of R*, 20 I&N Dec. 621 (BIA 1992).

[130] *Campos-Guardado v. INS*, 809 F.2d 285 (5th Cir. 1987).

[131] *Id.*

[132] *Id.*

[133] *Id.*

[134] *Young v. INS*, 759 F.2d 450 (5th Cir. 1985). *See also Girma v. INS*, 283 F.3d 664 (5th Cir. 2002); *Ontunez-Tursios v. Ashcroft*, 303 F.3d 341 (5th Cir. 2002) (the Fifth Circuit upheld BIA denials where the applicants failed to establish that the harm feared was "on account of" one of the five grounds.).

[135] *Young*, 759 F.2d 450.

[136] *INS v. Elias Zacarias*, 502 U.S. 478 (1992).

The five named grounds on which a claim may be based

There are five stated grounds upon which a claim to asylum may be made. Claims based on membership in a particular social group and political opinion are generally the most contested and common cases.

Membership in a particular social group

The *UNHCR Handbook* states that a "particular social group normally comprises persons of similar backgrounds, habits or social status."[137] The Ninth Circuit has defined "social group" as a collection of people closely affiliated with each other who are activated by some common impulse or interest.[138] Another court has offered the following definition: "Social group persecution must be based on a characteristic that either is beyond the power of an individual to change or is so fundamental to that individual's identity or conscience that it ought not to be required to be changed."[139]

In *Sanchez-Trujillo v. INS*, the Ninth Circuit laid out a four-part test for the determination of a claim based on social group persecution: (1) identification of a cognizable social group; (2) proof that the applicant is a group member; (3) proof that the persecution is aimed at one of the group's unifying characteristics; and (4) evidence of special circumstances that merit the recognition of a group-based claim.[140] Proof of membership in a targeted group satisfies the objective basis for a well-founded fear of persecution.[141]

The BIA has defined a social group as membership in a group of persons, all of whom share a common immutable characteristic such as sex, kinship, or, in some cases, former military leadership or land ownership.[142] For example, the BIA found that former national policemen in El Salvador were a social group and that this status was an immutable characteristic upon which a claim to political asylum might be based.[143] The family may be a social group, and a showing that a family member may be subject to harm because of the political activity or opinion of another family member constitutes a basis for political asylum.[144] Treatment of family members is a sig-

---

[137] *UNHCR Handbook*, *supra* note 14, para. 77.

[138] *See DeValle v. INS*, 901 F.2d 787, 793 (9th Cir. 1990).

[139] *Ananeh-Firempong v. INS*, 766 F.2d 621 (1st Cir. 1985).

[140] *Sanchez-Trujillo v. INS*, 801 F.2d 1571, 1574–75 (9th Cir. 1986).

[141] *Compare Kotasz v. INS*, 31 F.3d 847, 852 (9th Cir. 1994) ("It would not have been necessary for each individual Jew to await a personal visit to his door by Nazi storm troopers in order to show a well founded fear of persecution."), *with Avetova-Elisseva v. INS*, 213 F.3d 1192, 1204 (9th Cir. 2000) (holding that because some "Armenians are persecuted and some are not, Armenians in Russia do not face one of the more extreme situations in which members of an entire group … are systematically persecuted.").

[142] *Matter of Acosta*, 19 I&N Dec. 211 (BIA 1985).

[143] *Matter of Fuentes*, 19 I&N Dec. 658 (BIA 1988); *see also Velarde v. INS*, 140 F.3d 1305 (9th Cir. 1998).

[144] *Thomas v. Gonzales*, 409 F.3d 1177 (9th Cir. 2005); *Campos-Guardado v. INS*, 809 F.2d 285 (5th Cir. 1987); *see Matter of Acosta* 19 I&N Dec. 211, 216 (BIA 1985) (listing "kinship" as a characteristic of social group membership or political opinion); *Hernandez-Ortiz v. INS*, 777 F.2d 509, 516 (9th Cir. 1985) (peti-

continued

nificant factor in determining the reasonableness of an individual's fear of persecution on account of membership in a particular social group.[145]

Harm suffered because of membership in a clan or tribe may be persecution on account of membership in a particular social group. Clan membership is a characteristic fundamental to one's "identity or conscience" that one cannot change or should not be required to change.[146] The BIA found that young women of a particular tribe who fear FGM as practiced in that country constitute a particular social group.[147] Individuals associated with a former government and members of a tribe may be classified as a social group, as well as educated individuals and professionals.[148] Students may be classified as a social group only if the evidence shows that the persecutor persecutes students as a group.[149] Union members may constitute a social group for purposes of asylum if the members are persecuted on account of their union membership.[150]

The BIA has held that urban working-class males who have not served in the military or demonstrated their loyalty to the government are not a social group.[151] The fact that statistics show that many of the individuals who were persecuted fell into this category of people does not mean that they qualify as members of a particular social group.[152]

It also has been ruled that the term "particular social group" was not intended for the protection of members of the criminal class merely upon a showing that the foreign country deals with criminals even more harshly than this country does.[153]

GENDER-BASED CLAIMS

Gender-based claims have been the focus of several BIA decisions. DHS also has developed guidelines for adjudicating gender-related claims.[154] In 1996, the BIA found that fear of FGM by a woman from a certain tribe in Togo was a basis for asy-

---

tioner's evidence indicating that family had suffered threats and violence at the hands of Salvadoran security forces demonstrated a clear probability of persecution).

[145] *See Chen v. Ashcroft*, 289 F.3d 1113, 1115 (9th Cir. 2002) (distinguishing *Estrada-Posadas v. INS*, 924 F.2d 916, 919 (9th Cir. 1991), which held that "family is not a particular social group" by noting that the family in *Estrada-Posadas* consisted of a "cousin" of, an "uncle," and "relatives" while the family of petitioner Chen was the nuclear family and could be considered a particular social group); *see also Gebremichael v. INS*, 10 F.3d 28 (1st Cir. 1993); *Matter of V–T–S–*, 21 I&N Dec. 792 (BIA 1997) (BIA member Lory Rosenberg, dissenting).

[146] *Matter of H*, 21 I&N Dec. 337 (BIA 1996).

[147] *Matter of Kasinga*, 21 I&N Dec. 357, 365 (BIA 1996).

[148] *See Ananeh-Firempong*, 766 F.2d 621 (1st Cir. 1985).

[149] *See Matter of Villalta*, 20 I&N Dec. 142 (BIA 1990).

[150] *Bernal-Garcia v. INS*, 852 F.2d 144 (5th Cir. 1988).

[151] *Matter of Sanchez and Escobar*, 19 I&N Dec. 276 (BIA 1985).

[152] *Id.*

[153] *Bastanipour v. INS*, 980 F.2d 1129 (7th Cir. 1992).

[154] *See* "INS Publishes Gender Persecution Guidelines," 22 *Interpreter Releases* 771 (1995).

lum on account of membership in a particular social group.[155] In another case, a Haitian female activist in a church group that supported then-Haitian President Jean Bertrand Aristide had been repeatedly gang-raped and beaten; she was granted asylum by the BIA, which found that she was persecuted on account of her religious beliefs and her political support of Aristide.[156]

In *Matter of R–A–*, a precedent decision dealing with victims of domestic violence, the BIA stated that women who were victims of domestic violence were not a particular social group eligible for asylum.[157] The BIA found that it was not sufficient to establish merely the particular characteristics of the social group.[158] It held that the applicant must specifically show that the persecutor intends to harm the victim because of these characteristics—the nexus was missing.[159] In addition, where the government fails to provide protection to the victim—in this case, the spousal victim of domestic abuse—it must be shown that governmental authorities somehow are in favor of the harm suffered, and are not merely negligent in their duties.[160] Although the applicant had been "terribly abused" by her spouse and had a "genuine and reasonable fear of returning to Guatemala," she was denied asylum because she failed to prove that the intent of her husband's actions was to harm her because of her membership in a particular social group, and because she failed to prove the connection to the particular social group of which she was a member, *i.e.*, "Guatemalan women involved intimately with male companions who believe that women should live under male domination." Also, she failed to show that her husband's actions represented "desired behavior within Guatemala or that the Guatemalan government encourages domestic abuse."[161] Then–Attorney General Janet Reno withdrew the BIA's decision and remanded the case back to the BIA ordering reconsideration when proposed asylum regulations affecting gender-based claims become finalized.[162] DHS has since dropped the government's opposition to a grant of asylum. In February 2004, DHS stated that R–A– had a well-founded fear of persecution and that "married women in Guatemala who are unable to leave the relationship" qualify as a social group.[163] However, the current Attorney General (AG) has not yet taken action and rendered a final decision in this case as of the date of this publication.

---

[155] *Matter of Kasinga*, 21 I&N Dec. 357 (BIA 1996).

[156] *Matter of D–V–*, 21 I&N Dec 77 (BIA 1993).

[157] *Matter of R–A–*, 22 I&N Dec. 906 (BIA 1999, A.G. 2001).

[158] *Id.*

[159] *Id.*

[160] *Id.*

[161] *Id.*

[162] *Matter of R–A–*, 22 I&N Dec. 906 (A.G. 2001).

[163] DHS "Position on Respondent's Eligibility for Relief" (Feb. 20, 2004), available at the Center for Gender and Refugee Studies website, *http://cgrs.uchastings.edu/documents/legal/dhs_brief_ra.pdf.*

The federal courts also have taken up the issue of gender-related claims.[164] Women opposing offensive social norms in Iran may be a social group only if the opposition to such norms is so strong that the applicant would suffer persecution rather than comply.[165] One court has recently remanded a case to the BIA for further consideration of evidence on the government's failure to protect a woman from sexual abuse at the hands of her father, and the tribal conditions under which this took place.[166]

CLAIMS BASED ON SEXUAL ORIENTATION

The BIA has found that homosexuals are a social group and that harm resulting from their sexual orientation would be persecution on account of membership in a particular social group.[167] The Ninth Circuit agrees, and has held that homosexual men with female sexual identities in Mexico constituted a particular social group as such female sexual identity was immutable because it was inherent in their identity.[168]

PATTERN OR PRACTICE CLAIMS

The asylum regulations state that where an individual establishes that there is a *pattern or practice* of persecution in his or her country of nationality or last habitual residence of groups similarly situated to the applicant on account of race, religion, nationality, membership in a particular social group, or political opinion, the individual may qualify for political asylum without the necessity of showing that he or she would be singled out for persecution.[169]

Political opinion

The definition of what constitutes a "political opinion" for purposes of asylum is another contested issue. Political opinion does not necessarily mean the expression of allegiance to a certain political ideology. It may be much broader in meaning and may be expressed through actions rather than words. In determining whether the individual has a fear based on political opinion, the adjudicator must look to the victim's political opinion that is at issue.[170] In some countries, the mere act of working to improve basic living conditions may be an expression of a political opinion.[171]

---

[164] *Mayer v. INS*, 188 F.3d 514 (9th Cir. 1999); *Safaie v. INS*, 25 F.3d 636 (8th Cir. 1994).

[165] *Id.*; *see also Fisher v. INS*, 79 F.3d 955 (9th Cir. 1996) (denying the claim of an Iranian woman based on punishment for non-compliance with gender-specific laws).

[166] *Fiadjoe v. Att'y Gen.*, 411 F.3d 135 (3d Cir. 2005).

[167] *Matter of Tenorio*, No. A72-093-558 (BIA 1999), *reported in* 70 *Interpreter Releases* 1100 (Aug. 23, 1993); *see also Matter of Taboso-Alfonso*, 20 I&N Dec. 819 (BIA 1990).

[168] *Hernandez-Montiel v. INS*, 225 F.3d 1084 (9th Cir. 2000).

[169] 8 CFR §§208.13(b)(2)(iii), 1208.13(b)(2)(iii). Previously, INS had demanded that an individual prove that he or she would be "singled out" for persecution in order to be eligible for relief.

[170] *INS v. Elias-Zacarias*, 502 U.S. 478 (1992).

[171] *Compare Osorio v. INS*, 18 F.3d 1017, 1029–30 (2d Cir. 1994) (holding that because the government perceived the petitioner's union activities as threatening to its political power, his activities could be considered "political opinion"), *with Ontunez-Tursios v. Ashcroft*, 303 F.3d 341 (5th Cir. 2002)

continued

Failure to show a nexus to political opinion can often be the basis upon which a claim is denied.[172]

IMPUTED POLITICAL OPINION

The existence of a generalized political motive underlying a *persecutor's* actions is insufficient to establish that the feared persecution is on account of political opinion. However, there have been several cases that stand for the proposition that even where an individual may not actually have a particular political opinion, it may be "imputed" to him or her by the persecutor.[173] In *Hernandez-Ortiz v. INS*, the Ninth Circuit recognized that a claim to asylum based on an *imputed political opinion* had always been legitimate.[174] It was irrelevant whether a victim actually possessed the political opinion as long as the persecutor believed that he or she did.[175] *Hernandez-Ortiz* also stands for the proposition that an individual need not prove to a certainty what was in the mind of the persecutor; in some cases, it may be presumed. In *Hernandez-Ortiz*, the court stated:

> [W]here a government exerts its military strength against an individual or a group within its population, and there is no reason to believe that the individual or group has engaged in any criminal activity or other conduct that would provide a legitimate basis for governmental action, the most reasonable presumption is that the government actions are politically motivated.[176]

The Supreme Court's 1992 decision in *INS v. Elias-Zacarias* raised the issue as to whether imputed political opinion constitutes a valid basis for political asylum.[177] The then-INS General Counsel issued two legal opinions stating that, in his opinion, the Supreme Court has not ruled out the possibility of an "imputed" political opinion as the basis for a claim to asylum.[178] He stated that it could be proven by direct or circumstantial evidence that a law of general applicability is used to punish an individual in such a way that the punishment is "obviously directed at real or perceived enemies rather than the ordinary lawbreakers."[179] Direct evidence would include statements by the persecutor to the effect that violators of the law are to be regarded not just as ordinary lawbreakers, but as political enemies.[180]

(holding that the petitioner was not persecuted because of "political opinion" when it was evident that he, along with other *campesinos*, was being persecuted simply to vacate a piece of property).

[172] *See Campos-Guardado v. INS*, 809 F.2d 285 (5th Cir. 1987).

[173] *See Hernandez-Ortiz v. INS*, 777 F.2d 509, 516 (9th Cir. 1985); *see also Lazo-Majano v. INS*, 813 F.2d 1432 (9th Cir. 1987), *overruled on other grounds by Fisher v. INS*, 79 F.3d 955 (9th Cir. 1996)).

[174] *See Hernandez-Ortiz*, 777 F.2d 509.

[175] *Id.* at 517; *see also Argueta v. INS*, 759 F.2d 1395, 1397 (9th Cir. 1985).

[176] *Hernandez-Ortiz*, 777 F.2d at 516; *see also Desir v. Ilchert*, 840 F.2d 723 (9th Cir. 1988).

[177] *INS v. Elias-Zacarias*, 502 U.S. 478 (1992).

[178] Legal Opinions of Grover J. Rees III, *reproduced in* 14 *Interpreter Releases* 485 (Apr. 12, 1993).

[179] *Id.*

[180] *Id.*

Several federal court decisions issued subsequent to *INS v. Elias-Zacarias* have reaffirmed the principle of imputed political opinion.[181] The BIA also has indicated that imputed political opinion is a valid basis for a claim.[182] There are presently proposed regulations that, if enacted, will incorporate the doctrine that imputed political opinion is a legitimate ground for asylum.[183]

ACTIONS AS AN EXPRESSION OF POLITICAL OPINION

Actions that constitute a manifestation of a political opinion, as opposed to verbal expression of the opinion, also may be grounds for a claim to asylum.[184] Death threats by individuals on one side of a civil war against a person suspected of being on the other side may be considered to be on account of the victim's political opinion. Even if the origin of the threats was personal in nature, if it can be shown that there are ideological, as well as personal, aspects to the threats, those threats may reach a level of persecution on account of the victim's supposed political opinion vis-à-vis his or her actions.[185] For example, the BIA has ruled that a beating and death threats made by a guerrilla group against an individual who refused to pay guerrillas' "revolutionary tax" were not persecution on account of political opinion (*i.e.*, the refusal was not seen as an act of political opinion and thus, the victim was not harmed for her political opinion), but rather were criminal extortion efforts and, therefore, not sufficient for a claim to asylum.[186]

NEUTRALITY AND REFUSAL TO PERFORM MILITARY SERVICE

One of the major issues as to what constitutes a political opinion involves the question of neutrality. Several federal court decisions have recognized neutrality as a political opinion upon which a claim to asylum may be based. The Ninth Circuit has stated that refusal to perform military service is considered a political opinion; however, the applicant must prove that the decision to refuse service was a conscious choice.[187] This rationale has been followed in several other court decisions where the courts have overturned BIA denials on this issue.[188]

---

[181] *See, e.g.*, *Canas-Segovia v. INS*, 970 F.2d 599 (9th Cir. 1992); *Singh v. Ilchert*, 801 F. Supp. 313 (N.D. Cal. 1992).

[182] *Matter of C–A–L–*, 21 I&N Dec. 754 (BIA 1997).

[183] Asylum and Withholding Definitions, 65 Fed. Reg. 76588 (Dec. 7, 2000) (to be codified at 8 CFR §§208, 1208).

[184] *Turcios v. INS*, 821 F.2d 1396 (9th Cir. 1987); *see also Osorio v. INS*, 18 F.3d 1017 (2d Cir. 1994).

[185] *Gomez-Saballos v. INS*, 79 F.3d 912 (9th Cir. 1996).

[186] *Matter of T–M–B–*, 21 I&N Dec. 775 (BIA 1997). *But see Borja v. INS*, 175 F.3d 732 (9th Cir. 1999) (stating that harm as a result of refusal to pay extortion taxes to the revolutionary Communist group actively opposing the government was persecution on account of political opinion).

[187] *Bolanos-Hernandez v. INS*, 767 F.2d 1277, 1286 (9th Cir. 1984).

[188] *See, e.g.*, *Maldonado-Cruz v. INS*, 883 F.2d 788 (9th Cir. 1989); *Canas-Segovia v. INS*, 970 F.2d 599, 601 (9th Cir. 1992).

Even in cases where the federal courts have affirmed BIA denials of applications for political asylum in other circuit courts, there is an implication that neutrality may be a political opinion if certain criteria are met.[189] In *Umanzor-Alvarado v. INS*, the First Circuit has stated that neutrality may be a political opinion where the alien affirmatively chooses to stay neutral, articulates this opinion, and has been or reasonably could be singled out for persecution on this basis.[190]

In *Turcios v. INS*, the Ninth Circuit reaffirmed its holding that neutrality may be a political opinion.[191] The Fifth Circuit has indicated that a position of neutrality during a civil war may constitute a political opinion.[192] However, an individual who previously served in the military without voicing any opinion about alleged human rights violations has shown little possibility of future persecution on account of political opinion based on his or her opposition to the military's actions.[193]

Generally, the BIA has refused to accept neutrality as a political opinion.[194] In *Matter of Vigil*, the BIA indicated that neutrality might be a basis for a claim if the claimant clearly articulated his neutrality previously and proves a threat of persecution as a result thereof.[195] However, it is recognized that refusal to participate in a conflict because of a sincere belief that one will be forced to commit atrocities may be a valid basis for a claim to asylum.[196] The BIA stated that an individual may qualify for asylum based on his or her refusal to serve in a foreign-dominated army.[197] In *Matter of Salim*, the BIA stated that an Afghani man who refused to serve in the military was justified in doing so because the Afghani army was "under Soviet command."[198] Conversely, an asylum applicant whose claim was based on a refusal to serve in the Salvadoran army was not justified because the Salvadoran army was not under foreign control.[199] In another case, the BIA stated that an individual might qualify for asylum based on a fear of punishment by the government for serving in an anti-government military group. The punishment by the government was considered

---

[189] *Del Valle v. INS*, 776 F.2d 1407 (9th Cir. 1985).

[190] *Umanzor-Alvarado v. INS*, 896 F.2d 14 (1st Cir. 1990); *see also Novoa-Umania v. INS*, 896 F.2d 1 (1st Cir. 1990).

[191] *Turcios v. INS*, 821 F.2d 1396 (9th Cir. 1987).

[192] *Coriolan v. INS*, 559 F.2d 993, 1001 (5th Cir. 1977).

[193] *Gomez-Mejia v. INS*, 56 F.3d 700 (5th Cir. 1995).

[194] *Matter of Vigil*, 19 I&N Dec. 572 (BIA 1988).

[195] *Id.*

[196] *Matter of Juarez*, A29 624 076 (I.J. Feb. 22, 1990); *see UNHCR Handbook*, *supra* note 14, para. 172 (regarding religious beliefs as a basis for refugee status).

[197] *See Matter of Salim*, 18 I&N Dec. 311 (BIA 1982).

[198] *Id.*

[199] *Matter of A–G–*, 19 I&N Dec. 502 (BIA 1987), *overruled sub nom. M.A. v. INS*, 858 F.2d 210 (4th Cir. 1988), *rev'd* 899 F.2d 304 (4th Cir. 1990).

to be persecution, not prosecution, because the government was a "totalitarian" government with no process for peaceful change.[200]

Religion

The Universal Declaration of Human Rights[201] proclaims the right to freedom of thought, conscience, and religion, including the right to manifest one's religious beliefs through teaching, practice, worship, or observation, in public or in private.[202] The *UNHCR Handbook* states the following regarding persecution based on religious grounds:

> [P]ersecution for "reasons of religion" may assume various forms, e.g., prohibition of membership in a religious community, of worship in private or in public, of religious instruction, or serious measures of discrimination imposed on persons because they practice their religion or belong to a particular religious community.[203]
>
> Mere membership of a particular religious community will normally not be enough to substantiate a claim to refugee status. There may, however, be special circumstances where mere membership can be a sufficient ground.[204]

The BIA has taken a restrictive view in certain cases based on religion. In *Matter of Canas*, two brothers who were Jehovah's Witnesses refused to serve in the Salvadoran military based on the tenets of their religion that prohibited them from participating in military service of any kind.[205] The INS did not contest the fact that the brothers were legitimate members of the Jehovah's Witnesses or that their refusal to perform military service was based on their religious beliefs.[206] Rather, the BIA denied the claim because the respondents had not shown that the government of El Salvador was aware of their religious beliefs, or that members of their religion were being persecuted in general.[207] The Ninth Circuit overturned the BIA's decision and, upholding the brothers' claim, stated that even a facially neutral statute mandating conscription may impinge on the rights of specific groups of persons.[208] The Supreme Court later overturned the circuit court's decision in *Canas* and remanded it in light of the decision in *INS v. Elias-Zacarias*.[209] The Ninth Circuit reaffirmed its grant of

---

[200] *Matter of Izatula*, 20 I&N Dec. 149 (BIA 1990).

[201] Art. 18, G.A. Res. 217A, at 71, U.N. GOAR 3d Sess., 1st Plen. mtg., U.N. Doc A/810 (Dec. 12, 1948).

[202] *UNHCR Handbook*, *supra* note 14, para. 71.

[203] *Id.* para. 72.

[204] *Id.* para 73.

[205] *Matter of Canas*, 19 I&N Dec. 697 (BIA 1988).

[206] *Id.* at 703.

[207] *Id.* at 712.

[208] *Canas-Segovia v. INS*, 902 F.2d 717 (9th Cir. 1990).

[209] *INS v. Canas-Segovia*, 502 U.S. 1086 (1992); *INS. v. Elias-Zacarias*, 502 U.S. 478 (1992).

asylum status on remand, but on the basis of imputed political opinion rather than religious belief.[210]

The Ninth Circuit again reversed the BIA in 2000, in a case based on religious persecution in which the petitioners claimed persecution in India because they were an inter-religious family.[211] The court concluded that the physical attacks, death threats, and harassment that they had suffered were aimed at stamping out their inter-faith marriage and constituted persecution based on religion.[212]

The Seventh Circuit Court of Appeals overturned the BIA's denial of asylum to an Iranian male who claimed a well-founded fear of persecution on account of his religious beliefs after he abandoned Islam for Christianity.[213] The BIA originally denied the claim for discretionary reasons and because the applicant had not "established that he has in fact converted to Christianity."[214] The circuit court, in overturning the BIA's decision, found that the offense in Muslim religious law is apostasy, or abandoning Islam for another religion.[215] While the petitioner was not baptized, nor had he joined a church, he made it clear that he renounced Islam for Christianity.[216]

In another case based on religion, the BIA overturned an IJ's denial of an asylum claim by a 21-year old Moroccan woman who had been seriously beaten on several occasions by her father.[217] She was a member of the Muslim faith, as was her father. She testified that over several years, she had been subjected to severe physical mistreatment, isolation, and deprivation of freedom by her father. She stated that she would be subjected to future persecution at the hands of her father because of the differences in their religious views, especially related to the place and treatment of women in Islam. The BIA found that she had suffered past persecution and had a well-founded fear of future persecution at the hands of her father on account of religion. Her religious beliefs differed from those of her father concerning the proper role of women in Moroccan society.[218]

Race

According to the UNHCR, the word "race" should be interpreted in a broad sense that includes "all kinds of ethnic groups."[219] Discrimination on racial grounds may amount to persecution if, as a result of the discriminatory practice, the individual's

---

[210] *Canas-Segovia*, 970 F.2d 599, 601 (9th Cir. 1992).

[211] *Maini v. INS*, 212 F.3d 1167 (9th Cir. 2000).

[212] *Id.* at 1174.

[213] *Bastanipour v. INS*, 980 F.2d 1129 (7th Cir. 1992); *see also Matter of Salama*, 11 I&N Dec. 536 (BIA 1966).

[214] *Bastanipour*, 980 F.2d at 1132.

[215] *Id.*

[216] *Id.*

[217] *Matter of S–A–*, 22 I&N Dec. 1328 (BIA 2000).

[218] *Id.*

[219] *UNHCR Handbook*, *supra* note 14, para. 68.

human dignity is affected to such an extent as to be "incompatible with the most elementary and inalienable human rights."[220] Repeated and serious discriminatory practices may rise to the level of persecution, especially where combined with other forms of harm.[221]

While the mere fact of belonging to a certain racial group is not normally sufficient to prove eligibility for asylum, there may be situations where, due to the persecutor's treatment of that group as a whole, mere membership will be a sufficient ground to fear persecution.[222]

Nationality

There are few cases defining the term "nationality." Again, as in the interpretation of what constitutes persecution based on race, the best explanation of the term comes from the *UNHCR Handbook*. Paragraphs 74 through 76 define the term "nationality" as follows:

> [The] term "nationality" in this context is not to be understood only as "citizenship." It refers also to membership of an ethnic group or linguistic group and may occasionally overlap with the term "race". Persecution for reasons of nationality may consist of adverse attitudes and measures directed against a national (ethnic, linguistic) minority and in certain circumstances the fact of belonging to such a minority may in itself give rise to a well-founded fear of persecution.
>
> The co-existence within the boundaries of a State of two or more national (ethnic, linguistic) groups may create situations of conflict and also situations of persecution or danger of persecution. It may not always be easy to distinguish between persecution for reasons of nationality and persecution for reasons of political opinion when a conflict between national groups is combined with political movements, particularly where a political movement is identified with a specific "nationality".
>
> Whereas in most cases persecution by reason of nationality is feared by persons belonging to a national minority, there have been many cases in various continents where a person belonging to a majority group may fear persecution by a dominant minority.[223]

Persecution based on this ground is becoming more common as ethnic, racial, and linguistic minority groups within a country struggle for independence.[224] One circuit

---

[220] *Id.* para. 69.

[221] *Id.* paras. 53–55

[222] *Id.* para. 70.

[223] *Id.* paras. 74–76.

[224] *See Matter of O–Z– and I–Z–*, 22 I&N Dec. 23 (BIA 1998) (granting asylum to a father and son who suffered threats, beatings, and harassment by anti-Semitic individuals/groups in Russia).

court has stated that it is not even necessary for an individual to establish his or her nationality in order to qualify for asylum on the basis of this ground.[225]

Basis for Mandatory Asylum Denial—8 CFR §§208.13(c), 1208.13(c)

Conviction by a final judgment of a particularly serious crime

Conviction by a final judgment of a particularly serious crime means that the alien constitutes a danger to the United States. INA §208(b)(i) states that an alien who has been convicted of an aggravated felony (as defined at INA §101(a)(43)) "shall be considered to have committed a particularly serious crime." This definition applies to all convictions no matter when entered. Any alien convicted of an aggravated felony is barred from eligibility for asylum.[226] The BIA has ruled that this bar applies to asylum applicants who filed prior to the date of enactment of IMMACT90[227] where the appeal is heard by the BIA after the date of enactment since the law to be applied is the law existing at the time of "final adjudication."[228]

Firm resettlement in a third country

An applicant found to have been firmly resettled in a third country is not eligible for asylum in the United States.[229] Firm resettlement has been defined as an offer of permanent resident status, citizenship, or "some other type of permanent resettlement" in another country, unless it is shown that the stay in that country was a necessary consequence of flight and that the alien stayed only long enough to arrange further travel without establishing significant ties. Firm resettlement will not be found where the living conditions for the alien are "substantially and consciously restricted" in comparison to the living conditions, rights, and privileges available to other residents of the country.[230]

National security

Asylum will be denied if there are reasonable grounds for regarding the applicant as a danger to the security of the United States.[231]

Persecution of others

An asylum applicant is ineligible if he or she has participated in any way in the persecution of others.[232] This includes ordering, inciting, assisting, or otherwise par-

---

[225] *See Dulane v. INS*, 46 F.3d 988 (10th Cir. 1995).

[226] 8 CFR §§208.13(c), 1208.13(c).

[227] Immigration Act of 1990, Pub. L. No. 101-649, 104 Stat. 4978.

[228] *Matter of U–M–*, 20 I&N Dec. 327 (BIA 1991). The asylum claim, although filed prior to the date of enactment of IMMACT90, was pending with the court at the time of enactment, and the court ruled that the law to be applied was the law in effect at the time of adjudication.

[229] INA §208(b)(2); 8 CFR §§208.13(c)(2)(i)(B), 1208.13(c)(2)(i)(B).

[230] See 8 CFR §§208.15, 1208.15, for definition of firm resettlement.

[231] 8 CFR §§208.13(c)(2)(i)(C), 1208.13(c)(2)(i)(C).

[232] 8 CFR §§208.13(c)(2)(i)(E), 1208.13(c)(2)(i)(E).

ticipating in the persecution of another on account of any of the five statutory grounds.[233]

Terrorist activity

Terrorists or those likely to engage in terrorism are not eligible for asylum.[234]

Other bars to asylum eligibility—INA §208(a)(2)

Safe third country

Asylum is not available to an individual whom the AG has determined may be removed, pursuant to a bilateral or multilateral agreement, to a country where his or her life or freedom would not be threatened on account of one of the five statutory grounds and where he or she would have access to a fair refugee procedure, unless the AG finds that it is in the public interest for the alien to receive asylum.[235] Under the terms of the U.S.–Canada Safe Third Country Agreement,[236] an individual seeking asylum must apply in whichever country he or she reaches first.

Time limit

Asylum is not available to an individual who has not filed an application within one year of arrival into the United States unless he or she can show the existence of changed conditions materially affecting the applicant's eligibility for asylum or extraordinary circumstances relating to the delay in filing the application within the one-year period.[237] An individual who has had Temporary Protective Status (TPS), parole, or other lawful status is given a reasonable period of time to file after the expiration of such status.[238] The one-year filing deadline is generally measured as of the date the application is received by U.S. Citizenship and Immigration Services (USCIS); however, where the applicant can show clear and convincing evidence of having mailed the application within one year of arrival, the mailing date may be considered as the filing date rather than the date USCIS received the application. New applications for asylum filed with the immigration court must be filed in court before the IJ.[239] AG decisions regarding timeliness of asylum requests are not reviewable by any court. The Eleventh Circuit affirmed, pointing to the plain language of the statute

---

[233] *Id.*

[234] 8 CFR §§208.13(c)(2)(i)(F), 1208.13(c)(2)(i)(F).

[235] INA §208(a)(2)(A).

[236] Agreement Between the Government of Canada and the Government of The United States of America for Cooperation in the Examination of Refugee Status Claims from Nationals of Third Countries (Dec. 5, 2002), available at *www.cic.gc.ca/english/policy/safe-third.html.*

[237] INA §208(a)(2)(B) (effective for applications filed on or after April 1, 1998).

[238] 8 CFR §§208.4(a)(5), 1208.4(a)(5).

[239] 8 CFR §§208.4(a)(2), 1208.4(a)(2).

at INA §208(a)(3), that the statute clearly indicates that Congress intended to restrict judicial review.[240] Other circuits also have found there is no jurisdiction.[241]

EXCEPTIONS TO THE ONE-YEAR RULE: CHANGED OR EXTRAORDINARY CIRCUMSTANCES

The one-year deadline may be excused where there is a showing of "changed circumstances," including changes in country conditions; changes in the applicant's circumstances that materially affect the applicant's eligibility for asylum; and the loss of derivative status for an individual who had previously been considered a dependent in the principal family member's application for asylum.[242] The application must be filed within a "reasonable" period of time after the applicant becomes aware of the changed circumstances.

In addition, a showing of "extraordinary circumstances" may excuse a failure to file within the one-year deadline. The extraordinary circumstances must be directly related to the applicant's failure to apply within the one-year deadline and may include serious mental or physical disability, including effects of persecution; legal disability; and ineffective assistance of counsel if the applicant submits a detailed summary of legal agreement with counsel, a summary of the representations made by counsel and the failure to meet them, proof of notification of the allegations to the attorney, and an indication of whether the appropriate disciplinary authorities have been notified.

The BIA has found that any unaccompanied minor who is in the custody of U.S. Immigration and Customs Enforcement (ICE) pending removal proceedings during the one-year period following arrival has established extraordinary circumstances excusing his or her failure to file within one year of arrival.[243]

Previously denied application

If an individual has previously been denied asylum, he or she is not eligible for asylum unless there is a showing of changed conditions.[244]

Reinstatement of prior removal/deportation orders

DHS takes the position that those who have been previously deported, excluded, or removed, and later re-enter the United States illegally, are ineligible for asylum or other forms of relief (except withholding of removal) upon reinstatement of the prior order of deportation, exclusion, or removal.[245] Where a person re-entering the country subsequent to an order of removal comes to DHS's attention, he or she may express

---

[240] *Fahim v. INS*, 278 F.3d 1216 (11th Cir. 2002).

[241] *Bejet-Violi-al-Jojo v. Gonzales*, 424 F.3d 823 (8th Cir. 2005); *Sharari v. Gonzales*, 407 F.3d. 467 (1st Cir. 2005); *Hakeem v. INS*, 273 F.3d 812, 815 (9th Cir. 2001).

[242] 8 CFR §§208.4(a)(4), 1208.4(a)(4).

[243] *Matter of Y–C–*, 23 I&N Dec. 286 (BIA 2002).

[244] INA §208(a)(2)(C).

[245] 8 CFR §§241.8, 1241.8; INA §241(a)(5); .

fear of returning to his or her country and seek asylum. The individual will be given a reasonable fear interview and a chance to seek withholding of removal.[246]

Frivolous applications

An applicant who files for asylum after April 1, 1997, and is determined to have knowingly filed a frivolous application is *barred permanently from any benefits under the INA*. A frivolous application is one in which any of the material elements is deliberately fabricated.[247]

The First Circuit decision regarding frivolous asylum claims was adopted by the Eleventh Circuit in December 2001. The IJ held that a Cuban citizen who applied for asylum twice and lied on the first application was not a sincere applicant, but was only using the asylum claim as a ruse in an attempt to reunite with family members already present in the United States. Moreover, based on his prior frauds, his testimony was not credible. The BIA affirmed, holding that he knowingly filed a frivolous asylum application, as defined under INA §208(d)(6), and was not entitled to asylum or refugee status. The Eleventh Circuit held that it was obligated to give due deference to the agency's strict no-tolerance statutory interpretation that applicants must tell the truth or be removed.[248]

Termination of Asylum—8 CFR §§208.24(f), 1208.24(f)

A grant of asylum by the IJ or the BIA may be revoked where DHS establishes by a preponderance of the evidence that one of the following grounds is applicable:[249]

- country conditions have fundamentally changed so that there is no longer a well-founded fear; or
- a showing of fraud in the application such that the applicant was ineligible at the time the claim was granted; or
- the alien has committed an act that would be a ground for mandatory denial under 8 CFR §§208.13(c),1208.13(c), *e.g.*, a particularly serious crime; or
- for applications filed after April 1, 1997, the existence of one of the grounds listed in INA §208(c)(2).

Termination must be done pursuant to a motion to reopen proceedings.[250] Termination of the asylum status of the principal alien will result in the termination of the derivative status of the spouse or child whose status was based on a grant to the principal applicant.[251]

---

[246] 8 CFR §§208.31, 1208.31 and 241.8(e), 1241.8(e); *see also* AILF Practice Advisory, "Reinstatement of Removal" (Apr. 18, 2005), available at *www.ailf.org*.

[247] INA §208(d)(6); 8 CFR §§208.20, 1208.20.

[248] *Barreto-Clara v. INS*, 275 F.3d 1334 (11th Cir. 2001).

[249] 8 CFR §§208.24(a), 1208.24(a).

[250] 8 CFR §§208.24(f), 1208.24(f).

[251] 8 CFR §§208.24(d), 1208.24(d).

Accompanying or Following to Join—8 CFR §§208.21, 1208.21

Spouses (as defined in INA §101(a)(35)) or children (as defined in INA §101(b)(1)) may be granted asylum under INA §208(b)(3) if "accompanying or following to join" the principal alien.[252] The relationship must have existed at the time the principal's application was approved. If the derivative beneficiary is a child, it qualifies if it was *in utero* when the parent was granted asylum.[253]

Form I-730 is used to file for the spouse or children accompanying or following to join. The principal alien must submit evidence to prove the spousal or parent-child relationship. The application is filed with the Nebraska Service Center. If approved, it is forwarded to the appropriate consulate for processing of the spouse and children.

Elements of a Withholding of Removal Claim

Introduction

Withholding of removal (formerly withholding of deportation) is a form of relief distinct from asylum. Although similar in some ways to a claim for asylum, it carries a higher burden of proof and, if granted, provides less relief than asylum. Like asylum, there must be some past harm or threat of future harm by an entity and it must be "on account of" one of the five statutory grounds. Unlike asylum, it is a mandatory—not discretionary—form of relief, if eligibility is proven.

Generally, withholding of removal is an alternative form of relief for persons who have been refused asylum based on statutory ineligibility (resettlement, certain crimes, and failure to file within one year of arrival) or a discretionary denial by the asylum adjudicator.[254] An application for asylum is deemed to constitute at the same time an application for withholding of removal.

Clear probability standard

An individual seeking withholding of removal under INA §241(b)(3) must show that his or her life or freedom would be threatened upon return to his or her homeland on account of one or more of the five reasons enumerated above for an asylum claim—race, religion, nationality, political opinion, or membership in a particular social group. The applicant for withholding of removal must show a "clear probability" of the threat to life or freedom if deported to his or her country of nationality. The Supreme Court has interpreted the clear probability standard to mean that the

---

[252] 8 CFR §§208.21(a), 1208.21(a).

[253] 8 CFR §§208.21(b), 1208.21(b).

[254] INA §§208(a) *and* (b). *Cf. Desta v. Ashcroft*, 329 F.3d 1179 (10th Cir. 2003) (the BIA did not abuse its discretion in finding the aliens statutorily ineligible for asylum by reason of their firm resettlement in Canada because of their protracted stay in that country, their status as landed immigrants, and the birth of their son, a Canadian citizen); *Tarrawally v. Ashcroft*, 338 F.3d 180 (3d Cir. 2003) (court of appeals lacked jurisdiction to review an asylum petition that the IJ and BIA deemed untimely); *Tsevgemid v. Ashcroft*, 318 F.3d 1226 (10th Cir. 2003) (court of appeals lacked jurisdiction to review an asylum petition that the IJ and BIA deemed untimely).

alien must show that it is "more likely than not that the alien would be persecuted in the country to which he was deported."[255] This language has been incorporated into the regulations at 8 CFR §§208.16(b)(1), 1208.16(b)(1). The standard has been defined by the Supreme Court as a different and higher standard than the "well-founded fear" standard required to prove eligibility for asylum.[256] Since the withholding of removal standard is higher than that required for asylum, an alien who does not meet the "well-founded fear" standard required for asylum cannot meet the higher "clear probability" standard for withholding of removal.[257] If an applicant for asylum is denied solely for discretionary reasons, but the applicant is later granted withholding of removal, thereby precluding the admission of his or her spouse and children, the denial of the asylum claim shall be reconsidered.[258]

Differences between withholding of removal and asylum

Withholding of removal, unlike asylum, is a mandatory form of relief.[259] The approval of an application for withholding of removal, however, does not give the applicant legal residence or other status within the United States. It merely prohibits the return of the applicant to the specific country where his or her life or freedom has been threatened.[260] If the government can find a third country that will accept the alien, he or she may be removed to that country.[261]

Individuals granted withholding of removal are not eligible to seek adjustment of status after one year, as are individuals granted asylum, nor can their spouses or children gain any derivative status if accompanying or following to join the principal alien, as can family members of asylees.[262] However, certain bars to asylum do not apply to withholding of removal. For example, resettlement in a third country prior to coming to the United States is not a bar to withholding of removal,[263] nor is failing to file within one year of admission. Some individuals with convictions for aggravated felonies may be eligible to seek withholding of removal in certain (rare) circumstances, while an aggravated felon is never eligible for asylum.[264]

The evidentiary rules for adjudication of a request for withholding of removal are similar to those involved with the adjudication of an asylum request (see discussion on "Evidentiary Burden," *infra*). The testimony of the individual, if credible, may be

---

[255] *INS v. Stevic*, 467 U.S. 407, 429–30 (1984).

[256] *INS v. Cardoza-Fonseca*, 480 U.S. 421, 444 (1987).

[257] *Matter of Fuentes*, 19 I&N Dec. 658, 660 (BIA 1988).

[258] 8 CFR §§208.16(e), 1208.16(e).

[259] *See* INA §241(b)(3); *see also* 8 CFR §§208.16(d)(1), 1208.16(d)(1).

[260] *Matter of Salim*, 18 I&N Dec. 311 (BIA 1982).

[261] 8 CFR §§208.16(f), 1208.16(f).

[262] *See* 8 CFR §§208.21, 1208.21.

[263] *See* 8 CFR §§208.16(d)(2), 1208.16(d)(2).

[264] *Matter of S–S–*, 22 I&N Dec. 458 (BIA).

sufficient to sustain the burden without corroboration.[265] Upon a showing of past persecution, it may be presumed that life or freedom of the applicant would be threatened upon return unless there is evidence that conditions have changed, such that it is no longer "more likely than not" that he or she would be persecuted.[266] If there is a pattern or practice of persecution against a particular group, the applicant need not establish that he or she would be singled out for persecution upon return if he or she establishes inclusion in and identification with this group.[267]

Bars to withholding of removal

Certain individuals are disqualified from eligibility for withholding of removal.[268] They include:

- those who have ordered, assisted, incited, or otherwise participated in the persecution of any person on account of race, religion, nationality, political opinion, or membership in a particular social group;
- those who, having been convicted by a final judgment of a particularly serious crime, constitute a danger to the community of the United States. An aggravated felony is considered to be a particularly serious crime per se. An individual convicted of an aggravated felony and sentenced to a term of imprisonment of five or more years is barred from receiving withholding of removal.[269] Where the sentence for the aggravated felony conviction is less than five years, there is a rebuttable presumption that it is a particularly serious crime depending on the facts and circumstances of the crime;
- those about whom there are reasons for considering that they have committed a serious crime outside the United States prior to arrival; and
- those about whom there are reasonable grounds to believe that they pose a threat to the security of the United States.

DHS takes the position that an individual previously removed or deported who returns to the United States illegally after the prior order may have that prior order reinstated, and that person, therefore, would be ineligible for withholding of removal or asylum relief in immigration court.[270]

Evidentiary Burden in Asylum and Withholding of Removal Claims

There is no set rule defining the applicant's burden in proving a well-founded fear. The Second Circuit has held that a well-founded fear of persecution may be estab-

---

[265] 8 CFR §§208.16(b), 1208.16(b).

[266] 8 CFR §§208.16(b)(1)(i), 1208.16(b)(1)(i).

[267] 8 CFR §§208.16(b)(2)(i)–(ii), 1208.16(b)(2)(i)–(ii).

[268] 8 CFR §§208.16(d)(2), 1208.16(d)(2).

[269] *See In re Q–T–M–T–*, 21 I&N Dec. 639 (BIA 1996).

[270] *See* INA §241(a)(5); *see also* 8 CFR §§241.8(d), 1241.8(d).

lished where the possibility of persecution is less than 50 percent.[271] The Supreme Court has stated that there may be cases where an individual with a 10 percent chance of persecution may be eligible for asylum.[272] However, in all cases, an applicant must establish an objective basis for his or her subjective fear. No matter how real the fear feels, it will not suffice if an objective basis for the fear is not established.[273] For a withholding of removal claim, the burden is to prove that there is better than a 50 percent chance that life or freedom will be threatened.[274]

Corroborating evidence

In proving one's claim, the major problem is that most refugees arrive at U.S. borders with little more than the shirts on their backs. The BIA has recognized this problem and stated that an alien's own testimony, without corroborative evidence, may be sufficient to prove a well-founded fear of persecution when the testimony is believable, consistent, and sufficiently detailed to provide a plausible and coherent account of the basis for the fear.[275] However, in several precedent decisions, the BIA appears to be taking a more restrictive view on whether testimony alone is adequate to meet one's burden. For example, in *Matter of Y–B–*, a Mauritanian applicant who failed to produce documentation of his stay in a refugee camp or other corroborative evidence was denied.[276] The BIA held that the "general and vague nature of the respondent's testimony was not remedied by a showing of specific and detailed corroborative evidence."[277] The testimony was described as "sketchy"[278] and "meager."[279]

In *Matter of M–D–*, another Mauritanian asylum-seeker who did not produce documentary evidence to corroborate his purported identity, nationality, claim of persecution, or former presence in a refugee camp was denied asylum.[280] The BIA found that the applicant failed to submit documentation to support his testimony where it was "reasonable" to do so, and denied the claim.[281] There was no claim that the re-

---

[271] *Carcamo-Flores v. INS*, 805 F.2d 60 (2d Cir. 1986).

[272] *INS v. Cardoza-Fonseca*, 480 U.S. 421, 440 (1987).

[273] *Id.*

[274] *INS v. Stevic*, 467 U.S. 407 (1984).

[275] *See Matter of V–T–S–*, 21 I&N Dec. 792, 795 (BIA 1997) (citing *Matter of Dass*, 20 I&N Dec. 120 (BIA 1989)).

[276] *Matter of Y–B–*, 21 I&N Dec. 1136 (BIA 1998).

[277] *Id.* at 1139.

[278] *Id.* at 1138.

[279] *Id.* at 1136.

[280] *Matter of M–D–*, 21 I&N Dec. 1180 (BIA 1998). *But see Ladha v. INS*, 215 F.3d 889 (disapproving the BIA's decision in *Matter of M–D–*).

[281] *Matter of M–D–*, 21 I&N Dec. 1180.

spondent lacked credibility;[282] rather, the issue was the lack of documentation other than the background materials submitted.[283]

In *Matter of O–D–*, a Mauritanian applicant submitted an identification card from Mauritania found to be counterfeit by the Forensic Document Laboratory, and a birth certificate that was "probably counterfeit."[284] The BIA also found inconsistencies between his testimony and his application.[285] Thus, it was held that all of the testimony was tainted because of the submission of the fraudulent identity document.[286] In this same case, however, the BIA acknowledged that "there may be reasons, fully consistent with the claim of asylum that will cause a person to possess false documents, such as the creation and use of a false document to escape persecution by facilitating travel."[287]

The Third Circuit addressed the matter of corroborating evidence in *Abdulai v. Ashcroft*, and determined that the BIA could require a credible applicant for asylum or withholding to provide such evidence to meet his or her burden of proof.[288] However, in this case, the court found that the BIA had failed to identify what particular aspects of petitioner's testimony the petitioner could reasonably be expected to corroborate, and that this failure violated its own procedures and prevented meaningful appellate review.[289] Therefore, the court remanded the case to the BIA for further proceedings.[290]

Like the Third Circuit, the Second Circuit holds a similar view. It has found that courts can require corroboration or at least an explanation of a lack of corroboration, but that the BIA has erred in applying the appropriate standard by failing to rule explicitly on the credibility of petitioner's testimony, failing to explain why it was reasonable to expect additional corroboration, and failing to assess the sufficiency of petitioner's explanation for the absence of corroborating evidence.[291]

In contrast, the Ninth Circuit has specifically rejected the BIA's holding in *Matter of M–D–*.[292] Specifically, the court noted that it "did not require corroborative evidence from applicants for asylum and withholding of deportation who have testified

---

[282] *Id.*

[283] *Id.*

[284] *Matter of O–D–*, 21 I&N Dec. 1079 (BIA 1998).

[285] *Id.*

[286] *Id.* at 1084 ("[T]he respondent compromised the integrity of his entire claim by submitting at least one fraudulent document vis-à-vis a germane aspect of his claim and by failing to explain his fraud.").

[287] *Id.* at 1083.

[288] *Abdulai v. Ashcroft*, 239 F.3d 542 (3d Cir. 2001).

[289] *Id.* at 550.

[290] *Id.* at 555.

[291] *Diallo v. INS*, 232 F.3d 279 (2d Cir. 2000).

[292] *See Ladha v. INS*, 215 F.3d 889, 899 (9th Cir. 2000).

credibly."[293] In fact, the asylum regulations state that the testimony of the applicant, if credible, may be sufficient to prove the claim.[294] However, the above-referenced BIA decisions indicate that the statement of the applicant may not be sufficient if there is any issue regarding credibility or if it is not supported by supporting documentation where available and relevant.[295]

Congress recently spoke on this issue. The REAL ID Act of 2005 states that although the testimony of the applicant may be sufficient to sustain the burden without corroboration if it is credible, the trier of fact may determine that the applicant should provide supporting documentation, and if so, "such evidence must be provided unless the applicant does not have the evidence and cannot reasonably obtain the evidence."[296]

Adjudicators' obligations in weighing evidence

Where an individual submits substantial documentation regarding country conditions in his or her native land that shows the nature and causes of persecution of others, the federal courts have stated that immigration officials and IJs must consider this documentary evidence: "[G]eneral information concerning oppressive conditions and violence in particular countries is relevant,"[297] and "presents an additional reason to take the threat seriously."[298]

The BIA has found that not only the applicant, but DHS and/or the IJ has a role in making certain that background information on country conditions is included in the record.[299] It stated that DHS should play an "active" role in introducing evidence regarding current country conditions.[300] On the role of the IJ, the BIA stated that he or she must state the source of his or her knowledge of a particular country if he or she makes reference to country conditions.[301] In addition, the BIA stated, "presentation of evidence is a proper function of an immigration judge."[302]

---

[293] *Id.*

[294] 8 CFR §§208.13(a), 1208.13(a).

[295] *See Matter of Dass*, 20 I&N Dec. 120 (BIA 1989).

[296] Emergency Supplemental Appropriations Act for Defense, the Global War on Terror, and Tsunami Relief, 2005, Division B, Pub. L. No. 109-13, 119 Stat. 231.

[297] *Hernandez-Ortiz v. INS*, 777 F.2d 509, 515 (9th Cir. 1985).

[282] *Id.* (citing *Bolanos-Hernandez v. INS*, 767 F.2d 1277, 1285 (9th Cir. 1984). *See also Castaneda-Hernandez v. INS*, 826 F.2d 1526, 1531 (6th Cir. 1987) (remanding the case back to the BIA and stating that "the Board should provide a more detailed review of the affidavits and other materials in the record suggesting the possibility of a well-founded fear of persecution").

[299] *Matter of S–M–J–*, 21 I&N Dec. 722 (BIA 1997).

[300] *Id.*

[301] *Id.*

[302] *Id.*

Department of State opinions and other sources

According to the regulations, the application for asylum and supporting information must be forwarded to the Department of State (DOS) for an opinion on the application. DOS may comment at its option, and it may provide the following:

- an assessment of the assertions regarding country conditions and the applicant's experiences in that country;
- an assessment of likely treatment of the applicant upon return;
- information on the persecution of others "similarly situated";
- information on possible mandatory denials under 8 CFR §§208.14, 1208.14 (*e.g.*, firm resettlement); and
- other relevant information.[303]

The asylum regulations state that the asylum adjudicator may rely on credible sources of information regarding country conditions from sources other than the opinion from DOS, including "international organizations, private voluntary agencies or academic institutions."[304] The current regulations place a greater emphasis on the value of reports from human rights organizations and other "background" evidence while eliminating the requirement that a DOS opinion be received in every case. In addition, under regulations and the provisions of a 1990 class action settlement between DOJ, DOS, and the plaintiffs—Salvadoran and Guatemalan asylum-seekers in the United States—a DOS recommendation of denial must articulate reasons for the recommendation and the factual consideration upon which the recommendation was based.[305] The settlement also mandates that the DOS opinions state that they are advisory only and that they are "only one of the several sources of information relevant to the applicant's claim."[306]

Newspaper and magazine articles and affidavits showing other examples of persecution may establish objective reasonableness of a claim.[307] The dismissal of this type of evidence by an IJ or the BIA should be challenged.

In addition to the applicant's statement, human rights reports, and other country reports, sources of evidence may include expert and other witnesses testifying verbally or through written statements; documentary evidence such as medical or psychological reports; photographs; and letters.[308] Last, the *UNHCR Handbook* lays down some guidelines for measuring the claim. While the burden of proof is on the applicant,[309] he

---

[303] *Koval v. Gonzales*, 418 F.3d 798 (7th Cir. 2005) (court has held that the IJ erred in relying too heavily on the State Department reports and not recognizing their limitations, while ignoring expert testimony).

[304] 8 CFR §§208.12(a), 1208.12(a).

[305] *See American Baptist Churches v. Thornburgh*, 760 F. Supp. 796 (N.D. Cal. 1991) (settlement agreement at Section 22).

[306] *Id.*

[307] *See Carcamo-Flores v. INS*, 805 F.2d 60 (2d Cir. 1986).

[308] *See Basic Law Manual*, *supra* note 26, at 99–100.

[309] 8 CFR §§208.13(a), 1208.13(a).

or she should be given the benefit of the doubt unless there are good reasons to the contrary.[310] Evidentiary requirements should not be too strictly applied in view of the difficulty refugees may have in obtaining proof of their claims.[311] The IJ should use all the means at his or her disposal to produce the necessary evidence and help resolve inconsistencies.[312] Untrue statements by themselves are not reason for refusal of refugee status;[313] rather, the statements should be examined in light of all the circumstances.[314] Taking isolated incidents out of context may be misleading; thus, the cumulative effect of the applicant's experience must be taken into account.[315] The examiner must apply all criteria in a "spirit of justice and understanding."[316]

Confidentiality—8 CFR §§208.6, 1208.6

The regulations state that the application "shall not be disclosed" without the written consent of the applicant.[317] There are certain exceptions to the confidentiality requirement, including cases where legal action is taken regarding the adjudication or failure to adjudicate an asylum claim and cases involving a civil or criminal investigation.[318] The regulations provide for authentication of foreign documents by authorities of the country where the document is issued in certain cases, and DHS sometimes requests this foreign authentication in accordance with 8 CFR §§287.6(b) or (c), 1287.6(b) or (c). However, any contact with an official or other individual from a foreign country may violate the right to confidentiality, and any investigation by DHS into a claim should be questioned and challenged if there is a risk of breaching confidentiality and possibly jeopardizing the applicant's safety.

Credibility

The BIA has issued several precedent decisions on the issue of credibility.[319] In *Matter of A–S–*, it deferred to an adverse credibility finding by the IJ where the record showed: (1) discrepancies and omissions as stated by the IJ; (2) "specific and cogent" reasons outlined by the judge concerning the inconsistencies; and (3) a lack of a convincing explanation for the discrepancies.[320] In addition, the BIA deferred to the IJ's finding that the respondent's demeanor provided an additional reason to question the

---

310 *UNHCR Handbook*, *supra* note 14, paras. 196, 203.

311 *Id.* para. 197.

312 *Id.* paras. 196, 199; *see also* 8 CFR §§208.9(b), 1208.9(b).

313 *See Damaize-Job v. INS*, 787 F.2d 1332, 1337 (9th Cir. 1986).

314 *UNHCR Handbook*, *supra* note 14, para. 199.

315 *Id.* para. 201.

316 *Id.* para. 202.

317 8 CFR §§208.6(a), 1208.6(a)

318 8 CFR §§208.6(c), 1208.6(c).

319 *See, e.g.*, *In re O–D–*, 21 I&N Dec. 1079 (BIA 1998) (relating to fraudulent documentation and the effect on credibility).

320 *In re A–S–*, 21 I&N Dec. 1106 (BIA 1998).

respondent's credibility.[321] The BIA distinguished this case from its decision in *Matter of B*, where it overturned the IJ's negative credibility finding based entirely on the judge's observation of the applicant's demeanor.[322]

The Sixth Circuit overturned a BIA decision upholding an IJ's denial of asylum where the judge's determination of lack of credibility resulted from questionable translation.[323] As the denial of the asylum was specifically based on the petitioner's testimony, the lack of proper translation of the questions and responses constituted a denial of petitioner's due process right to a full and fair hearing.[324]

The Second Circuit found that an IJ was in error for failing to evaluate the applicant's explanations before making a finding that the testimony was inconsistent, vague, unresponsive, and, therefore, lacked credibility.[325]

The Ninth Circuit reversed the BIA where it made an independent credibility finding without giving the petitioner an opportunity to establish credibility.[326] The IJ had failed to make any finding as to the petitioner's credibility.[327] The circuit court found that the BIA's independent finding violated due process.[328] Where an applicant's credibility is questioned in the immigration court because of alleged contradictions between statements made at an affirmative USCIS asylum interview and the court proceeding, there must be a reliable record of what transpired at the interview.[329] At a minimum, there must be a meaningful, clear, and reliable written summary of the statements made by the applicant to the asylum officer.[330] However, where the inconsistencies alleged are between the affirmative application itself—not the oral statement—and the statement of the applicant in court, the application itself is sufficient even in the absence of a clear written record.[331]

The REAL ID Act of 2005 also addresses the issue of credibility.[332] Specifically, it allows the IJ to consider "demeanor, candor … responsiveness of the applicant," and "inherent plausibility" as factors. REAL ID states that "there is no presumption of credibility, however if no adverse credibility determination is made, the applicant or witness shall have a rebuttable presumption of credibility on appeal."[333]

---

[321] *Id.*

[322] *Matter of B*, 21 I&N Dec. 66 (BIA 1995).

[323] *Amadou v. INS*, 226 F.3d 724 (6th Cir. 2000).

[324] *Id.*

[325] *Lin v. Dep't of Justice*, 428 F.3d 391 (2d. Cir. 2005).

[326] *Abovian v. INS*, 234 F.3d 492 (9th Cir. 2000).

[327] *Id.*

[328] *Id.*

[329] *Matter of S–S–*, 21 I&N Dec. 121 (BIA 1995).

[330] *Id.*

[331] *Matter of M–S–*, 21 I&N Dec. 125 (BIA 1995).

[332] REAL ID Act of 2005, *supra* note 74.

[333] *Id.*

Finally, the *UNHCR Handbook* addresses the issue of credibility. It has been recognized by the courts as a valuable tool for preparing and adjudicating asylum claims.[334] In addition, the *Basic Law Manual* contains an excellent summary of criteria for evaluating credibility and evidence submitted in support of a claim for asylum. Among other criteria, the *Manual* states that asylum officers should recognize and take into account the difficulty of obtaining documentary evidence as well as linguistic and cultural barriers that may cause gaps or discrepancies in the statement of the applicant, and remember that decisions to deny asylum carry serious consequences.[335]

On the issue of credibility, the *Manual* states that claims may be credible even when not made at the earliest opportunity or where the alien did not apply for asylum in a third country through which he or she passed. Minor inconsistencies are to be expected even where a second examination produces information different from or omitted from the first examination.[336] The absence of past persecution or of detection by the authorities should not lead to an assumption that the claim is not credible.[337] Even where an applicant lies about one part of a claim, the IJ may give weight to the parts of the testimony found to be credible and approve the claim based on those parts.[338]

In sum, the *Basic Law Manual* and the *UNHCR Handbook* provide a realistic and common sense approach to evaluating the credibility of an asylum applicant and the evidence submitted in support of the asylum claim.

Relief Under the Convention Against Torture

Introduction

Relief is available under the Convention Against Torture (CAT)[339] if an individual fears torture at the hands of the government in his or her country, or from individuals who have the acquiescence of that government. The CAT can provide relief if the respondent is not eligible for asylum or withholding of removal under INA§241(b)(3) because of a lack of nexus to one of the five statutory grounds, or because of a bar to asylum or withholding of removal (crime, prior persecutory acts, etc.). Furthermore,

---

[334] *Cardoza-Fonseca v. INS*, 767 F.2d 1448 (9th Cir. 1985).

[335] *See Basic Law Manual*, *supra* note 26, at 107–10.

[336] *Id.* at 102–03.

[337] *Id.* at 103.

[338] *Id.* at 108.

[339] U.N. Convention Against Torture and Other Cruel, Inhumane or Degrading Treatment or Punishment, Dec. 10, 1984, *opened for signature* Feb. 4, 1985, G.A. Res. 39/46, 39 U.N. GAOR Supp. No. 51, at 197, U.N. Doc. A/RES/39/708 (1984) (entered into force June 26, 1987), *reprinted in* 1465 U.N.T.S. 85, 23 I.L.M. 1027 (1984), *modified* 24 I.L.M.535 (1985). The United States signed the treaty on April 18, 1988, but the Senate did not adopt its resolution until October 27, 1990, and President Clinton did not deposit the ratification with the U.N. Secretary General until November 20, 1994. *See* U.N. Doc. 571 Leg./SER. E/13, IV.9 (1995). *See also* 8 CFR §§208.16–18, 1208.16–18.

the CAT does not require that the applicant show that the torture is "on account of" a specific reason.

Article 3 of the CAT prohibits the return of an individual to a country where there are substantial grounds for believing that he or she would be subject to torture. Specifically, it states that "no state shall expel, return ('refouler') or extradite a person to another state where there are substantial grounds for believing that he would be in danger of being subjected to torture."[340] The BIA has stated this in different words: "Article 3 of the Convention Against Torture prohibits refoulement of an alien to a country where it is more likely than not that he will be subjected to torture.[341] This is a relatively new form of relief available from the immigration court as of March 22, 1999. The regulations governing CAT relief are found at 8 CFR §§208.16–18, 1208.16–18. The CAT and the implementing regulations require a showing that it is more likely than not that an individual will be tortured by the government or with the acquiescence of the government if returned to his or her country.[342]

Under the CAT and the implementing regulations, the individual must establish in essence that:

- it is more likely than not;
- that he or she would be subjected to "torture";
- inflicted by, at the instigation of, or with the consent or acquiescence of;
- a public official or other person acting in an official capacity.[343]

Torture Defined

Torture is defined as "any act by which severe pain or suffering, whether physical or mental, is intentionally inflicted on a person" for such purposes as:[344]

- obtaining a confession;
- punishment for commission or suspicion of commission of an offense;
- intimidation or coercion; or
- for any reason based on discrimination of any kind.

It is an extreme form of cruel and inhuman treatment and does not extend to lesser forms of cruel, inhuman, or degrading treatment of punishment.[345] It must be inflicted at the instigation of or with the "consent or acquiescence of" a public official or other

---

340 *Id.* art. 3.

341 *Matter of G–A–*, 23 I&N Dec. 366, 367 (BIA 2002).

342 *Matter of A–H–*, 23 I&N Dec. 774 (BIA 2005).

343 8 CFR §§208.16(c)(2), 1208.16(c)(2) and 208.18(a)(1), 1208.18(a)(1).

344 8 CFR §§208.18(a)(1), 1208.18(a)(1). *See Matter of J–E–*, 23 I&N Dec. 291 (BIA 2002) (finding that indefinite detention of criminal deportees by Haitian authorities does not constitute torture where there is no evidence that the authorities intentionally and deliberately detain deportees to inflict torture).

345 8 CFR §§208.18(a)(2), 1208.18(a)(2); *see also Matter of J–E–*, 23 I&N Dec. 291.

person acting in an official capacity.[346] Torture does not include harm or suffering arising only from lawful sanctions. The regulations outline a series of actions that may constitute torture.[347] Although mental pain or suffering may constitute torture, it must be "prolonged" and caused by (or result from): the threat of death; the intentional infliction or threatened infliction of severe pain; the real or threatened application of mind altering substances or procedures calculated to disrupt "profoundly" the senses or personality; or the threat that another person will be subjected to any of the above.[348] Significantly, it need *not* be "on account of" any of the five grounds specified for asylum or withholding or removal; however, it must be intentional and not an act that results in unanticipated or unintended pain or suffering.[349] Torture must be inflicted by a person in the offender's custody or physical control.[350]

Standard of Proof—More Likely than Not

The burden is on the applicant to establish that there is a clear probability that life or freedom will be threatened if the applicant were returned to his or her country of nationality. The BIA has found that the ratification history of the CAT shows that the standard was to be the same as that of withholding of removal, *i.e.*, a clear probability.[351] The Supreme Court has determined in the withholding of removal context that the "clear probability" standard means that it is "more likely than not."[352] The applicant must show that it is "more likely than not" that he or she would be tortured if removed and returned to the home country.[353] In determining whether the burden has been met, all evidence must be considered, including:

- evidence of past torture of the applicant;
- evidence of possible relocation to a part of the country with little likelihood of torture;
- evidence of gross, flagrant, or massive human rights violations in country of removal; and
- other relevant information on conditions in the country of removal.[354]

Evidence of massive or severe human rights violations by itself does not constitute sufficient grounds for determining that the CAT claim should be approved. Specific grounds must exist to show that the person is at risk.[355] For example, "pervasive and widespread" acts of torture against Iranian prisoners resulted in a grant of a CAT

---

[346] 8 CFR §§208.18(a)(1), 1208.18(a)(1).

[347] 8 CFR §§208.18(a)(4), 1208.18(a)(4).

[348] *Id.*

[349] 8 CFR §§208.18(a)(5), 1208.18(a)(5).

[350] 8 CFR §§208.18(a)(6), 1208.18(a)(6).

[351] *Matter of J–E–*, 23 I&N Dec. 291, 302 (BIA 2002).

[352] *INS v. Stevic*, 467 U.S. 407 (1984).

[353] 8 CFR §§208.16(c)(2), 1208.16(c)(2).

[354] *Matter of J–E–*, 23 I&N Dec. 291 at 303.

[355] *Id.*

claim for an Iranian who was likely to be imprisoned based on a combination of factors including his drug-related convictions in the United States.[356] On the other hand, the fact that human rights violations are not widespread does not mean that the applicant cannot establish a claim.[357] While the individual's statement may in itself establish a claim if credible, failure to give detailed information or supporting documentation will result in a denial of the claim.[358] An application will be denied where the applicant cannot produce reliable evidence (which may be his or her testimony) to show that it is more likely than not that he or she will be subjected to torture.[359]

Instigation, Consent, or Acquiescence of a Public Official

An application for CAT relief will be denied unless some governmental connection is shown. An applicant who cannot show that the harm will be inflicted by, or with the acquiescence of the government, a public official, or other person acting in an official capacity, cannot qualify.[360] The fact that government officials may seek retribution against an individual for personal reasons does not mean that it is torture by a government official in an official capacity.[361] CAT relief does not extend to persons who will be tortured by individuals or groups merely because the government cannot control them. Torture includes acts that occur in the context of governmental authority. The government must be "willfully accepting of the acts of torture, not merely powerless to stop it."[362] Acquiescence encompasses both actual knowledge and "willful blindness."[363] Acquiescence of a public official means that the public official has awareness of the possibility of the torture prior to the activity, and, thereafter, breaches his or her duty to intervene to prevent such activity.[364]

Bars to Withholding of Removal

The CAT relief granted, if the burden is met, is withholding of removal. Withholding of removal means that the alien cannot be removed to the country of claimed persecution. The individual is permitted to remain in the United States and is granted employment authorization.[365] The applicant is ineligible for withholding of removal under the CAT if he or she has assisted in the persecution of others, presents a danger to security of the United States, has been convicted of a particularly serious crime, or if there are serious reasons to believe he or she has committed a serious nonpolitical crime

---

[356] *Matter of G–A–*, 23 I&N Dec. 366 (BIA 2002).

[357] *Id.*

[358] *Id.*

[359] *Matter of Y–L–*, 23 I&N Dec. 270 (BIA 2002).

[360] *Id.*

[361] *Id.*

[362] *Matter of S–V–*, 22 I&N Dec. 1306, 1311 (BIA 2000).

[363] *Id.*

[364] 8 CFR §§208.18(a)(7), 1208.18(a)(7).

[365] 8 CFR §§274a.12(a)(10), 1274a.12(a)(10).

prior to arrival.[366] However, there may be relief in the form of "deferral of removal" under the CAT (discussed, *infra*). Regarding the "particularly serious crime" bar, there may be an exception in certain cases where the sentence is less than five years.[367] However, the AG has been very strict in limiting this exception.[368] There is no requirement to file the CAT application within one year; nor is there a resettlement bar.

Deferral of Removal

For those individuals who meet the "more likely than not" standard, but are barred from withholding for one of the grounds enumerated in INA §241(b)(3)(B) (crime, persecution of others, etc), there may be eligibility for "deferral of removal."[369] An alien's criminal convictions in the United States, no matter how serious, are not a bar to deferral of removal under the CAT.[370] Frequently, applicants with serious criminal records seek this form of relief because there is no bar. However, it provides limited relief, in that the applicant receives no "lawful status" or release from custody if detained. In addition, deferral of removal may be terminated at any time (even without a motion to reopen) and the applicant is subject to removal at any time if an IJ determines that it is no longer likely that the alien would be tortured in the country to which removal has been deferred.[371] The IJ must inform the individual granted deferral of removal that removal has been deferred only regarding the country in which it is likely that he or she will be tortured; that is, the individual may be removed to any other country where he or she is not likely to be tortured.[372]

Motion to Terminate Deferral of Removal

The government attorney may file at any time with the court where the deferral has been granted a motion to consider whether the deferral of removal should be terminated.[373] The motion will be granted if there is some evidence relevant to the possibility that the individual would be tortured in the native country and that evidence was not presented at the original hearing where deferral was granted.[374] This motion is not subject to the time and numerical limitations of a motion to reopen.[375] The individual must be given notice of the time and place for the termination hearing and given a chance to respond. DOS also is given a copy of the application and supplemental information from the alien

---

[366] INA §241(b)(3)(B); 8 CFR §208.16(d)(2), 1208.16(d)(2).

[367] 8 CFR §208.16(d)(3), 1208.16(d)(3).

[368] *Matter of Y–L–*, 23 I&N Dec. 270 (BIA 2002).

[369] 8 CFR §§208.17(a), 1208.17(a); *see also Matter of G–A–*, 23 I&N Dec. 366 (BIA 2002).

[370] *Matter of G–A–*, 23 I&N Dec. at 368.

[371] 8 CFR §§208.17(b)(1), 1208.17(b)(1).

[372] 8 CFR §§208.17(b)(2), 1208.17(b)(2).

[373] 8 CFR §§208.17(d)(1), 1208.17(d)(1).

[374] *Id.*

[375] *Id.*

or the government, and it has the option of responding.[376] DOS may forward to the AG any assurances received from a foreign government that an individual will not be tortured upon return. The AG decides in conjunction with the Secretary of State whether the assurances from the foreign government are reliable.[377] Once these assurances are received from the foreign government, the IJ and the BIA lose jurisdiction of the case and it can be adjudicated only by the AG, Deputy AG, or "INS Commissioner."[378]

Procedure

There is no form for seeking withholding or deferral under the CAT other than the I-589 application form used for asylum and withholding. It also may be initiated verbally or where an individual submits evidence as part of an asylum or withholding claim that indicates that the individual may be tortured upon returning to his or her country.[379] However, he or she must indicate in some manner—verbally, through the submission of documentation, or by marking the appropriate section on the I-589—that he or she will be seeking CAT relief. Failure to seek CAT relief at the relief hearing will result in a loss of the opportunity to seek this relief.[380] The CAT is a last resort form of relief used most often when an applicant is barred from asylum or cannot establish a nexus between the harm feared and one of the five grounds.

Reinstatement of Removal and Administrative Removal Orders

Any alien who, during an administrative removal process under INA §238(b) or reinstatement procedures under INA §241(a)(5), expresses a fear of returning to the country of removal is referred to an asylum officer for a reasonable fear interview to determine if there is a reasonable fear of persecution or torture.[381] DHS has exclusive power to make a determination as to whether there is a "reasonable fear" and the IJ has exclusive jurisdiction to review such a finding.[382] The interview is conducted by an asylum officer in a nonadversarial manner. The individual may be represented by counsel at no expense to the government. This is a screening process and there are no bars at this phase.[383] If the asylum officer determines that the individual does have a reasonable fear of persecution or torture, the person is informed of this and referred to the IJ for consideration of the withholding/deferral of removal under the CAT claim. If the asylum officer finds that the person does not have a reasonable fear of persecution or torture, the alien is so informed and given the opportunity to request review of

---

[376] 8 CFR §§208.17(d)(2), 1208.17(d)(2).

[377] 8 CFR §§208.18(c), 1208.18(c).

[378] 8 CFR §§208.18(c)(3), 1208.18(c)(3) (also, because there is no longer an "INS Commissioner," this authority must be exercised by other officials).

[379] 8 CFR §§208.13(c)(1), 1208.13(c)(1).

[380] *Matter of R–S–H–*, 23 I&N Dec. 629 (BIA 2003).

[381] 8 CFR §§208.31(b), 1208.31(b).

[382] 8 CFR §§208.31(a), 1208.31(a).

[383] 8 CFR §§208.31(c), 1208.31(c).

this decision before the IJ.[384] If no review is sought, the person is removed. If review is sought of a negative reasonable fear finding, the IJ may do the following:

- review the case and determine if the asylum officer was correct, in which case the case is returned to DHS for removal of the alien; or
- review the case and determine that the alien does have a reasonable fear in which case the alien is given the opportunity to file an I-589 and have a hearing on the withholding claim; the court may only grant withholding or deferral of removal.[385]

BIA Review

Appeal of an IJ decision on the withholding or deferral of removal claim is made to the BIA. The BIA may only review respondent's eligibility for withholding or deferral of removal and nothing else.[386]

Judicial Review

There is no judicial review of a claim under the CAT except as part of the review of a final order of removal under INA §242. If an appeal is authorized under INA §242, and an appeal is taken, it does not authorize the appeal of any other issues that are restricted or barred under INA §242.[387]

---

[384] 8 CFR §§208.31(f), 1208.31(f).

[385] 8 CFR §§208.31(g), 1208.31(g).

[386] 8 CFR §§208.31(g)(2)(ii), 1208.31(g)(2)(ii).

[387] 8 CFR §§208.18(e)(1), 1208.18(e)(1).

CHAPTER 6

OTHER FORMS OF RELIEF FROM REMOVAL

Cancellation of Removal for Certain Non–Permanent Residents

Introduction

Historically, there has been a form of relief for aliens who had been present in the United States for long periods of time, avoided problems with the criminal authorities, and could show that their forced removal from the country would result in a high level of hardship to certain individuals. Prior to 1996, this form of relief was called "suspension of deportation" and was found under Immigration and Nationality Act (INA)[1] former §244. This form of relief required a combination of seven years' physical presence in the United States, good moral character, and a showing of extreme hardship to the alien and/or U.S. citizen or lawful permanent resident (LPR) spouse, parents, or children.

In 1996, with the passage of the Illegal Immigration Reform and Immigrant Responsibility Act (IIRAIRA),[2] Congress eliminated the former suspension of deportation as a form of relief from deportation. In its place, Congress enacted a form of relief called "cancellation of removal for certain non–permanent residents," found under INA §240A(b)(1). The statutory requirements for cancellation are much higher than those of the former suspension statute. An individual seeking cancellation of removal under this statute can no longer claim eligibility based on hardship to him- or herself. It is now hardship to the alien's U.S. citizen or LPR spouse, parents, or children that must be shown. Also, the level of hardship that must be

---

[1] Immigration and Nationality Act of 1952, Pub. L. No. 82-414, 66 Stat. 163 (codified as amended at 8 USC §§1101 *et seq.*).

[2] Illegal Immigration Reform and Immigrant Responsibility Act of 1996, Division C of the Omnibus Appropriations Act of 1996 (H.R. 3610), Pub. L. No. 104-208, 110 Stat. 3009.

proven has risen from "extreme hardship" to "exceptional and extremely unusual hardship."

In addition, while under the old statute, an individual had to show only seven years of continuous physical presence; cancellation of removal requires 10 years' physical presence in the United States. Finally, the applicant must show that he or she is a person of good moral character and has been a person with good moral character for the 10-year period. Individuals who have been convicted of certain crimes including crimes involving moral turpitude and aggravated felonies are ineligible, as are individuals who are believed to be threats to security. The ineligible classes will be discussed below.

There are other variations of the cancellation of removal statute with differing standards. Spouses and children of U.S. citizens or LPRs who have been the victims of domestic violence or extreme cruelty may petition for cancellation of removal through the Violence Against Women Act (VAWA).[3] These individuals may seek cancellation of removal under more lenient standards. Also, there is a special rule for cancellation of removal for certain individuals who seek relief under the Nicaraguan Adjustment and Central American Relief Act (NACARA).[4] Again, cancellation of removal under this statute has more lenient standards than the 10-year cancellation of removal under INA §240A(b)(1). Each form of cancellation of removal will be discussed below, and the standards for each—as well as the standards under the former suspension of deportation statute—will be outlined (prior to 1996, the grounds of deportability were found under former INA §241, "General Classes of Deportable Aliens"). Individuals who may be in "deportation" proceedings rather than in "removal" proceedings are still eligible to seek suspension of deportation under the pre-IIRAIRA statute.

Cancellation of removal is a discretionary form of relief; not only must the individual meet the statutory standards as outlined in the INA, the individual must prove that he or she is discretionarily deserving of this benefit. Cancellation of removal leads to LPR status (Green Card) and is a valuable form of relief. Unfortunately, there is no derivative status for spouses or children of those seeking cancellation of removal, be it the 10-year, NACARA, or VAWA cancellation of removal (although NACARA has more lenient standards for immediate family members, they still must have applied and qualified under those reduced standards). Each individual must qualify on his or her own merits. In addition, cancellation of removal is a "defensive" form of relief (except under NACARA); thus, it may only be sought and received in removal proceedings as a defense to deportation after an individual has been found removable. An individual who may have a strong cancellation case and is not in removal proceedings may have to decide whether he or she wishes to take the chance of being placed in removal proceedings and risk a removal order if the application is not approved (*e.g.*, someone with an ill immediate family member who needs to remain

---

[3] Violence Against Women Act of 1994, Pub. L. No. 103-322, 108 Stat. 1902–1955.

[4] Nicaraguan Adjustment and Central American Relief Act, Pub. L. No. 105-100, 111 Stat. 2160, 2193.

in the United States for medical treatment or another LPR benefit, or another exceptional and extremely unusual hardship factor). On the other hand, if the application is approved, the individual receives a Green Card and becomes a legal permanent resident in the United States.

Elements of Cancellation of Removal Under INA §240A(b)(1)— 10-Year Cancellation of Removal

The statute requires the following:

- 10 years of physical presence immediately preceding the date of the application;
- good moral character during this 10-year period;
- exceptional and extremely unusual hardship to the U.S. citizen or LPR spouse, parent, or child of the applicant;
- no convictions for crimes involving moral turpitude, drugs, weapons, or domestic violence, failure to register with the Department of Homeland Security (DHS), or the commission of document fraud; and
- positive showing of discretionary merit.[5]

Continuous physical presence for 10 years

The cancellation of removal statute requires continuous physical presence for a period of not less than 10 years. That period begins when an alien first physically enters the United States, whether that entry is legal or illegal. That period terminates when an alien is served a charging document placing him or her in deportation or removal proceedings, or when the alien commits an offense referred to in INA §212(a)(2) that renders him or her inadmissible under INA§212(a)(2) or removable from the United States under INA §§237(a)(2) (certain crimes) or 237(a)(4) (security reasons).[6] That period of physical presence is also broken when an alien departs the United States for any period in excess of 90 days or for any period in the aggregate exceeding 180 days.[7]

There have been a series of decisions interpreting this physical presence requirement at the administrative and judicial level. The Seventh Circuit, for example, has found that there is no break in the continuity of one's physical presence where an individual departs the United States, attempts to re-enter the United States, and is returned to Mexico, if the individual is not placed into any type of administrative proceedings.[8] The attempt at re-entry and being turned away did not constitute a break of continuous presence for cancellation purposes.[9] Likewise, the Board of Immigration Appeals (BIA) has found that a two-week absence from the United States did not break an individual's physical presence even where that individual was refused re-

---

[5] INA §240A(b)(1).

[6] INA §240A(d)(1).

[7] INA §240A(d)(2).

[8] *Morales-Morales v. Ashcroft*, 384 F.3d 418 (7th Cir. 2004).

[9] *Id.*

admission at a port of entry after departing the United States, but was never threatened or placed into any type of deportation or exclusion proceedings.[10] However, the BIA has found that the period of continuous physical presence is deemed to end at the time an alien is compelled to depart the United States under threat of the commencement of deportation or removal proceedings.[11]

Where an individual was previously deported and then re-enters the United States and ultimately accumulates 10 years' of physical presence, he or she may be eligible for cancellation of removal. The "stop-time rule," which stops the accrual of physical presence for cancellation purposes, applies only when the charging document in the current proceeding is issued against the alien. The charging document in a prior proceeding that resulted in the alien's departure does not serve to stop an individual from re-accruing physical presence upon a later re-entry to the country.[12] However, in such a situation, an individual may be subject to reinstatement of removal.[13] Additionally, a lawful entry into the United States allows an individual to accrue physical presence for cancellation purposes even after that individual has been convicted on a prior visit of a controlled substance offense.[14]

The physical presence requirement for cancellation of removal under §240A(b) does not apply to an alien who has served a minimum of 24 months in active duty status in the U.S. Armed Forces and, if separated from that service, was separated under honorable conditions, and was in the United States at the time of enlistment or induction into the military.[15]

The "stop-time" provisions of INA §240A(b)(1) were enacted in 1996 as part of IIRAIRA. However, the stop-time rule also applies to former INA §244 suspension of deportation relief even though the individual may have been placed into proceedings prior to the 1996 enactment.[16] The BIA, in 1997, found that the stop-time provisions of IIRAIRA applied to all cases not *completed* prior to the effective date of IIRAIRA—September 30, 1996.[17] This decision was later vacated by the Attorney General (AG).[18] However, Congress, by means of amendments enacted through NACARA, made it clear that the stop-time rules were to be applied retroactively and that time stopped accruing for individuals in deportation proceedings at the time of the issuance of the Order to Show Cause (OSC).[19] As a result, the stop-time provi-

---

[10] *Matter of Avilez-Nava*, 23 I&N Dec. 799 (BIA 2005).

[11] *Matter of Romalez-Alcaide*, 23 I&N Dec. 423 (BIA 2002).

[12] *Matter of Cisneros-Gonzalez*, 23 I&N Dec. 668 (BIA 2004).

[13] INA §241(a)(5).

[14] *Okeke v. Gonzales*, 407 F.3d 585 (3d Cir. 2005).

[15] INA §240A(d)(3).

[16] *Matter of Mendoza-Sandino*, 22 I&N Dec. 1236 (BIA 2000)

[17] *Matter of N–J–B–*, 22 I&N Dec. 1057 (BIA 1997); *overturned* by A.G. (Aug. 20, 1999).

[18] *Id.*

[19] NACARA, *supra* note 4.

sions applied retroactively to cut off the time at the point of service of the OSC or the commission of an act that would be a ground of inadmissibility under INA §212(a), thereby, eliminating the former suspension of deportation relief for individuals in deportation proceedings. Additionally, these individuals were not eligible for cancellation of removal because they were in deportation—not removal—proceedings.

The effect of this law was extremely harsh in certain cases, and, as a result, the BIA with the cooperation of the Immigration and Naturalization Service (INS) established a means by which there could be agreement to close cases in *deportation* proceedings and recharge the individuals in *removal* proceedings, thereby removing the tolling effect of the OSC issuance. Those "repapered" individuals could then accrue the time after the issuance of the OSC right up to the time that the "repapering" occurred, *i.e.*, the time that the NTA was issued placing the person into removal proceedings. The requirements for "repapering" are:

- the respondent is not an LPR;
- the respondent would have been eligible for suspension under the seven- or 10-year provisions of suspension of deportation but for the stop-time rule under INA §240A(d)(1); and
- the respondent is eligible for cancellation of removal and is not barred under any of the provisions of INA §240A(d)(1).

There are no repapering regulations; the failure to translate this procedure into regulations by the government is not considered a due process or equal protection violation; nor does it create estoppels claims.[20]

Good moral character

The cancellation statute requires that an individual show that he or she has been a person of good moral character during the 10-year physical presence period.[21] There is no definition for the term "good moral character"; however, the INA does indicate who cannot be persons of good moral character, including:

- habitual drunkards;
- prostitutes or individuals involved in commercialized vice;
- individuals who have been convicted of, or admitted the commission of, a crime involving moral turpitude;
- individuals with multiple criminal convictions;
- individuals who have been convicted of, or admitted of commission of, crimes related to controlled substances;
- controlled substance traffickers;
- smugglers;

---

[20] *Rojas-Reyes v. INS*, 235 F.3d. 115 (2d Cir. 2000).

[21] INA §240A(b)(1)(B).

- certain aliens who have been previously removed (INA §212(a)(9)(A));
- individuals whose income is derived principally from illegal gambling, and individuals who have been convicted of two or more gambling offenses;
- anyone who has given false testimony to obtain an immigration benefit;
- anyone who has been confined to a penal institution for 180 days or more in the aggregate; and
- anyone convicted of an aggravated felony under INA §101(a)(43).[22]

This list is not all-inclusive. The statute states that other individuals may be found to lack good moral character even if not included on this list.[23]

The period during which an individual must establish good moral character is measured backward from the date on which the application for cancellation of removal is resolved by the immigration judge (IJ) or the BIA.[24]

An alien who is convicted of an aggravated felony under INA §101(a)(43) is barred from establishing good moral character if the aggravated felony conviction occurred on or after November 29, 1990.[25] An individual who is convicted of murder is forever precluded from establishing good moral character.[26] Individuals who have been convicted of conspiring to obtain, possess, or use illegal immigration documents are barred on good moral character grounds.[27] An individual who gives false testimony during an asylum interview is barred from establishing eligibility for cancellation of removal on good moral character grounds.[28] Assisting in illegally smuggling a spouse and/or child into the United States also makes one ineligible for cancellation on good moral character grounds.[29] Incarceration in a county jail for a period of 365 days makes an individual ineligible for cancellation for a lack of good moral character.[30] An individual convicted of terroristic threats, *i.e.*, to commit a crime of violence with the purpose of terrorizing another, is ineligible for cancellation of removal based on moral character grounds.[31] An individual who has been ordered removed from the United States and seeks admission within five years of the date of removal is ineligible for cancellation of removal based on moral character grounds.[32]

---

[22] INA §101(f); *see also* 8 CFR §316.10 (which applies to citizenship cases).

[23] See also 8 CFR §316.10 for other classes of individuals who are found to be lacking good moral character; this relates to applicants for citizenship who must prove good moral character.

[24] *Matter of Ortega-Caberera*, 23 I&N Dec. 793 (BIA 2005).

[25] *Matter of Reyes*, 20 I&N Dec. 789 (BIA 1994).

[26] *Id.*

[27] *Omagah v. Ashcroft*, 288 F.3d 254 (5th Cir. 2002).

[28] *Quadra v. Gonzales*, 417 F.3d 947 (8th Cir. 2005); *Medina v. Gonzales*, 404 F.3d 628 (2d Cir. 2005).

[29] *Moran v. Ashcroft*, 395 F.3d 1089 (9th Cir. 2005).

[30] *Gomez-Lopez v. Ashcroft*, 393 F.3d 882 (9th Cir. 2005).

[31] *Chanmouny v. Ashcroft*, 376 F.3d 810 (8th Cir. 2004).

[32] *Avendano- Ramirez v. Ashcroft*, 365 F.3d 813 (9th Cir. 2004); *see also* INA §212(a)(9)(A).

To compare, in a recent decision, the Fifth Circuit found that attempted misdemeanor child abandonment with intent to return the child was not a crime involving moral turpitude and, therefore, not a bar to the good moral character requirement for cancellation of removal.[33] Also, the BIA has held that an individual who is convicted of a petty offense, *i.e.*, the sentence is less than six months and the crime is a misdemeanor offense, is not barred from eligibility for cancellation of removal on good moral character grounds, if that is the only offense.[34]

The cancellation statute has a separate subsection indicating that individuals who have been convicted of offenses under INA §§212(a)(2), 237(a)(2), or 237(a)(3) are barred from this form of relief.[35] Thus, individuals who are convicted of crimes relating to moral turpitude (unless it is a petty offense), controlled substance violations, prostitution or a commercialized vice, firearms offenses, domestic violence offenses, document fraud, falsification of documents, or failure to register with the government are barred from cancellation of removal.

Other classes of ineligible aliens

The INA also makes the following groups of aliens ineligible for cancellation of removal for non–permanent residents:[36]

- aliens who entered the United States as crewmen after June 30, 1964;
- individuals who have entered the United States as, or acquired the status of, J visa holders under INA §101(a)(15)(J) in order to receive graduate medical training, regardless of whether the alien is subject to, or has fulfilled, the two-year foreign residence requirement;
- A "J" visa holder, subject to the two-year foreign residence requirement who has not fulfilled that requirement;
- individuals inadmissible or deportable as security threats;
- individuals who have been persecutors as defined at INA §241(b)(3)(B)(i); and
- individuals whose removal has previously been cancelled under INA §§240A(a) or (b), or who have been granted suspension of deportation under INA §244 or relief under INA §212(c), as these sections were in effect prior to IIRAIRA.

Exceptional and extremely unusual hardship

A statutory requirement for cancellation of removal for non–permanent residents is that the applicant must establish that removal would result in "exceptional and extremely unusual hardship" to the applicant's U.S. citizen or LPR spouse, parent, or child. Prior to 1996, the standard for hardship was "extreme."[37] The BIA outlined

---

[33] *Rodriguez-Castro v. Gonzales*, 427 F.3d 316 (5th Cir. 2005).

[34] *Matte of Garcia-Hernandez*, 23 I&N Dec. 590 (BIA 2003).

[35] INA §240A(b)(1)(C).

[36] INA §240A(c).

[37] *See* (former) INA §244(a).

several factors under the previous statute that could be measured to determine whether the individual could establish "extreme hardship," including age of the individual; family ties in the United States and abroad; length of residence in the United States; condition of health; conditions in the country to which the alien was returnable; economic and political conditions in applicant's native country; financial status including business and occupational ties; the possibility of other means of adjustment of status; position in the community; community ties; and, finally, an individual's immigration history.[38] The hardship considered could be the alien's or the immediate family members'.

In 2001, the BIA finally defined what was meant by "exceptional and extremely unusual" hardship. It stated that "exceptional and extremely unusual" was a higher standard of hardship than "extreme hardship." Thus, it must be "truly exceptional."[39] However, the BIA went on to state that hardship need not be "unconscionable."[40] It is hardship that is substantially beyond that which ordinarily would be expected to result from the alien's deportation.[41] The BIA identified several factors to be considered on the issue of hardship—age; serious health issues; and compelling special needs in school of qualifying LPR and U.S citizen relatives. Generally, lower standards of living, while relevant, will be insufficient to support a finding of exceptional and extremely unusual hardship.[42] Hardship factors should be considered in the aggregate.

The BIA found that in weighing hardship to U.S. citizen or LPR children, the court should consider the heavy burden imposed on the children where there is only one provider for six children.[43] In that case, in addition to the hardship to the six children with only one provider, the BIA looked at the lack of family ties in the native country; the children's lack of familiarity with the Spanish language; and the unavailability of any other means of immigrating to the United States by the alien parent in proceedings.[44] However, the BIA also has found that an unmarried mother did not establish eligibility for cancellation of removal where she failed to demonstrate that her six- and eleven-year-old U.S. citizen children would suffer exceptional and extremely unusual hardship upon return to Mexico.[45] This case is distinguishable because the father was contributing financially to the family and was a presence in the lives of the children; he also was able to assist the children in Mexico.[46]

---

[38] *Matter of Anderson*, 16 I&N Dec. 596 (BIA 1978).

[39] *Matter of Monreal*, 23 I&N Dec. 56 (BIA 2001).

[40] *Id.*

[41] *Id.*

[42] *Id.*

[43] *Matter of Recinas*, 23 I&N Dec. 467 (BIA 2002).

[44] *Id.*

[45] *Matter of Andazola-Rivas*, 23 I&N Dec. 319 (BIA 2002).

[46] *Id.*

The BIA has stated that the hardship standard is "not so restrictive that only a handful of applicants, such as those who have a qualifying relative with a serious medical condition, will qualify for relief."[47] Although it has arrived at different decisions in the three precedent cases defining the term "exceptional and extremely unusual hardship," the BIA developed some pattern. The BIA has stated clearly in several decisions that it is not a requirement that a U.S. citizen or LPR child or family member have a serious medical condition. It may be sufficient to prove that it is extremely difficult or impossible to support children in the country where the alien will be living in poverty. This was restated in both the *Recinas* decision as well as the *Andazola-Rivas* decision. In addition, the BIA highlighted the higher lever of difficulty faced by a single parent. It stated in *Recinas* that this set of facts was probably the outer limits of where the BIA would go in finding exceptional and extremely unusual hardship.[48]

Discretion

The decision on cancellation of removal, like most forms of relief, is discretionary, which means that in addition to showing the statutory factors (hardship, good moral character, and physical presence), an individual should be prepared to establish discretionary merit. For example, although hardship to the alien may not prove the exceptional and extremely unusual hardship standard, it may be presented on the issue of discretion. The hardship to children who are not U.S. citizens or LPRs, although not a statutory factor, may be admitted on the issue of discretion. Counsel should be prepared to put forth as much as possible under the umbrella of discretionary factors.

Quota

The quota for cancellation of removal grants under INA §240A(b) is 4,000 in any fiscal year.[49] It applies to the aggregate number of decisions to cancel removal or suspend deportation of any alien in the fiscal year. This quota does not apply to grants of cancellation of removal under NACARA.[50]

Suspension of Deportation Under Former INA §244(a)

For individuals who are in "deportation" proceedings rather than removal proceedings, there may be a possibility for suspension of deportation under the former INA §244. Individuals in deportation proceedings are those who were issued OSCs prior to April 1, 1997. Such individuals are eligible to seek suspension of deportation under the relaxed standards on hardship and physical presence of former INA §244(a).[51] Following are the requisite statutory elements under the prior suspension statute:

---

[47] *Matter of Recinas*, 23 I&N Dec. 467.

[48] *Id.*

[49] INA §240A(e)(1).

[50] INA §240A(e)(3).

[51] 8 CFR §§240.65(b), 1240.65(b).

- Physical presence for a period of seven years or longer. The issuance of the OSC stops the clock for suspension purposes; therefore, the individual must measure from the date of entry to the date on which the OSC was issued.
- Good moral character—the applicant must show good moral character during all requisite periods of physical presence.
- Extreme hardship—the alien must show that deportation would result in extreme hardship to the alien or his or her U.S. citizen or LPR spouse, parent, or child.[52]
- Discretionary merit—suspension of deportation, like cancellation of removal, is a discretionary form of relief.[53]

Individuals who were deportable on criminal or other grounds under the former INA §§241(a)(2)–(4) (relating specifically to crimes involving moral turpitude, controlled substances, aggravated felonies, firearms, espionage, sabotage, treason, violations of the Military Selective Service Act, violations of the Trading with the Enemy Act, failure to register or file changes of address with INS, falsification of documents, document fraud, or security threats) were required to establish that they had 10 years of physical presence the United States.[54] The 10 years of physical presence follows the commission of the criminal act or the assumption of the status that made the individual deportable. Finally, the individual had to establish "exceptional and extremely unusual hardship" to the alien or his or her U.S. citizen or LPR spouse, parent, or child.

VAWA Cancellation of Removal for Abused Immigrants

Introduction

A second form of cancellation of removal specifically for battered spouses and children of U.S. citizens or LPRs exists under VAWA, which provides for cancellation of removal for immigrant victims of domestic violence.[55] There also is a separate form of relief under VAWA called "self-petitioning" that enables victims of domestic violence at the hands of a U.S. citizen or LPR spouse or parent to petition for permanent residence through a "self petition" (Form I-360), which, if approved, enables the victim to adjust status without a USC or LPR petitioner. (Self-petitioning is not discussed in detail in this section.)[56] The requisite elements to qualify for VAWA cancellation of removal are more lenient than those for the 10-year cancellation of removal described above. The applicant for VAWA cancellation must establish the following:

- the appropriate relationship to a U.S. citizen or LPR (relatives discussed below);

---

[52] *Id.*

[53] 8 CFR §§240.64(a), 1240.64(a).

[54] *See* former INA §§244(a) and 241(a)(2)–(4) (eliminated by IIRAIRA, Sept. 30, 1996).

[55] INA §240A(b)(2).

[56] INA §§204(a)(1)(A)(ii) and (iii).

- battery or extreme cruelty at the hands of the U.S. citizen or LPR (relatives discussed below);
- physical presence in the United States of not less than three years immediately preceding the date of application;
- good moral character during the three-year period;
- not inadmissible under INA §§212(a)(2) or (3) and not deportable under INA §§237(a)(1)(G) or 237(a)(2)–(4); and
- extreme hardship to the alien, the alien's child, or the alien's parent if the alien is removed.[57]

In addition to these enumerated elements, the applicant must prove that he or she is discretionarily deserving of this relief. The application is filed on the same form as the 10-year cancellation of removal under INA §240A(b)—the EOIR-40. There is a waivable $100 filing fee. The application for VAWA cancellation is a defensive claim, and can only be filed in removal proceedings before the immigration court. Below is a brief outline of the statutory and regulatory requirements for seeking cancellation or removal under VAWA.[58]

Who may seek VAWA cancellation of removal

The following classes of individuals may be qualified to seek cancellation of removal under VAWA if the other elements are proven:

- spouses of U.S. citizens or LPRs who have been abused;
- sons and daughters of U.S. citizens or LPRs who have been abused;
- parents of abused children of U.S. citizens or LPRs, even where the parent is not married to the U.S. citizen or LPR abuser—the abused child need not be a U.S. citizen or LPR; and
- intending spouses of U.S. citizens or LPRs who have been abused by a spouse to whom they believed themselves lawfully married but the marriage was not legitimate because of the abuser's bigamy.[59]

Where a parent of an abused child is seeking a benefit under this statute, it must be proven that the abused individual is a "child" under INA §101(b). Under this section, a "child" must be single, under the age of 21, and one of the following:

- born in wedlock;
- step-child where the marriage creating the step-relationship took place before the child's 18th birthday;
- a legitimated child if the legitimation takes place before the child's 18th birthday, and the child was in the legal custody of the legitimating parent;

---

[57] INA §240A(b)(2)(A).

[58] INA §240A(b)(2).

[59] INA §240A(b)(2)(A).

- a child born out of wedlock where it is the natural mother claiming the benefit; or the natural father if he has established a bona fide parent-child relationship with the child;
- adopted children where the adoption has taken place prior to the child's 16th birthday and the child has resided with, and been in the legal custody of, the adopting parent for at least two years. However, under the Violence Against Women and Department of Justice Reauthorization Act of 2005 (VAWA 2005),[60] Congress removed the two-year requirement of lawful custody and residence with the adoptive parent, allowing the child to obtain LPR status even if the child has not been in the lawful custody, or residing with the adoptive parent for two years, if the child has been battered by the adoptive parent or family member;[61] or
- orphans as defined under INA §101(b)(1)(F).

Differences between VAWA adjustment of status self-petitions and VAWA cancellation of removal

Following are several differences between VAWA cancellation of removal and the self-petitioning process under VAWA:

- VAWA cancellation requires a showing of three years' physical presence in the United States; the self-petitioning process does not.
- VAWA cancellation requires a showing of extreme hardship; the adjustment of status through the self-petitioning process does not require extreme hardship.
- The VAWA cancellation or removal application must be filed before an IJ. The self-petition is not filed in court, nor does an IJ have authority to adjudicate a self-petition. However, if an individual is in proceedings and the self-petition has been approved, the IJ has the authority to, and will, adjudicate the adjustment of status application.
- VAWA cancellation of removal has no public charge ground of inadmissibility, whereas this may be a bar to adjusting through the self-petitioning process.
- VAWA cancellation of removal gives no derivative permanent resident status to the children of the cancellation applicant. An approval of the self-petition does give derivative status to the "children" of the self-petitioner.
- Last, the cancellation of removal process has no time requirement during which the application must be filed. It can be filed even after the marriage is terminated through divorce or death of the abuser. It also can be filed after an LPR abuser has been removed from the United States. In the self-petitioning process, the application must be filed within two years of the termination of the marriage.

---

[60] Violence Against Women and Department of Justice Reauthorization Act of 2005, Pub. L. No. 109-162 (VAWA 2005).

[61] *Id.* §805(d).

Standard of abuse—battery or extreme cruelty

The cancellation of removal section of the INA uses the same term "battery or extreme cruelty" that is used in the self-petitioning statute.[62] The regulations define "battery or extreme cruelty"[63] to include (but not to be limited to) the following: acts of violence; threatened acts of violence; forced detention resulting in physical or mental injury; threats of physical or mental injury; and psychological or sexual abuse or exploitation including rape, molestation, incest, or forced prostitution. A pattern of this type of activity also may rise to the level of "battery or extreme cruelty" even where the individual actions themselves may not rise to this level.[64]

Evidence of this abuse may include reports and affidavits from police, judges and other court officials, medical personnel, school officials, clergy, social workers, and other social service agency personnel. In addition, evidence of prior protective orders against the abuser may be helpful.[65] Any "credible evidence" relevant to the application "shall" be considered by the IJ.[66]

Legal status of the abuser

The abuser must be an LPR or a U.S. citizen at the time of the abuse. This is true whether the abuse is based on a spousal relationship or a parent-child relationship. In the cancellation process, it does not matter that the LPR abuser has lost his or her status or been deported as long as he or she was an LPR at the time of the abuse and, in a spousal situation, the abuse took place during the course of the marriage. Evidence of the marital relationship should be submitted with the application.[67] Furthermore, the evidence submitted with the application also should prove that any prior marriage in which either party was involved has been terminated, and that the abuser lived together in a bona fide marital relationship with the cancellation of removal applicant.[68]

Physical presence

The statute requires three years of continuous physical presence in the United States.[69] The statute specifically states that the issuance of a charging document placing an individual into removal proceedings does not "toll" the three-year period of continuous physical presence, as it does in the 10-year cancellation of removal application under INA §240A(b). In addition, the special rules relating to breaks in physical presence, whereby physical presence is broken for a departure in excess of 90 days or in the aggregate for 180 days, do not apply in the VAWA cancellation of re-

---

[62] INA §204(a)(1)(A)(iii).

[63] 8 CFR §204.2(c)(1)(vi).

[64] *Id.*

[65] 8 CFR §204.2(c)(2)(iv).

[66] INA §240A(b)(2)(D).

[67] 8 CFR §204.2(c)(2)(ii).

[68] 8 CFR §204.2(c)(2).

[69] INA §240A(b)(2)(A)(ii).

moval application "if the alien demonstrates a connection between the absence and the battery or extreme cruelty perpetrated against the alien."[70] That is, any break of time where an individual is outside of the United States as a result of violence or threatened violence will not be computed in measuring the amount of time during which the individual has been physically present.[71]

Good moral character

A VAWA applicant must prove that he or she is a person of good moral character at the time that the application is adjudicated and has been during the three years immediately proceeding the date of the application.[72] The individual will not necessarily be found to lack good moral character even if he or she is a person described in INA §101(f) (which sets out those individuals barred from a finding of good moral character). Note that VAWA 2005 amends INA §101(f)(3) so that those who have prior orders of removal under INA §212(a)(9)(A) are no longer barred as persons lacking good moral character.[73]

For VAWA applicants, the regulations state that extenuating circumstances may be taken into account for individuals who have admitted to the commission of actions that show a lack of good moral character, but have not been convicted.[74] For example, an individual who has been subjected to forced prostitution, or who has been forced to engage in other actions that would render the person inadmissible under INA §212(a) on good moral character grounds, may be found to be a person a good moral character if this activity was a form of abuse perpetrated by the abuser on the applicant.[75]

The regulation states that a VAWA applicant may be found to lack good moral character if he or she willfully failed or refused to support dependents, or admitted other actions that reflect poorly on his or her moral character.[76]

Extreme hardship

The applicant for VAWA cancellation of removal must prove extreme hardship.[77] This is a more lenient standard than the "exceptional and extremely unusual hardship" standard described above. The interpretation of "extreme hardship" in the VAWA context also is a more lenient standard than the interpretation of the "extreme hardship" standard of the former suspension of deportation context because there are more hardship factors that may be measured in a VAWA case than can be considered

---

[70] INA §240A(b)(2)(B).

[71] *Id.*

[72] INA §240A(b)(2)(A)(iii); *see also* INA §240A(b)(2)(C).

[73] VAWA 2005, *supra* note 60, §812.

[74] 8 CFR §204.2(c)(1)(vii).

[75] *Id.*

[76] *Id.*

[77] INA §240A(b)(2)(A)(v).

under the former suspension hardship standard. The BIA outlined the basic hardship factors to be measured in determining whether an individual showed "extreme hardship" in the suspension of deportation context.[78] The BIA stated that the following factors could be considered in measuring extreme hardship under the former INA §244(a): age of the applicant; length of residence in the United States; family ties in the United States and abroad; health of the applicant and qualifying relatives; financial status; occupation of the applicant; ties to the community; economic and political conditions in the native country; immigration history; applicant's position in the community; and other means of adjusting to lawful status.[79]

In adjudicating a VAWA cancellation of removal application, the IJ may consider all of the above plus the following: major extent of the physical and psychological consequences of abuse; the effect of loss of access to U.S. courts and the criminal justice system including the ability to obtain and enforce a protection order; the possibility that the batterer's friends and family or others connected to the batterer in the home country could physically and psychologically harm the applicant; the applicant's needs, or those of the applicant's children, for social, medical, mental health, or other supportive services that may be required as a result of the domestic violence and that are unavailable or not accessible in the home country; the existence of laws and social practices in the home country that punish the applicant because he or she has been a victim of domestic violence or has taken steps to leave an abusive situation; the abuser's ability to travel to the home country; and the willingness or ability of the authorities to protect the applicant in the home country.[80] As in all cancellation of removal applications, the hardship factors may be considered in the aggregate. Even if an individual factor does not rise to the level of extreme hardship, when taken together with other factors they may rise to this level cumulatively.

The regulations state that evidence of extreme hardship may include affidavits, birth certificates of children, medical reports, protection orders and other court documents, police reports, and other relevant credible evidence.[81]

Statutory bars

The statute at INA §240A(b)(2)(A)(iv) specifically states that certain classes of inadmissible aliens are barred from cancellation of removal. These include individuals who are inadmissible for crimes of moral turpitude, controlled substance violations, or prostitution; those for whom there is reason to believe have been involved in controlled substance trafficking; those involved in serious criminal activity who have sought immunity from prosecution and departed the United States as a result; foreign government officials who have engaged in particularly severe violations of religious

[78] *Matter of Anderson*, 16 I&N Dec. 596 (BIA 1978).

[79] *Id.*

[80] 8 CFR §1240.58(c).

[81] 8 CFR §204.2(c)(2)(vi).

freedom; traffickers in persons; and money launderers. In addition, individuals who are inadmissible or removable on security and related grounds are not eligible.[82]

Also, individuals who are deportable for the following grounds are ineligible for VAWA cancellation of removal: individuals who have been involved in marriage fraud; certain individuals who have been convicted of crimes of moral turpitude; individuals who have been convicted of aggravated felonies; those who are removable based on high speed flight from immigration checkpoints; individuals convicted of controlled substance violations (other than a single offense of simple possession of 30 grams or less of marijuana); individuals who have been drug abusers or addicts; individuals with convictions for firearm offenses; individuals who have been convicted of domestic violence, stalking, or child abuse; individuals who have violated portions of protective orders that were meant to protect against threats of violence or bodily injury; individuals who are deportable for failing to register with the government; and those who are removable because of document fraud.[83]

VAWA 2005 includes a provision that makes immigrants who had been convicted of crimes of domestic violence or stalking and were, therefore, removable under INA §237(a)(2)(E)(i) eligible for a waiver of these offenses if that person: (1) had been the victim of battery and extreme cruelty; (2) was not the main perpetrator; and (3) was either acting in self-defense in violating a protection order that was meant to protect him or her, or involved in a crime that did not result in serious bodily injury and could show that there was a connection between the crime and the violence suffered by the victim.[84] This provision allows the IJ to give a waiver for this type of offense if the applicant can prove that he or she meets the condition laid out at INA §237(a)(7).

Applying for VAWA cancellation of removal

The application for VAWA cancellation of removal can be submitted only before the IJ after an individual has been found to be removable. In many cases, the IJ will continue a VAWA cancellation of removal case where there is a VAWA self-petition pending. However, there are situations where the IJ cannot or will not continue or administratively close a removal case; the alien will be forced to go forward on the VAWA cancellation of removal. At a minimum, the following documents should be included with the application:

- Form EOIR-42B (application for cancellation of removal);
- proof of payment of the filing fee ($100) or a motion to go forward "*informa pauperis*";
- declaration of the applicant (detailing the abuse and detailing the relationship);
- applicant's identity document (birth certificate, passport, or other identity documents with translations pursuant to 8 CFR §1003.33);

---

[82] INA §§212(a)(3).

[83] INA §240A(b)(2)(A)(iv).

[84] VAWA 2005, *supra* note 60, §813(c).

- proof of the marriage—marriage certificate, termination of any prior marriage; proof of the good faith nature of a marital relationship (if the claim is based on abuse by a spouse, proof of cohabitation should be submitted); if the claim is based on abuse by a parent, proof of the parental relationship between the U.S. citizen or LPR abuser should be submitted;
- proof of the abuser's U.S. citizen or LPR status;
- proof of three-year physical presence in the United States; and
- proof of good moral character (including letters or proof of contributions to the community).

The documentation should be submitted in accordance with the local court rules in the jurisdiction where the case is heard. Some courts have rules on tabbing, indexing, highlighting, or paginating documentation. Copies of all documents must be submitted to the DHS trial attorney; the court will want a certificate of service with the court's packet to prove that the government attorney has been served. Many courts have filing deadlines of 10 business days prior to the date of the hearing on the cancellation of removal application. Finally, it is the burden of the alien to make certain that he or she has been fingerprinted. DHS charges a $70 fingerprint (biometrics) fee that is submitted along with the application for cancellation of removal. The court cannot grant a cancellation of removal request if the background checks have not been completed.

Hearing on the cancellation of removal application before the immigration court

In any cancellation of removal request, it is the burden of the applicant to prove eligibility. After the IJ reviews the documentation and rules on admissibility of the documentation, he or she will request that the applicant, through the attorney if represented, present the case for the applicant. The direct examination of the applicant is given focusing on the factors outlined above and found at INA §240A(b)(2). The government attorney is given an opportunity to cross-examine the applicant and any witnesses presented by the applicant on any of the issues. Frequently, certain issues can be negotiated prior to the hearing. Often, the government will concede to the good moral character and physical presence elements of the claim if there is clear proof through the documentation that the alien has been in the United States and has not been in any trouble with the law.

Quota on VAWA cancellation of removal grants

The quota restrictions mentioned for the INA §240A(b)(1) 10-year cancellation of removal also cover VAWA cancellation. No more than 4,000 aliens may be granted cancellation of removal in any physical year.[85]

Children of battered aliens and parents of battered alien children

Cancellation of removal is an individual application; there is no derivative status. Unlike the self-petitioning process, the child of the victim of domestic violence in a

---

[85] INA §240A(e).

cancellation of removal application does not derive any benefit through the parent's approval. However, the INA does state that children of an alien granted VAWA cancellation of removal are granted parole under INA §212(d)(5).[86] In addition, the parent of a child who has been abused and granted cancellation also will be granted parole.[87] This parole extends from the time the relief is granted to the time that the parolees ultimately are able to adjust status.

Confidentiality

The Executive Office for Immigration Review (EOIR) has issued a memorandum to all immigration courts stating clearly that VAWA cancellation of removal applications are confidential. The file is marked when the IJ becomes aware that a case is a VAWA cancellation of removal. In addition, the IJ is to clear the courtroom on the date of a hearing with a VAWA cancellation of removal applicant. No information regarding the VAWA cancellation of removal case can be given to any individual outside the court. There can be no finding of removability or inadmissibility using information furnished by the accuser or any member of the household. The files of those seeking VAWA cancellation of removal are given not only a separate stamp, but a separate code within the EOIR computer file management system.[88]

NACARA Cancellation of Removal

Another common form of cancellation of removal can be pursued via NACARA.[89] This relief, known as NACARA cancellation of removal, is found under §203 of the NACARA statute. Congress provided that certain groups of individuals from El Salvador, Guatemala, and the countries of the former Soviet Union are eligible for cancellation of removal under relaxed standards. Specifically, the statute provides that these groups of individuals be eligible to seek relief under the standards of the former suspension of deportation rather than the more strict cancellation of removal standards found at INA §240A(b). However, the standards are different for each group; that is, this form of relief is country specific. Only individuals from the designated countries who meet the requirements for that particular country may seek this form of relief. Following are the requirements for eligibility for each group:

Requirements to apply for NACARA cancellation of removal

- *El Salvador*—To be considered eligible to apply for NACARA cancellation of removal, Salvadorans must show:
  - entry into the United States on or before September 19, 1990;

---

[86] INA §240A(b)(4)(A).

[87] *Id.*

[88] *See* EOIR Operating Procedures and Policy Memorandum 97-7, at *www.usdoj.gov/eoir*.

[89] NACARA, *supra* note 4.

- registration for Temporary Protected Status (TPS); registration as a class member in the *American Baptist Churches* (*ABC*)[90] class action on or before October 31, 1991; or filing an application for asylum prior to April 1, 1990; and
- not apprehended at the time of entry after Dec. 19, 1990.

▪ *Guatemalans*—Guatemalans must show:

- entry into the United States on or before October 1, 1990; and
- registration as an *ABC* class member on or before December 31, 1991 (Guatemala has never been designated as a TPS country); or filing for asylum prior to April 1, 1990.

Guatemalans and Salvadorans who filed applications for asylum with the government on or before April 1, 1990, are eligible to seek NACARA cancellation of removal even if they did not register for the *ABC* class.[91]

Eastern Europeans—For Eastern Europeans, the requirements are:

- entry into the United States on or before December 31, 1990;
- filing of an application for asylum on or before December 31, 1991;
- proof of citizenship in the former Soviet Union or Eastern bloc countries under the control of the Soviet Union at the time of filing.[92]

Jurisdiction to adjudicate NACARA cancellation of removal applications

El Salvador

For Salvadorans who have registered for *ABC* or TPS as outlined above and filed an application for asylum (pursuant to the *ABC* settlement agreement), their cancellation of removal applications are adjudicated by the U.S. Citizenship and Immigration Services (USCIS) asylum section if the asylum claim is still pending. However, if the application for asylum was "referred" to the immigration court, or if a charging document has been issued against the alien placing him or her in removal proceedings, the application is adjudicated by the IJ unless those proceedings have previously been administratively closed.[93]

Guatemalans

For Guatemalans who have registered for the *ABC* class settlement and who have filed an application for asylum with the asylum office prior to January 3, 1995 (in accordance with the *ABC* settlement agreement), USCIS adjudicates their cancellation applications if those asylum applications are still pending. If the application has

---

90 *American Baptist Churches v. Thornburgh*, 760 F. Supp. 796 (N.D. Cal. 1991). The *American Baptist Churches* lawsuit was a class action against the Department of Justice (DOJ) for the discrimination and treatment of asylum claims filed by El Salvadoran and Guatemalan applicants.

91 8 CFR §§240.61, 1240.61.

92 8 CFR §§240.61(a)(3), 1240.61(a)(3).

93 8 CFR §§240.62(b), 1240.62(b).

been referred to the immigration court, the IJ adjudicates the application for cancellation.

Eastern Europeans

For Eastern Europeans who meet the requirements outlined above, the cancellation or removal applications are submitted to the USCIS asylum office, which adjudicates the asylum and the NACARA cancellation of removal applications. However, if the individual has previously been referred to the immigration court and removal proceedings are pending, the IJ adjudicates the NACARA claim.

Application process

The application is submitted on Form I-881 (Application for Suspension of Deportation or Special Rule Cancellation of Removal). The application must be filed with the appropriate filing fee (currently $285) and the fee for the fingerprinting (currently $70).[94] The fee is the same whether the application is filed with the asylum office or with the immigration court.

If the application is before the IJ, it is filed in accordance with the court's local rules or instructions by the IJ. The applicant should be very clear in understanding the exact procedures used by the court, and should not leave the court on the day of the master calendar without understanding exactly how the court wants the application filed (where, when, fingerprinting, court's instructions for the preparation and presentation of applications and evidence, etc.). All supporting documentation to prove the eligibility requirements outlined below should be attached to the application. Any application submitted to the court also should be submitted to the DHS trial attorney.

Elements

Physical presence

The applicant for NACARA cancellation of removal must prove to the asylum officer or IJ that he or she meets the requirement of seven years' physical presence in the United States.[95] Any absence of 90 days, or 180 days in the aggregate for multiple absences, breaks the continuity of physical presence.[96] The applicant must meet the standard by a preponderance of the evidence showing eligibility. Even if the break was less than 90 days, the applicant still may be required to show that it was "casual and innocent" and not meaningfully interruptive of the period of continuous physical presence.[97] Removal of an alien from the United States is a break

---

[94] 8 CFR §§240.63(a), 1240.63(a).

[95] 8 CFR §§240.66(b)(2), 1240.66(b)(2).

[96] 8 CFR §§240.64(b), 1240.64(b).

[97] 8 CFR §§240.64(b)(2), 1240.64(b)(2).

in physical presence.[98] There are exceptions for individuals who have served in the U.S. Armed Forces.[99]

Good moral character

The applicant for NACARA cancellation of removal must establish that he or she would have met the requirements for suspension of deportation under former INA §244. This statute requires not only that an individual have physical presence for seven years, but that he or she maintain good moral character during this time.[100]

Rebuttable presumption of extreme hardship

The groups of individuals from El Salvador, Guatemala, and Eastern Europe who are eligible to seek NACARA cancellation of removal are the beneficiaries of a presumption of extreme hardship that can be rebutted by the government. Hardship is presumed as a result of deportation or removal.[101] This presumption can be rebutted if the evidence in the record establishes that it is more likely than not that neither the applicant nor a qualified relative would suffer extreme hardship if the applicant were deported. It is the burden of the government to rebut this presumption.[102]

Motions to reopen

Individuals with prior final orders of deportation or removal from El Salvador, Guatemala, or Eastern Europe were required to file a motion to reopen proceedings during the period beginning in January 1998 and ending on September 11, 1998. Failure to file this motion to reopen results in loss of eligibility.[103]

Spouses and children of principal aliens

The NACARA statute states that an alien who is a spouse or child of a principal alien granted NACARA cancellation of removal also may be eligible for cancellation without having to meet the individual requirement that the principal had to prove. In addition, unmarried sons and daughters (children 21 years of age or older) of the eligible principal aliens may be eligible for cancellation of removal if they can prove that they entered the United States on or before October 1, 1990.[104]

Referral of application to the immigration court

If the asylum officer adjudicates the application for NACARA cancellation of removal and determines that the individual is ineligible for NACARA cancellation of

[98] 8 CFR §§240.64(b)(3), 1240.64(b)(3).

[99] 8 CFR §§240.64(b)(4), 1240.64(b)(4).

[100] *See* discussion on good moral character, above; INA §101(f). *See also* 8 CFR §§240.66(b)(3), 1240.66(b)(3).

[101] 8 CFR §§240.64(d)(1), 1240.64(d)(1).

[102] 8 CFR §§240.64(d)(3), 1240.64(d)(3).

[103] 8 CFR §1003.43(e)(2).

[104] 8 CFR §§240.61(a)(4) and (5), 1240.61(a)(4) and (5).

removal, the application is referred to the immigration court for adjudication in deportation or removal proceedings. If the officer determines that the individual is eligible, the application is to be granted. The applicant must admit deportability or inadmissibility at the interview before the application can be granted. If the applicant refuses to admit deportability, removability, or inadmissibility, the asylum officer must refer the application to the court even though the applicant may be eligible for NACARA cancellation.[105]

Cancellation of Removal for Certain Permanent Residents

Introduction

Cancellation of removal for permanent residents under INA §240A(a) is a form of relief by which an alien who has been an LPR for at least five years and who has resided continuously in the United States for a period of seven years may apply to retain that lawful resident status even if he or she takes an action that would make him or her inadmissible under INA §212(a), or deportable under §237(a). It is, in effect, a second chance for LPRs who have been in trouble with the law. The only class of criminal aliens that is specifically barred from this form of relief is the aggravated felon class.

The INA historically has had a form of relief by which LPRs could seek to retain that status if they had run afoul of the law. The form of relief in effect prior to the enactment of IIRAIRA in 1996 was relief under former INA §212(c) (see §212(c) discussion, *infra*, for individuals who may be eligible to seek §212(c) relief if they are deportation proceedings). Both forms of relief are humanitarian in nature. Both are meant to give an individual who has established ties in the United States, and lived for a long period as a lawful resident, an opportunity to rehabilitate him- or herself and retain his or her status. Both are "defensive" applications, *i.e.*, they can be sought only in a proceeding before an IJ after the individual has been found inadmissible under INA §212(a) or deportable under INA §237(a), as relief from removability.

Statutory Requirements

Section 240A(a) of the INA makes cancellation of removal available to certain LPRs if they meet the following qualifications:

- lawful admission for permanent residence for five years or more;
- continuous residence in the United States for seven years after having been admitted in any status;
- lack of convictions for any aggravated felony.[106]

---

[105] 8 CFR §§240.70(d)(3), 1240.70(d)(3).

[106] INA §240A(a).

Although not explicitly stated in the statute, the applicant must prove that he or she merits a positive exercise of discretion. Therefore, the applicant must prove to the IJ that the positive equities outweigh the negative factors. These discretionary factors will be discussed below.

Lawful admission for permanent residents

Cancellation of removal for LPRs requires that an individual prove that he or she has been lawfully admitted for permanent residence and that the period of lawful resident status is "not less than 5 years."[107] The INA states that the term "lawfully admitted for permanent residence" means that the alien has been accorded the privilege of residing permanently in the United States as an immigrant and such status has not changed.[108] The phrase "lawful permanent residence" means that the residence must have been obtained lawfully.[109] An alien who has acquired permanent resident status through fraud has never been lawfully admitted for permanent residence.[110] Therefore, even though an individual has a Green Card, if that card was obtained by fraud, it is not "lawful permanent residence" for relief purposes. In short, an applicant for cancellation of removal must, as a threshold issue, show that he or she has been an LPR for five or more years and that residence was lawfully obtained.

Continuous residence for seven years after admission

The second requirement under INA §240A(a) is that an applicant must show seven years of continuous residence after admission "in any status." The INA states that the terms "admission" and "admitted" mean "the lawful entry of the alien into the United State after inspection and authorization by an immigration officer."[111] The seven years' continuous residence can accrue after admission in any lawful status—immigrant or nonimmigrant.[112] It is clear that this statute does not include unlawful entry into the United States. Admission under INA means inspection and authorization to be admitted into the United States; "admission" also means adjustment of status within the United States.[113] The BIA has stated that an alien's residence in the United States after admission as a nonimmigrant may be considered in calculating the seven years of continuous residence required to establish eligibility for cancellation of removal.[114] In *Matter of Blancas-Lara*, the alien entered the United States in 1986 with a border crossing card and then obtained lawful status as a permanent resident in 1991. He was placed into deportation proceedings six years later. The government argued that he did not qualify for cancellation of removal because he had only six

---

[107] INA §240A(a)(1).

[108] INA §101(a)(20).

[109] *Matter of Ayala*, 22 I&N Dec. 398 (BIA 1998).

[110] *Matter of Koloamatangi*, 23 I&N Dec. 548 (BIA 2003).

[111] INA §101(a)(13)(A).

[112] *Matter of Blancas-Lara*, 23 I&N Dec. 458 (BIA 2002).

[113] *Matter of Shanu*, 23 I&N Dec. 754 (BIA 2005).

[114] *Blancas-Lara*, 23 I&N Dec. 458.

years as a lawful permanent resident. The BIA found that the five years after admission with a border crossing card could be added to the six years of lawful permanent residence in order to meet the seven-year requirement.[115]

One federal circuit court also has found that the lawful admission and legal permanent residence of a parent could be imputed to a minor unemancipated child for purposes of calculating the period of continuous residence.[116]

In 1996, through IIRAIRA, Congress added the "stop-time" rule in measuring continuous residence or physical presences for relief purposes. The rule states that any period of continuous residence or physical presence in the United States for cancellation of removal purposes shall be deemed to end when the individual is served an NTA, or when the individual commits an offense "referred to" in INA §212(a)(2) that renders the individual inadmissible to the United States or deportable from the United States under INA §§237(a)(2) or (4), whichever is earliest.[117] The time is stopped as of the date of *commission* of the crime, not the conviction.[118]

The "stop-time" provisions also apply retroactively to individuals placed into deportation proceedings prior to the enactment of IIRAIRA. Although it was unclear in the wording of IIRAIRA whether this stop-time rule was to be applied retroactively, Congress, in 1997, via NACARA, made clear that the stop-time provision was to be applied retroactively even to those placed into pre-IIRAIRA deportation proceedings.[119]

The BIA has found that where an individual was convicted of two misdemeanor crimes and did not become inadmissible under INA §212(a)(2) until the commission of the second crime, the clock did not stop for cancellation of removal purposes until the second crime was committed. The first crime that did not make the applicant inadmissible by itself did not stop the clock.[120]

No convictions for aggravated felonies

Section 240A(a) states clearly that an individual is ineligible for cancellation of removal if he or she has been convicted of an aggravated felony.[121] There are no exceptions to this rule for cancellation of removal for LPRs. Conviction is defined as the following:

- a formal judgment of guilt entered by a court; or if adjudication of guilt is withheld, a judge or jury has found the alien guilty, or he has entered a plea of guilty or *nolo contendere*, or admitted sufficient facts to warrant a finding of guilt; and

[115] *Id.*

[116] *Cuevas-Gaspar v. Gonzales*, 430 F.3d 1015 (9th Cir. 2005).

[117] INA §240A(d)(1).

[118] *Matter of Perez*, 22 I&N Dec. 689 (BIA 1999).

[119] NACARA, *supra* note 4; *see also Ashki v. INS*, 233 F.3d 913 (6th Cir. 2000).

[120] *Matter of Deanda-Romo*, 23 I&N Dec. 597 (BIA 2003).

[121] INA §240A(a)(3).

- the judge has entered some form of punishment, penalty, or restraint on the liberty of the alien.[122]

In sum, a finding or admission of guilt coupled with some restraint on a person's liberty is a conviction for purposes of INA §240A(a). However, if either of these elements is missing, there is no conviction for immigration purposes. Once a conviction is entered by the criminal court, the fact that it is later dismissed or expunged under a state rehabilitative statute for purposes of eliminating an immigration hardship (as opposed to substantive or procedural defects) will not alter its finality for removal purposes. It is still a conviction and can be a basis for removal and a finding of ineligibility for relief.[123] However, where the conviction is overturned for a substantive reason (*e.g.*, failure to admonish the defendant of the immigration consequences of a guilty plea), it may not be used as a conviction for removal purposes.[124] One circuit court has implied that where a conviction is vacated for any reason, it can still be used as a basis for removal by the immigration authorities.[125] However, the BIA's position is that if the conviction is vacated for substantive or procedural reasons unrelated to avoiding immigration hardships, the conviction cannot be used as a basis for removal or denial of relief.[126] The BIA has recognized that where a criminal court has reduced a defendant's sentence below the one-year period required for an aggravated felony, that defendant cannot be classified as an aggravated felon.[127]

In the cancellation of removal context, there are two questions to be addressed: (1) has there been a conviction?; and (2) if so, is the crime an aggravated felony?[128]

Aliens Ineligible for Cancellation of Removal

The statute states that there are certain classes of individuals who are ineligible for cancellation of removal for permanent residents under INA §240A(a) and for non–permanent residents under INA §240A(b)(1).[129] These include:

- aliens who entered as crewmen after June 30, 1964;
- holders of J visas who came to the United States for graduate medical education or training, regardless of whether they are subject to the two-year foreign residence requirement;

---

[122] INA §101(a)(48).

[123] *Matter of Pickering*, 23 I&N Dec. 621 (BIA 2003).

[124] *Matter of Adamiek*, 23 I&N Dec. 878 (BIA 2006).

[125] *Renteria-Gonzalez v. INS*, 322 F.3d 804, 812 (5th Cir. 2002).

[126] *Matter of Rodriguez-Ruiz*, 22 I&N Dec. 1378 (BIA 2000).

[127] *Matter of Song*, 23 I&N Dec. 173 (BIA 2001).

[128] For individuals amenable to §212(c) relief, the situation is different. Some individuals with convictions for aggravated felonies (defined under INA §101(a)(43)) may still be eligible for §212(c) relief, depending on the date of the plea agreement, the nature of the crime, or the sentence imposed. This will be discussed further, *infra*.

[129] INA §240A(c).

- holders of J visas who are subject to the two-year foreign residence requirement and have not completed it or obtained a waiver;
- individuals inadmissible under INA §212(a)(3) or removable under INA §237(a)(4) for security reasons;
- persecutors of others under INA §241(b)(3)(B)(i); and
- individuals previously granted cancellation of removal, or suspension of deportation or §212(c) relief under the Act as in effect prior to the changes made by IIRAIRA in 1996.

Discretionary Factors

If an individual is not barred from relief and meets the statutory residence and lawful permanent residence status requirements of §240A(a), he or she then must merit the positive exercise of discretion. The BIA has issued one major precedent decision on the issue of the discretionary factors that should be weighed to determine eligibility for cancellation of removal. In *Matter of C–V–T–*, the BIA found that an applicant had to establish that cancellation of removal relief was warranted as a matter of discretion.[130] In exercising that discretion, the BIA stated that the standards developed in the prior §212(c) precedent decisions would apply in the cancellation of removal situation as well. Citing *Matter of Marin*,[131] the BIA stated that the IJ, upon review of the record as a whole, "must balance the adverse factors evidencing the alien's undesirability as a permanent resident with the social and humane considerations presented in his (or her) behalf to determine whether the granting of … relief appears to be in the best interest of this country."[132] The BIA then listed the positive and negative factors, *i.e.*, the "*Marin*" factors.

On the positive side are family ties within the United States; residence of long duration in the United States (particularly when the residence starts at a young age); evidence of hardship to the respondent and his or her family if deportation occurs; service in this country's armed forces; a history of employment; the existence of property or business ties; evidence of value and service to the community; proof of genuine rehabilitation if a conviction exists; and other evidence attesting to a person's good character.[133]

On the negative side are the following: nature and underlying circumstances of the exclusion or deportation (now removal) ground(s) at issue; the presence of other significant violations of the country's immigration laws; the existence of a criminal record and its nature, recency, and seriousness; and the presence of other factors indicative of poor character or undesirability as a permanent resident of this country.[134]

---

[130] *Matter of C–V–T–*, 22 I&N Dec. 7 (BIA 1998).

[131] *See Matter of Marin*, 16 I&N Dec. 581, 584–85 (BIA 1978).

[132] *C–V–T–*, 22 I&N Dec. 7.

[133] *Id.*

[134] *Id.*

As the negative factors grow more serious, it is incumbent on the alien to counterbalance these with additional favorable factors.[135] In some cases, this may mean outstanding or unusual equities.[136] A heightened standard is used when there is a serious criminal record, such as a serious drug offense like trafficking. A heightened showing of equities also may be required where there is one serious offense or a succession of criminal acts that taken together establish a pattern of serious criminal misconduct.[137] However, a showing of outstanding and unusual equities is not a threshold requirement in order to consider all of the factors. All factors bearing on discretion—positive and negative—must be considered.[138] The BIA, in *Matter of Edwards*, goes on to state that even where outstanding and unusual equities are shown, the crime may be so serious that a positive exercise of discretion is not possible.[139] This language is irrelevant in the cancellation of removal context in most cases because if a crime is very serious, it is most likely already classified as an aggravated felony and the individual is statutorily not eligible for cancellation of removal. Additionally, the BIA has indicated that rehabilitation is not an absolute prerequisite to a grant of relief, although it is a factor to be considered.[140]

Relief Under INA §212(c)

Introduction—Brief Historical Background of Relief Under INA §212(c)

Immigration and Nationality Act (1952)

Between 1952 and 1996 (before IIRAIRA's cancellation of removal for LPRs), individuals who had been lawfully present in the United States for many years, but who faced exclusion or deportation proceedings because of some action they had taken (often resulting in a criminal conviction) had only one possibility for retaining their lawful resident status—relief under INA §212(c). The 1952 INA provided relief under §212(c) to individuals who met the following requirements: (1) lawful admission for permanent residence; (2) departure from the United States voluntarily and not under an order of deportation; and (3) excludable from the United States, but not on subversive charges. Although literally applicable to exclusion (now inadmissibility) proceedings, relief under §212(c) also waived most forms of deportability including those for individuals who had been convicted of drug trafficking, smuggling aliens, or other serious crimes, so long as those grounds of deportability had comparable exclusion grounds. It was a discretionary form of relief.

---

[135] *Id.*

[136] *Matter of Edwards*, 20 I&N Dec. 191, 195–96 (BIA 1990).

[137] *Id.* at 195, 196; *see also Matter of Buscemi*, 19 I&N Dec. 628 (BIA 1988); *Matter of Roberts*, 20 I&N Dec. 294 (BIA 1991).

[138] *Edwards*, 20 I&N Dec. at 195.

[139] *Id.* at 196.

[140] *Id.*

Section 212(c) was initially used like other waivers as a means of obtaining, in advance, the removal of a ground of inadmissibility for individuals seeking entry or adjustment of status. However, the issue later arose as to whether it could be used in deportation proceedings involving respondents who had been lawfully admitted for permanent residence and had continuously resided in the United States for seven years. The federal courts, and subsequently the immigration courts, authorized the use of the waiver in deportation proceedings where the deportation ground was analogous to a ground of inadmissibility.[141]

Immigration Act of 1990 (IMMACT90)

There were no significant legislative changes to the waiver until 1990. The Immigration Act of 1990 (IMMACT90)[142] barred §212(c) relief for individuals who had been convicted of certain aggravated felonies and had served prison terms of at least five years. IMMACT90 expanded the definition of aggravated felonies to include not only those included in the omnibus Anti-Drug Abuse Act of 1988 (ADAA)[143] (those convicted for murder, illicit trafficking in controlled substances, and illicit trafficking in firearms or destructive devices), but also money laundering under 18 USC §1956 and crimes of violence as defined in 18 USC §16. IMMACT90 made an individual who had been convicted of any of these offenses, and who had served a period of incarceration of at least five years, ineligible for relief.

IMMACT90 was not clear as to the effective date after which such convictions would bar relief under §212(c). Several circuits held that IMMACT90 applied retroactively to convictions for aggravated felonies defined in the ADAA that occurred prior to the enactment of IMMACT90.[144] However, convictions for aggravated felonies added by IMMACT90, specifically crimes of violence and crimes relating to money laundering, were only to be applied prospectively on or after the effective date of enactment—November 29, 1990.[145] In 1991, the statute was amended so that aggregate sentences for multiple aggravated felonies amounting to five or more years barred an individual from relief. This change was effective "as if included in the Immigration Act of 1990." The BIA later determined that the bar to §212(c) relief applied to aggravated felons convicted prior to 1988.[146]

AEDPA

In 1996, Congress enacted two laws that drastically affected the availability of relief under §212(c) for LPRs—the Antiterrorism and Effective Death Penalty Act

---

[141] *See Francis v. INS*, 532 F.2d 268 (2d Cir. 1976); *Matter of Silva*, 16 I&N Dec. 26 (BIA 1976).

[142] Immigration Act of 1990, Pub. L. No. 101-649, 104 Stat. 4978.

[143] Pub. L. No. 100-690.

[144] *Ignacio v. INS*, 955 F.2d 295 (5th Cir. 1992).

[145] *Matter of A–A–*, 20 I&N Dec. 492 (BIA 1992).

[146] *Matter of Gomez-Giraldo*, 20 I&N Dec. 957 (BIA 1995).

(AEDPA) and the Illegal Immigration Reform and Immigrant Responsibility Act (IIRAIRA).

AEDPA was enacted on April 24, 1996, and made a number of changes to the law. It made relief under §212(c) unavailable to various classes of LPRs found deportable for criminal problems other than aggravated felonies, including: individuals with convictions for controlled substances that were not aggravated felonies; those convicted for firearms offenses; and various classes of individuals with convictions for crimes involving moral turpitude and crimes involving national security.[147] The then-Attorney General took the position that AEDPA was immediately effective and barred relief to any individual with a pending claim before an IJ or the BIA regardless of the date of the commission of the offense, the date of conviction, or the date of filing the relief application, thus applying retroactively to pleas in the underlying criminal cases that were entered prior to AEDPA's passage.[148] There were numerous successful federal court challenges to the retroactive application by the AG.[149] AEDPA also eliminated judicial review of deportation orders against aliens who had been ordered deported based on criminal convictions. Moreover, it contained mandatory detention provisions for certain classes of criminal aliens. The bar to §212(c) relief under AEDPA was applicable to those in deportation proceedings, but not to individuals in exclusion proceedings.[150]

IIRAIRA

Several months after the enactment of AEDPA, Congress passed IIRAIRA, which was enacted on September 30, 1996.[151] IIRAIRA was a massive overhaul of the immigration laws. It eliminated INA §212(c), replacing it with cancellation of removal for permanent residents under INA §240A(a) (discussed, *supra*).

IIRAIRA greatly expanded the classes of crimes that are defined as aggravated felonies, thereby barring most LPRs from the new cancellation of removal form of relief. In addition to the prior classes of aggravated felony crimes, such as murder, rape, and illicit trafficking in controlled substances and firearms, the new statute added theft, perjury, forgery, counterfeiting, bribery, obstruction of justice, failure to appear in court, certain fraud crimes, and crimes of violence under 18 USC §16 to the list, as long as there was a conviction and a "term of imprisonment" of at least one year.[152]

---

[147] Antiterrorism and Effective Death Penalty Act, Pub. L. No. 104-132, §440(d), 110 Stat. 1214 (Apr. 24, 1996).

[148] *Matter of Soriano*, 21 I&N Dec. 516 (A.G. 1997).

[149] *See Wallace v. Reno*, 194 F.3d 279 (1st Cir. 1999); *Magana-Pizano v. INS*, 200 F.3d 603 (9th Cir. 1999).

[150] *Matter of Fuentes-Compos*, 21 I&N Dec. 905 (BIA 1997).

[151] IIRAIRA, *supra* note 2.

[152] INA §101(a)(43).

IIRAIRA made the definition of "aggravated felony" apply to convictions entered "before, on, or after" the date of enactment—September 30, 1996. The retroactive effect makes an individual removable and ineligible for relief even for crimes committed many years in the past and prior to IIRAIRA. The aggravated felony bar therefore eliminates cancellation of removal relief for most LPRs regardless of the length of residence in the United States or the equities accumulated during that period of time.

The statute also changed the definition of the term "conviction" so that a conviction requires merely a formal adjudication of guilt, a plea of guilty or nolo contendere, or an admission of sufficient facts to warrant a finding of guilt together with some form of punishment or restraint on liberty. A "term of imprisonment" under IIRAIRA includes periods of incarceration ordered by a court even where there is a suspension of the imposition or execution of imprisonment.[153]

In sum, the changes to immigration law under AEDPA and IIRAIRA effectively wiped out the possibility of retention of lawful permanent residence for the majority of Green Card-holders with any type of criminal conviction. In addition, IIRAIRA eliminated judicial review for those denied this form of relief.[154]

Soriano regulations

After the enactment of AEDPA, the Department of Justice (DOJ) published what came to be known as the *Soriano* regulations.[155] The *Soriano* regulations stated that the amendments made by §440(d) of AEDPA were not applicable to individuals placed into deportation proceedings prior to April 24, 1996—the effective date of AEDPA. Thus, individuals who were placed into deportation proceedings prior to April 24, 1996, were considered to be still eligible for INA §212(c) relief regardless or whether their conviction resulted from a trial or from a plea agreement, and regardless of the date of the final hearing before the immigration court. The only issue was the date that deportation proceedings were commenced. The §212(c) regulations (discussed below) retain the provisions of the *Soriano* regulations in their entirety. The only limitation is that in effect for those convicted after 1990 under IMMACT90; that is, individuals who have served five or more years for an aggravated felony conviction are ineligible for §212(c) relief.

St. Cyr decision

In June of 2001, the Supreme Court addressed two of the major issues raised by IIRAIRA's changes to the immigration laws. The Court in *INS v. St. Cyr*,[156] was faced with the issue of whether the federal courts still had habeas corpus jurisdiction under 28 USC §2241 to review removal orders in light of the judicial review restric-

---

[153] INA §101(a)(48).

[154] INA §242(a)(2)(C).

[155] 8 CFR §§212.3(g), 1212.3(g). *See also Matter of Soriano*, 21 I&N Dec. 516 (BIA 1996, A.G. 1997).

[156] 553 U.S. 289, 323 (2001).

tions of AEDPA and IIRAIRA. The second issue that the Court addressed was whether IIRAIRA §304(b) had an illegal retroactive effect when applied to an individual seeking §212(c) relief if he or she was eligible for this relief at the time he or she entered a guilty plea.

The Court found that habeas relief was still available to individuals seeking review of removal orders under 28 USC §2241. It stated that there was a "strong presumption in favor of judicial review" and that there must be a "clear statement of congressional intent" to repeal habeas jurisdiction. The Court also noted that there is a historically different meaning for the terms "judicial review" and "habeas corpus."

The second finding made by the Court in *St. Cyr* was that relief under §212(c) remains available to aliens whose convictions were obtained through plea agreements and who would have been eligible for such relief under the law in effect at the time the plea was made. The Court stated that Congress's intentions concerning the application of the cancellation of removal procedure were ambiguous, and found that the government's interpretation of the statute imposed an impermissible retroactive effect on aliens who, in reliance on the possibility of §212(c) relief, pleaded guilty to aggravated felonies.[157] Among the findings made by the Court were the following:

- Congressional enactments will not be construed to have retroactive effect unless the language clearly requires this result. Congress has the power to enact laws with retroactive effect; however, it may not do so absent clear indication that it intended such a result.
- Elementary considerations of fairness dictate that individuals have an opportunity to know what the law is and to conform their conduct accordingly.
- The legal effect of conduct should ordinarily be assessed under the law that existed when the conduct took place.
- Elimination of §212(c) relief for people who entered into plea agreements with the expectation that they would be eligible for such relief clearly attaches a new disability and therefore has retroactive effect.
- The potential for unfairness in the retroactive application of IIRAIRA is significant and manifest.

In his opinion, Justice John Paul Stevens stated that the possibility of §212(c) relief would have been one of the principal benefits sought by a defendant in deciding whether to go to trial or accept a plea. He went on to state that it would be contrary to "familiar considerations of fair notice, reasonable reliance and settled expectations" to hold that IIRAIRA's subsequent restrictions deprived individuals of any possibility of such relief.[158]

The decision in *St. Cyr* and the language used by the majority have opened up new possibilities for LPRs seeking relief. The decision made possible §212(c) relief for

---

[157] *Id.* at 312.

[158] *Id.* at 323, 324.

thousands of individuals previously found to be ineligible. In effect, the Supreme Court's decision resurrected a form of relief that is no longer found in the INA. Unfortunately, many who would have benefited by the decision of the Court in *St. Cyr* already had been removed. Others, however, still present in the United States with pending cases before the immigration court or BIA are able to seek relief under INA §212(c) depending on a number of factors, discussed below. Individuals who are present with administratively final orders of removal also may apply for §212(c) relief. The decision in *St. Cyr* left open several procedural and substantive issues, some of which were addressed in the "*St. Cyr*" regulations (outlined below).

St. Cyr regulations

On September 28, 2004, DOJ issued a final rule on §212(c) relief in light of the decision of the Supreme Court in *INS v. St. Cyr*.[159] The new rule answered several questions. First, it made clear who was eligible for relief under former §212(c) and whether this relief was available to individuals who had been deported based on the interpretation of the law by the courts prior to the *St. Cyr* decision. It also gave deadlines for filing a "Special Motion" to seek §212(c) relief. The rule restated the legal conclusions of the Supreme Court in *St. Cyr*—generally, that the law in effect at the time the plea was made is the law that governs. Specifically, the rule states the fact that the plea in the criminal proceedings had to have taken place prior to the enactment of AEDPA—April 24, 1996—for §212(c) relief to apply without regard to AEDPA's restrictions on the relief. The *St. Cyr* regulations retain the *Soriano* regulations; thus, if the plea occurred between April 24, 1996, and April 1, 1997, the petitioner is eligible for the §212(c) relief that exists with AEDPA's restrictive amendments.[160] If the plea agreement takes place after April 1, 1997, the individual does not get any benefit of this regulation even if the criminal conduct took place prior to April 24, 1996.[161] It is the date of the plea that controls. Under the rule, those who have been found guilty after a trial, rather than as a result of a plea agreement, are not eligible to seek §212(c) relief even if the verdict was issued prior to April 24, 1996. Only those who have pleaded can be considered eligible for this relief because a plea (as opposed to a verdict) can be given based on reliance claims (*i.e.*, a defendant might forego a trial where he or she could be found not guilty and instead plead guilty or nolo contendere in reliance on a form of immigration relief available).

Who is eligible to seek §212(c) relief under the regulations

The rule at 8 CFR §1003.44(b) states that an applicant must meet the following requirements in order to establish eligibility:

- lawful permanent residence;
- subject to a final order of deportation or removal;

---

[159] 8 CFR §1003.44. In addition, other regulations relating to §212(c) relief are found at 8 CFR §§212.3, 1212.3.

[160] 8 CFR §1212.3(h)(2).

[161] *Domond v. INS*, 244 F.3d 81 (2d Cir. 2001).

- plea of guilty of nolo contendere to an offense rendering the alien deportable or removable pursuant to a plea agreement made before April 1, 1997;
- seven consecutive years of lawful unrelinquished domicile in the United States prior to the date of a final administrative order of deportation or removal; and
- otherwise eligible to apply for §212(c) relief under the standards in effect at the time the plea was made.[162]

Who is not eligible to §212(c) relief under the regulations

In addition to those who do not meet the above requirements, the final rule specifically excludes the following classes of individuals from eligibility:

- individuals who have been deported from the United States and are either outside of the United States or have re-entered illegally;[163]
- individuals who have been found guilty after a trial, rather than through a plea agreement;[164]
- individuals who pleaded to an aggravated felony conviction on or after April 1, 1997;[165]
- individuals found deportable on grounds of deportability that do not have a statutory counterpart under the §212(a) grounds of inadmissibility;[166]
- aliens who have not been admitted or paroled;[167]
- individuals who are inadmissible under certain security provisions of INA §212(a)(3);[168] and
- individuals previously denied §212(c) relief.[169]

Aggravated felons

Section 1003.44 has various provisions relating to aggravated felons depending on the law in effect at the time of the plea agreement.

- *Individuals who pleaded before November 29, 1990*: Individuals are not excluded from §212(c) relief on account of a plea agreement to an aggravated felony conviction made prior to November 29, 1990.
- *Individuals who pleaded between November 29, 1990, and April 24, 1996:* Individuals who pleaded to an aggravated felony conviction on or after November 29,

---

[162] 8 CFR §1003.44(b).

[163] 8 CFR §1003.44(k).

[164] 8 CFR §1212.3(h); *see also Rankine v. Reno*, 319 F.3d 93 (2d Cir. 2003).

[165] 8 CFR §1212.3(h)(3).

[166] 8 CFR §§212.3(f)(5), 1212.3(f)(5).

[167] 8 CFR §1003.44(k)(3).

[168] 8 CFR §§212.3(f)(3), 1212.3(f)(3).

[169] 8 CFR §1003.44(d).

1990, but prior to April 24, 1996, are eligible for §212(c) relief unless that individual served a term of imprisonment of five or more years for one or more aggravated felonies (terms can be aggregated).

- *Individuals who pleaded between April 24, 1996 and April 1, 1997:* See section on the *Soriano* regulations, above, relating to the effect of AEDPA §440(d) on §212(c) relief eligibility.

Date of plea agreement

For purposes of 8 CFR §1003.44, the date of the plea agreement is considered to be the date on which the plea agreement was agreed to by the parties, as opposed to the date the court accepted the plea.[170]

- *Pleas prior to April 24, 1996:* For those who pleaded prior to April 24, 1996, the effective date of AEDPA, the law in effect at the time of the plea governs.[171]
- *Pleas from April 24, 1996, to April 1, 1997:* The amendments made by AEDPA §440(d) (restricting eligibility for individuals convicted of certain crimes involving moral turpitude, aggravated felonies, firearms offenses, and controlled substance violations where the sentence imposed was five years or more) apply.[172]
- *Pleas on or after April 1, 1997:* Section 212(c) relief is not available;[173] cancellation of removal under INA §240A(a) is the only possible relief.

Establishing Eligibility for Relief Under INA §212(c)

Once it is established that an individual is eligible to seek relief under former INA §212(c)—either because of having pleaded to a crime prior to April 24, 1996, or because the individual is in deportation (as opposed to removal) proceedings, the basic requirements for establishing eligibility remain the same whether the person is seeking §212(c) relief in deportation or removal proceedings.

- The applicant must be an alien lawfully admitted for permanent residence.
- He or she must be returning to (or continuing) a lawful unrelinquished domicile of at least seven years.
- If convicted of one or more aggravated felonies, he or she must not have served five years in the aggregate for those felonies (relates to pleas between November 29, 1990 and April 24, 1996).
- If he or she is applying for §212(c) relief in order to waive a ground of deportability (under current INA §237 or former §241), there must exist a corresponding ground of inadmissibility.[174]

---

[170] 8 CFR §1212.3(h).

[171] 8 CFR §1212.3(h)(1).

[172] 8 CFR §1212.3(h)(2).

[173] 8 CFR §1212.3(h)(3).

[174] INA §212(c) (1995); *see also* 8 CFR §§212.3(f), 1212.3(f).

Lawful admission for permanent residence

The statute defines "lawfully admitted for permanent residence" as "the status of having been lawfully accorded the privilege of residing permanently in the United States as an immigrant in accordance with the immigration laws, such status not having changed."[175] One who was wrongly granted permanent residence (*i.e.*, by failing to reveal an existing ground of inadmissibility) did not obtain permanent residence "in accordance with the immigration laws" and so would not be eligible for §212(c) relief.[176] One who holds a Green Card may be ineligible for §212(c) relief if his or her status has changed; for example, if he or she is found to have abandoned his or her residence by virtue of the length and nature of absences from the United States.[177] Lawful permanent residence ends with an administratively final order of deportation.[178]

Lawful unrelinquished domicile

Section 212(c) does not explicitly require seven years as an LPR; nor does it require seven years' physical presence. Rather, it requires seven years' "lawful unrelinquished domicile." For years, the INS insisted and the BIA agreed that "lawful domicile" commenced only with a grant of permanent residence.[179] The Second Circuit disagreed with the BIA's conclusion, which essentially equated the term "permanent resident status" with "lawful unrelinquished domicile." On remand from the circuit court, the BIA in *Lok*[180] found that there was a distinction between lawful permanent resident status and lawful unrelinquished domicile. The BIA stated that in order to establish lawful unrelinquished domicile, the individual must establish: (1) physical presence in the United States; (2) intent to reside in the United States permanently; and (3) lawful presence.[181] There was further disagreement with the BIA's conclusion by some federal courts.[182] One court has stated the following: "for a domicile to be lawful, an alien need not obtain lawful permanent residence but must have the ability under the immigration laws to form the intent to remain in the United States."[183] The BIA has found that the period of time an alien accumulates after admission as a nonimmigrant may be calculated in determining lawful unrelinquished domicile.[184] Tem-

---

[175] INA §101(a)(20).

[176] *Matter of Longstaff*, 716 F.2d 1439 (5th Cir. 1983); *Monet v. INS*, 791 F.2d 752 (9th Cir. 1986); *see also Matter of Michel*, 21 I&N Dec. 1101 (BIA 1998).

[177] *Matter of Quijencio*, 15 I&N Dec. 95 (BIA 1974).

[178] 8 CFR §1003.44(b)(3); *Garcia-Hernandez v. INS*, 821 F.2d 222 (5th Cir. 1987).

[179] *Matter of Anwo*, 16 I&N Dec. 293 (BIA 1977).

[180] *Lok v. INS*, 548 F.2d 37 (2d Cir. 1977); *see also Castellon-Contreras v. INS*, 45 F.3d 149 (7th Cir. 1995).

[181] *Matter of Lok*, 18 I&N Dec. 101, 108 (BIA 1981).

[182] *See Marti-Xiques v. INS*, 741 F.2d 350 (11th Cir. 1984) (holding that lawful domicile ended on the date that "INS commenced the deportation proceedings.").

[183] *White v. INS*, 75 F.3d 213 (5th Cir. 1996).

[184] *Matter of Blancas-Lara*, 23 I&N Dec. 458 (BIA 2002).

porary resident status under the legalization program[185] is also considered lawful domicile.[186] Additionally, domicile of a parent can be attributed to his or her unemancipated minor child for purposes of "lawful unrelinquished domicile" under INA §212(c).[187]

Note: Time spent unlawfully in the United States cannot count toward "lawful" unrelinquished domicile.[188]

Once lawful domicile begins for §212(c) purposes, the BIA considers it to continue until an administratively final decision is rendered in the alien's immigration proceedings.[189] The *St. Cyr* regulations confirm this decision.[190] In other words, neither the commission of an offense rendering the applicant deportable, nor a finding of deportability will stop the accrual of lawful domicile. Lawful domicile continues to accrue even when an IJ orders the alien deported so long as an appeal is properly filed, and ends only when the BIA renders a final order of deportation. However, it does not continue to run where a permanent resident takes up "commuter" status, in that the alien no longer has the intention to reside in the United States.[191]

Five-year term of imprisonment served—pleas between Nov. 29, 1990, and April 24, 1996

IMMACT90 §511(a) instituted a preclusion on §212(c) relief where the alien had been convicted of an aggravated felony and had served a term of imprisonment of at least five years for that offense. Section 306(a)(10) of the Miscellaneous and Technical Immigration and Naturalization Amendments of 1991 (MTINA)[192] further amended §212(c) to provide that an alien is barred from receiving §212(c) relief whether he or she has been convicted of one aggravated felony for which he or she has served five years or more or where he or she has been convicted of more than one aggravated felony for which he or she has served five years or more in the aggregate.[193]

This bar only applies where the five years have been actually served, not where the sentence was suspended or the alien was sentenced to five years but actually served a lesser period. Only time served for *aggravated felonies*—not for lesser offenses—should be used in computing the time relevant for this purpose. Even in situations where DHS is in error in initially ruling a detained individual ineligible for

---

[185] INA §§210 and 245A.

[186] *See* 8 CFR §§212.3(f)(2), 1212.3(f)(2).

[187] *Cuevas-Gaspar v. Gonzales*, 430 F.3d 1013 (9th Cir. 2005).

[188] *Madrid-Tavares v. INS*, 999 F.2d 111 (5th Cir. 1993).

[189] *Matter of Lok*, 18 I&N Dec. 101 (BIA 1981).

[190] 8 CFR §1003.44(b)(3).

[191] *Carrasco-Favela v. INS*, 563 F.2d 1220 (5th Cir. 1977).

[192] Miscellaneous and Technical Immigration and Naturalization Amendments of 1991, Pub. L. No. 102-232, 105 Stat. 1733.

[193] The §212(c) regulations restate this. *See* 8 CFR §§212.3(f)(4)(ii), 1212.3(f)(4)(ii).

the relief, if the individual accumulates the five-year incarceration during the appeal period, he or she is still ineligible based on the five-year bar, and not entitled to a *nunc pro tunc* ruling based on the facts as they existed at the time of the government's error.[194]

Corresponding ground of inadmissibility

Because §212(c) relief was originally designed to benefit LPRs who were found inadmissible when returning to the United States after a temporary absence, the BIA and the courts have held that, where the alien is charged with being deportable (as opposed to inadmissible), a §212(c) waiver is only available if there exists a corresponding ground of inadmissibility.[195] The courts of appeal uniformly have agreed with this formulation.[196] It has been held that §212(c) relief is not available where the ground of deportability is entry without inspection,[197] or conviction for a firearms offense.[198] As a result, relief may be available for one who has committed a very serious crime involving moral turpitude, for example, but not for an alien who has been convicted of unlawfully carrying a weapon or of entering the United States without inspection.

When the BIA attempted to expand §212(c) relief to include grounds of deportability for which there is no corresponding ground of inadmissibility, the AG vacated the BIA's order, ruling that, even where the alien might be deportable on a ground for which there is a corresponding ground of inadmissibility, he or she is not eligible for §212(c) relief unless INS/DHS chooses to charge the alien on that ground.[199]

The addition of the "aggravated felony" ground of deportability in 1988 (via the ADAA) further complicated matters. There is no "aggravated felony" ground of inadmissibility per se; thus, former INS argued that §212(c) relief was precluded for all aggravated felons. In 1990, however, Congress amended §212(c) to specifically preclude relief for any alien who was convicted of an aggravated felony *and* served five or more years for that offense. Congress apparently contemplated that §212(c) relief would be available to at least some aggravated felons who had served less than five years.

The BIA has acknowledged that an aggravated felon may be eligible for §212(c) relief even though there is no specific ground of inadmissibility mentioning aggravated felonies.[200] The BIA ruled in *Matter of Meza* that §212(c) relief is available for aliens who are aggravated felons by virtue of a conviction for trafficking in a con-

---

[194] *Fernandes-Pereira v. Gonzales*, 417 F.3d 38 (1st Cir. 2005).

[195] *Matter of Wadud*, 19 I&N Dec. 182 (BIA 1984).

[196] *Chow v. INS*, 12 F.3d 34 (5th Cir. 1993).

[197] *Matter of Hernandez-Casillas*, 20 I&N Dec. 262 (BIA 1990).

[198] *Matter of Montenegro*, 20 I&N Dec. 603 (BIA 1992).

[199] *Matter of Hernandez-Casillas*, 20 I&N Dec. 262 (A.G. 1991).

[200] *Matter of Meza*, 20 I&N Dec. 257 (BIA 1991) ("a waiver under section 212(c) is not unavailable to an alien convicted of an aggravated felony simply because there is no ground of exclusion which recites the words, 'convicted of an aggravated felony'").

trolled substance.[201] It reasoned that any alien who was *deportable* for trafficking in a controlled substance also would necessarily be *inadmissible* under then-INA §212(a)(23) (current INA §§212(a)(2)(A)(i)(II) and 212(a)(2)(C)).

The BIA's ruling in *Meza* was limited by the facts of the case to aggravated felons who are deportable for drug trafficking offenses. In recent cases, the BIA has shown that it is taking a strict interpretation of what is a comparable ground of inadmissibility. For example, an individual found deportable for sexual abuse of a minor, an aggravated felony, was not eligible for §212(c) because there was no corresponding ground of inadmissibility.[202] Likewise, an individual deportable as an aggravated felon for the offense of unauthorized use of a motor vehicle was not eligible for §212(c) relief because there was no corresponding ground of inadmissibility under INA §212(a).[203] Deportability for a conviction under 18 USC §1546(a) for fraud and misuse of documents for entry does not have a comparable ground of inadmissibility, and, therefore, §212(c) relief is not available to an individual found deportable for this offense.[204]

In addition to the cases mentioned above involving aggravated felonies (crimes of violence, sexual abuse of a minor, etc.), the following grounds of deportability do not have corresponding grounds of inadmissibility under INA §212(a):

- Firearms: *Matter of Chow*, 20 I&N Dec. 647 (BIA 1993); *Matter of Montenegro*, 20 I&N Dec. 603 (BIA 1992); *Matter of Granados*, 16 I&N Dec. 726 (BIA 1979); *Matter of Esposito*, 21 I&N Dec. 1 (BIA 1995).
- Document Fraud and Misuse of Documents: *Matter of Jimenez-Santillano*, 21 I&N Dec. 567 (BIA 1996); *Matter of Wadud*, 19 I&N Dec. 182 (BIA 1984).
- Entry Without Inspection: *Matter of Hernandez-Casillas*, 20 I&N Dec. 262 (A.G. 1991).
- Domestic Violence: See INA §237(a)(2)(E).

DHS is opposing §212(c) eligibility for many *St. Cyr* relief applicants by arguing that there is no ground of inadmissibility corresponding to the aggravated felony ground with which the applicant is charged. In addition, DHS can be selective in the way that it charges offenses so that an alien may have difficulty showing a comparable ground of inadmissibility, and, thus, eligibility for §212(c) relief. Courts have on occasion restricted INS's/DHS's prosecutorial discretion in selecting which deportation charges to bring. One court rejected the INS's attempt to "thwart congressional intent through its unfettered discretion to charge a violation of a lesser offense and so nullify the forgiveness provisions" (of then-INA §241(f)).[205] However, other courts

---

[201] *Id.*

[202] *Matter of Blake*, 23 I&N Dec. 722 (BIA 2005).

[203] *Matter of Brieva-Perez*, 23 I&N Dec. 766 (BIA 2005).

[204] *Matter of Jimenez-Santillano*, 21 I&N Dec. 567 (BIA 1996).

[205] *Persaud v. INS*, 537 F.2d 776, 779 (3d Cir. 1976).

have held that the government's prosecutorial discretion is immune from review.[206] The BIA has stated that it has no authority over what charges the government lodges.[207]

It may be necessary to argue that the entire *category* of offenses in question is composed of crimes that are necessarily crimes involving moral turpitude. The BIA stated in one case that the focus "is not whether the deportable alien's particular offense, in this case a conviction for a [document fraud and misuse offense] could form the basis for a ground of exclusion and therefore be waivable; rather, the focus is whether the ground of deportability against the alien has a comparable ground of exclusion."[208] An individual is not barred from §212(c) relief based on deportability for commission of a certain crime unless he or she is actually charged with deportability, and found deportable, for that crime.[209]

§212(c) Application in Conjunction with an Adjustment of Status Application

There are situations where an individual is charged with both a ground of inadmissibility for which §212(c) relief is appropriate, and a ground of removability that does not have a comparable ground of inadmissibility. For example, an LPR married to a U.S. citizen is convicted of possession of a controlled substance, a ground of inadmissibility, and unlawful possession of a firearm, a deportable offense. The §212(c) petition will address only the ground of inadmissibility (drugs), but there is no relief or waiver to address the ground of deportability (firearm). In such situations, it is possible to file a §212(c) application along with an adjustment of status application if the individual might be eligible for adjustment of status with a waiver of the ground of inadmissibility. It should be remembered that a §212(c) waiver is a waiver of inadmissibility that may be used in any context where the alien is an "applicant for admission," including when the alien is eligible for adjustment of status.[210] The BIA has ruled that an LPR who fired a gun at an occupied vehicle, and was, therefore, both removable for the weapons offense and the aggravated felony (crime of violence), as well as inadmissible for the crime involving moral turpitude, could jointly file a §212(c) waiver and an adjustment of status application. The §212(c) grant waived the ground of inadmissibility, and the aggravated felony and weapons offenses are not bars to adjustment.[211]

---

[206] *Johns v. Dep't of Justice*, 653 F.2d 884, 893 (5th Cir. 1981).

[207] *Matter of Ramirez-Sanchez*, 17 I&N Dec. 503 (BIA 1980).

[208] *Matter of Esposito*, 21 I&N Dec. 1 (BIA 1995).

[209] *Matter of Fortiz-Zelaya*, 21 I&N Dec. 1199 (BIA 1998).

[210] *Matter of Gabryelsky*, 20 I&N Dec. 750 (BIA 1993).

[211] *Matter of Azurin*, 23 I&N Dec. 695 (BIA 2005); *see also Matter of Gabryelsky*, 20 I&N Dec. 750 (BIA 1993).

Establishing Discretionary Eligibility for §212(c) Relief

In addition to establishing the statutory prerequisites of admission for lawful permanent residence and lawful unrelinquished domicile for the specified period of time, there are various discretionary factors to be measured in determining eligibility for §212(c) relief. These factors have been outlined by the BIA.[212] There is a "balancing test" between various positive and negative factors. The positive factors outlined by the BIA include family ties in the United States, residency of long duration, hardship to the respondent and family as a result of deportation, service in the armed forces, history of employment, property or business ties, community service, proof of genuine rehabilitation, and general evidence attesting to a person's good character.[213] The negative include the nature and underlying circumstances of the ground of exclusion or deportation at issue, additional significant violations of the immigration laws, existence of a criminal record, and any other evidence of poor character or undesirability.[214] Equities accrued after knowledge of possible deportation or the issuance of a final order of deportation are given less weight.[215] Heightened equities are required where the individual has an extensive criminal record.[216] The individual must be prepared with sufficient evidence to establish that the positive factors outweigh the negative factors in order to obtain relief. The burden is on the applicant.

One limitation on the discretion to grant §212(c) relief is that neither the court nor DHS may grant an application for advance parole to enter under §212(c) if the applicant:

- has not been lawfully admitted for permanent residence;
- has not had seven years of lawful unrelinquished domicile as an LPR, temporary resident, or special agricultural worker;
- is inadmissible under certain security grounds (INA §§212(a)(3)(A), (B), (C), or (E)); or
- has been convicted of an aggravated felony and served at least five years in prison.

Adjustment of Status

Introduction

Adjustment of status is a term of art in the immigration world. It generally refers to the procedure for seeking LPR status in the United States without having to leave the country. For those individuals placed in removal proceedings, it can serve as an

---

212 *Matter of Marin*, 16 I&N Dec. 581 (BIA 1978).

213 *Id.*

214 *Id.*; *see also Matter of Buscemi*, 19 I&N Dec. 628 (BIA 1988).

215 *Matter of Correa*, 19 I&N Dec. 130, 134 (BIA 1984); *Ghassan v. INS*, 972 F.2d 631, 635 (5th Cir. 1992).

216 *Matter of Edwards*, 20 I&N Dec. 191 (BIA 1990); *Matter of Roberts*, 20 I&N Dec. 294 (BIA 1991).

available form of relief. Generally, adjustment of status requires an approved visa petition through a U.S. citizen family member, an employer, or a diversity (a/k/a lottery) visa. There also are requirements regarding manner of entry into the country, visa availability, and admissibility. The adjustment of status procedure is found at INA §245 and the regulations at 8 CFR §§245.1(a), 1245.1(a). There are other forms of adjustment of status based on the length of time an individual has lived in the United States (registry), an individual's nationality (NACARA, Haitian Refugee Immigration Fairness Act of 1998 (HRIFA),[217] Cuban Adjustment Program), status as a victim of domestic violence (VAWA), and refugee/asylee status.

The following section will first discuss the "regular" adjustment of status under INA §245(a). Second, it will summarize the other means by which one may adjust status outside of §245(a), including §245(i), which provides an exception so that adjustment of status is available to illegal entrants and those in unlawful status who have filed an application for an immigrant visa or labor certification on or before April 30, 2001, regardless of whether the petition was approved, denied, or still is pending.

Adjustment of Status—Requirements Under INA §245(a)

The INA sets out the statutory requirements for those who apply for adjustment of status in the United States, including:

- inspection and admission or parole into the United States;
- eligibility to receive an immigrant visa;
- admissibility to the United States under INA §212(a); and
- immediate availability of a visa.

The regulations further clarify the requirements for adjustment of status. The statutory and regulatory requirements are outlined below.

Physical presence

An individual must be physically present in the United States in order to apply for adjustment of status.[218]

Inspection and admission

The statute requires inspection and admission to the United States. Admission means the lawful entry of the alien into the United States after inspection and authorization by an immigration officer.[219] An inspection occurs when the alien physically presents him- or herself for questioning and makes no false claims to citizenship even if he or she is asked no questions by the immigration officer and volunteers no informa-

---

[217] Haitian Refugee Immigration Fairness Act of 1998, Pub. L. No. 105-277, 112 Stat. 2681 (div. A, title IX).

[218] 8 CFR §§245.1, 1245.1.

[219] INA §101(a)(13).

tion.[220] The BIA has stated that "admission" occurs when the inspecting officer indicates to the individual that he or she is not inadmissible.[221] That communication occurs when the inspector permits the alien to enter. DHS has argued since the passage of INA §101(a)(13) in 1996, the BIA's decision is no longer the law and that more is required now to prove an inspection and admission than simply appearing before an officer at the border and refraining from making a false claim to citizenship. DHS's claim is based on the language in INA §101(a)(13) that indicates that admission now means lawful inspection and admission into the United States. The BIA, however, has not retreated from its position in *Areguillin*.

Parolees also are permitted to adjust status, although there are some limits. The statute clearly states that those paroled into the United States are eligible to adjust.[222] However, the regulations classify parolees as "arriving aliens."[223] Former Attorney General John Ashcroft promulgated a regulation making arriving aliens in removal proceedings ineligible for adjustment.[224] The government has since taken the position that parolees are no longer eligible to adjust status unless they were paroled into the United States specifically for the purpose of adjustment of status, or given advance parole so that they could resume an adjustment of status application. Several courts have found that the regulation contravenes the statutory provision permitting paroled aliens to adjust status even in removal proceedings, and, therefore, the regulation is invalid.[225] However, at least one circuit court has upheld the regulation and found that parolees may not adjust status in removal proceedings even if they meet the other adjustment requirements.[226]

The government is usually strict in demanding proof of admission, including, most commonly, an I-94, a visa inspection stamp in the passport, or a border crossing card. An individual who entered without inspection cannot adjust; there are certain exceptions including VAWA applicants,[227] special immigrants (including special immigrant children who are considered to have been paroled),[228] asylees,[229] and applicants under INA §245(i).

---

[220] *Matter of Areguillin*, 17 I&N Dec. 308 (BIA 1980); *Morelos–Ontiveros v. INS*, 927 F.2d 610 (9th Cir. 1991).

[221] *Id.*

[222] INA §245(a).

[223] 8 CFR §§1.1(q), 1001.1(q).

[224] 8 CFR §§245.1(c)(8), 1245.1(c)(8).

[225] *Succar v. Ashcroft*, 394 F.3d 8 (1st Cir. 2005); *Rivera v. Ashcroft*, 394 F.3d 37 (1st Cir. 2005); *Bona v. Gonzales*, 425 F.3d 663 (9th Cir. 2005); *Zheng v. Gonzales*, 422 F.3d 98 (3d Cir. 2005).

[226] *Mouelle v. Gonzales*, 416 F.3d 923 (8th Cir 2005).

[227] INA §245(a).

[228] INA §101(a)(27)(J); *see also* 8 CFR §§245.1(a), 1245.1(a).

[229] INA §209.

Maintaining lawful status

The regulations require, in addition to inspection and admission, or parole, that an applicant for adjustment of status maintain lawful status in the United States.[230] There are exceptions to this requirement; the following groups need not have maintained continuous lawful status in the United States in order to adjust status:

- applicants under INA 245(i);[231]
- immediate relatives of U.S. citizens applying under INA §201(b);[232]
- special immigrants under INA §101(a)(27)(H) (foreign medical graduates);[233]
- special immigrants under INA §101(a)(27)(J) (special immigrant children);[234]
- individuals under INA §101(a)(27)(I) (former employees of international organizations and family members);[235] and
- individuals under INA §101(a)(27)(K) (immigrants who have served honorably in the U.S. military).[236]

In addition, applicants for adjustment of status under certain special programs such as HRIFA, the prior NACARA relief, and the Immigration Reform and Control Act of 1986 (IRCA)[237] programs have not had to maintain lawful status, or even have had a lawful entry, in order to qualify for adjustment to permanent status. Asylees adjusting under INA §209 need not have maintained lawful status, nor are registry applicants under INA §245 required to do so.[238]

Availability of visas

In order to adjust status under INA §245(a), there must be a visa immediately available.[239] Thus, the beneficiary of the visa petition must be an immediate relative of a U.S. citizen,[240] or qualify for one of the family- or employment-based preferences and have a current "priority date."[241] The priority date is the date on which the family visa petition is filed with USCIS, or the labor certification is filed with the

---

230 8 CFR §§245.1(b)(5), 1245.1(b)(5).

231 8 CFR §§245.1(b), 1245.1(b).

232 8 CFR §§245.1(b)(4)(i), 1245.1(b)(4)(i).

233 8 CFR §§245.1(b)(4)(ii), 1245.1(b)(4)(ii).

234 *Id.*

235 8 CFR §§245.1(b)(10), 1245.1(b)(10).

236 *Id.*

237 Immigration Reform and Control Act of 1986, Pub. L. No. 99-603, 100 Stat. 3359.

238 INA §249.

239 INA §245(a); 8 CFR §§245.1(g)(1), 1245.1(g)(1).

240 INA §201(b)(2)(A) defines immediate relative as the spouse, children (under 21 and single), and parents of U.S. citizens (for the parent to be an immediate relative, the U.S citizen child petitioning must be 21 or over).

241 INA §§203(a) and (b) define the four family-based preferences and five employment-based preferences.

Department of Labor (DOL) (previously, labor certifications were filed with state work commissions or agencies). The priority date is important because it is the date on which the alien gets in the waiting line for his or her visa. The waiting line is caused by a quota for all family- and employment-based categories, except for immediate relatives who have no quota or waiting time for approval. There are quotas on all the preferences, and, therefore, backlogs, because many preferences have more applicants than available visas.

As visa applicants are approved at the consulate or adjusted to permanent resident status in the United States, more visas become available and the dates of processing change until the day when the government reaches the date on which the visa for the alien was filed. At that time, the priority date is said to be current, and the alien is eligible to adjust status under INA §245(a) if he or she meets the other statutory requirements and discretion is merited in his or her favor. In addition to the quotas and waiting times for the family- and employment-based categories, there are quotas for diversity visa applicants[242] and refugee adjustment of status applicants.[243] The movement and availability of the visa numbers for the family-, employment-, and diversity-based visa applicants are monitored monthly through the U.S. State Department's Visa Bulletin.[244]

Note: For an individual seeking adjustment of status in removal proceedings, the IJ has no authority over the family-, employment-, or diversity-based visa petition, which USCIS adjudicates. It is quite common for an individual to be prima facie eligible to adjust status with the visa petition adjudication lagging. Where the approval of the visa petition would make the respondent in proceedings prima facie eligible to adjust status, the IJ should continue the removal proceedings to permit USCIS time to adjust the visa petition.[245]

Admissibility

The statute also requires that the individual be admissible. The grounds of inadmissibility have been covered in Chapter 3. The main grounds of inadmissibility fall into five general categories—health-related grounds of inadmissibility; crime; security; public charge; and immigration violations. In an adjustment of status application, the health-related grounds of inadmissibility are examined through the required medical examination, which evaluates an individual for communicable diseases and required vaccinations.[246] There is a waiver available for mental or physical conditions and the vaccination requirements (waivers are discussed, *infra*).[247]

---

[242] INA §201(e).

[243] INA §§207(a)(1) and 209(b).

[244] *See www.travel.state.gov.*

[245] *Matter of Velarde-Pacheco*, 23 I&N Dec. 253 (BIA 2002).

[246] 8 CFR §§245.5, 1245.5.

[247] INA §212(g).

In order to address the criminal and immigration grounds of inadmissibility, DHS or the IJ will require a biometrics (fingerprint) check whereby the prints are sent to the appropriate government law enforcement agency to conduct a check into the person's background to determine whether there are prior criminal or immigration offenses that make the individual inadmissible. An individual is inadmissible for a conviction, or the admission of crimes, listed at INA §212(a)(2), relating to crimes involving moral turpitude; crimes relating to controlled substances; multiple criminal convictions; trafficking in controlled substances; and prostitution. If an individual is inadmissible for crimes involving moral turpitude, multiple criminal convictions, prostitution, or a single marijuana possession offense of 30 grams of less of marijuana, he or she is not admissible without obtaining a waiver for these offenses.[248] Any drug offense more serious than the single marijuana possession offense is a permanent bar and cannot be waived, except in those situations where the person already is an LPR and may be able to use a waiver under former §212(c) together with an adjustment of status application.[249] There also is an exception to the criminal ground of inadmissibility for "petty offenses,"[250] and certain offenses committed while one is a juvenile.[251]

For immigration violations, there are waivers for certain immigration-related fraud offenses[252] and prior removal orders.[253] These and other waivers are discussed below.

In addressing the public charge ground of inadmissibility, Congress has required in all family-based, and in certain employment-based (those where the employer-petitioner is a family member under INA §203(b)) adjustment of status applications, that an affidavit of support (Form I-864) be submitted by the petitioner "to establish that the alien is not excludable as a public charge."[254] The affidavit of support form with the prior three years' tax returns and proof of current financial status must be submitted with the adjustment of status application. Failure to do so results in a denial of the application. If the petitioner does not earn a sufficient income or possess sufficient assets to support the individual at an annual income of 125 percent of the federal poverty guidelines,[255] an alternate affiant may be used.[256]

There are numerous grounds of inadmissibility that cannot be waived, including drug trafficking offenses; most drug possession offenses; fraud involving false claims to citizenship; murder; and crimes relating to torture and human trafficking. Individu-

---

[248] INA §212(h).

[249] *Matter of Gabryelsky*, 20 I&N Dec. 750 (BIA 1993).

[250] INA §212(a)(2)(A)(ii) (a petty offense is one where the maximum possible sentence does not exceed one year and the alien is not sentenced to more than six months).

[251] *Id.*; *see also Matter of Devison*, 22 I&N Dec. 1362 (BIA 2000).

[252] INA §212(i).

[253] INA §212(a)(9)(A)(iii).

[254] INA §213A(a)(1).

[255] INA §213A(a)(1)(A).

[256] INA §213A(f)(5).

als who are deportable under INA §237(a)(4)(B) (terrorism ground) cannot adjust status, nor can they obtain a waiver for terrorism-related grounds of inadmissibility under INA §212(a)(3) or deportability under INA §237(a)(4)(B).[257] Those who have been deported or illegally present for one year and return without a waiver are ineligible to adjust status or seek a waiver until they have remained outside the United States for 10 years.[258]

The IJ determines the grounds of inadmissibility and the required waivers in deportation or removal proceedings. He or she also adjudicates the waiver as part of the adjustment hearing. USCIS is responsible only for the visa petition when an individual is in removal proceeding. If DHS wishes for USCIS to adjudicate the adjustment of status petition, the proceedings must be terminated; the IJ is the only person who can make that determination.

Ineligible aliens

The following individuals are listed as ineligible for adjustment of status in the United States:[259]

- nonpreference immigrant seeking to work without a valid labor certification;
- exchange visitor subject to the two-year foreign residency requirement who has not obtained a waiver under INA §212(e);
- immediate relative or preference immigrant without an approved visa petition;
- alien already in conditional resident alien status;
- fiancé(e) with a K-1 visa applying to adjust status through someone other than the original fiancé(e), or who has not married the fiancé(e) within 90 days of admission;
- fiancé(e) with a K-3 visa who seeks to adjust status based on a marriage to someone other than the U.S. citizen who filed the original K visa petition;
- alien admitted on an S (witness) visa applying to adjust status unless through the request of a law enforcement agency;
- alien seeking to adjust status based on a marriage that occurred on or after November 10, 1986, and while the alien was in exclusion or deportation proceedings, unless the alien proves by clear and convincing evidence that the marriage was bona fide and not entered into for the purpose of procuring the alien's entry into the United States; or the alien meets one of the other exceptions to this bar.[260]

---

[257] 8 CFR §§245.10(g), 1245.10(g).

[258] INA §212(a)(9)(C).

[259] 8 CFR §§245.1(c), 1245.1(c).

[260] 8 CFR §§245.1(c)(9), 1245.1(c)(9).

Adjustment of Status Under INA §245(i)

To adjust status under INA §245(a)—the normal adjustment procedure—the applicant must always show proof of inspection and admission, and in many preference-based cases, proof of maintaining lawful status. However, there is a section of the §245 adjustment of status statute that permits certain individuals to adjust status even if they have not entered lawfully or maintained lawful status in the United States—INA §245(i). It is a law that "grandfathers" certain applicants for permanent resident status who filed the family-based visa petition or labor certification application prior to April 30, 2001. Following are the requirements for adjustment under §245(i):

- physical presence in the United States;[261]
- an approved visa petition (employment- or family-based);
- a family-based visa petition that was filed before April 30, 2001, or an employment-based labor certification that was filed before that date and was prima facie approvable when filed;[262]
- physical presence in the United States since December 21, 2000, if the qualifying visa petition or labor certification was filed after January 14, 1998;
- eligibility to receive an immigrant visa and an immediate available immigrant visa;[263]
- admissibility as an immigrant;[264]
- payment of a penalty sum of $1,000 (not required for children under the age of 17, or spouses and children of aliens granted Special Agricultural Worker or legalization status under IRCA who have been present in the United States since May 5, 1988, have been in a relationship with the legalized alien (as a spouse or child) since that date, and have applied for Family Unity benefits).[265]

An alien who has previously filed for adjustment of status under INA §245(a) and who has been denied may file a new application for adjustment of status pursuant to INA §245(i) if eligible and if he or she files the penalty sum.[266] The denial, withdrawal, or revocation of the visa petition filed before April 30, 2001, does not preclude eligibility under the grandfather clause as long as it was approvable when filed.[267]

---

[261] 8 CFR §§245.10(b)(1); 1245.10(b)(1).

[262] 8 CFR §§245.10(a)(1)(i)(A) and (B), 1245.10(a)(1)(i)(A) and (B); *see also* 8 CFR §§245.10(a)(2), 1245.10(a)(2). Diversity and asylum petitions do not qualify under the grandfather clause. *See* 8 CFR §§245.10(h), 1245.10(h).

[263] 8 CFR §§245.10(b)(2), 1245.10(b)(2).

[264] 8 CFR §§245.10(b)(3), 1245.10(b)(3).

[265] 8 CFR §§245.10(b)(6), 1245.10(b)(6); 245.10(c), 1245.10(c).

[266] 8 CFR §§245.10(f)(2), 1245.10(f)(2).

[267] 8 CFR §§245.10(i), 1245.10(i).

The procedure and documentary requirements for filing under INA §245(i) are outlined at 8 CFR §§245.10, 1245.10. Supplement A along with the penalty sum must be submitted with Form I-485.[268] The penalty sum is separate and apart from the fee. Unlike the fee, it cannot be waived.[269]

The regulations highlight several groups of aliens who may only adjust through INA §245(i) (and who are not in one of the ineligible categories defined at 8 CFR §§245.1(c), 1245.1(c)),[270] including:

- aliens who entered in transit without a visa;
- aliens serving aboard a vessel or aircraft on arrival or aliens destined to serve on a U.S. vessel;
- aliens not admitted or paroled following inspection into the United States;
- aliens employed without authorization in the United States after January 1, 1977 (unless he or she was an immediate relative, special immigrant juvenile, or files with one of the other exceptions at 8 CFR §§245.1(b)(4), 1245.1(b)(4));
- aliens not in lawful status after November 6, 1986, unless immediate relatives or in special immigrant juvenile status; or in certain cases, those foreign medical graduates under INA §101(a)(27)(H) or employees and family members of international organizations under INA §101(a)(27)(I);[271]
- aliens admitted on the visa waiver program or Visa Waiver Pilot Program, other than immediate relatives;
- aliens seeking adjustment of status based on employment visa petitions who have not maintained lawful status; and
- aliens who have engaged in unauthorized employment in the United States, unless they are immediate relatives or special immigrants under INA §§101(a)(27)(H), (I), (J), or (K).

Adjustment of Status for Battered Spouses and Children

INA §245(a) provides for adjustment of status for individuals who qualify under INA §204 as battered spouses or children of U.S. citizens or LPRs.[272] Specifically, this section of the INA states that an individual who qualifies as a victim of domestic violence at the hands of U.S. citizen or LPR spouse and or parent may adjust status even if he or she has not entered the United States lawfully, or maintained lawful resident status. In addition, victims of domestic violence seeking adjustment of status

---

[268] 8 CFR §§245.10(b)(5), 1245.10(b)(5).

[269] *Matter of Fesale*, 21 I&N Dec. 114 (BIA 1995).

[270] 8 CFR §§245.1(b), 1245.1(b).

[271] 8 CFR §§245.1(b)(6), 1245.1(b)(6).

[272] *See* INA §245(a) (referring to §§204(a)(1)(A)(iii)–(iv) and (B)(ii) and (iii), referencing spouses and children of abusive U.S. citizens or LPRs).

need not file the affidavit of support (Form I-864), which is required of most other adjustment applicants pursuant to INA §213A.

Adjustment of status applicants seeking permanent residence as spouses or children of U.S. citizen or LPR abusers must still meet the following requirements:

- approved Form I-360 (Special Immigrant Petition);
- availability of a visa as the immediate relative or second preference relative of a U.S. citizen or LPR;
- admissibility under INA §212(a);
- proof that he or she will not be a public charge, even though the affidavit of support is not required; and
- completion of all background checks and payment of all fees unless a waiver of the fees has been granted.

Victims of domestic violence who meet the above conditions may adjust status before the immigration court if they are in proceedings. However, as in the family visa situation, the IJ may not proceed with the adjustment application until there is an approved petition—in this case, an approved I-360 Special Immigrant Petition. Even with an approved petition based on battery or extreme cruelty at the hands of the U.S. citizen or LPR spouse or parent, the applicant for adjustment of status before the IJ still should be prepared to answer questions about domestic violence should this issue come up.

VAWA 2005[273] contains certain provisions regarding adjustment of status for victims of domestic violence. Specifically, it allows spouses and children who would have been eligible to seek adjustment of status as Cuban or Nicaraguan beneficiaries under Section 202 of NACARA to adjust status if the abuser did not apply for such status on their behalf, even though the deadline for adjustment under NACARA has passed.[274] In addition, spouses and children of alien abusers who were eligible to adjust status under HRIFA, but did not apply for such status, may now apply for adjustment of status under VAWA 2005.[275] Finally, spouses of Cuban nationals who were abusers may seek adjustment of status under the Cuban Adjustment Act[276] for two years after the date on which the abusing spouse died or the marriage terminated, if the victim of the domestic violence can demonstrate a connection between the termination of the marriage and being battered or subjected to extreme cruelty by the Cuban abuser.[277]

---

[273] VAWA 2005, *supra* note 60.

[274] *Id.* §815.

[275] VAWA 2005, *supra* note 60, §824.

[276] Pub. L. No. 89-73.

[277] *Id.* at 823.

Adjustment of Status for Special Immigrants

Certain classes of special immigrants under INA §101(a)(27) may adjust status without meeting all of the requirements required under the regular adjustment provisions.

Special immigrant veterans who have served honorably in the U.S. Armed Forces, described in INA §101(a)(27)(K), may apply to adjust status. These are immigrants who served honorably in the armed forces after October 15, 1978, for periods aggregating 12 years and who were separated under honorable conditions, or who have six years in the armed forces and have agreed to re-enlist for another six years.[278] Spouses and children may adjust, too.

Special immigrant juvenile children under INA §101(a)(27)(J) also may adjust status. They must be declared dependent by a juvenile court or placed by a juvenile court under the custody of an agency or department of the state, and declared by that court as eligible for long-term foster care due to abuse, abandonment, or neglect. The requirements regarding lawful entry and lawful presence do not apply, nor do the grounds of inadmissibility relating to public charge, valid labor certification, or unlawful presence.[279]

Special immigrants under INA §§101(a)(27)(H) (foreign medical graduates) and (I) (relating to retired officers or employees of international organizations and their families) may adjust status even if they have been in unlawful status or employed without authorization.[280]

Cuban Adjustment Act

The Cuban Adjustment Act provides for the adjustment of status of Cuban nationals one year after they have arrived in the United States.[281] Under this law, the AG may adjust to LPR status any Cuban national who meets the following requirements:

- inspected and admitted or paroled after January 1, 1959;
- physical presence for at least one year;
- applied for adjustment of status;
- eligible for immigrant visa; and
- admissible for permanent residence.

In April, 1999, INS issued a memorandum stating that even Cubans who arrived at locations other than designated ports of entry without inspection may adjust status.[282]

---

[278] INA §101(a)(27)(K).

[279] 8 CFR §§245.1(e)(2)(vi)(B)(3), 1245.1(e)(2)(vi)(B)(3).

[280] 8 CFR §§245.1(b)(6) and (10), 1245.1(b)(6) and (10).

[281] Cuban Adjustment Act, *supra* note 276.

[282] Memorandum from Doris Meissner "Eligibility for Permanent Residence under the Cuban Adjustment Act Despite Having Arrived at other than a Designated Port of Entry," *reproduced in* 76 *Interpreter Releases* 676 (May 3, 1999).

The application for adjustment of status may be adjudicated by the immigration court.[283] The application is filed on Form I-485 together with the biographical form (G-325). With the application should be the required fee (or fee waiver request), proof of Cuban nationality, physical presence, and medical examination, and fingerprints. If there has been an admission or parole, the I-84, passport stamp, or other proof should be included. The grounds of inadmissibility relating to inspection and admission, public charge, unlawful presence, and valid entry documentation do not apply.

Registry

Certain individuals who have had long-term residence in the United States may adjust status under INA §249, regardless of the manner of entry or unlawful status. The requirements for registry include the following:

- entry into the United States prior to January 1, 1972;
- continuous residence since that time (individual breaks of 90 or more days, or 180 days in the aggregate, may break the continuity of the residence);[284]
- good moral character (the BIA has stated that this is not required for the entire period, but for a "reasonable period");[285]
- not inadmissible under INA §212(a) as a procurer or immoral person, criminal, subversive, smuggler, or violator of narcotics laws; and
- not ineligible for citizenship or deportable as a terrorist under INA §237(a)(4)(B).

This is a discretionary application. It may be filed directly with the court on Form I-485 with the required supporting documentation relating to identity, physical presence, good moral character, fees (or fee waivers), medical exams, and completed background checks.[286]

Adjustment of Status Under NACARA

There have been specific laws for adjustment of status targeted at nationals of certain countries. For many of these nationalities, the deadlines have passed for application; however; the more common of these adjustment of status statutes are summarized below.

Section 202 of NACARA allowed for the adjustment of status of Nicaraguans and Cubans who had been physically present in the United States on or before December 1, 1995. However, the deadline for applying under this program was April 1, 2000. The only exceptions are those Nicaraguan and Cuban victims of domestic violence as outlined in VAWA 2005, as discussed above.

NACARA adjustment under §202 carries the following requirements:

---

[283] *Matter of Artigas*, 23 I&N Dec. 99 (BIA 2001).

[284] INA §240A(d)(2).

[285] *Matter of Sanchez-Linn*, 20 I&N Dec. 362 (BIA 1991).

[286] 8 CFR §§249.2, 1249.2.

- proving nationality as a Cuban or Nicaraguan;
- physical presence in the United States since December 1, 1995, or prior to that date;
- admissibility under INA §212(a); however, certain grounds of inadmissibility were waived, including public charge, lack of valid labor certification, unlawful presence, and lack of valid inspection and admission.

The regulations also state that certain grounds of inadmissibility may be waived. The grounds of inadmissibility under INA §§212(a)(9)(A) and (C), relating to prior removal orders and physical presence in the United States after immigration violations, may be waived.[287] Finally, the regulations are specific regarding the types of documentation of physical presence that should be presented in order to meet the continuous presence requirement under the statute.[288]

Haitian Refugee and Immigrant Fairness Act (HRIFA)

HRIFA allowed for the adjustment of status of certain Haitian nationals present in the United States on terms similar to those granted to Cubans and Nicaraguans under §202 of NACARA.[289] However, like NACARA, the time for application has passed, with the exception of those victims of domestic violence listed above in VAWA 2005. Applications for benefits under HRIFA were to be filed between the period of June 11, 1999, and April 1, 2000.[290] Applicants for adjustment of status under HRIFA are to meet the following requirements:

- must fall within one of the following groups:[291]
  - filed for asylum before December 31, 1995;
  - paroled into the United States prior to December 31, 1995, after having been identified as having a credible fear of persecution; or paroled for reasons deemed in the public interest; or
  - unmarried and under 21 years old on December 31, 1995, and had arrived without parents and remained without parents, became orphaned after arrival, or was abandoned by his or her parents prior to April 1, 1998, and had remained so.
- must be present in United States at the time the application was filed;[292]
- must properly file the application (Form I-485);[293]
- must be admissible;[294] and

---

[287] 8 CFR §§245.13(c)(2), 1245.13(c)(2).

[288] 8 CFR §§245.13(a), 1245.13(a).

[289] HRIFA, *supra* note 217.

[290] 8 CFR §§245.15(f)(1), 1245.15(f)(1).

[291] 8 CFR §§245.15(b)(1), 1245.15(b)(1).

[292] 8 CFR §§245.15(c)(1), 1245.15(c)(1).

[293] 8 CFR §§245.15(c)(2), 1245.15(c)(2).

[294] 8 CFR §§245.15(c)(3), 1245.15(c)(3).

- must have physical presence in the United States on or before December 31, 1995, and ending on the date the application for adjustment is granted; a period of six months' (180 days) absence in the aggregate was permitted in meeting the physical presence requirement.[295]

In addition, dependents of the principals described above may qualify for adjustment of status under HRIFA even if not individually eligible under these criteria.[296]

The procedure for HRIFA applications is outlined at 8 CFR §§245.15(h), 1245.15(h). The application had do be received at a INS/USCIS service center by March 31, 2000.[297]

Waivers

Introduction

There are various violations of the immigration laws that require waivers in order for an individual to remain within the United States, to be admitted to the United States, or to obtain lawful residency status. A waiver under the immigration laws is essentially a pardon of some past offense. In this section, there will be a summary of the more common waivers under the INA that may be required in representing an individual before the immigration court. Some of the more common waivers are: (1) waiver for criminal activity under INA §212(h); (2) waiver under INA §212(i) for immigration fraud; (3) smuggling waiver found at INA §212(d)(11); and (4) waiver for document fraud under INA §212(d)(12).

The INA also contains waivers for health-related grounds of inadmissibility. Section 212(g) provides possible waivers for individuals who are not inadmissible because of a communicable disease, psychological or behavioral disorders, or lack of vaccinations.

Individuals who have had certain prior immigration violations can obtain waivers. An individual who is inadmissible because of prior unlawful presence may be eligible for a waiver under INA §212(a)(9)(B)(v). Individuals with prior removal orders may be able to waive this ground of inadmissibility by seeking a waiver under §212(a)(9)(A)(iii). Individuals who have re-entered unlawfully after being removed or having spent one year unlawful presence in the United States are inadmissible under INA §212(a)(9)(C)(i). There is, however, a waiver of this ground of inadmissibility at §212(a)(9)(C)(ii), but the individual must have remained outside the United States for a period of 10 years.

Finally, as discussed above, there are waivers available to LPRs who have resided in the United States for long periods of time if they have been found removable or

---

[295] 8 CFR §§245.15(c)(4), 1245.15(c)(4).

[296] 8 CFR §§245.15(b)(2), 1245.15(b)(2).

[297] 8 CFR §§245.15(c)(2), 1245.15(c)(2).

inadmissible for criminal activity. These waivers are found at former INA §212(c), or under current INA §240A(a) (*i.e.*, cancellation of removal for LPRs).

Waiver for Criminal Activity Under INA §212(h)

INA §212(h) contains a waiver for certain crimes or certain criminal grounds of inadmissibility, including crimes involving moral turpitude;[298] controlled substance violation relating to a single offense for possession of marijuana of less than 30 grams;[299] prostitution;[300] crimes by individuals who are eligible for immunity from prosecution;[301] and individuals with multiple criminal convictions for which the aggregate sentences to confinement were five or more years (not including controlled substance violations).[302]

Requirements for §212(h) waiver

There are three means by which an individual may claim eligibility for a §212(h) waiver.

First, if the person's inadmissibility would result in extreme hardship to that person's U.S. citizen or LPR parent, spouse, son, or daughter, a waiver might be granted.[303]

Second, an individual could qualify for this waiver by showing that he or she is inadmissible under INA §212(a)(2)(D) for prostitution or commercialized vice, and that the activities that render him or her inadmissible occurred more than 15 years before the date of application for a visa, admission, or adjustment of status; that the admission of the individual to the United States would not be contrary to the national welfare, safety, or security of the United States; and the individual has been rehabilitated.[304]

Third, spouses and children who qualify as victims of domestic violence under INA §§204(a)(1)(A)(iii) and (iv) or 204(a)(1)(B)(ii) and (iii) are eligible for the INA §212(h) waiver.[305]

The §212(h) waiver is explicitly not available to individuals who have been convicted of murder or criminal acts that involve torture or any attempt to commit murder or torture. There also are limitations on this relief relating specifically to LPRs. The §212(h) waiver is unavailable to an LPR unless he or she can show the following:

---

[298] INA §212(a)(2)(A)(I).

[299] INA §212(a)(2)(A)(i)(II).

[300] INA §212(a)(2)(D).

[301] INA §212(a)(2)(E).

[302] INA §212(a)(2)(B).

[303] INA §212(h)(1)(B).

[304] INA §212(h)(1)(A).

[305] INA §212(h)(1)(C).

- lawful residence in the United States for a period of seven years since the date of admission; and
- no aggravated felony convictions.

This waiver may be granted "nunc pro tunc" in removal proceedings in order to cure a ground of inadmissibility at the time of a prior entry.[306]

In determining whether an individual has established extreme hardship for this waiver, the IJ must balance the adverse factors evidencing an individual's undesirability as a permanent resident with the social and humane considerations presented on the alien's behalf.[307] In *Matter of Mendez-Moralez*, the BIA followed the precedent followed set in *Matter of Marin*[308] and balanced the positive factors—such as family ties, employment, property and community ties, hardship to family members, long period of residence in the United States, service in the armed forces, employment history, and evidence of rehabilitation—against the negative factors—the exclusion ground at issue, prior criminal history as well as immigration history, and other evidence showing poor moral character.

The BIA has found that LPRs who have been convicted of aggravated felonies are not eligible for this form of relief.[309] LPRs who have not lawfully resided continuously in the United States for a period of seven or more years immediately preceding the date of initiation of proceedings also are not eligible.[310] However, an individual who has never been an LPR and has an aggravated felony conviction is allowed to seek this waiver in conjunction with an adjustment of status application.[311]

Battered spouses and children

Section 212(h) also serves as a waiver for criminal activity available to spouses and children who have been the victims of domestic violence at the hands of U.S. citizens or LPRs.[312] The waiver under this subsection does not require the showing of extreme hardship.

Waiver for Fraud of Willful Misrepresentation of a Material Fact

The INA provides a waiver to individuals who are found inadmissible under §212(a)(6)(C)(i) for fraud or willful misrepresentation of a material fact at §212(i) The waiver is authorized at INA §212(a)(6)(C)(iii). The §212(i) waiver is not avail-

---

[306] *Matter of Sanchez*, 17 I&N Dec. 218 (BIA 1980).

[307] *Matter of Mendez-Moralez*, 21 I&N Dec. 296 (BIA 1996).

[308] *Matter of Marin*, 16 I&N Dec. 581 (BIA 1978).

[309] *Matter of Yeung*, 21 I&N Dec. 610 (BIA 1996).

[310] INA §212(h) (last paragraph); *see also Matter of Ayail*, 22 I&N Dec. 398 (BIA 1998); *Matter of Pineda-Castellanos*, 21 I&N Dec. 1017 (BIA 1997).

[311] *Matter of Michel*, 21 I&N Dec. 1101 (BIA 1998).

[312] INA §212(h)(1)(C).

able to individuals who have made a false claim to U.S. citizenship. The requirements for the waiver follow:[313]

- The applicant must be the spouse, son, or daughter of a U.S. citizen or alien lawfully admitted for permanent residence;[314] and
- The refusal of admission to the United States would result in extreme hardship to the citizen or LPR relative; or
- The applicant is the spouse or child of a U.S. citizen or LPR and has been the victim of domestic violence and shows that refusal of admission would result in extreme hardship to him- or herself, or the U.S. citizen or LPR relative(s).

The statute is clear that there is no jurisdiction of any court to review the decision of the AG in granting or denying this waiver.[315]

The BIA has stated that the factors to be used in determining whether an alien has established extreme hardship under this waiver include, but are not limited to, the following: LPR or U.S. citizen family ties; conditions in the country to which the individual would be removed and family members within that country: the financial impact of departure from the United States; conditions of health, particularly when tied to the unavailability of suitable medical care in the country to which the alien would be removed.[316] It has stated that the standard to be used in measuring hardship is the same as that applied in the former suspension of deportation cases.[317]

The BIA has found that one of the negative factors that may be weighed in adjudicating the waiver is the underlying fraud or misrepresentation for which the individual seeks the waiver.[318]

The fraud ground of inadmissibility at §212(a)(6)(C)(i)(II) states that a waiver is not required and an individual is not considered inadmissible for fraud if each parent is or was a citizen of the United States; the individual resided permanently in the United States prior to the age of 16; and the individual reasonably believed that at the time of making a misrepresentation as to U.S. citizenship that he or she was a citizen.[319]

Smuggling Waivers

For individuals who are inadmissible as smugglers under INA §212(a)(6)(E), there is a waiver available pursuant to INA §212(d)(11) (authorized under INA §212(a)(6)(E)(iii)). The requirements for this waiver are the following:

---

[313] INA §212(i)(1).

[314] Note that this waiver is not available to the parent of U.S. citizens or LPRs.

[315] INA §212(i)(2).

[316] *Matter of Cervantes*, 22 I&N Dec. 560 (BIA 1999).

[317] *Matter of Kao and Lin*, 23 I&N Dec. 45 (BIA 2001).

[318] *Id.*

[319] INA §212(a)(6)(C)(ii).

- the alien is an LPR;
- he or she temporarily left the United States voluntarily and not under an order of removal;
- the alien has encouraged, induced, assisted, abetted, or aided only an individual who at the time of the smuggling action was his or her spouse, parent, son, or daughter (and no other individual); and
- the alien's admission would be to ensure family unity, for humanitarian purposes, or in the public interest.

This waiver also is available to individuals who are seeking admission or adjustment of status as immediate relatives or immigrants under INA §203(a), if the individual has encouraged and assisted only a spouse, parent, son, or daughter to enter the United States in violation of law.

The BIA has found that in order to qualify for this waiver, the individual must show that the object of the smuggling attempt was the spouse, parent, son, or daughter.[320] It also has stated that this relationship must exist at the time of the smuggling.[321]

Waiver of Deportation/Removal for Inadmissibility at Time of Admission

The INA provides a waiver of the ground of deportability under INA §237(a)(1) for individuals who were inadmissible at the time of admission for fraud or misrepresentation.[322] This INA §237(a)(1)(H) waiver is available even for willful misrepresentations at the time of admission if the applicant meets the following requirements:

- he or she is the spouse, parent, son, or daughter of a U.S. citizen or an LPR;
- he or she was in possession of an immigrant visa or equivalent document; and
- he or she is otherwise admissible at the time of admission except for lack of labor certification (INA §212(a)(5)) and lack of valid documentation (INA §212(a)(7)) that were a direct result of that fraud or misrepresentation.

The waiver is available also to spouses and children of U.S. citizens or LPRs who have been victimized by domestic violence under INA §§204(a)(1)(B)(ii) or (iii) or §§204(a)(1)(A)(iii) or (iv). This waiver, however, is not available to waive fraudulent claims to U.S. citizenship at the time of admission.[323] If granted, it waives removal under the ground of inadmissibility resulting from the fraud or misrepresentation. This is a discretionary waiver if the statutory elements are proven. The IJ, in exercising discretion, should balance the alien's undesirability as a permanent resident with the social and humane considerations present to determine whether a grant of relief is in the best interests of the country.[324] Adverse factors should include consideration of the underly-

---

[320] *Matter of Compean*, 21 I&N Dec. 51 (BIA 1995).

[321] *Matter of Farias-Menoza*, 21 I&N Dec. 269 (BIA 1996, A.G. 1997).

[322] INA §237(a)(1)(H).

[323] *Reid v. INS*, 492 F.2d 225 (2d Cir. 1974).

[324] *Matter of Tijam*, 22 I&N Dec. 408, 412 (BIA 1998).

ing fraud.[325] In addition, other negative factors include any criminal record and other evidence of bad character or undesirability as a permanent resident. Favorable factors to be considered include family ties in the United States; residency of long duration in the country, particularly if it began at a young age; hardship to the alien or family if deportation occurs; stable employment history; property or business ties; evidence of value and service to the community; and evidence of good character.[326]

The grant of a waiver under INA §237(a)(1)(H) (previously found at INA §241(f)) waives not only the alien's deportation but also the underlying fraud or misrepresentation and renders LPR status upon the waiver recipient from the time of initial entry, if he or she entered and was admitted as an LPR.[327] The grant of this waiver, therefore, makes the waiver recipient lawful from the point of initial entry, and that time accumulated from that point is lawful residence for §212(c) purposes.[328]

Waiver for Unlawful Presence

IIRAIRA added a new ground of inadmissibility in 1996—the three- or ten-year bar for unlawful presence.[329] Aliens who have accumulated between 180 days and 365 days of unlawful presence face a three-year bar, while those who have been unlawfully present for one year or more face a ten-year bar to admission. The INA provides a waiver of the unlawful presence bar if the following conditions are met:

- the alien is the spouse, son, or daughter of a U.S. citizen or LPR (note that it does not include parents of a U.S. citizen or LPR children); and
- the refusal of admission would result in extreme hardship to the U.S. citizen or LPR relative.

This is a discretionary waiver and the courts have no jurisdiction to review the administrative decision.

Unlawful presence means that the alien "is present" in the United States after the expiration of the period authorized by the AG or is present in the United States without being admitted or paroled.[330] Unlawful presence does not accrue in the following situations:

- time during which an alien is under the age of 18;
- period during the pendency of a bona fide asylum application unless the alien was employed without authorization;
- period of time in which the alien has family unity benefits under §301 of IMMACT90;

---

[325] *Id.*

[326] *Id.*; *see also Hernandez-Robledo v. INS*, 777 F.2d 536 (9th Cir. 1985).

[327] *Matter of Sosa-Hernandez*, 20 I&N Dec. 758 (BIA 1993).

[328] *Id.*

[329] INA §212(a)(9)(B).

[330] INA §212(a)(9)(B)(ii).

- the alien is a child or spouse of a U.S. citizen or LPR and the victim of domestic violence, and there is a substantial connection between the unlawful presence and the battery or cruelty; or
- the alien is a victim of a severe form of trafficking in persons.[331]

The unlawful presence stops accruing for an alien lawfully admitted or paroled during the pendency of an application to change or extend lawful status if the application is filed prior to the expiration of status, is a nonfrivolous application, and the alien has not been unlawfully employed during that period.[332]

Waiver of "Permanent" Bar Under INA §212(a)(9)(C)

Any alien who enters, or attempts to enter the United States after a prior aggregate period of more than one year in an unlawful status, or after an order of removal, is inadmissible.[333] There is a possible waiver of this ground of inadmissibility; however, it cannot be sought until the alien remains outside the United States for a period of 10 years following the alien's last departure.[334] For the 10 years following the departure, there is no possible waiver—hence, the penalty often is referred to as the permanent bar.

In order to qualify for a waiver under INA §212(a)(9)(C)(ii), the alien must:

- remain outside the United States for 10 years;
- file for permission to be admitted with the AG (the INA states "Attorney General"; however, this refers to the officer directing the district office who now is part of DHS); and
- obtain the consent of the AG.

In addition, there is a waiver of this ground of inadmissibility for immediate family members of U.S. citizens and LPRs victimized by domestic violence who meet the following requirements:

- they have been granted classification as VAWA self-petitioners under INA §§204(a)(1)(A)(iii), (iv), or (v), or §§204(a)(1)(B)(ii),(iii), or (iv); and
- there is a substantial connection between the battery or extreme cruelty and the alien's removal, departure from the United States, re-entry (or re-entries) into the United States, or attempts to re-enter.[335]

Waiver of Prior Removal Order

An alien who has been ordered removed is inadmissible for a period of several years depending on the type of removal proceeding or the reason for removal. Indi-

---

[331] INA §212(a)(9)(B)(iii).

[332] INA §212(a)(9)(B)(iv). For an excellent summary of what constitutes unlawful presence, see "Nuances of Unlawful Presence," *Immigration & Nationality Law Handbook* 847 (AILA, 2005–06 ed.).

[333] INA §212(a)(9)(C)(i).

[334] INA §212(a)(9)(C)(ii).

[335] *Id.*

viduals who have been ordered removed in an expedited removal proceeding under INA §235(b) or removal proceedings under INA §240 initiated upon the alien's arrival in the United States, may not seek admission for five years. Individuals already present in the United States who have been ordered removed may not seek admission within 10 years of departure. An individual who has been ordered removed more than once must wait 20 years before seeking admission. Last, individuals ordered removed who have been convicted of aggravated felonies may not seek admission "at any time."[336] There is a statutory waiver under INA §212(a)(9)(A)(iii) for aliens who have been removed who meet the following conditions:

- the alien filed an application for permission to apply for admission;
- prior to re-embarkation at a place outside the United States; and
- the AG consents to the alien's reapplying for admission.

The waiver is now generally adjudicated by DHS; however, an IJ may adjudicate the waiver and grant it *nunc pro tunc*, but only if granting the waiver is appropriate and necessary for the complete disposition of the case.[337] If granting the waiver would resolve completely the issues in the case, the IJ may adjudicate the waiver. If the applicant still would remain deportable or excludable, even with the grant of the waiver, the judge may not adjudicate it.[338] An IJ may not grant "advance" permission to apply. This authority is reserved to the district director.[339]

The BIA revisited this issue in 1996, and again stated that the IJ may not grant a *nunc pro tunc* waiver of a prior deportation order permitting the alien to reapply for admission if the alien would remain deportable or inadmissible even with a grant of the waiver.[340] In *Matter of Garcia-Linares*, an alien who returned to the United States following deportation with a visa but without obtaining advance permission to reapply was not eligible to apply for *nunc pro tunc* permission to reapply in conjunction with a §212(c) waiver since the grant of the waiver under INA §241(a)(1)(H) (now §237(a)(1)(H)) would not effect a complete disposition of the case.[341] In spite of the decision in *Garcia-Linares*, there are precedent decisions where the BIA has granted a *nunc pro tunc* application for permission to reapply for admission after deportation in conjunction with another waiver application.[342]

---

[336] INA §212(a)(9).

[337] *Matter of Vrattakos*, 14 I&N Dec. 593 (BIA 1974).

[338] *Id.*

[339] *Id.* at 602.

[340] *Matter of Garcia-Linares*, 21 I&N Dec. 254 (BIA 1996).

[341] *Id.*

[342] *Matter of Farinas*, 12 I&N Dec. 467 (BIA 1967) (permission to reapply with a §212(c) waiver and waiver of documentary requirements under INA §211(b); *Matter of Rapacon*, 14 I&N Dec. 375 (R.C. 1973) (*nunc pro tunc* permission to reapply for admission combined with adjustment of status application; *Matter of Sosa-Hernandez*, 20 I&N Dec. 758 (BIA 1993) (*nunc pro tunc* permission to reapply combined with a waiver under INA §212(c)).

There are certain grounds of removal for which an alien can never gain admission to the United States because these individuals are inadmissible for reasons based on controlled substance convictions (other than a single offense for possession of less that 30 grams of marijuana); murder; criminal acts involving torture; or attempt or conspiracy to commit murder or a criminal act involving torture.[343] In addition, there are no waivers for false claims to citizenship, smuggling (other than immediate family members), or document fraud under INA §237(a)(3)(C).

Finally, for an individual who returns to the United States with a deportation, exclusion, or removal order, the concern is that the government will merely re-instate the old order, detain, and remove the individual under INA §241(a)(5). That section states that the order may be reinstated upon the alien's return, the alien shall be removed, and the alien is not eligible for "any" relief.

Other Waivers

In addition to the waivers listed above for removal and immigration violations, there are other waivers that may be relevant in certain situations.

Waiver for document fraud—INA §212(d)(12)

This waiver is available to those inadmissible under INA §212(a)(6)(F) for document fraud if:

- the alien is an LPR who proceeded abroad temporarily (not under a removal order) and is otherwise admissible as a returning resident, or is seeking admission as an immediate relative or family member within one of the family preferences;
- the offense was committed solely to assist, aid, or support the alien's spouse or child (and no other individual); and
- there has been no other civil money penalty under INA §274C.

In addition, the document fraud ground of deportability[344] may be waived for LPRs with no prior document fraud penalty and the LPR is assisting only his or her spouse or child.[345]

Waiver of two-year foreign residence requirement—INA §212(e)

This waiver is for "J" visa holders subject to the two-year foreign residence requirement. There are several possible grounds for this waiver, including:

- a favorable recommendation by the director of the U.S. Information Agency (USIA), pursuant to a request by an interested U.S. government agency;
- a determination by USCIS that departure from the United States would pose an extreme hardship on the U.S. citizen or LPR child or spouse of the alien;

---

[343] INA §212(h).

[344] INA §237(a)(3).

[345] INA §237(a)(3)(C).

- the alien cannot return to the country of nationality because he or she would be subject to persecution on account of race, religion, or political opinion;
- a finding by the AG that the alien's admission is in the public interest; and
- a waiver by the AG of the obligation upon the favorable recommendation of the USIA director, where the foreign country of the alien's nationality or last residence has furnished a "no objection" letter.

Waiver of health grounds of inadmissibility—INA §212(g)

Certain health-related grounds of inadmissibility may be waived in accordance with the conditions stated in INA §212(g). The health-related grounds of inadmissibility that may be waived (provided the conditions of INA §212(g) are met) include:

- communicable diseases (HIV, TB, hepatitis, sexually transmitted diseases);
- vaccination requirements;[346] and
- physical or mental disorders.[347]

This section contains no waiver for the drug abuser or addict ground of inadmissibility.[348]

Waiver for admission of aliens without proper documents—INA §212(k)

An individual inadmissible for lacking a proper immigrant visa or other valid entry document may be admitted if the DHS officer is satisfied that the alien: (1) is in possession of an immigrant visa; (2) is otherwise admissible; and (3) could not have ascertained by due diligence prior to departure that he or she was inadmissible.

Public charge waiver—posting bond under INA §213

An alien inadmissible as a public charge under INA §212(a)(4) may be admitted, if otherwise admissible, upon the posting of a suitable bond as decided by the AG, and subject to the requirement of an affidavit of support under INA §213A.

Waiver of documentary requirements for returning residents—INA §211(b)

The AG may admit returning LPRs inadmissible under INA §212(a)(7) for lack of proper entry documentation, if otherwise admissible.[349]

Waivers for special immigrant juveniles—INA §237(c)

The grounds of removability relating to illegal status, including inadmissibility at time of admission, being present in violation of law, violation of terms of admission,

---

[346] INA §212(a)(1)(A)(ii).

[347] INA §212(a)(1)(A)(iii).

[348] INA §212(a)(1)(A)(iv).

[349] INA §211(b).

and failure to file change of address notices, are waived for individuals who are special immigrant juveniles under INA §101(a)(27)(J).

Waivers for refugees—INA §209(c)

Section 209 of the INA provides for adjustment of status for those granted refugee status under INA §207 or asylum under INA §208 if they have been physically present in the United States, continue to be a refugee under INA §101(a)(42), and are admissible.

The grounds of inadmissibility for being a public charge,[350] lacking a valid labor certification,[351] or valid entry documentation[352] are waived for purposes of adjusting status under INA §209.[353]

In addition, any other ground of inadmissibility may be waived for the refugee adjustment applicant except INA §§212(a)(2)(C) (relating to controlled substances) and 212(a)(3)(A), (B), (C), and (E) (relating to security grounds of inadmissibility). The ground of inadmissibility under INA §212(a)(3)(D) (relating to membership in a totalitarian party) may be waived. The AG has stated that aliens who have committed violent or dangerous crimes will not be granted a discretionary waiver under INA §209(c) except in extraordinary circumstances, such as those involving national security or foreign policy considerations, or cases in which the alien demonstrates that the denial of adjustment of status would result in exceptional and extremely unusual hardship.[354]

Executive Pardon—INA §237(a)(2)(A)(v)

The grounds of removability relating to crimes involving moral turpitude, multiple criminal convictions, aggravated felonies, and high speed flight[355] are waived with regard to criminal convictions if subsequent to the conviction, the alien obtains a lawful and unconditional pardon by the President or by the governor of any state. However, the pardon waives only the grounds of removal specifically set forth at INA §§237(a)(2)(A)(i)–(iv), and no implicit waivers may be read into the statute. An individual convicted of sexual abuse of a minor—an aggravated felony—is not removable on that ground if the waiver is granted; however, where the alien is also removable for the same offense under INA §237(a)(2)(E)(i)—crime of domestic violence—he or she remains removable for that offense even with the pardon because the offense is not waived by that pardon.[356]

---

[350] INA §212(a)(4).

[351] INA §212(a)(5).

[352] INA §212(a)(7)(A).

[353] INA §209(c).

[354] *Matter of Jean*, 23 I&N Dec. 373 (A.G. 2002).

[355] INA §§237(a)(2)(A)(i), (ii), (iii), and (iv).

[356] *Matter of Suh*, 23 I&N Dec. 626 (BIA 2003).

Voluntary Departure

Introduction

Voluntary departure is a limited form of relief. It provides no permanent status, nor does it allow the individual to remain in the country for any extended period of time. Voluntary departure provides a short period of time for an individual to wrap up his or her affairs in the United States and depart at his or her own expense in lieu of deportation. There are no provisions for work authorization during this period. The main benefit is that the recipient of a grant of voluntary deportation is free to leave under his or her own power on a day of his or her choosing and his or her record is kept clean of a removal order. The maximum period for which a grant of voluntary departure can be given is 120 days. In certain cases, to be discussed below, the maximum period is 60 days. Failure to depart within this period of time granted by the IJ carries severe consequences, *i.e.*, the voluntary departure order converts into a removal order and the person cannot return for a period of 10 years, nor is he or she eligible for most forms of relief for that same period. There are two types of voluntary departure—voluntary departure prior to completion of proceedings and voluntary departure at the conclusion of proceedings. The two types of voluntary departure have different requirements and provide different benefits. They will be discussed individually below.

Voluntary Departure Prior to Completion of Proceedings—INA §240B(a)

This form of voluntary departure is usually sought by itself when there will be neither other relief sought, nor any other contested issues.

Statutory and regulatory requirements—INA §240B(a)(1) and 8 CFR §1240.26(b)

- Not deportable as an aggravated felon;
- Not deportable as a terrorist under INA §237(a)(4)(B);
- Must be able to leave at his or her own expense;
- Concedes removability;[357]
- Waives all appeal issues;[358] and
- Makes no additional request for relief.[359]

Arriving aliens

If an alien is an arriving alien for whom removal proceedings under INA §240 are started at the time of arrival, he or she is not eligible for voluntary departure.[360]

---

[357] 8 CFR §1240.26(b)(1)(i)(C).

[358] 8 CFR §1240.26(b)(1)(i)(D).

[359] 8 CFR §1240.26(b)(1)(i)(B).

[360] INA §240B(a)(4).

Period of time granted

The maximum period allowed for this type of voluntary departure is 120 days.[361]

Documentary requirements

The alien must present a travel document (*e.g.*, passport) to prove he or she will be permitted entry into the country of departure unless the country does not require it, or U.S. Immigration and Customs Enforcement (ICE) already possesses it.[362]

Bond

The AG (and DHS) may require the posting of a voluntary departure bond to be surrendered upon proof that the person deported the United States.[363]

When sought

The request must be made prior to or at the master calendar hearing at which the case is initially calendared for a hearing on the merits.[364] If a request for other relief has been made and a case is set for a merits hearing, the individual still may be able to obtain voluntary departure prior to the completion of proceedings if the request for relief is withdrawn prior to the grant of any voluntary departure.[365]

Appeal

In order to obtain this type of voluntary departure, the applicant must abandon all challenges and appeals of any issue, and accept the voluntary departure decision of the judge.[366] The IJ has the duty to inform an eligible immigrant of the availability and requirements of voluntary departure and to provide the alien the opportunity to apply for this relief. An alien does not forfeit the right to apply for voluntary departure prior to completion of proceedings by appealing an erroneous denial of this relief.[367]

Voluntary Departure at the Conclusion of Proceedings—INA §240B(b)

This type of voluntary departure is generally sought as an alternative form of relief if other forms of relief (*e.g.*, asylum, adjustment of status) are denied. It is requested from the IJ at the master calendar hearing along with whatever other primary forms of relief are sought. Seeking this form of voluntary departure does not mean that one must abandon any contested issues or appeals.

---

[361] INA §240B(a)(2); *see also* 8 CFR §240.25(c).

[362] 8 CFR §1240.26(b)(3)(i).

[363] *Id.*

[364] 8 CFR §1240.26(b)(1).

[365] 8 CFR §1240.26(b)(1)(i)(B).

[366] *Matter of Ocampo*, 22 I&N Dec. 1301 (BIA 2000); *see also* 8 CFR §240.25(c).

[367] *Matter of Cordova*, 22 I&N Dec. 966 (BIA 1999).

Statutory requirements—INA §240B(b)(1)

- Physical presence in the United States for one year immediately proceeding the service of the NTA;
- The alien is and has been a person of good moral character for a period of five years immediately preceding his or her application for voluntary departure;
- The alien is not deportable based on aggravated felony or security-related grounds;
- The alien has the financial means to depart the United States and has established this by clear and convincing evidence; and the alien has established that he or she intends to depart the United States.

The requirements to show good moral character and the means to depart apply only to those who seek voluntary departure at the conclusion of proceedings under INA §240B(b), not to those seeking it prior to the completion of proceedings under INA §240B(a).[368]

Ineligible aliens

- Those deportable under INA §237(a)(2)(A)(iii) for aggravated felonies;[369]
- Individuals deportable under INA §237(a)(4) on terrorist grounds;[370]
- Individuals previously permitted to depart after having been found inadmissible under INA §212(a)(6)(A);[371]
- Individuals who have not accumulated one year of physical presence prior to the issuance of the NTA.

The bar to voluntary departure for those previously granted voluntary departure applies to those previously granted voluntary departure under INA §240B. It does not apply to those granted voluntary departure prior to April 1, 1997, under former INA §244(e).[372]

Bond

For voluntary departure at the conclusion of proceedings, an individual must post a voluntary departure bond of $500 at minimum to ensure departure. It is returned upon proof that the alien has departed.[373]

---

[368] *Matter of Arguelles*, 22 I&N Dec. 811 (BIA 1999).

[369] INA §240B(b)(1)(C).

[370] *Id.*

[371] INA §240B(c).

[372] *Matter of Arguelles*, 22 I&N Dec. 811 (BIA 1999).

[373] INA §240B(b)(3); *see also* 8 CFR §1240.26(c)(3).

Period of time granted

The grant of voluntary departure at the conclusion of proceedings shall not exceed 60 days.[374] While in some cases, extensions of voluntary departure may be granted by DHS after the IJ makes an initial grant, the extension may not go beyond the statutory period.[375]

Documentary requirements

The voluntary departure regulations require that the alien present a passport or other travel document to ensure lawful entry into the country to which the alien is departing.[376] The regulations also provide that ICE will have a full opportunity to inspect and photocopy the travel document, and if necessary challenge its validity before voluntary departure is granted.[377]

Civil penalty for failure to depart—INA §240B(d)

If an alien is granted voluntary departure and fails to depart voluntarily, he or she is subject to a civil penalty of not less than $1,000 or more than $5,000. In addition, he or she is ineligible for the following relief for a period of 10 years:

- cancellation of removal under INA §240A;
- adjustment of status under INA §245;
- change of nonimmigrant status under INA §248; and
- registry under INA §249.

An alien who is ordered deported "in absentia" has not remained beyond a granted period of voluntary departure since no voluntary departure is granted in an in absentia proceeding, and the 10-year bar is not applicable.[378]

No judicial review—INA §240B(f)

No court has jurisdiction over an appeal from a denial of a request for an order of voluntary departure, nor may any court stay an order of removal pending any claim with respect to voluntary departure.

Grants of Voluntary Departure by ICE

Certain ICE officials, including district directors, assistant directors in inspections and examinations, certain officers in charge, chief patrol agents, and directors and assistant directors for examinations at service centers may grant voluntary depar-

---

[374] INA §240B(b)(2).

[375] 8 CFR §1240.26(f).

[376] 8 CFR §1240.26(c)(2).

[377] *Id.*

[378] *Matter of Singh*, 21 I&N Dec. 998 (BIA 1997).

ture.[379] This is prior to the commencement of proceedings and is similar to what was previously called "pre-hearing" voluntary departure in the pre-IIRAIRA era.

The application is made with ICE. Generally, the alien must present a travel document to ICE proving that he or she will be able to enter the country of departure lawfully.[380] This is photocopied by ICE and may be subject to investigation or forensic examination.[381] The maximum period allowed is 120 days.[382] The alien need not show good moral character; however, other conditions may be set by ICE, including the requirement of a bond.[383]

Procedure for Seeking Voluntary Departure

There is not a form for seeking voluntary departure from ICE or the IJ, nor is there a fee; although a voluntary departure bond of at least $500 must be paid to ICE within five business days of the grant if made "at the conclusion of proceedings."[384] The following issues should be considered, depending on when and before which decision-maker voluntary departure is sought:

- *Passport:* Required if voluntary departure is sought before the court; it may be required if sought with ICE;
- *Proof of Good Moral Character:* Required if the request is made "at the conclusion" of proceedings, but not required if sought from ICE or prior to the completion of proceedings with the IJ;
- *Date of Applying:* Not eligible if sought in deportation proceedings and the alien has not been present for one year prior to the service of the NTA;
- *Aggravated Felons and Terrorists:* Not eligible;
- *Arriving Aliens:* Not eligible unless applying at the conclusion of proceedings and can show one year's physical presence prior to service of NTA.

Finally, there is an issue as to whether voluntary departure should be sought at all. If the alien has no intention of departing, he or she is not eligible, and is only creating an additional bar to future admission under INA §240B(d) should he or she seek it, receive it, then refuse to depart. In this scenario, he or she has both the bar to admissibility under INA §212(a)(9)(A) for the removal and the bar for failure to comply with the voluntary departure conditions. Many experienced practitioners will often forego seeking voluntary departure where there is a significant possibility that the person will not depart, or will not be able to do so. The decision to seek or forego voluntary departure is one that must be analyzed with several other factors kept in

---

379 8 CFR §240.25(a).

380 8 CFR §240.25(b).

381 *Id.*

382 8 CFR §240.25(c).

383 8 CFR §240.25(b).

384 INA §240B(b)(3).

mind, including the effect that voluntary departure, or the failure to depart, will have on other possible future forms of relief.

Relief from DHS

Introduction

Partially as a result of the drastic reduction in the availability of relief after the implementation of IIRAIRA, frequently, there is no relief available from the immigration court. Almost all forms of relief discussed in Chapters 5 and 6, with the possible exceptions of Convention Against Torture and VAWA relief, were limited by IIRAIRA, if not eliminated altogether. As a result, IJs often are quite helpless to grant relief even in the most extraordinarily humanitarian situations. The only authority in such situations that may grant relief to avoid or postpone removal is DHS—either through ICE or U.S. Customs and Border Patrol (CBP).

Below is a brief summary of possible relief that may be sought from DHS. These forms of relief are not listed in the INA, but are recognized as within DHS's discretion to grant in appropriate situations.

Prosecutorial Discretion

Prosecutorial discretion is a device by which DHS may choose not to enforce a statute or regulation that it has the power to enforce in a particular situation. It can refer to a broad array of discretionary decisions by DHS such as: (1) choosing to institute proceedings; (2) agreeing to terminate or administratively close proceedings; (3) the allocation of resources; (4) whether to stop or arrest an individual; and (5) what charges to make against an individual.

The General Counsel for INS (now DHS) issued a memorandum on when prosecutorial discretion might be the appropriate action and what factors might be considered, including:[385]

- "Overcriminalization"—existence of laws on the books that the society did not wish to enforce as strongly as written;
- Limitation in available enforcement resources and the need to prioritize the use of such resources; and
- The need to be able to address the individual equities of particular cases in a way that a rigid application of a broadly drawn statute cannot do.

The idea of prosecutorial discretion applies to decisions to enforce, or not to enforce, a law—it does not mean granting a benefit.[386] Prosecutorial discretion means that the government may choose not to take action to place someone in proceedings, bring certain charges, obtain a finding of removability, or remove an alien.

---

[385] Bo Cooper, General Counsel, "INS Exercise of Prosecutorial Discretion," HQCOU 90/16-P.

[386] *Id.* at 4.

DHS decisions to commence deportation proceedings or execute removal orders are not reviewable.[387]

In 2000, shortly before she left her position as INS Commissioner, Doris Meissner issued a memorandum outlining guidelines for the exercise of prosecutorial discretion. She set out a number of factors to be considered. Where the government does not have a substantial interest in enforcing the immigration laws against an individual, the choice may be to exercise discretion not to prosecute.[388] She stated that enforcement officers were expected to use prosecutorial discretion at all phases of the enforcement process. She outlined the following (but not limited) factors to be taken into account in exercising prosecutorial discretion:

- immigration status;
- length of residence in the United States;
- criminal history;
- humanitarian concerns;
- likelihood of ultimately removing the alien;
- likelihood of ultimately achieving enforcement goals by other means;
- eligibility or likelihood of alien becoming eligible for relief;
- effect of action on future admissibility;
- current or past cooperation with law enforcement;
- honorable U.S. military service;
- community attention or public opinion on the case; and
- resources available to the government.

The exercise of prosecutorial discretion in the immigration area often involves asking DHS to agree not to initiate proceedings against a child, or other individual, for whom removal or the removal procedure would be especially harsh. It also may involve requesting the DHS attorney to agree to administratively close or postpone a proceeding where an individual might be eligible in the future for relief, or where removal would have a very damaging effect. Almost always, it involves strong equities or humanitarian factors on the part of the alien that might cause the government not to proceed with a removal procedure even where it might win a removal order.

Deferred Action

Deferred action is a program that allows the government to defer or postpone taking action to remove an individual where there is no other relief available to the individual. It is a policy decision by the government to place a case in a low priority category and defer taking any further action on it. It is not an action that an IJ can take. If

---

[387] *Reno v. American-Arab Anti-Discrimination Committee*, 525 U.S. 471 (1999).

[388] INS Memorandum, Doris Meissner, "Exercising Prosecutorial Discretion," HQOPP 50/4 (Nov. 17, 2000), available at *http://uscis.gov/graphics/lawsregs/handbook/discretion.pdf*.

the government issues a charging document and moves to prosecute the case, the IJ has no option but to go forward and adjudicate the charges brought and relief applications made. Deferred action was previously found in INS Operating Instructions.[389] There is no right to deferred action and its denial has not been successfully challenged in court. The factors that the government generally considers in making the decision include:

- presence of humanitarian or sympathetic factors;
- likelihood of ultimately removing the alien;
- likelihood of generating bad publicity by enforcing the law; and
- the person's membership in a group whose deportation has been given high priority status (*e.g.*, criminal aliens in detention).

Deferred action usually is sought at the end of proceedings and, frequently, the government trial attorney will seek to get a final deportation order or order of voluntary departure before agreeing to consider a request for deferred action. Historically, the decision on a deferred action request had to be referred to the regional INS office. However, deferred action is most common now in VAWA situations; where an I-360 is approved based on battery or extreme cruelty to the spouse or child of a U.S. citizen or LPR, the beneficiary of the self-petition is given deferred action along with the approval of the petition. One of the major benefits to receiving deferred action, in addition to the relief that the government will not be seeking to remove the person, is the grant of employment authorization for which the person is eligible upon receiving deferred action.[390] There is no application form for deferred action; it is a request supported by documentation to prove sympathetic and other favorable factors. There is no fee for this request. However, if granted and the individual wishes to seek employment authorization, the I-765 must be filed with the appropriate fee or request for fee waiver.

Administrative Closure

Administrative closure of a case is a vehicle used to temporarily remove a case from the docket of an IJ or the BIA. It does not result in a final order. The case is merely taken from the list of active cases and placed in inactive status by the court. Administrative closure is used frequently where the individual may qualify for another type of relief that would render removal impossible or inappropriate because the person has another means to obtain lawful status, such as TPS. It also is sometimes used in sympathetic situations where there may be good reasons to refrain from going forward with a deportation procedure but the government does not want to completely terminate the case. The difference between a termination and an administrative closure is that when a case is administratively closed it is still alive, just not active. In order to make it active, either side need merely to file a motion to calendar the

---

[389] INS Operations Instruction 242.1(a)(22).

[390] 8 CFR §§274a.12(c)(14), 1274a.12(c)(14).

case, and it goes back on the docket. When a case is terminated, it is officially dead unless an appeal of the termination is filed with the BIA. If there is a final decision of termination and the government wishes to prosecute a removal proceeding against an individual, a motion to reopen proceedings must be made or the government must commence with a new proceeding by issuing a new charging document. In addition, the IJ has the authority to terminate a case over the objection of DHS counsel.[391] Administrative closure, however, cannot be forced on the government. A case may not be administratively closed if opposed by either party.[392] Where an alien requests administrative closure pursuant to the *ABC* settlement,[393] and the person is not an aggravated felon or within the listed categories of public concern in the settlement, the proceedings must be administratively closed pursuant to the *ABC* agreement to permit the individual his or her right to pursue benefits under the agreement.[394]

Temporary Protected Status

The AG (now USCIS) may grant an individual TPS if the individual is from a foreign state designated by the AG as a TPS state. The requirements for such designation are a finding by the AG:

- that there is an ongoing armed conflict within the state and because of this conflict, requiring the person to return home would pose a severe risk to his or her personal safety; or
- that there has been an earthquake, flood, epidemic, or other environmental disaster resulting in a substantial but temporary disruption of living conditions in the area affected; the foreign state is unable temporarily to handle adequately the return of the nationals of that country and has requested designation as a TPS country.[395]

The designation is temporary and continues until AG determines that the state no longer meets the requirements outlined above. The initial designation period is between six and 18 months.[396]

The requirements for applicants are the following:[397]

- proof that he or she is a national of the designated country;
- proof of physical presence in the United States since the date of TPS designation;
- continuous residence in the United States since the date designated by the AG;

---

[391] 8 CFR §1240.12(c).

[392] *Matter of Gutierrez-Lopez*, 21 I&N Dec. 489 (BIA 1996).

[393] *American Baptist Churches v. Thornburgh*, 760 F. Supp. 797 (N.D. Cal. 1991).

[394] *Matter of Morales*, 21 I&N Dec. 130 (BIA 1996).

[395] INA §244(b).

[396] INA §244(b)(2).

[397] INA §244(c)(1).

- admissibility as an immigrant (the grounds of inadmissibility relating to documentary requirements and labor certification are waived[398]); and
- no convictions of any felony or two or more misdemeanors.[399]

If TPS is granted, work authorization is mandatory.[400] In addition, DHS "shall not remove" the alien from the United States during the period in which TPS is in effect.[401] Because the person cannot be removed, DHS frequently will agree to an administrative closure, but this cannot be forced on the government. The application is filed on Form I-821 with the required fees, photographs, and proof of nationality, physical presence, and eligibility.[402] If the application is denied, or if the person is served an NTA with a denial of the TPS application, the application may be renewed before an IJ, and, if denied in immigration court, appealed to the BIA.[403]

Stay of Deportation/Removal

An individual with a final order of deportation or removal always may seek a stay of the deportation/removal order with DHS. It must be filed on Form I-246.[404] It is filed with the district director (now ICE director) at the place where the alien is at the time of filing.[405] The regulations provide DHS/ICE with broad latitude in the granting of the stay. It may be granted "for such time or under such conditions" as the director may deem appropriate.[406] The form should be filed with the appropriate fee and documentation to explain why the stay of deportation/removal is needed. A stay of deportation/removal also may be obtained from the IJ or the BIA while a motion to reopen or reconsider is pending.[407]

---

[398] INA §244(c)(2)(A).

[399] INA §244(c)(2)(B)(i).

[400] INA §244(a)(1)(B); 8 CFR §§274a.12(a)(12), 1274a.12(a)(12).

[401] INA §244(a)(1)(A).

[402] 8 CFR §§244.6 and 244.9, 1244.6 and 1244.9.

[403] 8 CFR §§244.11, 1244.11.

[404] 8 CFR §241.6.

[405] *Id.*

[406] *Id.*

[407] 8 CFR §1003.23(b)(1)(v).

CHAPTER SEVEN

APPEALS AND MOTIONS TO REOPEN AND RECONSIDER

Appeals to the Board of Immigration Appeals

Introduction

Review of the decision of an immigration judge (IJ) is generally accomplished in one of two ways: (1) direct appeal to the Board of Immigration Appeals (BIA)[1] or (2) a motion to reopen or reconsider the decision of the IJ,[2] which is filed with the judge. The following section outlines the bases and procedures for appealing the decision of an IJ to the BIA and, ultimately, to the Attorney General (AG). This discussion focuses on decisions by the IJ relating to removability/deportability, inadmissibility, relief, and bond/custody redetermination.

Board of Immigration Appeals

Who serves on the BIA

The BIA was created in 1940 by the AG, and members serve at his or her discretion. It is a creation of regulation, not statute.[3] In 1983, the BIA, along with the immigration court system, was removed from the former Immigration and Naturalization Service (INS) and made part of a new agency, the Executive Office for Immigration Review (EOIR), within the Department of Justice (DOJ).[4] The BIA is an 11-member body appointed by the AG. It was reduced from a 21-member body to the current membership of 11 in 2002 after then–Attorney General John Ashcroft's "streamlining" regulations (discussed below). A chairman of the BIA also is designated by the AG.

---

[1] 8 CFR §1003.3.

[2] 8 CFR §1003.23.

[3] 8 CFR §1003.1 *et seq.*

[4] *See* Anna Marie Gallagher, "Practice and Procedure Before the Board of Immigration Appeals: An Update," 03-2 *Immigration Briefings* (Feb. 2003).

BIA jurisdiction

The BIA has jurisdiction over all appeals from the decisions of the IJs under 8 CFR §1003.1(b), as well as certain administrative decisions made by the Department of Homeland Security (DHS). The following issues may be appealed to the BIA:[5]

- Final decisions of the IJ in exclusion and deportation cases (unless the only issue is the length of time granted for voluntary departure).
- Final decisions in removal cases (unless it is an in absentia order under Immigration and Nationality Act (INA)[6] §240(b)(5)(C), or a decision on the length of time granted for voluntary departure by the IJ).
- Decisions on relief from removal, including cancellation of removal (lawful permanent residents (LPRs) or non–LPRs under INA §§240A(a) and (b); adjustment of status under INA §245; asylum under INA §208; withholding of removal under INA §241(b)(3); relief under the Convention Against Torture (CAT) (8 CFR §§208.16–208.18); and waivers adjudicated by the IJ including INA §§212(h); 212(i); 212(d)(11); and former §212(c).
- Decisions on applications for Temporary Protected Status (TPS) under INA §244.
- Decisions involving fines and penalties including mitigation of fines.
- Decisions on visa preference issues, except employment-based and orphan petitions under INA §101(b)(1)(F).
- Bond/custody decisions by the IJ except for mandatory detention cases (unless mandatory detention is being challenged); there is no jurisdiction by the BIA to review custody decisions in exclusion proceedings.
- Determinations by the IJ to detain a person beyond the removal period under 8 CFR §1241.14.
- IJ decisions on rescission of adjustment of status under INA §246.
- Decisions on certain adjustment applications from nationals of Cuba, Nicaragua, and Haiti.[7]
- Decisions on applications for individual and agency accreditation and listing on the legal services list under 8 CFR §1292.2.
- Decisions of IJs in attorney disciplinary proceedings.[8]

Issues on which the BIA has no jurisdiction

The BIA has no jurisdiction to review the following issues:

---

[5] 8 CFR §1003.1(b).

[6] Immigration and Nationality Act of 1952, Pub. L. No. 82-414, 66 Stat. 163 (codified as amended at 8 USC §§1101 *et seq.*).

[7] 8 CFR §§245.13(n)(2) and 245.15(n)(3), 1245.13(n)(2) and 1245.15(n)(3).

[8] *Matter of Gadda*, 23 I&N Dec. 645 (BIA 2003).

- The length of the voluntary departure period granted by the court under INA §240B (there is jurisdiction to appeal a denial of voluntary departure altogether);
- In absentia removal orders;
- Credible fear determinations;
- Applications for advance parole;
- Orphan petitions;
- Employment-based visa petitions;
- Waivers of two-year foreign residency requirements for J-1 exchange visitors;
- H, L, and K-1 petitions;
- Employer sanctions;
- DHS decisions on administrative fines for aircrafts and vessels; and
- DHS decisions to reinstate deportation or removal orders.[9]

Review Powers of the BIA

On September 25, 2002, final regulations took effect that amended the procedures and powers of the BIA in reviewing appeals.[10] In addition to reducing the size of the BIA from 21 to 11 members, there were several other significant changes including the scope of review by the BIA.

Scope of review

On questions of "law, discretion, and judgment," the BIA maintains de novo review power.[11] However, on questions of fact, the BIA's power to review an IJ's findings is greatly reduced. It now defers to the IJ's factual and discretionary findings, including findings on credibility, unless they are "clearly erroneous."[12]

The BIA may not engage in "fact-finding" except to take administrative notice of commonly known facts. If a party to an appeal alleges that further fact-finding is necessary, a motion to remand must be filed. The BIA may then remand the case to the immigration court, or DHS, where appropriate.[13] The BIA may review all questions of fact or law "de novo" on decisions rendered by DHS officers.[14]

---

[9] *See BIA Practice Manual* §1.4(b), available at *www.usdoj.gov/eoir*.

[10] 8 CFR §1003.1(a)(1) *et seq.*

[11] 8 CFR §1003.1(d)(3)(ii).

[12] 8 CFR §1003.1(d)(3)(i); *Matter of S–H–*, 23 I&N Dec. 462 (BIA 2002).

[13] 8 CFR §1003.1(d)(3)(iv).

[14] 8 CFR §1003.1(d)(3)(iii).

Summary dismissal of appeals

A single BIA member or a panel may summarily dismiss any appeal or portion of an appeal in any of these situations:[15]

- failure to specify the reason for the appeal;
- the appeal is on a question of law or fact conceded by the appellant at the hearing;
- the appeal is of an order granting the appellant the relief requested;
- the appeal filed for an improper purpose, such as to cause delay, or an appeal lacking an arguable basis in law or fact (unless the BIA determines the appeal is supported by a good faith argument to modify or reverse existing law);
- failure to file a brief after indicating on the Notice of Appeal that one would be filed;[16]
- the appeal is not within the BIA's jurisdiction;
- the appeal is untimely;
- the party waived appeal clearly on the record; however, an unrepresented alien who accepts the judge's decision as "final" does not waive his or her right to appeal when the judge does not explain that acceptance of the decision as final constitutes an irrevocable waiver of appeal rights;[17]
- the appeal is expressly excluded by statute or regulation; or
- the appeal fails to meet essential statutory or regulatory requirements.

The BIA may sanction an attorney or representative who files an appeal that is summarily dismissed if the BIA finds that the filing of the appeal constitutes "frivolous" behavior.[18]

Jurisdiction by certification

Certification is separate and distinct from the appeal process. While normally the BIA takes jurisdiction of an administrative appeal via the filing of a Notice of Appeal (Form EOIR-26) by the respondent or DHS, the BIA may take jurisdiction by certification.[19] The DHS attorney, the IJ, any other duly authorized government officer, or even the BIA may "certify" a case to the BIA for review, and the BIA, in its discretion, may review the case.[20] An IJ may certify his or her decision to the BIA in any case under INA §240 "when it involves an unusually complex or novel question of

---

[15] *See* 8 CFR §1003.1(d)(2).

[16] *See Rioja v. Ashcroft*, 317 F.3d 514 (5th Cir. 2003).

[17] *Matter of Rodriguez Diaz*, 22 I&N 1320 (BIA 2000).

[18] 8 CFR §1003.102(j).

[19] 8 CFR §1003.1(c).

[20] 8 CFR §§1003.1(c) and 1003.7.

law or fact."[21] The case has to fall within the classes of cases outlined in 8 CFR §1003.1(d) that the BIA is permitted to review.

The IJ and DHS may only certify a case to the BIA after an initial decision has been rendered, but before an appeal is taken.[22] The case is certified and the record forwarded to the BIA by DHS and the immigration court having administrative control over the record. The BIA may accept or refuse to accept such certified case for review. If a case is certified to the BIA, both parties must be notified that the case is required to be certified and that they have the right to make representations before the BIA including the right to seek oral argument and to submit briefs.[23]

The BIA's discretionary power to certify a case for review is not unlimited. Certification by the BIA for review is limited to "exceptional" circumstances and is not meant to be used as a general cure for filing defects or to otherwise circumvent the regulations where enforcing them might result in hardship.[24]

If the BIA, in its discretion, decides to certify a case for review, it may do so without giving oral argument or an additional briefing schedule where it determines the parties already have had a fair opportunity to present their case to the BIA.[25] The certification of a case to the BIA does not relieve the affected party of the requirements for taking an appeal if the affected party wishes to do so. A separate appeal in accordance with the appeal provisions in the regulations must be filed, and no extension of time is given to take the appeal.[26]

In cases where the time for filing the appeal has passed, certification by the BIA may be a way to get before the BIA a meritorious issue that cannot be otherwise considered because of the passage of the appeal time.[27]

Rules of practice

The BIA has the authority, with the approval of the director of EOIR, to prescribe procedures governing proceedings.[28] The BIA has set out these procedures in the *BIA Practice Manual* (available on the EOIR website, *www.usdoj.gov/eoir*).

Discipline of practitioners

The BIA has the power to "regulate the conduct" of attorneys, representatives of organizations, and others who appear in a representative capacity before the BIA, the

---

[21] 8 CFR §1240.1(a)(2).

[22] 8 CFR §1003.7.

[23] *Id.*

[24] *Matter of J–J–*, 21 I&N Dec. 976, 984 (BIA 1990).

[25] 8 CFR §1003.1(e); *see also* 8 CFR §1003.7.

[26] 8 CFR §1003.3(d).

[27] *Garcia v. Bolden*, 691 F.2d 1172, 1181 (5th Cir. 1982).

[28] 8 CFR §1003.1(d)(4).

immigration courts, and DHS. It determines whether any organization or representative listed in 8 CFR §1292.2 meets the requirements as set out in that section.[29]

Procedures in Filing Appeals

What can be appealed

- See section on BIA jurisdiction, above.
- See also 8 CFR §1003.1(b).

Who can file an appeal

The alien—An alien who is the subject of a decision by the immigration court or, where appropriate, DHS may file an appeal. The attorney representing the alien may file the appeal on his or her behalf. The Notice of Appeal (Form EOIR-26) must designate the party appealing and the alien registration number.[30] If the representative for the alien files the appeal, a Notice of Appearance (EOIR-27) must be filed with the Notice of Appeal. An alien has a right to legal representation in the appeal process at no expense to the government. The attorney may file the appeal on behalf of the alien. Any such representative must be within the classes of permitted individuals outlined in 8 CFR §1292.2.

DHS—The government also may appeal. Any government appeal must identify the person whose case the government is appealing.

When to file

The Notice of Appeal (Form EOIR-26) must be filed within 30 days of the oral decision of the IJ; the service of a summary decision; or the mailing of the written decision.[31] *It must be received at the EOIR clerk's office within that 30-day period.*[32] Mailing on the 30th day is not sufficient. The 30-day deadline applies whether the person is detained or not detained. If the 30th day falls on a Saturday, Sunday, or legal holiday, the due date falls to the following business day.[33] A Notice of Appeal may not be filed if the party has waived appeal.

The time period for appeal begins to run immediately upon the issuance of a final disposition of the case.[34] If the appeal is not filed within the time specified, it is not considered properly filed and the decision of the IJ becomes the final decision.[35] The

---

[29] 8 CFR §1003.1(b)(13).

[30] 8 CFR §1003.3(a)(1); *see also BIA Practice Manual*, *supra* note 9, §4.3.

[31] 8 CFR §1240.15.

[32] 8 CFR §1003.38(c).

[33] 8 CFR §1003.38(b).

[34] *Matter of Jean*, 23 I&N Dec. 373 (A.G. 2002).

[35] 8 CFR §1003.38(d).

IJ may not extend this time.[36] Failure to file a timely appeal by counsel has been found not to constitute ineffective assistance of counsel.[37]

There is no regulatory authority for extending the deadline; however, the BIA has done so on rare occasions. Where the BIA dismisses an appeal as untimely without addressing the merits of the appeal, it has the authority to reconsider its dismissal of the appeal where the basis of the motion to reconsider is the BIA's finding of untimeliness or the reasons for the untimely filing of the appeal.[38] The BIA may take a case on certification to address an issue in a case where the appeal is untimely filed.[39] When the BIA takes jurisdiction of a case by certification, it "may reach a meritorious question presented by an untimely or otherwise questionable appeal."[40]

Where to file

Appeals of the decisions by the immigration court are filed with the clerk's office for the BIA in Falls Church, Va. The addresses (depending on how the appeal is sent) are below:

For courier, overnight, or personal delivery:

Office of the Clerk
Board of Immigration Appeals
5107 Leesburg Pike, Suite 2000
Falls Church, VA 22041
Phone: (703) 605-1007

For regular mailing:

Board of Immigration Appeals
Office of the Clerk
P.O. Box 8530
Falls Church, VA 22041

What forms to file

The following documents should be filed for an appeal to the BIA:

- Notice of Appeal (Form EOIR-26).
- Fee or fee waiver—the filing fee is $110. If the appellant cannot afford the fee, there is a fee waiver application (Form EOIR-26A). There is no fee for bond appeals.

---

36 *Matter of Correa-Garces*, 20 I&N Dec. 451 (BIA 1992).

37 *Matter of Assaad*, 23 I&N Dec. 553 (BIA 2003).

38 *Matter of Edilzar-Lopez*, 22 I&N Dec. 16 (BIA 1998).

39 *Matter of Correa-Garces*, 20 I&N Dec. 451 (BIA 1992); *see also Matter of Gallares*, 14 I&N 250 (BIA 1972).

40 *Garcia v. Bolden*, 691 F.2d 1172, 1181 (5th Cir. 1982).

- Notice of Entry of Appearance—on appeals to the BIA, a separate notice of appearance form (Form EOIR-27) is filed. The BIA does not accept the EOIR-28, which is the form used for the immigration court. On appeals of DHS decisions over which the BIA has jurisdiction, the notice of entry of appearance is Form EOIR-29.
- Change of Address—if the appellant has changed addresses, the Form EOIR-33/BIA is submitted.
- Certificate of Service—any document filed with EOIR, including appeals to the BIA, must be served on DHS counsel. The appeal form has a certificate of service section that must be completed. On all filings with the BIA, make certain there is a certificate of service verifying service on DHS counsel.[41]

Contents of notice of appeal (Form EOIR-26)

In order to avoid a summary dismissal of the appeal, the contents of the notice of appeal must be consistent with 8 CFR §1003.3(b). The regulation states that the notice of appeal must meet the following requirements or the appeal will be summarily dismissed.

- *Basis for appeal:* The findings of fact and the conclusion(s) of law being challenged must be "specifically" identified.[42] If additional space is needed, additional pages can be added.
  - question of law—if a question of law is presented, supporting authority must be included;
  - question of fact—the contested issues of fact must be identified with specificity; and
  - discretionary relief—if the appeal concerns discretionary relief, the Notice of Appeal must state whether the appeal goes to grounds of eligibility; that is, the appeal must indicate whether the alleged error relates to statutory grounds or discretionary issues.
- *Oral argument:* The appeal form must note whether oral argument is desired. It is not always granted; however, it must be noted on the Form EOIR-26 if it is sought. If granted, the parties will present their oral arguments to a panel of three or more BIA members.[43]
- *Notice of brief:* The Notice of Appeal must indicate whether a written brief will be filed in support of the appeal. Failure to file a brief after indicating that a brief will be filed may result in the dismissal of the appeal.[44]

---

[41] 8 CFR §1003.3(a)(1).

[42] 8 CFR §1003.3(b).

[43] *BIA Practice Manual*, *supra* note 9, §4.2(g).

[44] 8 CFR §1003.1(d)(2)(i)(E). *See also BIA Practice Manual*, *supra* note 9, §4.16.

- *Notice of three-member panel:* The party appealing may note in the Notice of Appeal that a three-member BIA panel is required. (See discussion below about single- and three-member panel BIA review.) If a party asserts that three-member panel review under 8 CFR §1003.1(e)(6) is warranted, the Notice of Appeal should indicate the factual and/or legal basis for the need of three-member panel review.[45]
- *Detained persons:* If the individual is detained, the Notice of Appeal should indicate such detention. Detained persons are subject to the 30-day appeal deadline as persons not in detention.[46]

Interlocutory appeals

An interlocutory appeal is a request for BIA review of a decision by an IJ *before* the judge renders a final decision. These are disfavored by the BIA because the BIA normally reviews the final decision of the IJ. The BIA only will accept an interlocutory appeal in cases involving important jurisdictional issues regarding the administration of the immigration laws, or recurring questions in the adjudication of cases by the immigration court.[47]

An interlocutory appeal is filed on Form EOIR-26 (Notice of Appeal). It should be noted on the form that it is an interlocutory appeal. The form additionally should note: (1) the nature of the disposition being appealed; (2) the date of that disposition; and (3) the precise issue appealed. If there is a written adjudication by the IJ (*e.g.*, decision on motion), it should be attached. Any brief to be filed should accompany the Notice of Appeal form. The case will not be suspended or delayed during the adjudication of the interlocutory appeal.[48]

Stay of execution of decision

Direct appeals

The filing of a direct appeal on a decision by the IJ in a timely manner (within the 30-day period) results in a stay of the execution of that order.[49] The decision of the IJ shall not be executed during the 30-day period allowed for the filing of the appeal, unless the party waives the right to appeal. Nor can the decision be executed while the appeal is pending or while a case is with the BIA following certification.

---

45 8 CFR §1003.3(b).

46 *BIA Practice Manual*, *supra* note 9, §4.5(c).

47 *Matter of K–*, 20 I&N Dec. 418 (1991).

48 *See BIA Practice Manual*, *supra* note 9, §4.14.

49 8 CFR §1003.6(a).

Motions

There is no stay of execution where the appeal is on a motion to reopen or reconsider unless a stay is expressly granted by the court or the BIA.[50] However, on all decisions involving motions to reopen "in absentia" orders, there is an automatic stay of the order upon filing the motion. This stay remains in effect during the appeal of the denial of the motion.[51]

Bond appeals

There is no stay of execution of the decision of deportation, inadmissibility, or removal proceedings during the appeal of a bond decision.[52] Bond proceedings are considered a separate phase of proceedings.[53] Appeal of the bond decision is taken within 30 days of the bond decision (not the final decision on removability).[54] It requires a separate notice of appeal (Form EOIR-26), but requires no fee.[55] However, an appeal of the amount of a voluntary departure bond[56] requires a fee of $110, unless waived by the BIA.[57] The removability and relief phase of the case may proceed forward while the appeal of the bond decision is pending before the BIA. If the alien is ordered removed, denied relief by the BIA, or departs the country, the bond appeal is considered moot. The AG retains authority to review a BIA decision in bond proceedings.[58]

DHS may stay the execution of a bond decision by the IJ. Where the bond amount initially set by DHS is $10,000 or greater, or DHS has refused to set bond, the bond decision by the IJ is automatically stayed upon DHS's filing of a "Notice of Service Intent to Appeal Custody Determination" (Form EOIR-43) with the immigration court within one business day of the issuance of the order. Failure to file this notice within one business day removes the stay provisions.[59] DHS also may seek an emergency stay with the BIA. The automatic stay provisions have been ruled unconstitutional by several courts.[60]

---

[50] 8 CFR §1003.6(b).

[51] *Id.*

[52] 8 CFR §§236.1(d)(4), 1236.1(d)(4).

[53] 8 CFR §1003.19(d).

[54] 8 CFR §1003.19(f) referring to 8 CFR §1003.38; *see also* 8 CFR §1003.38(b).

[55] *BIA Practice Manual*, *supra* note 9, §7.3(a)(iii).

[56] 8 CFR §1240.26(c)(3).

[57] *BIA Practice Manual*, *supra* note 9, §7.3(a)(iii).

[58] *Matter of D–J–*, 23 I&N 572 (A.G. 2003).

[59] 8 CFR §1003.19(i)(2).

[60] *Zavala v. Ridge*, 310 F. Supp. 2d 1071 (N.D. Cal. 2004); *Ashley v. Ridge*, 288 F. Supp. 2d 662 (D.N.J. 2003).

Appearances before the BIA

The same basic right to representation before DHS and the immigration judges applies to representation before the BIA. Immigrants have a right to be represented "at no expense to the government."[61] The classes of individuals authorized to represent parties before EOIR and DHS are outlined at 8 CFR §1292.1(a).

Attorneys who are members in good standing of the bar of any state, possession, territory, the District of Columbia, or commonwealth and who are not under a court order suspending or restraining them from practice are authorized to represent parties before EOIR and DHS.[62] Law students may represent individuals in immigration court and before DHS if they meet the following requirements: (1) they are enrolled in an accredited law school; (2) they appear at the party's request; (3) they receive no remuneration; (4) they appear under the supervision of a licensed attorney and faculty member; and (5) they appear via a legal aid program conducted by a law school or nonprofit organization. Law graduates who are not yet licensed may represent under the supervision of a licensed attorney as long as they receive no remuneration.

Certain accredited representatives of accredited organizations under 8 CFR §1292.1(a)(5) may represent parties before DHS and EOIR. Additionally, reputable individuals who are of good moral character; appearing on an individual case basis; at the request of the alien; with whom he or she has a pre-existing relationship; and who receives no remuneration may represent an individual before DHS and an IJ.

Note: Law students, law graduates, reputable individuals, and certain foreign-licensed attorneys may represent individuals *only* with the permission of the tribunal.[63] It is not a right.

Waiver of right to appeal

An IJ's order becomes final upon an individual's waiver of the right to appeal.[64] An unrepresented alien who accepts as final the decision of the IJ, however, does not waive the right to appeal where the judge does not explain clearly to the individual that the acceptance of the decision as final constitutes an irrevocable waiver of appeal rights.[65] A party wishing to challenge the validity of an appeal waiver may timely file either a motion to reconsider with the IJ or a direct appeal to the BIA.[66] Voluntary departure "prior to completion" of removal proceedings may not be granted without an express waiver of the right to appeal.[67]

---

[61] INA §240(b)(4)(A); 8 CFR §1240.3.

[62] 8 CFR §1001.1(j).

[63] 8 CFR §§292.1(a)(2)–(6), 1292.1(a)(2)–(6).

[64] *Matter of L–V–K–*, 22 I&N Dec. 976 (BIA 1999).

[65] *Matter of Rodriguez-Diaz*, 22 I&N Dec. 1320 (BIA 2000).

[66] *Matter of Patino*, 23 I&N Dec. 74 (BIA 2001).

[67] *Matter of Ocampo*, 22 I&N Dec. 1301 (BIA 2000).

Appeal Briefs

After a timely notice of appeal is filed with the BIA, both sides are sent a written notice of receipt. The BIA then obtains the record of proceedings (tapes and documentary material) from the immigration court. Transcripts are prepared in those cases where the proceedings are taped. Once the transcript is complete, it is forwarded to the IJ for review and correction. He or she has 14 days from receipt of the transcript to review it and forward it to the BIA.[68] Copies of the transcript are then sent to both sides along with a briefing schedule. In noncustody cases, the appellant is given 21 days to file the brief. The appellee has the same period to file a response brief. The BIA may extend the deadline for an appeal brief or reply brief for up to 90 days for good cause. In custody cases, both sides get 21 days to file simultaneous briefs.[69] The briefs must arrive at the BIA by the dates set in the briefing schedule. If it arrives late, the BIA may reject the brief.[70]

Transcripts

In certain types of proceedings—appeals of bond decisions by IJs, denials of motions to reopen or reconsideration, or interlocutory appeals—there is generally no transcript made. These proceedings may be transcribed at the BIA's discretion.[71] If there is no transcription of the record, the tapes stay in the possession of the immigration court. Any party may ask for a transcription of the proceedings—even in bond cases—if they have been taped. In addition, if there are defects in the transcript (*e.g.*, parts of the record are missing), a party may ask for a correction of the transcript. The party seeking the correction must notify the BIA clerk's office with a cover page titled "request for correction of transcript." The party should identify the defect and its significance. The BIA has the discretion to correct the record with a new or amended transcription. However, unless and until the party seeking the correction receives notice otherwise, the parties are bound by the original briefing schedule.[72]

Briefing guidelines

There is no limit on the number of pages in a given brief, but the BIA suggests a limit of 25 pages or less. Briefs should always be paginated.[73] The "A" number should be on the cover page of the brief and on the bottom right corner of each page thereafter.[74] Finally, captions and cover pages should be included with all filings.

---

[68] 8 CFR §1003.5(a).

[69] 8 CFR §1003.3(c).

[70] *BIA Practice Manual*, *supra* note 9, §4.7(b).

[71] *Id.* §4.2(b).

[72] *Id.* §4.2(f)(iii).

[73] *Id.* §4.6(b).

[74] *Id.* §4.6(e)(iii).

Contents

Each appellate brief should contain a concise statement of the facts; the procedural history of the case; the statement of issues presented for review; the standard of review; a summary of the argument; the argument itself; and a short conclusion stating the precise relief or remedy sought.

References to parties

- *Respondent*—the individual in deportation or removal, or bond proceedings.
- *Applicant*—the individual in exclusion/inadmissibility proceedings.
- *Petitioner*—the sponsoring person in visa petition appeals.
- *Beneficiary*—the individual being petitioned for in a visa petition.
- *DHS*—the government should be referred to as the Department of Homeland Security or DHS.
- *Immigration Judge*—should be referred to as "the Immigration Judge" in all immigration court appeals.[75]

Statement of facts

If the facts of the case are not at issue, the brief should simply adopt the IJ's factual summary. If the facts are in dispute, or are not fully developed, they should be laid out fully and/or supplemented, and the brief should clearly state the facts in contention. The facts also should be identified by their page number in the record (*e.g.*, Tr. at ____). If the error is in the IJ's decision, then the page number of the decision should be cited (*e.g.*, Immigration Judge at ____). Likewise, any reference to the brief by the opposing party should contain the page number (*e.g.*, DHS brief at ____ or Respondent's brief at ____). Exhibits also should be identified by number (*e.g.*, Ex. ____ or Motion to Reopen, Ex. ____).[76]

Citations

- *BIA precedent decisions:* Citations to precedent BIA decisions should not be to the Interim Decision number, but rather to the "I & N Dec." form (*e.g.*, *Matter of Jones* 2 I&N Dec. 1 (BIA 2000)). Use the "Matter of" format, not the "In re" format.
- *Nonprecedent BIA decisions:* Generally, the BIA discourages citation of nonprecedent decisions.[77] However, where it is necessary, cite the name of the alien, the "A" number, and the decision date. Include a copy of the nonprecedent decision with the brief.

---

[75] *Id.* §4.6(c)(v).

[76] *Id.* §4.6(c)(vi).

[77] *Id.* §4.6(d)(ii).

- *AG precedent decisions:* These are cited in the same format as BIA decisions; however, in the parenthetical after the volume and page citation, it should be noted that it is an "Attorney General" decision, not a BIA decision (*e.g.*, *Matter of Jones*, 20 I&N Dec. 1 (A.G. 1999)).
- *Federal and state court decisions:* Use the same format as identified in *A Uniform System of Citations*, *i.e.*, the "Blue Book." It is prudent to attach a copy of any unpublished state or federal decision.
- *Statutes and regulations:* As with federal and state court decisions, follow the format in "The Blue Book." A citation to any source not readily available to the BIA (international law decisions, for example), should include a copy of the decision.

Response and supplemental briefs

Response briefs

The appellee may file a response brief in accordance with the briefing schedule set by the BIA. Normally, this is 21 days after receipt of the brief in support of the appeal.[78]

Reply briefs

Briefs in reply to the appellee's brief are disfavored; however, if a party wishes to file a reply brief, a "Motion to Accept Reply Brief" should be filed, outlining (1) the "surprise" at the assertions of the other party; (2) the nature of the assertion in the appellee's brief; (3) challenges to these assertions; and (4) that the motion and brief are filed in response to these assertions. The brief should accompany the motion.[79]

Supplemental briefs

Supplemental briefs outside of the scheduling guidelines are rarely accepted; where there is new legal authority and the individual wishes to submit a new argument based on previously unavailable legal authority, a "Motion to Accept Supplemental Brief" may be filed setting forth the reasons why the brief with the new legal authority should be accepted.[80]

Amicus curiae briefs

The BIA may grant permission to file an amicus curiae brief if the public interest will be served.[81] A written "Request to Appear as Amicus Curiae" must be filed with the clerk's office and served on all parties. In addition to filing briefs, parties seeking

---

[78] 8 CFR §1003.3(c)(1).

[79] *Id.* §4.6(c).

[80] *Id.* §4.6(g).

[81] 8 CFR §§292.1(d), 1292.1(d).

to appear as "amicus curiae" may request the opportunity to present oral argument; such requests are granted "sparingly."[82]

Consolidation of briefs

Where cases have been consolidated, one brief may be submitted on behalf of all aliens in the consolidated proceeding if the names and "A" numbers of each party appear.

BIA Case Management—"Streamlining"

Once an appeal is received at the BIA, it is assigned to a single BIA member unless a case meets the standards for assignment to a three-member panel.[83]

Initial screening and summary dismissal

All cases go to an initial screening panel for review and decision on whether there is a basis for summary dismissal.[84] Any appeal subject to "Summary Dismissal" is dismissed at this stage. Cases subject to summary dismissal include those listed above in the section on "summary dismissal of appeals."

Merits review by single BIA member

If not summarily dismissed, a case is assigned to a single BIA member who determines the appeal on the merits through the "Affirmance Without Opinion" (AWO) system,[85] or a "brief order" affirming, modifying, or remanding the decision below.[86] The AWO decision does not include any explanation or reasoning.[87]

For the single member "brief order" procedure, an individual BIA member may reverse the decision of the IJ if the reversal is consistent with the INA, regulations, or case precedent. A single BIA member affirms, modifies, or remands the decision unless the case is designated for three-member review.

Three-member panel review

The screening panel may assign the case for three-member panel review in certain circumstances, including those outlined below.[88] The BIA may decide on its own that a case merits three-member panel review;[89] however, the better practice is to request three-member panel review and spell out in the appeal notice and brief or by separate

---

[82] *BIA Practice Manual, supra* note 9, §§2.10 and 4.6(c)(i).

[83] 8 CFR §§1003.1(e) and 1003.1(e)(6).

[84] 8 CFR §1003.1(e)(1).

[85] 8 CFR §1003.1(e)(4).

[86] 8 CFR §1003.1(e)(5).

[87] 8 CFR §1003.1(e)(4).

[88] 8 CFR §1003.1(e)(6).

[89] 8 CFR §1003.1(e)(5).

motion why the case fits into one of the following categories justifying three-member panel review:

- need to settle inconsistencies in rulings by different IJs;
- need to establish precedent construction of law;
- need to review decision not consistent with the law or relevant precedent cases;
- case or controversy of national import;
- clearly erroneous factual determination by IJ;
- need to reverse the IJ or DHS decision (other than a single member reversal).

En banc review

A majority of the "permanent" BIA members constitutes a quorum for purposes of convening the BIA en banc. (The Director of EOIR may designate "temporary" BIA members and immigration judges, including retired BIA members and immigration judges, and administrative law judges with EOIR or those retired from EOIR to serve as BIA members for terms not to exceed six months.[90]) The BIA may consider a case en banc by a majority vote of the permanent BIA members or by direction of the chair. They may consider en banc review in any case that has been considered by a three-member panel. The en banc review process is used only where necessary to address an issue of particular importance, or maintain the consistency of the BIA's decisions.[91]

Oral argument

A three-member panel or the BIA en banc may grant oral argument as a matter of discretion.[92] If so, it is held at the BIA offices unless the AG's office designates a different location.

Timeliness of BIA appeal processing

The BIA has placed an emphasis on speed in the adjudication process. It has organized and prioritized its caseload as outlined below.

- *Summary dismissals*—must be entered "promptly."[93]
- *Detained aliens*—take priority over those not detained.[94]
- *Single BIA member decisions*—shall be adjudicated within 90 days of completion of the record on appeal.[95]

---

[90] 8 CFR §1003.1(a)(4)

[91] 8 CFR §1003.1(a)(5).

[92] 8 CFR §1003.2(h).

[93] 8 CFR §1003.1(e)(8).

[94] *Id.*

[95] *Id.*

- *Three-member panel decisions*—shall be adjudicated within 180 days of the completion of the record on appeal.[96]
- *Extensions*—the BIA chair may grant an extension of up to 60 days as a matter of discretion for the members to complete the decision. If the panel cannot reach a decision, the BIA chair takes the case or refers it to the vice chair for a decision within 14 days.[97] The BIA also may extend a decision deadline if there is an impending decision from a federal circuit court, the U.S. Supreme Court, the BIA en banc, or pending regulatory changes that may substantially impact the outcome of the case.[98]

These deadlines create no right on the part of the alien before the administrative or judicial courts.[99]

Finality

The BIA decisions are final administrative decisions unless the case has been referred to the AG.[100] In addition, if the case is remanded back to DHS or to the immigration court for further action, the case is not final and may be appealed again to the BIA by either party after the action on remand is completed.

Designation as precedent

By majority vote of the permanent members, select decisions of the BIA may be designated as precedent decisions. All BIA selected decisions, as well as decisions by the AG and DHS Secretary, shall serve as precedent decisions. Decisions of the BIA and AG are binding on all DHS officers and employees as well as IJs.[101]

Attorney General Review

The following cases are referred to the AG for review:

- cases directed for referral by the AG;
- cases in which the BIA chair, or majority of BIA members, direct for referral to the AG; and
- cases in which DHS officials, with the concurrence of AG, refer to the AG for review.[102]

---

[96] 8 CFR §1003.1(e)(8)(i).

[97] 8 CFR §1003.1(e)(8)(ii).

[98] 8 CFR §1003.1(e)(8)(iii).

[99] 8 CFR §1003.1(e)(8)(vi).

[100] 8 CFR §1003.1(d)(7).

[101] 8 CFR §1003.1(g).

[102] 8 CFR §1003.1(h).

Where the AG renders a decision, it is in writing and transferred to the BIA as well as the DHS Secretary for transmittal and service.[103] The AG has de novo review powers of all issues. Precedent decisions of the BIA that have been certified to the AG remain binding as precedent on the same or similar issues until they are modified or overturned by the AG.[104]

Avoidance of Summary Dismissal of Appeals

The American Immigration Law Foundation (AILF) has published several "Practice Advisories" on representing individuals before the BIA on appeal. The advisories are extremely practical and helpful.[105] In order to avoid a summary dismissal of the appeal under the 2002 BIA "streamlining" provisions found at 8 CFR §1003.1(e), the advisory regarding the streamlining provisions recommends addressing this issue in the Notice of Appeal, noting in the EOIR-26 that the appeal is not suitable for the BIA "Affirmance Without Opinion" by a single member procedure. In supporting this position, make clear in the Notice of Appeal where relevant any or all of the following:

- the legal issues;
- the contested factual issues; be clear and detailed on the facts in dispute;
- the reason(s) the facts as stated are erroneous and the relevance of these errors;
- any legal errors on the part of the IJ; describe the legal errors and give supporting authority;
- any other material and significant errors made by the IJ, or by the trial attorney and permitted by the judge;
- the reason(s) the appellant is eligible for relief under the correct legal standards; and
- how the proceedings deprived the respondent of rights under the INA or the due process clause of the Fifth Amendment.

In addition to stating the above in the Notice of Appeal, the appeal brief should contain a section substantiating that position in detail, including citations to the law and the administrative record, and the factual and legal arguments as to why three-member panel review is appropriate.

Challenges to the Affirmance Without Opinion (AWO) Procedure

The federal courts that have reviewed the BIA's AWO procedure under 8 CFR §1003.1(e)(4) generally have found that the use of this procedure is not violative of

---

[103] 8 CFR §1003.1(h)(2); *Matter of D–J–*, 23 I&N Dec. 572 (A.G. 2003).

[104] *Matter of E–L–H–*, 23 I&N Dec. 700 (A.G.2004).

[105] *See, e.g.*, AILF Advisory, "Practicing Before the Board Under the New Procedural Reforms Rule" (amended Jan. 10, 2003), available at *www.ailf.org*.

due process.[106] However, federal courts have found that the manner in which this procedure is applied may be subject to federal court review. The BIA must follow its own regulations in issuing an AWO opinion.[107] In *Dia v. Ashcroft*, the Third Circuit found that it did have jurisdiction to decide whether the BIA followed properly its own nondiscretionary factors as outlined in 8 CFR §1003.1(e)(4).

Another challenge to the AWO procedure may be where there are alternate bases for an IJ's decision, one of which is subject to judicial review while the other is not. If the use of the AWO procedure makes it impossible for the federal court to determine whether it has jurisdiction upon which to review the administrative decision, *i.e.*, the court cannot determine if it was based on the reviewable or nonreviewable ground, the use of the AWO procedure is improper.[108] The AILF practice advisory cited above contains a helpful chart outlining the various positions of the circuit courts on the AWO procedure.

Several courts have examined the actual application of the AWO procedure and have found that, at times, it has been misapplied in contravention of the BIA's own regulations.[109] However, other courts have refused to review the application by the BIA of the AWO regulation.[110]

Withdrawal of Appeal

The party appealing may at any time prior to the entry of a decision by the BIA withdraw the appeal.[111] The withdrawal should be in writing. If no decision has been made on the appeal, the initial decision shall be final to the same extent as if no appeal had been taken. If a decision already has been made by the BIA, then "further action shall be taken in accordance therewith."[112] An appellant's departure from the United States subsequent to the filing of the appeal, but prior to the decision, constitutes a withdrawal of the appeal (except for arriving aliens).[113] If an individual withdraws the appeal of an IJ's decision where voluntary departure has been granted, the decision of the judge becomes immediately effective and the voluntary departure period runs from the date of original decision of the judge, not the date of the withdrawal.[114]

---

[106] *Soadjede v. Ashcroft*, 324 F.3d 830 (5th Cir. 2003); *Zhang v. Dep't of Justice*, 362 F.3d 155 (3d Cir. 2004).

[107] *Dia v. Ashcroft*, 353 F.3d 228 (3d Cir. 2003).

[108] *Zhu v. Ashcroft*, 382 F.3d 521 (5th Cir. 2004). *See also* AILF Practice Advisory, "BIA 'Affirmance Without Opinion': What Federal Court Challenges Remain" (Apr. 27, 2005), available at *www.ailf.org*.

[109] *Smirko v. Ashcroft*, 387 F.3d 279 (3d Cir. 2004); *Chen v. Ashcroft*, 378 F.3d 1081 (9th Cir. 2004).

[110] *Ngure v. Ashcroft*, 367 F.3d 975 (8th Cir. 2004).

[111] 8 CFR §1003.4.

[112] *Id.*

[113] *Id.*

[114] *BIA Practice Manual*, *supra* note 9, §4.11.

Motions to Reopen and Reconsider

Introduction—Purpose of a Motion to Reopen

The authority for filing a motion to reopen with the BIA is found at 8 CFR §1003.2. For the immigration court, the relevant regulation is found at 8 CFR §1003.23. The purpose of the motion to reopen is to have the court or the BIA review the case for either of the following reasons:

- There is new material evidence that was not available and could not have been discovered or presented at the time of the hearing before the court or review by the BIA.[115]
- There are changed conditions, including a change in the law or facts that may make the individual eligible for relief from removal. The application for relief must accompany the motion.[116]

The BIA or court may deny a motion to reopen in the following instances:

- failure to make a prima facie case for relief;[117]
- failure to meet the requirements of 8 CFR §§1003.2 and 1003.23 regarding new material evidence that could not have been presented; or
- denial on discretionary grounds.[118]

Filing Procedure

Who may file

Motions to reopen can be filed by either party, or the court or BIA on their own motion.[119]

Where to file

The motion to reopen is filed with the immigration court that last had jurisdiction unless jurisdiction rests with the BIA after an appeal.[120]

When to file—time limitations

Either party may file a motion to reopen within 90 days of the final administrative order, with certain exceptions outlined below. The motion to reopen must be filed within 90 days of the date on which the IJ or the BIA entered a final administrative order. It is measured from the date of the decision and it is not affected by any subse-

---

115 8 CFR §§1003.2(c)(1) and 1003.23(b)(3).

116 *Id.*

117 *See INS v. Abudu*, 485 U.S. 94 (1988).

118 8 CFR §§1003.2(a) and 1003.23(b)(3) .

119 8 CFR §§1003.2(a) and 1003.23(b)(1).

120 8 CFR §1003.23(b)(1)(ii).

quent action taken by the government in the course of executing the order.[121] The court or BIA may move to reopen sua sponte at any time.[122]

Fee and form for filing

The motion is written and signed by the respondent or representative (or DHS attorney if filed by the government), and supported by affidavits and other evidentiary material. It must be in English or have a certified English translation.[123] The fee is $110, unless waived.[124] There is no fee in the following cases:[125]

- a motion based on applications that have no fee (*e.g.*, asylum);
- consolidated proceedings (only the principal pays);
- a motion that is filed while an appeal or motion to reopen or reconsider is pending with the BIA;
- a motion that is agreed upon by all parties; and
- a motion filed by DHS.

Certificate of service on DHS counsel

As in all other situations where a document is filed with the immigration court or the BIA, a certificate of service proving that DHS counsel has been served must be included.

Notice of appearance

If the respondent is represented by counsel, a notice of appearance must be filed with the appropriate tribunal. The immigration court and the BIA have separate notice of appearance forms (EOIR-28 for motions with the court; EOIR-27 for motions with the BIA).

Contents

The motion to reopen must be in writing and state the new facts to be proven at the reopened hearing. It should be supported by documentation sufficient to prove a prime facie case for reopening, including the following:

- Affidavits and supporting evidentiary material.[126]

---

[121] *Matter of Goolcharan*, 23 I&N Dec. 5 (BIA 2001).

[122] 8 CFR §§1003.2(a) and 1003.23(b)(1).

[123] 8 CFR §§1003.2(g)(1) and 1003.23(b)(1)(i).

[124] 8 CFR §§1003.8(a)(3) and 1003.24(b)(1).

[125] 8 CFR §§1003.8(a)(2) and 1003.24(b)(2).

[126] 8 CFR §§1003.2(c)(1) and 1003.23(b)(3).

- Supporting evidence showing prima facie eligibility for relief requested.[127] If the motion is based on an approved visa petition in order to adjust status, a copy of the visa petition approval should be included.
- Translations of all documents in a foreign language along with a certificate of translation.[128]
- Copy of application for relief should accompany the motion if the motion is made based on relief eligibility.[129]
- Fee receipt or fee waiver form—when the motion is filed with the immigration court, a copy of the fee receipt for $110 must be included unless the motion is based on an application where there is no fee, such as asylum.[130] Since the court does not accept fees, the fee is generally paid to USCIS and the receipt or the fee waiver form is attached to the motion. If filed with the BIA, the fee is included generally in the form of a money order or cashier's check and filed directly with the BIA. Fees may be waived where the movant is unable to pay.[131] If there is a fee waiver to be filed with the BIA, the waiver form is EOIR-26A. If the fee waiver request is made to the court, an affidavit showing indigence and a motion to waive the fee should be included.[132] If the motion includes an application for relief, the fee for the relief application is not included but must be paid later if the case is reopened at the time specified by the IJ.[133]
- Copies of prior orders by an IJ or the BIA should be included if the motion is made to reopen or reconsider a prior order of the IJ or BIA.[134]
- Where the motion is based on the overturning or modification of a prior criminal court conviction, evidence must be included that clearly shows the overturned or modified decision.[135]
- The motion must indicate whether the validity of the order has been or is the subject of any prior proceeding and also whether there are any pending criminal proceedings.[136]
- Signatures—all motions must be signed by the movant or the representative.[137]

---

[127] *Id.*

[128] 8 CFR §§1003.2(g)(1) and 1003.23(b)(1)(i).

[129] 8 CFR §§1003.2(c)(1) and 1003.23(b)(3).

[130] 8 CFR §§1003.8(a)(2) and 1003.24(b)(2)(i).

[131] 8 CFR §§1003.8(a)(3) and 1003.24(b)(1).

[132] 8 CFR §1003.24(d).

[133] 8 CFR §1003.24(c)(2).

[134] *BIA Practice Manual*, *supra* note 9, §5.2(e).

[135] *Id.* §5.6(e).

[136] 8 CFR §§1003.2(e) and 1003.23(b)(i).

[137] *BIA Practice Manual*, *supra* note 9, §5.2(c); 8 CFR §1003.23(b)(1)(i).

- Briefs—while not mandated, if a brief is to be filed, it should accompany the motion.[138] The opposition brief should be filed within 13 days of the service of the motion.[139] There is no briefing schedule set by the BIA on motions to reopen or reconsider.[140]
- Notice of appearance—the notice of appearance (EOIR-28 (court) or EOIR-27 (BIA)) must be included if the person is represented.[141]
- Transcripts—in a motion to reopen before the court or BIA, there is generally no transcript prepared (unless an appeal of an order has been previously filed with the BIA); however, if a party seeks a transcript of a prior proceeding, this request should be made in writing.[142]
- If the motion is made by, or on behalf of, a detained individual, it should be marked clearly as a detention case. The BIA in its *Practice Manual* recommends that the cover page be marked "Detained."[143]
- There must be evidence of service on the opposing party.[144] To serve the government, service is made on the district counsel for the DHS district where the case was completed.

Exceptions to Time Limitations

The motion to reopen is to be filed within 90 days of the final administrative order.[145] However, the 90-day time limitation does not apply in the circumstances outlined below.

Asylum or withholding claims based on changed circumstances

An applicant may move to reopen proceedings even beyond the 90-day deadline to apply or re-apply for asylum or withholding of removal based on changed circumstances arising in the country of his or her nationality.[146] If evidence is presented that is material and was not available and could not have been discovered or presented at the former hearing, a motion to reopen for changed circumstances is appropriate.[147] However, a motion to reopen based on changed circumstances will be denied if there is insufficient evidence that country conditions have materially changed.

---

[138] 8 CFR §1003.2(g)(3).

[139] *Id.*

[140] *BIA Practice Manual*, *supra* note 9, §5.4.

[141] 8 CFR §§1003.2(g)(1) and 1003.23(b)(1)(ii).

[142] *BIA Practice Manual*, *supra* note 9, §5.5.

[143] *See id.* §5.2(b).

[144] 8 CFR §§1003.2(g)(1) and 1003.23(b)(1)(ii).

[145] 8 CFR §§1003.2(c)(2) and 1003.23(b)(1).

[146] 8 CFR §§1003.2(c)(3)(ii) and 1003.23(b)(4)(i).

[147] *In re J–J–*, 21 I&N Dec. 976 (BIA 1997).

In absentia proceedings/lack of notice

There is no appeal of an "in absentia" removal order; it can be reviewed only in a motion to reopen. If there was no proper notice of the removal proceedings given to the alien, the motion to reopen can be filed at any time.[148] A motion to reopen deportation proceedings conducted in absentia that demonstrate a lack of notice of the hearing to the alien is an exception to the regulatory time limitations on motions.[149] An IJ may not enter an order of removal in the alien's absence where the alien does not receive the charging document. The charging document contains the advisal to the alien regarding his or her obligations to notify the court of any change of address, as well as consequences for failure to do so. If the alien has not received this advisal because the charging document was not served, the IJ may not enter an order of removal in his or her absence.[150] An alien who fails to appear because of an "illegible" hearing notice has the burden to establish that the notice was not legible.[151] While the alien has the burden of keeping the government notified of any change of address, a letter written to the BIA is sufficient notice to the court, even if not on the specified change of address form.

Failure to appear/exceptional circumstances

If the party received notice but could not go to the hearing due to exceptional circumstances, the motion to reopen must be filed within 180 days.[152] An alien may file a motion to reopen a deportation hearing held "in absentia" within 180 days after the date of the order of deportation if the alien demonstrates that the failure to appear was because of exceptional circumstances beyond the control of the alien.[153] The INA defines exceptional circumstances as "serious illness of the alien, or serious illness or death of the spouse, parent or child of the alien, but not including less compelling circumstances."[154] Heavy traffic is not considered to be an exceptional circumstance.[155] A foot injury on the day before the hearing does not establish exceptional circumstances.[156] A serious headache on the day of the hearing does not constitute an exceptional circumstance.[157]

The BIA has stated that the claim of ineffective assistance of counsel does not constitute an exception to the 180-day statutory limit for the filing of a motion to re-

---

[148] 1003.23(b)(4)(ii).

[149] *Matter of Mancera*, 22 I&N Dec. 79 (BIA 1998).

[150] *Matter of G–Y–R–*, 23 I&N Dec. 181 (BIA 2001).

[151] *Matter S–M–*, 22 I&N Dec. 49 (BIA 1998).

[152] 8 CFR §1003.23(b)(4)(ii).

[153] 8 CFR §1003.23(b)(4)(iii).

[154] INA §240(e).

[155] *Matter of S–A–*, 21 I&N Dec. 1050 (BIA 1997).

[156] *Matter of B–A–S–*, 22 I&N Dec. 57 (BIA 1998), *rev'd, Singh v. INS*, 213 F.3d 1050 (9th Cir. 2000).

[157] *Matter of J–P–*, 22 I&N Dec. 33 (BIA 1998).

open to rescind an in absentia order of deportation.[158] An alien seeking to reopen proceedings based on ineffective assistance of counsel must meet the requirements set out by the BIA in *Matter of Lozada.*[159] Thus, the alien must notify the attorney of the problem, present a copy of the contract outlining the attorney's obligation, and file a grievance with the state bar association regarding the attorney's conduct. The BIA acts within its discretion in denying motions to reopen that fail to meet the *Lozada* requirements.[160] Where a claim to ineffective assistance of counsel is the basis for the motion to reopen, this claim must be made before the administrative authorities first, otherwise, the federal court is without jurisdiction to hear the issue.[161]

Where an attorney has defrauded his or her client, preventing the alien from discovering the mishandling of his or her case, there is an "equitable tolling" of the 180-day period. This fraud would constitute an "extraordinary circumstance" excusing the alien's failure to appear at the hearing and excusing the failure to file the motion to reopen within the 180-day time limit.[162] An alien who asserts that his or her failure to appear at a deportation hearing was the result of ineffective assistance of counsel must show "reasonable cause" for the failure to appear.[163] An alien who was mistaken about the law in believing that filing a change of address report would result in a change of venue did not show an exceptional circumstance that would form the basis for reopening.[164]

Joint agreement by all parties

Neither the time nor the one-motion numerical limitation[165] applies where the DHS attorney is willing to join in a motion to reopen.[166]

Sua sponte

A sua sponte motion to reopen by the IJ or BIA is an exception to the statutory time limitation.[167] Even where a deadline has passed to file a motion to reopen, the IJ or the BIA retains jurisdiction to reopen on their own motion without time limitation.[168] In order for the BIA to reopen sua sponte based on a change in the law, the change must be fundamental in nature and not merely an incremental development in

---

158 *Matter of A-A-*, 22 I&N Dec. 140 (BIA 1998).

159 *Matter of Lozada*, 19 I&N Dec. 637, 639 (BIA 1988).

160 *Asaba v. Ashcroft*, 377 F.3d 9 (1st Cir. 2004).

161 *Goonsuwan v. Ashcroft*, 252 F.3d 383 (5th Cir. 2001).

162 *Borges v. Gonzales*, 402 F.3d 398 (3d Cir. 2005).

163 *Cruz-Garcia*, 22 I&N Dec. 1155 (BIA 1999).

164 *Kkay v. Ashcroft*, 387 F.3d 664 (7th Cir. 2004).

165 8 CFR §1003.23(b)(1).

166 8 CFR §§1003.2(c)(3)(iii) and 1003.23(b)(4)(iv).

167 8 CFR §§1003.2(a) and 1003.23(b)(1) .

168 *Id.*

the state of the law.[169] The BIA may reopen on its own motion where there are "exceptional circumstances."[170] It has taken this action where there is a sufficient change in the law that affects an individual's removability.[171] Likewise, the BIA reopened on its own motion where there was a sufficient change in the applicable asylum law.[172] However, the BIA will not reopen even where there is a significant change in circumstances where the individual already has been deported or has departed from the United States. Federal courts have upheld this position.[173] The BIA lacks jurisdiction over motions to reopen where the motion is withdrawn by the departure of the alien from the United States.[174]

Respondent in state or federal custody

Proceedings may be reopened at any time if the alien was ordered removed in absentia and was in state or federal custody at the time.[175]

DHS motions

The time and numerical limitations on motions to reopen do not apply to DHS in removal proceedings.[176]

Fraud

A motion filed by the government to reopen deportation or exclusion proceedings based on fraud in the original proceedings is not subject to the time limitations.[177]

Exceptions to Numerical Limitations

There is a numerical limitation of one motion to reopen whether before the BIA or the immigration court.[178] The regulations state that an alien may file "only one motion to reconsider and one motion to reopen proceedings."[179] Even if a motion to reopen is submitted in the form of a "motion to remand" during the pendency of an appeal, it must meet the numerical limitations of the regulation.[180] A motion to reopen "proceedings" refers to the hearing as opposed to a subsequent administrative deci-

---

169 *Matter of G-D-*, 22 I&N Dec. 1132 (BIA 1999).

170 *Matter of J-J-*, 21 I&N Dec. 976 (BIA 1997).

171 *Matter of Vasquez-Muniz*, 23 I&N Dec. 207 (BIA 2002).

172 *Matter of X-G-W-*, 22 I&N Dec. 71 (BIA 1998).

173 *Navarro-Miranda v. Ashcroft*, 330 F.3d 672 (5th Cir. 2003).

174 *Matter of Crammond*, 23 I&N Dec. 179 (BIA 2001); 8 CFR §1003.23(b)(1).

175 8 CFR §1003.23(b)(4)(ii).

176 8 CFR §1003.23(b)(1).

177 8 CFR §1003.2(c)(3)(iv).

178 8 CFR §§1003.2(b)(2) and 1003.23(b)(1).

179 8 CFR §1003.23(b)(1).

180 *Matter of Oparah*, 23 I&N Dec. 1 (BIA 2000).

sion on a motion to reconsider.[181] However, the one-motion limitation does not apply in the situations below:

- In pre-IIRAIRA[182] deportation or exclusion cases, motions filed to reopen "in absentia" deportation or exclusion proceedings do not count toward the one-motion limit if the alien was in federal or state custody and failed to appear through no fault of his or her own, or did not appear due to exceptional circumstances.[183]
- DHS motions to reopen (no limit).[184]
- Joint agreement by all parties on the motion to reopen.[185]
- Motions to reopen asylum applications based on changed conditions.[186]
- Motions filed by DHS in deportation or exclusion proceedings where the motion is based on fraud.[187]

Stays

The filing of the motion to reopen generally does not stay the effect of the initial order by the IJ or the BIA.[188] The exception to this rule is a motion to reopen an in absentia proceeding where the filing of this motion automatically stays the order.[189] Other than "in absentia" orders, the movant must seek a stay from the tribunal. Until the stay is granted, execution of the decision may proceed. A stay on a pending motion to reopen also may be granted by the BIA.[190]

Proving a Prima Facie Case for Relief

Where an alien seeks to file an untimely motion to reopen, the burden of proof rests with the alien to show not only the reason that the motion is untimely, but also to establish that the case warrants reopening, and that if reopened, there is a substantial likelihood that the result in the case may be changed.[191] In addition, the regula-

---

[181] *William v. INS*, 217 F.3d 340 (5th Cir. 2000).

[182] Illegal Immigration Reform and Immigrant Responsibility Act of 1996, Division C of the Omnibus Appropriations Act of 1996 (H.R. 3610), Pub. L. No. 104-208, 110 Stat. 3009.

[183] 8 CFR §1003.23(b)(4)(iii)(D); *BIA Practice Manual*, *supra* note 9, §5.6(f)(v).

[184] 8 CFR §1003.23(b)(1).

[185] 8 CFR §1003.23(b)(4)(iv).

[186] 8 CFR §§1003.2(c)(3)(ii) and 1003.23(b)(4)(i).

[187] 8 CFR §1003.2(c)(3)(iv).

[188] 8 CFR §1003.23(b)(1)(v).

[189] 8 CFR §§1003.23(b)(4)(iii)(C) and 1003.2(f).

[190] *Matter of Herrera*, 23 I&N Dec. 43 (BIA 2001).

[191] *Matter of Beckford*, 22 I&N Dec. 1216 (BIA 2000).

tions state that any application filed to seek relief must include a copy of the application and supporting documentation.[192]

A motion to reopen for adjustment of status based on a pending visa petition should be granted where the motion is timely filed and not barred by numerical limitations or other bars or any other procedural grounds, and there is clear and convincing evidence presented to show that relief will be granted. Where the visa petition is based on a marriage and evidence showing a bona fide marriage is attached, the motion to reopen for adjustment purposes should be granted.[193]

Response to a Motion

If a motion to reopen is filed with the BIA, the opposing party has 13 days from the date of service of the motion to file a brief in opposition to the motion. It must be filed directly with the BIA.[194] If the motion to reopen is filed with the immigration court, the court may set and extend time limits for replies.[195] A motion is deemed unopposed unless a response is filed.[196]

Oral Argument and Decision

A request for oral argument before the BIA must be incorporated into the motion.[197] Like the motion itself, the decision must be made in writing.[198]

Termination upon Departure from United States

A departure from the country terminates any pending motion to reopen. In addition, no motion to reopen may be filed once a person leaves the country.[199]

Tolling of Voluntary Departure during Motion to Reopen

A timely filed motion to reopen submitted prior to the expiration of the voluntary departure time granted to the alien in proceedings saves or tolls the time allotted for voluntary departure.[200]

Motions to Reconsider

A motion to reconsider a decision by the IJ or the BIA is a request, not to submit new evidence, but rather a request to revisit and reconsider the decision on the record that al-

---

[192] 8 CFR §§1003.2(c)(1) and 1003.23(b)(3).

[193] *Matter of Velarde-Pacheco*, 23 I&N Dec. 253 (BIA 2002).

[194] 8 CFR §1003.2(g)(3).

[195] 8 CFR §1003.23(b)(iv).

[196] 8 CFR §§1003.2(g)(3) and 1003.23(b)(2)(iv).

[197] 8 CFR §1003.2(h).

[198] 8 CFR §1003.2(i).

[199] 8 CFR §§1003.2(d) and 1003.23(b)(1).

[200] *Kanivets v. Gonzales*, 424 F.3d 330 (3d Cir. 2005).

ready has been made. It is generally based on legal issues.[201] A motion to reconsider the decision of the IJ or the BIA must be filed within 30 days after entry of, or the mailing of, the decision, respectively.[202] Motions to reconsider, like motions to reopen, are numerically limited. An individual is limited to one motion to reconsider.[203] An individual may not seek reconsideration of a decision denying a prior motion to reconsider.[204]

A motion to reconsider a decision rendered by an IJ that is pending when an appeal is filed, or that is filed subsequent to the filing of the appeal with the BIA, may be deemed a motion to remand the decision for further proceedings before the IJ. Such a motion may be consolidated with the appeal and considered by the BIA in connection with the appeal.[205] The motion to reconsider must state the reason for the motion by specifying the errors of fact or law in the IJ's prior decision and be supported by pertinent authority.[206] A motion to reconsider based solely on the argument that the case should not have been affirmed by a single BIA member or three-member panel in an AWO is barred.[207]

Until an appeal is properly before the BIA, the IJ has continuing jurisdiction to entertain motions regarding proceedings previously before him or her. An IJ may entertain a motion to reconsider that contests the validity of an appeal waiver provided that the motion is timely and otherwise satisfies the regulation.[208] A timely filed motion to reconsider may "toll" the voluntary departure period.[209]

Judicial Review

Introduction

When an individual has exhausted all possible administrative remedies, federal court may be the only remaining source of relief. Judicial review of administrative decisions has been greatly reduced during the past 10 years. In 1996, Congress enacted IIRAIRA, which substantially limited the possibilities in seeking review of administrative decisions in the federal court. In May 2005, the REAL ID Act of 2005[210] was enacted. REAL ID removed from federal district courts' jurisdiction to review

---

201 *Matter of G–D–*, 22 I&N Dec. 1132 (BIA 1999).

202 8 CFR §§1003.2(b)(2) and 1003.23(b)(1).

203 *Id.*

204 8 CFR §1003.2(b)(2).

205 8 CFR §1003.2(b)(1).

206 8 CFR §1003.23(b)(2).

207 8 CFR §1003.2(b)(3).

208 *Matter of Patino*, 23 I&N Dec. 74 (BIA 2001).

209 *Barrios v. Attorney General*, 399 F.3d 272 (3d Cir. 2005).

210 Emergency Supplemental Appropriations Act for Defense, the Global War on Terror, and Tsunami Relief, 2005, Division B, Pub. L. No. 109-13, 119 Stat. 231 (May 11, 2005) (REAL ID).

removal orders, specifically eliminating habeas corpus as a means for reviewing administrative removal orders, and placing jurisdiction exclusively with the federal circuit court through a petition for review of an agency action or decision. Habeas is still available as a means to challenge unlawful detention, but not a vehicle for challenging an agency decision on removal (except for expedited removal).[211] Below is a brief summary of the possibilities for judicial review of administrative decisions and outline of the changes made by REAL ID. Section 242 of the INA summarizes the matters that are amenable to judicial review.

Jurisdiction

Notwithstanding any other provision of law (statutory or nonstatutory), including 28 USC §2241, or any other habeas corpus provision, a petition for review filed with the appropriate court of appeals is the sole and exclusive means for judicial review of an order of removal entered or issued under the immigration laws.[212] Congress, through REAL ID, eliminated habeas corpus as a means of reviewing removal decisions by the immigration court or BIA.[213] However, REAL ID does preserve habeas corpus as a means of challenging the administrative determination to review expedited removal proceedings under INA §235(b)(1).

The changes in the law brought about by REAL ID allow for judicial review of constitutional claims or questions of law raised through a petition for review.[214] The statute also specifically states that claims under the United Nations Convention Against Torture and Other Forms of Cruel Inhuman or Degrading Treatment or Punishment may be raised within the courts of appeal through a petition for review.[215]

Matters Not Subject to Judicial Review

The statute states that the following are not reviewable by the court of appeals in a petition for review:[216]

- Any determinations on an individual case relating to an expedited removal order including: the procedures and policies adapted to implement expedited removal provisions; a decision to invoke the expedited removal procedures; or a decision on an individual case.

---

[211] *See* INA §242(e).

[212] INA §242(a)(5).

[213] *Bonhometre v. Gonzales*, 414 F.3d 442 (3d Cir. 2005).

[214] INA §242(a)(2)(D).

[215] INA §242(a)(4).

[216] INA §242(a)(2)(A)–(C). *But see* INA §242(e).

- Any judgment regarding the granting of relief under the waiver provisions of INA §§212(h) and 212(i);[217] cancellation of removal for certain LPRs or non–permanent residents;[218] or adjustment of status.
- Any final orders of removal against an alien who is removable for certain criminal grounds covered in the grounds of inadmissibility, including:
  - crimes of moral turpitude;
  - controlled substance violations;
  - drug trafficking;
  - prostitution;
  - multiple criminal convictions;
  - human traffickers;
  - money launderers; and
  - certain diplomats who have escaped prosecutions for criminal activity.[219]
- Final order of removal based on convictions for aggravated felonies, controlled substance violations, and firearms offenses.[220]
- Deportation orders based on multiple crimes involving moral turpitude not arising out of a single scheme of criminal misconduct.[221]
- Deportation orders based on convictions for any of the crimes outlined at INA §237(a)(2)(D) relating to espionage, sabotage, treason, sedition, or other offenses outlined under that subsection.[222]

Requirements for Judicial Review of Orders of Removal

The petition for review, if permitted, must be filed not later than 30 days after the date of the final order of removal.[223] It must be filed with the court of appeals for the judicial circuit in which the IJ completed the proceedings.[224] The named government party in any such proceedings is the AG. The petition shall be served on the AG and on the office or employee of DHS in charge of the immigration district in which the final order of removal under INA §240 was entered.[225] There is no automatic stay of

---

[217] INA §242(a)(2)(B)(i).

[218] INA §§240A(a) and (b).

[219] INA §§212(a)(2) and 242(a)(2)(C).

[220] INA §§237(a)(2)(A)(iii) and 237(a)(2)(B) and (C).

[221] INA §237(a)(2)(A)(ii).

[222] INA §242(a)(2)(C).

[223] INA §242(b)(1).

[224] INA §242(b)(2).

[225] INA §242(b)(3)(A).

removal upon the filing of the petition for review. It must be separately requested.[226] A copy of the order sought to be removed must be attached to the motion.[227] In addition, the petition must state whether the court has upheld the validity of the order in any prior proceeding, and, if so, the name of the court, the type of proceeding, and the date of the proceeding must be specified.[228]

The brief in support of the petition for review must be filed no later than 40 days after the date on which the administrative record is available (unless the court sets a different briefing schedule). The individual also is given an additional 14 days after the service of the government's brief in which to file a reply brief. There is no extension of these deadlines except upon motion for good cause shown.[229]

The adjudication of the petition for review is limited to the administrative record on which the removal order was based. The facts found by the administrative court are conclusive "unless any reasonable adjudicator would be compelled to conclude to the contrary."[230] Any decision that an alien is not eligible for admission to the United States is conclusive unless "manifestly contrary to law." Any "discretionary" judgment whether to grant relief under the asylum statute at INA §208 is conclusive "unless manifestly contrary to the law and an abuse of discretion."[231]

No reviewing court may reverse a determination made by the administrative court with respect to the availability of corroborating evidence for asylum claims,[232] withholding of removal claims,[233] or other forms of relief under the immigration laws, unless the court finds that a reasonable trier of fact is compelled to conclude that such corroborating evidence is unavailable.[234]

Nationality Claims

If the petitioner claims to be a national of the United States and the court of appeals is satisfied that there is no genuine issue of material fact about his or her nationality claim, it will decide the nationality claim.[235] However, if the court finds that there is a genuine issue of material fact about the petitioner's nationality, the court will transfer the proceeding to the district court of the United States for the judicial

---

[226] INA §242(b)(3)(B).

[227] INA §242(c)(1).

[228] INA §242(c)(2).

[229] INA §242(b)(3)(C).

[230] INA §242(b)(4)(B).

[231] INA §242(b)(4)(D).

[232] INA §208(b)(1)(B).

[233] INA §241(b)(3)(C).

[234] INA §242(b)(4).

[235] INA §242(b)(5)(A).

district in which the petitioner resides for a hearing on the nationality claim and a decision on the claim.[236]

Consolidation of Motion to Reopen

When a petitioner seeks review of an order of removal entered by the administrative court, and there is a subsequent motion to reopen or reconsider filed while the appeal of the administrative decision is pending, the review of the motion order will be consolidated with the review of the original order by the administrative court.[237]

Exhaustion of Administrative Remedies

A court may review a final administrative order only if the alien has exhausted all administrative remedies available to him or her and no other court has decided the validity of order.[238] However, if the reviewing court finds that the petition presents grounds that could not have been presented in the prior judicial proceedings or that the remedy provided by the prior proceeding was inadequate or ineffective, the court may take action.[239]

Effect of Filing Petition for Review

The filing of the petition for review of a final order of removal does not prevent the AG from detaining the alien under INA §241(a).[240] Nor does it stay the order of removal until a separate stay is granted by the court.[241]

Limit on Injunctive Relief

No court shall have the authority or jurisdiction to enjoin or restrain the operation of the apprehension, examination, exclusion, or removal provisions of the INA, as amended by IIRAIRA, other than with respect to the application of such provisions to an individual alien against whom proceedings under such part already have been initiated.[242]

Habeas Corpus

REAL ID eliminates habeas corpus as a means of reviewing an order of removal.[243] Any pending habeas corpus petition seeking review of an order of removal was transferred from the federal district court to the federal circuit to be adjudicated

---

[236] INA §242(b)(5)(B).

[237] INA §242(b)(6).

[238] INA §242(d)(1).

[239] INA §242(d).

[240] INA §242(b)(8)(A).

[241] INA §242(b)(8)(C).

[242] INA §242(f)(1).

[243] *Amunikoro v. Secretary, Dep't of Homeland Security*, 423 F.3d 383 (2d Cir. 2005).

as a petition for review.[244] Notwithstanding any other provision of law, including 28 USC §2241 (habeas corpus), no court shall have jurisdiction to hear any cause or claim by or on behalf of an alien arising from the decision or action by the government to commence proceedings, adjudicate cases, or execute orders against an alien.[245] When the court says that there is no jurisdiction or judicial review of a certain type of case, the terms "judicial review" and "jurisdiction to review" include habeas corpus provisions under 28 USC §2241.[246]

The jurisdiction-stripping provisions of REAL ID do not deprive the district court of jurisdiction over a petition for writ of habeas corpus where the issue being challenged before the court is the detention of the alien, not a review of the removal order.[247] In addition, the district court maintains jurisdiction through habeas to issue a stay of execution of bond decisions in custody redetermination cases.

REAL ID does preserve habeas corpus as a means of challenging the administrative determination to review expedited removal proceedings under INA §235(b)(1). Specifically, if an individual is ordered removed under an expedited removal proceeding, he or she may challenge this order but is limited to the determination of the following: (1) whether the individual is an alien; (2) whether the individual was ordered removed under expedited removal proceedings; and (3) whether the individual can show by a preponderance of the evidence that he or she is an LPR or a refugee under INA §207, or has been granted asylum under INA §208 and that status has not yet been terminated.[248]

Reinstatement of Removal Orders

Introduction

The AG may reinstate a prior order of removal against any alien who has re-entered the United States illegally after having been removed or having departed voluntarily under an order of removal.[249] The prior order of removal is reinstated from its original date and is not subject to being reopened or reviewed. The alien is not eligible and may not apply for any relief under the INA.[250] The only exceptions to this rule are for those with prior deportation/removal orders who have re-entered and are eligible for withholding of removal under INA §241(b)(3).[251] In addition, there are certain other "country specific" forms of relief (*e.g.*, NACARA) outlined below for

---

[244] *Jama v. Gonzales*, 431 F.3d 230 (5th Cir. 2005); *Gittens v. Menefee*, 428 F.3d 382 (2d Cir. 2005).

[245] INA §242(g).

[246] INA §242(a)(5).

[247] *Hernandez v. Gonzalez*, 424 F.2d 42 (1st Cir. 2005).

[248] INA §242(e)(2).

[249] INA §241(a)(5).

[250] *Id.*

[251] 8 CFR §§241.8(e), 1241.8(e).

which an alien may seek eligibility even where a prior removal order has been reinstated. Where the order has been reinstated, the alien has no right to a hearing before an IJ on the reinstatement issue.[252] Where there is a prior order of removal, the immigration officer must obtain that order of exclusion, deportation, or removal against the alien. The alien must be provided with written notice that the officer intends to reinstate the prior order.[253] While the statute specifically mentions "removal" orders, the reinstatement provisions have been interpreted to encompass prior orders of deportation and exclusion as well.[254]

Applicants for Relief Exempt from Reinstatement of Removal

The regulations outline several groups of individuals who are exempt from the reinstatement provisions, including:

- applicants for adjustment under the Haitian Refugee Immigrant Fairness Act (HRIFA) of 1998;
- applicants for adjustment of status under §202 of the Nicaraguan Adjustment and Central American Relief Act (NACARA);
- applicants for cancellation of removal under §203 of NACARA; and
- applicants for adjustment of status under the legalization provisions of INA §245A who are protected under several class action lawsuits filed in relation to the INA.[255]

Requirements for Reinstatement Order

In order for an individual to be subject to a reinstatement order, there must have been a final order of deportation, exclusion, or removal against the alien. Second, the alien must have departed the United States under that order. Last, the alien must have returned to the United States without having sought or obtained a waiver of the removal order.[256]

Retroactivity

In the application of the reinstatement provisions, the main issue has been whether the reinstatement provisions are applicable to individuals who have departed the United States and returned prior to the effective date of INA §241(a)(5)—April 1,

---

[252] 8 CFR §§241.8(a), 1241.8(a).

[253] 8 CFR §§241.8(b), 1241.8(b).

[254] 8 CFR §§241.8(a) and (c), 1241.8(a) and (c).

[255] Class action lawsuits include *Catholic Social Services, Inc. v. Meese*, *vacated sub nom.*, *Reno v. Catholic Social Services, Inc.*, 509 U.S. 43 (1993); *League of United Latin American Citizens v. INS*, *vacated sub nom.*, *Reno v. Catholic Social Services, Inc.*, 509 U.S. 43 (1993). The CSS and LULAC lawsuits were consolidated for review at the Supreme Court. *See also Zambrano v. INS*, *vacated sub nom.*, *INS v. Zambrano*, 509 U.S. 918 (1993).

[256] INA §212(a)(9)(A)(iii).

1997. Several circuits have held that where the alien has departed and returned to the United States prior to the effective date of the provision, it cannot be applied retroactively.[257]

Other courts have held that where an alien had departed and returned and had an application for relief pending prior to the effective date of the reinstatement provision, reinstatement could not be applied retroactively, in that it would attach new consequences to actions that had been previously taken.[258] However, where no application for relief was filed prior to April 1, 1997, courts have found that there was no impermissible retroactive effect since the individuals had no request for relief pending.[259]

Several courts have found that there is no impermissible retroactive effect for individuals who have returned to the United States with a deportation order after the effective date of the statute (April 1, 1997).[260]

In sum, several courts are in accord that an individual who has been removed and who has returned to the United States and applied for some benefit prior to the effective date of April 1, 1997, may be protected from the reinstatement provisions, in that there is a strong argument that this is a retroactive application of the law. However, for individuals who return to the United States after the effective date of the statute, those courts that have looked at this issue are in agreement that there is no issue regarding "retroactive" application of the law.

---

[257] *Bejjani v. INS*, 271 F.3d 670 (6th Cir. 2001); *Castro-Cortez v. INS*, 239 F.3d 1037 (9th Cir. 2001).

[258] *Cisneros v. Att'y General*, 381 F.3d 277 (11th Cir. 2004).

[259] *Ojeda-Terrazas v. Ashcroft*, 290 F.3d 292 (5th Cir. 2002); *see also Latabb v. Ashcroft*, 384 F.3d (1st Cir. 2004).

[260] *Garcia-Marrufo v. Ashcroft*, 376 F.3d 1061 (10th Cir. 2004); *Alvarengo-Villalobos*, 271 F.3d 1169 (9th Cir. 2001). *See also Perez-Gonzalez v. Ashcroft*, 379 F.3d 783 (9th Cir. 2004). For an excellent analysis of reinstatement and the holdings of various circuit courts, see AILF Practice Advisory, "Reinstatement of Removal" (Apr. 18, 2005), available at *www.ailf.org*.

ABBREVIATIONS

AEDPA	Antiterrorism and Effective Death Penalty Act of 1996, Pub. L. No. 104-132, 110 Stat. 1214
BIA	Board of Immigration Appeals
CAT	Convention Against Torture
CBP	U.S. Customs and Border Protection
DHS	Department of Homeland Security
DOJ	Department of Justice
DOS	Department of State
EOIR	Executive Office for Immigration Review
HRIFA	Haitian Refugee Immigration Fairness Act of 1998, Pub. L. No. 105-277, 112 Stat. 2681
ICE	U.S. Immigration and Customs Enforcement
IIRAIRA	Illegal Immigration Reform and Immigrant Responsibility Act of 1996, Division C of the Omnibus Appropriations Act of 1996 (H.R. 3610), Pub. L. No. 104-208, 110 Stat. 3009
IJ	Immigration Judge
IMMACT90	Immigration Act of 1990, Pub. L. No. 101-649, 104 Stat. 4978
INA	Immigration and Nationality Act of 1952 (INA), Pub. L. No. 82-414, 66 Stat. 163
IRCA	Immigration Reform and Control Act of 1986, Pub. L. No. 99-603, 100 Stat. 3359
LPR	Lawful Permanent Resident
MTINA	Miscellaneous and Technical Immigration and Naturalization Amendments of 1991, Pub. L. No. 102-232, 105 Stat. 1733
NACARA	Nicaraguan Adjustment and Central American Relief Act, Pub. L. No. 105-100, 111 Stat. 2160
NTA	Notice to Appear
OSC	Order to Show Cause
USA PATRIOT Act	Uniting and Strengthening America by Providing Appropriate Tools Required to Intercept and Obstruct Terrorism Act of 2001, Pub. L. 107-56, 115 Stat. 272
USCIS	U.S. Citizenship and Immigration Services
VAWA	Violence Against Women Act of 1994, Pub. L. No. 103-322, 108 Stat. 1902-1955
VAWA 2005	Violence Against Women and Department of Justice Reauthorization Act of 2005, Pub. L. No. 109-162

TABLE OF APPENDICES

APPENDIX 1—ASYLUM AND WITHHOLDING OF REMOVAL CHECKLISTS

Asylum—Preparation and Filing

Eligibility

Requirements

- ❑ Unable or unwilling to return;
- ❑ To country of nationality;
- ❑ On account of persecution (past); or
- ❑ A well-founded fear of future persecution;
- ❑ On account of race, religion, nationality, political opinion, or membership in a particular social group.

Bars

- ❑ Convictions for particularly serious crimes in the United States;
- ❑ Commission of serious nonpolitical crimes outside the United States;
- ❑ Any past persecutory acts;
- ❑ Danger to the security of the United States;
- ❑ Firm resettlement in another country;
- ❑ Failure to file within one year of admission (may be exceptional or extraordinary circumstances for failure to file);
- ❑ Prior denials of asylum;
- ❑ Prior removal, deportation, or exclusion order (reinstatement);
- ❑ Safe third country;
- ❑ Changed conditions in country of feared persecution;
- ❑ Negative discretionary factors.

Documentation/Evidence

Application

- ❑ I-589;
- ❑ Supporting affidavit;
- ❑ Fingerprints taken (at application support center (ASC));
- ❑ Proof that fingerprinting has been completed;
- ❑ Photos.

Documentation

Identification

- ❑ Birth certificate/translation (accompanied by certificate of translation, 8 CFR §1003.33);
- ❑ National I.D. (passport, cedula, or other identity document);
- ❑ Immigration documents (I-94, visa stamp, parole document, etc.);
- ❑ Proof of marital status and translation (if spouse following to join, or is part of the claim);

- ❑ Birth certificates of children and translation.

Individualized Documentation of Persecution

- ❑ Medical records from native country (if treated for persecution there);
- ❑ Medical evaluation from U.S. doctor (evaluating scars or evidence of harm);
- ❑ Psychological evaluation for PTSD;
- ❑ Photos from native country (proof of persecution, political involvement, etc.);
- ❑ Arrest or conviction records from country where harm or threat lies;
- ❑ Statements of witnesses (to verify persecution, political involvement, etc.);
- ❑ Other documentation relating specifically to the applicant.

Documentation on Causation/Motivation

- ❑ I.D. or membership card showing group membership or position in group;
- ❑ Letters or statements from group leaders or members;
- ❑ Publicity (newspaper/magazine articles, fliers, transcripts of broadcasts, etc.);
- ❑ Photos proving group, political, or religious involvement;
- ❑ Books or articles written by applicant;
- ❑ Witness statements or letters documenting involvement;
- ❑ Awards, certificates, recognition of involvement with group;
- ❑ Governmental or nongovernmental documentation of involvement;
- ❑ Any other evidence connecting harm to race, religion, nationality, political opinion, or membership in a particular social group.

Evidence on Country Conditions

- ❑ Documentation on harm to others similarly situated to the applicant (*e.g.*, harm to union members, religious personnel, ethnic minorities, etc.);
- ❑ Documentation on harm to family members of others similar to applicant;
- ❑ Evidence that current country conditions have not improved;
- ❑ Letters/affidavits from experts on political, social, or religious conditions in that country;
- ❑ Human rights reports, government reports, newspaper or magazine articles.

Note: The documentation carries more weight if from well-known, reliable sources. The regulations specifically mention the State Department reports on country and human rights conditions. U.S. government records carry the most weight with the court, but human rights reports from well-known organizations (Amnesty International, etc.), newspaper and magazine articles from reliable sources (*Time*, *NYT*, *WP*, etc.) also are relevant.

Evidence to Address Any Bars to Eligibility

- ❑ Proof of admission (if one-year filing date is at issue);
- ❑ Proof to rebut any criminal bars (copies of charges, convictions, statutes, police, or court records showing that there is no bar);
- ❑ If resettlement in third country is an issue, evidence on conditions in third country (lack of rights or privileges for noncitizens; evidence of forced departure; other evidence on resettlement factors—*see* 8 CFR §§208.15, 1208.15);
- ❑ Letters from witnesses, character references, or other evidence if there is any other issue that may impact statutory eligibility or discretionary merit.

Witness List (may be submitted with documentary packet or separately)

- ❑ Name, age, and address of witness;
- ❑ Immigration status (if relevant);
- ❑ Relationship to the applicant;
- ❑ Points on which he or she will testify (if telephonically, then state so);
- ❑ How he or she knows this information (family member, witness to harm, member of same organization, etc.—if it is an expert witness, include evidence of expertise, c.v., résumé, etc).

Index (detailed listing of each piece of documentation)

- ❑ Name of each document (*e.g.*, birth certificate of respondent);
- ❑ Source and date if an article is from publication (*e.g.*, *New York Times*, Jan. 1, 2001);
- ❑ Summary of each article, or relevant part, and purpose for which it is submitted;
- ❑ Translations with a certificate of translator for each foreign document;
- ❑ If photos submitted, then summarize where and when photos were taken.

Filing Application and Documentation with the Court

- ❑ File copy of I-589, EOIR-28 (notice of appearance) and "Instructions for Submitting Certain Applications in Immigration Court" with the USCIS service center (*see* Appendix 19 for instructions for court filing);
- ❑ USCIS service center returns a receipt and a date for the respondent to be fingerprinted at the ASC;
- ❑ The respondent appears for fingerprinting and is given a receipt for this;
- ❑ Respondent then files with the court the original and one copy of the application for asylum, copy of fingerprint notice and ASC receipt, documentation, and witness list with the court;
- ❑ Make certain to read and comply with any local court rules regarding date and procedure for filing relief application with the court;
- ❑ Highlight relevant areas of documentation;
- ❑ File one copy of the application and supporting documentation with the trial attorney;
- ❑ If it is an original application, it may have to be filed with the court in person.

Asylum—Presentation in Court

By the time the asylee appears before the immigration judge for the "hearing on the merits" of the claim, several things will have already taken place in prior proceedings, including the following:

Pre–Merits Hearing

- ❑ The immigration judge has made findings on the issues of removability. The applicant has been found removable on at least one ground;
- ❑ The applicant has designated the forms of relief for which he or she wishes to apply usually including asylum, withholding of removal, and possible relief under the removal Convention Against Torture (CAT);

- ❑ The applicant has designated (or declined to designate) a country for removal if all relief applications are denied;
- ❑ All relief applications have been filed with the court by the dates set by the court at the "master calendar" hearing. Copies have also been served on the DHS trial attorney. Any amendments to the application should have been made;
- ❑ The court has been informed at the master calendar hearing of the language in which the hearing on the merits will take place and arrangements have been made by the court for an interpreter to be present at the merits hearing;
- ❑ If there will be several witnesses, witness list with a brief synopsis of the testimony of each has been submitted;
- ❑ It is helpful, although not required, to submit a prehearing brief or memorandum of law;
- ❑ Find out who the judge and trial attorney are, prior to the hearing. Talk to experienced practitioners to find out any specific tendencies, issues, or rules in that court, or with the local DHS legal section;
- ❑ Contact DHS trial attorney to do the following:
  - ❑ See if FBI fingerprint report is back;
  - ❑ Make certain documentation packet has been received;
  - ❑ See if there are any issues upon which stipulations may be made.

Initial Phase of the Hearing—Getting Documents into the Record

At the outset of the merits hearing, the immigration judge will review all documentary exhibits and then number them (*e.g.*, Exhibit 1 is the Notice to Appear, Exhibit 2 is the I-589, etc.). Make certain that any changes in the applications (*e.g.*, address changes) and the personal statement are made before the application is signed and sworn to before the judge. The immigration judge will go through each exhibit and ask both sides if there are any objections to the admission of the document. The following is a list of common documentary objections and cases, regulations, or statutes addressing them. It is not all inclusive; there may be other bases for objections, or responses to objections. The standard for admission is whether the evidence is probative and its usage would not be fundamentally unfair. *Ezeagwuna v. Ashcroft*, 325 F.3d 396 (3d Cir. 2003).

DHS Objections to Documents

- ❑ Authentication: If it is an "official" foreign or domestic document, the government may argue that it must be authenticated. 8 CFR §§287.6, 1287.6; (this regulation is not found in the asylum regs at 8 CFR §§208, 1208); FRCP Rule 44(c) states that "any other method authorized by the law" may be used to authenticate; *see also Khan v. INS*, 237 F.3d 1143(9th Cir. 2001).
- ❑ Right to cross-examination—written witness statement: The government may object to written statements or evaluations by personal witnesses when witness is not in court to be cross-examined. *Bustos-Torres v. INS*, 898 F.2d (5th Cir. 1990); *but see Hernandez-Garza v. INS*, 882 F.2d 945 (5th Cir. 1989); *Olabanji v. INS*, 973 F.2d 1232 (5th Cir. 1992); *Renteria-Gonzalez v. INS*, 322 F.3d 804 (5th Cir. 2002). *Matter of Mejia*, 16 I&N Dec. 6 (BIA 1976). Hearsay is admissible if it is probabive and its usage would not be fundamentally unfair. *Ezeagwuna v. Ashcroft*, 325 F.3d 405 (3d Cir. 2003).

- ❑ Expert affidavit: The government may object to an expert's affidavit or written statement if the expert is not present in court to be examined. *See Dia v. Ashcroft*, 353 F.3d (3d Cir. 2003). If possible, have the expert available telephonically.
- ❑ Forensics analysis: The government may object to going forward without a forensic analysis from the government forensic laboratory.
- ❑ Original documents: 8 CFR §§103.2(b)(4) and (5). If copies are submitted, originals should be available for comparison.
- ❑ Translations: 8 CFR §1003.33. All foreign documents must be translated and have a certificate of translation.
- ❑ Completeness: If part of a report is submitted, make certain that the complete original is available for review.
- ❑ Relevance: At relief phase almost all evidence is relevant.
- ❑ Timeliness: See local court rules. Documents must be filed by date set in court or as stated in local court rules.
- ❑ Compliance with local court rules: The format of the packet should be in accordance with the local rules.

Objecting to DHS Documents

- ❑ Right to cross-examine: INA §240(b)(4)—Respondent has a right to confront witnesses against him or her. This includes available government witnesses (asylum officers, DHS officers) if a statement from a government witness is submitted. *But see Bustos-Torres v. INS*, 898 F.2d 1053, 1055 (5th Cir. 1990).
- ❑ Authentication: 8 CFR §§287.6, 1287.6; *see also* INA §240(c)(3)(B)—if it is an "official document" has it been "authenticated"? See also INA §240(c)(2)(B) on authentication of correction records.
- ❑ Timeliness: Any court rules on filing deadlines apply also to the DHS trial attorney. Where trial attorney files documents in court on day of the hearing, objections based on timeliness and right to examine evidence (INA §240(b)(4)) are appropriate.
- ❑ The objections listed above as a basis for DHS objection to admission of documentation are also the basis for the respondent's objections: completeness; translations; authentication if original document not presented; etc.

Direct Examination of the Respondent

After the judge completes the marking and admission of documents into the record, he or she will have the applicant sign and swear to the application if it has not already been done, and will then ask the attorney if he or she is ready to proceed with the testimony. The testimonial phase of the hearing is basically the following: direct examination; cross-examination; followed by re-direct and re-cross. The judge in most cases will ask questions, often interrupting a line of questioning on direct or cross-examination of the witness. As in all courts, the level of the judge's involvement varies with the style and temperament of the judge. The following are a few hints on direct and cross-examination of the applicant.

Understanding Questions:

Remind the witness not to answer questions that he or she does not understand. Remind the witness it is O.K. to say that he or she did not understand the question. Bring out the witness's shortcomings—he or she lacks education, illiteracy, problems with memory, etc. that might explain difficulty in responding.

Monitoring Translator:

If the attorney does not speak the language of the witness, it is wise to bring an interpreter to keep track of the court interpreter. Even the best make mistakes.

Chronology:

In directing the questions to the witness try to keep the events in chronological order.

Lack of chronological order may confuse the immigration judge. Go through all of the information regarding the first event before letting the witness jump to another event.

Completion of Answers:

In a long answer, the interpreter may cut off the witness before the answer is completed, in order to translate part of the answer. Make certain that the witness goes back and completes the answer. The witness may feel that she can say no more on that subject when the interpreter stops him or her in order to translate.

Times and Dates:

For many asylum applicants, time is not an important or familiar cultural concept. They may not know the exact date or month of an incident. If so, make certain that the witness has the events in chronological order and can at least make an estimate as to what year (or part of the year) the event took place. Estimates about the time of an event are permissible if the witness cannot remember the exact time and date. If no estimate can be made, then relate it to another event (*e.g.*, it happened right after the birth of child).

Specificity:

The applicant should be as specific as possible about names, places, and time of events.

What Happened and Why:

After the applicant explains what has happened to him or her or someone else, he or she should then be questioned as to why he or she thinks the persecutor did the act (or will do the act).

The reason for past or future persecution must be explained on account of one of the statutory grounds; *i.e.*, religion, political opinion, etc. In most cases it is best to save the "why" until after the "what" is done.

Hearsay Is Admissible but:

The applicant or witness testifying about an event at which he or she was not present must explain how he or she knows that the event took place. Clarify as much as possible the basis for the hearsay information.

Countrywide Persecution:

The applicant should make an effort to show that the danger or persecution feared extended beyond a small section of the country. The more widespread the persecutor's power and control, the more likely the possibility that asylum will be granted.

Family in the Home Country:

The strength of the claim may be diminished if family members or others close to the applicant are living openly in relative peace in the applicant's home country. If there are family members living in the home country, the applicant should explain why they are not being persecuted but he or she will be. Question the applicant about the differences between his or her situation and their situation.

Time Between Persecution and Departure:

If the applicant remained in the country for a long period of time between the last incident of persecution and his or her departure, he or she will need to explain to the immigration judge what he or she was doing this period; *i.e.*, how did he or she avoid being bothered by the persecutor for such a long period?

Exit Visa and Passports:

The circumstances surrounding an individual's departure from his or her home country may be questioned by the DHS attorney or judge. For example, if the applicant fears persecution from the government, but he or she was able to go to a government office to obtain a passport and exit visa, and then passed through a government inspection station in departing the country, how was he or she able to do this? The client should be able to explain how he or she was able to exit the country.

Motive for Departure:

The asylum applicant should be able to show that his or her motive for departure from the native country was fear of persecution. Were there other motives for fleeing the country, *e.g.*, unemployment, job offer in the United States? On direct examination the attorney should establish that the fear of persecution was a central motivation for fleeing the country—that leaving was not simply an economic or personal issue.

Changed Conditions in Home Country:

If conditions have changed in the home country since the time of the applicant's departure, evidence should be submitted to show that the changed conditions in the home country have not measurably lessened or removed the danger to the applicant.

The Negatives:

If there is negative information that may impact the case and possibly result in a denial, it should, in most cases, be addressed on direct examination.

Do Not Lead:

Avoid leading questions. The trial attorney will object in most cases, and be sustained by the judge.

Voluntary Departure:

If the applicant is statutorily eligible for voluntary departure and it is in his or her best interest to seek it after a denial of asylum, the following issues must be addressed:

- Length of time in the United States;
- Willingness to depart voluntarily from the United States if so ordered;
- Ability or means by which to depart the country at no expense to the government;
- Absence of arrests or convictions that would show that the applicant is not a person of good moral character;
- Does he or she have a passport, or can he or she obtain one;
- Can he or she proffer a voluntary departure bond of at least $500 within five business days.

Cross-Examination of the Respondent

There are certain standard issues that DHS attorneys regularly pursue during cross-examination. Several have been mentioned above as items to be covered on direct examination.

Dates and Times:

The DHS attorney's questions may confuse the client about when certain events took place. Prior to the hearing, the applicant should be advised that it is permissible to approximate or answer in general terms about the time of an event if he or she cannot remember the exact date and time of an event. Be ready to object if the trial attorney is repetitive in his or her questioning after the applicant has responded and has no further information to give.

Motivation:

The trial attorney may attempt to show that the motivation of the applicant in fleeing was not fear of persecution but some other (usually financial) reason. In preparing the applicant for direct and cross-examination, spend time discussing his or her motivation for flight. It is also important to discuss his or her opinions on the motivation of the persecutor, and his or her main reason for leaving.

Departure from Native Country:

The time and the manner of the applicant's departure from the native country are areas that the DHS may question. Specifically, the length of time the applicant remained in the country after he or she was persecuted (or threatened) may be an issue.

If the applicant remained for a relatively long period (several months or years), he or she must be able to explain why he or she did not leave and where he or she resided during that period. In addition, if possible, the applicant should explain how he or she managed to flee the country without being stopped by the persecutor.

Countrywide Persecution:

The trial attorney may question whether there were other safer areas of the country where the applicant could have remained without fear. The applicant should be prepared to explain why it is not reasonable to relocate internally.

Family:

Are relatives of the applicant residing in the home country without being persecuted?

The client should be prepared to explain why he or she would be persecuted but other family members have not been persecuted. Highlight the differences between the applicant and the family members.

Intimidation by DHS:

Occasionally DHS trial attorneys may question the applicant on minor violations of the immigration law unrelated to the actual claim for political asylum. The trial attorney may ask a series of questions designed to show how the client entered the country illegally, disregarding U.S. immigration laws. The applicant should be prepared for this so that he or she is not confused or made to feel like a criminal. If the issue has already been addressed at the removability phase, there may be an objection based on relevancy or that it was previously asked and answered.

Objections to DHS Questions:

While there are no formal rules of evidence and the parties are permitted wide latitude in questioning witnesses, there may be grounds for objections to questions by government counsel in cross-examination.

Misstatement of testimony—The trial attorney's questions misstate an answer given by the witness on direct examination.

Argumentative—A question may be argumentative where repetitive or meant not to gain information but rather to argue, demean, or incite.

Relevancy—The question is not relevant to the issue of asylum or the exercise of discretion.

Vagueness—The question is badly worded, vague, or confusing.

Asked and answered/repetitive—The question has previously been asked and answered. (Most judges will permit the trial attorney to ask again during cross-examination questions previously answered on direct examination. However, where the question is repetitive, an objection should be made.)

Re-Direct and Re–Cross-examination of the Respondent

The applicant's attorney will have the opportunity to conduct a re-direct examination of the witness, and the trial attorney may conduct a re-cross examination. While neither side should be permitted to raise new issues on re-direct or re-cross, this is permitted in some cases. If the DHS attorney attempts to question about new issues not previously addressed on direct or cross in his or her re-cross, an objection should be raised. Likewise the DHS attorney may object if the respondent's attorney opens new areas on re-direct. The immigration judge can and usually will ask questions at any time.

Testimony of Other Witnesses

In addition to the testimony of the applicant there may be other witnesses. Usually they are either personal (*i.e.*, individuals with direct knowledge of the applicant's case) or expert witnesses who may testify regarding medical and psychological issues facing the respondent, country and human rights conditions, or a more specific area of expertise relating to the claim. The following are some pointers for each:

Personal Witnesses: Keep questions short, objective, and easy to understand. Keep the witness focused on the issue. Questions should cover: identity of the witness; relationship to the applicant; knowledge of the applicant's situation and asylum claim; how does the witness know this; what the witness thinks would happen to the applicant if returned; and why.

Expert Witnesses: Question status as an expert. Submit curriculum vitae with the following (if relevant):

- ❑ Name, age, place of employment, position;
- ❑ Educational background (degrees, titles, etc.);
- ❑ Employment history;
- ❑ Publications on the issue involved;
- ❑ Travel to the country involved;
- ❑ Other evidence of expertise (awards, membership in organizations, etc.);
- ❑ Prior experience in testifying as an expert.

Testimony on the Subject:

- ❑ Knowledge of the particular issue;
- ❑ Knowledge of the issue facing the applicant;
- ❑ Opinion about what has happened to the applicant or might happen (plausibility);
- ❑ Basis for this opinion.
- ❑ Opinion as to what might happen to respondent if returned, and why.

Closing Argument

Many judges do not permit closing arguments. In most cases it will have to be requested, although a small percentage of judges request it. For those who do permit it, they want it short and focused. Some judges will permit it and tell the attorney specifically what issue(s) he or she wants addressed. Judges do not want a restatement of all the testimony in the case. It is important to remember that this is not a jury being addressed but rather a judge who has heard hundreds, and possibly thousands, of asylum cases. The following is a list of items to be addressed in closing:

- ❑ Credibility—remind the judge that the applicant was credible on the major points;
- ❑ Brief summary of the case (*e.g.*, this case is based on past persecution on account
- ❑ of political opinion, direct and imputed);
- ❑ Statutory requirements—the applicant must prove these elements;
- ❑ Evidence—summarize the evidence submitted that proves each element; make reference to the documentary record where appropriate to prove a point;
- ❑ Weaknesses—if there are any weaknesses in the case, address them and explain how they should not negate a grant of asylum (take note of the questions asked by the judge—these are the issues on the judge's mind);
- ❑ Summary—summarize for the judge the elements of the claim and how the evidence proved these elements, and therefore the claim should be granted.

Decision and Appeal

At the end of the closing argument (if permitted), the immigration judge will usually render his or her decision. The attorney can ask to have it translated to the applicant as it is rendered, but this is not required. On occasion, the immigration judge will reserve decision and send it out by mail or call the parties back to court for the decision at a subsequent time. The decision should restate the evidence and the court's findings as well as the relevant case law and basis for the court's decision.

The appealing party is given 30 days from the date of the oral decision (or date of mailing if the decision is written) to file an appeal with the BIA. If the judge denies the claim for asylum, the right to appeal should be reserved unless the applicant is absolutely certain that he or she does not wish to appeal. Reserving the right to appeal does not mandate that the appeal must be filed; it only preserves the right to do so. The original notice of appeal must be received by the BIA within 30 days with the appropriate fee ($110) paid to the United States Department of Justice. A copy must be given to DHS. There are preoisions for proceedings "in forma pauperis."

Withholding of Removal Checklist

Statutory Eligibility

Requirements

- ❑ Clear probability (more likely than not); that
- ❑ Life or freedom will be threatened;
- ❑ On account of race, religion, nationality, political opinion, or membership in a particular social group.

Bars

- ❑ Conviction for a particularly serious crime (sentence to five or more years for a particularly serious crime is an absolute bar);
- ❑ Commission of a serious nonpolitical offense;
- ❑ Persecution of others.

Note: Resettlement is not a bar, nor is the one-year filing deadline.

No Discretion: If statutorily eligible, relief is mandatory.

Application

- ❑ I-589 (application for asylum is an application for withholding);
- ❑ Birth certificate or proof of nationality (passport, cedula);
- ❑ Photos (two passport size);
- ❑ Evidence of completion of biometrics (fingerprints).

Documentation

The documentation used to support a claim to withholding of removal is similar to most, if not all, respects to the documentation used for proving an asylum claim. A claim of asylum is considered a claim to withholding, hence the form (I-589) and supporting documentation used to support a claim to asylum under INA §208 is that also used for withholding of removal under INA §241(b)(3).

Appendix 2—Checklist for Cancellation of Removal Cases for Non–Lawful Permanent Residents

Eligibility

- ❑ Continuous physical presence for 10 years;
- ❑ Good moral character during that period;
- ❑ Exceptional and extremely unusual hardship.

Application and Documentation

Application

- ❑ Form EOIR-42;
- ❑ Fee $100 (or fee waiver under 8 CFR §103.7);
- ❑ Fingerprint fee $70;
- ❑ Photos (see USCIS website for requirements, *www.uscis.gov*);
- ❑ Statement of applicant, factual background, and basis for claim;
- ❑ Birth certificate and translation (with certification of translator);
- ❑ Other identity documentation (marriage certificate, name change, etc);
- ❑ Passport (if available).

Documentation

Proof of physical presence

- ❑ Proof of entry (I-94, passport stamps, visas, if available);
- ❑ Pay stubs or other employment records;
- ❑ Bank records or credit card receipts;
- ❑ Utility bills or apartment leases;
- ❑ School or vaccination records of children;
- ❑ Income tax returns and/or W-2 forms;
- ❑ Immigration records (DHS receipts, employment authorization, etc);
- ❑ Church records or contributions to community organizations;
- ❑ Medical records;
- ❑ Prior mail received with postmarks;
- ❑ Photos that might show presence in United States;
- ❑ Dated receipts from purchases;
- ❑ Affidavits of witnesses (name, address, relationship—neighbor, family member, co-worker, what he or she knows, how he or she knows it);
- ❑ Any other documentation proving physical presence.

Good moral character

- ❑ Fingerprint check (make sure completed at application support center (ASC));
- ❑ Police letter(s) (places where applicant has lived six months or more);
- ❑ Letters of recommendation (should state: name, address, age of affiant; relationship to applicant; information on applicant's character; may also include hardship information, if possible); notarized (but not required);

- ❑ Other evidence of good character—contributions to community, etc.

Exceptional and extremely unusual hardship

- ❑ USC/LPR family ties;
- ❑ Birth certificates of USC or LPR family spouse, parents, children;
- ❑ Copies of Green Cards;
- ❑ Marriage certificate;
- ❑ Divorce records showing custody or child support obligations;
- ❑ Other evidence of family ties in United States;
- ❑ Medical records and doctors' letters if claim based on health;
- ❑ Evidence of health insurance;
- ❑ Evidence of lack of medical care in native country (if claim based on health);
- ❑ Emotional hardship—psychological evaluation if claim based on emotional hardship;
- ❑ Statements from counselors or teachers at childrens' school;
- ❑ Death certificates of deceased immediate family members;
- ❑ Community ties, evidence of community involvement of USC/LPR children or spouse;
- ❑ School records;
- ❑ Academic awards;
- ❑ Membership in religious or community groups;
- ❑ Letters from neighbors/community members as evidence of ties to the community (documentation of participation in church or other community events by applicant or immediate family);
- ❑ Ownership of property, business, or evidence of investment;
- ❑ Mortgage documents;
- ❑ Employment records, tax returns;
- ❑ Conditions in native country—economic, political, social (State Department, CIA, or other country reports; human rights reports; newspaper and magazine articles, etc.), showing lack of health care, educational opportunities, employment, security;
- ❑ Any other evidence of hardship.

Filing Procedure for Application and Supporting Documentation

- ❑ Mail copy of the above EOIR-42 form with fees ($100); biometrics fee ($70); and EOIR-28 to the service center. Ask the court for the "Instructions for Submitting Certain Applications in Immigration Court." See Appendix 19 for a copy.
- ❑ A USCIS notice and instructions to appear at an ASC is sent out by the service center for completion of biometrics (fingerprints) within three weeks. If not received, call 800-375-5283.
- ❑ Applicant is fingerprinted when notified and obtains biometrics (fingerprint) receipt.
- ❑ File with the court the original application, fee receipt, and all supporting documentation along with the USCIS notice instructing applicant to report for biometrics at the ASC. The biometrics receipt is proof that fingerprinting was

completed. Include certificate of service on DHS trial attorney. (Check local court rules on filing guidelines.)

- ❑ Send copy of application, documentation, USCIS receipt, to the DHS attorney by certified or express mail. Keep proof of service—the DHS mail room sometimes does not get documents to the legal section.
- ❑ Check with DHS trial attorney prior to the hearing to:
  - ❑ verify receipt of documentation;
  - ❑ see if biometrics (fingerprint) check is completed; and
  - ❑ see if any issues can be resolved or conceded prior to the hearing.

Checklist for VAWA and NACARA Cancellation

VAWA Cancellation

Application and Documentation

- ❑ EOIR-42;
- ❑ Filing fee ($100 or fee waiver);
- ❑ Biometrics fee ($70);
- ❑ Photographs (2);
- ❑ Birth certificate plus translation;
- ❑ Passport (if available);
- ❑ Documentation of marriage:
  - ❑ Marriage certificate;
  - ❑ Evidence of cohabitation establishing bona fide marriage;
  - ❑ Proof of termination of prior marriages;
- ❑ Documentation of abuse/domestic violence;
- ❑ Documentation of good moral character:
  - ❑ Results of fingerprint check (obtain from DHS/TA);
  - ❑ Local police letter;
  - ❑ Letters of good moral character from friends, family, and community members.
- ❑ Documentation of at least three years' physical presence.
- ❑ Evidence of extreme hardship to the applicant and/or USC/LPR immediate family member if deported.

NACARA Cancellation

Application and Documentation

- ❑ Form I-881;
- ❑ Filing fee ($100 or fee waiver);
- ❑ Biometrics fee ($70);
- ❑ Birth certificate plus translation.

Salvadorans

- ❑ Evidence of registration for TPS or *ABC* class litigation; or proof that asylum claim was filed prior to April 1, 1990;

- ❑ Documentation to prove entry on or before September 19, 1990;
- ❑ Documentation to prove seven years' physical presence;
- ❑ Documentation to prove good moral character (results of fingerprint check, police letter, letters of recommendation);
- ❑ Documentation on extreme hardship (Salvadoran and Guatemalans get a presumption of extreme hardship so there is no need for extensive documentation).

Guatemalans

- ❑ Evidence of registration for *ABC* class litigation or proof that asylum claim was filed prior to April 1, 1990;
- ❑ Documentation proving entry on or before October 1, 1990;
- ❑ Documentation to prove seven years' physical presence;
- ❑ Documentation establishing good moral character;
- ❑ Documentation on extreme hardship (there is a presumption of hardship).

Eastern Europeans

- ❑ Documentation establishing entry on or before December 31, 1990;
- ❑ Proof of filing for asylum before December 31, 1991;
- ❑ No convictions for aggravated felonies;
- ❑ Documentation establishing seven years' physical presence;
- ❑ Documentation showing good moral character;
- ❑ Documentation of extreme hardship to alien and/or USC/LPR spouse, parents, or children.

Instructions for Filing NACARA Cancellation Application

- ❑ File form I-881, EOIR-28, filing fee ($285 or fee waiver), biometrics fee ($70) with Immigration Court Instructions (see Appendix 19) with the service center.
- ❑ Service center returns receipt for fees with instructions for appearance at ASC for biometrics. ASC gives applicant a receipt for biometrics.
- ❑ Original application with supporting documentation, fee receipts, proof of completion of biometrics, witness list, and certificate of service is filed with the court (see local court rules for filing instructions).
- ❑ Send copy to the DHS trial attorney.

APPENDIX 3—CHECKLIST FOR CANCELLATION OF REMOVAL CASES FOR CERTAIN PERMANENT RESIDENTS

Eligibility

- ❑ Lawful admission for permanent residence for not less than five years;
- ❑ Continuous residence for not less than seven years;
- ❑ No convictions for aggravated felonies.

Not Eligible

- ❑ Crewmen entering after June 30, 1964;
- ❑ Exchange visitors (J visa holders) subject to two-year foreign residency requirement;
- ❑ Alien admitted on (or later acquired) J visa for graduate medical training;
- ❑ Alien inadmissible or removable on security grounds;
- ❑ Alien who assisted, aided, or abetted in the persecution of others;
- ❑ Alien previously granted §212(c) relief or suspension of deportation under the former INA §244(a) prior to 1996 IIRAIRA amendments.

Application and Supporting Documentation

- ❑ EOIR-42A
- ❑ G-325A
- ❑ Birth certificate of applicant plus translation (or other identification);
- ❑ Filing Fee ($100 or EOIR-26A fee waiver form);
- ❑ Fingerprint Fee ($70);
- ❑ Copy of resident alien card (passport stamp, I-94, other evidence of LPR status);
- ❑ Notice of appearance (EOIR-28, if not already filed).

Evidence of Continuous Residence

- ❑ Tax returns or W-2 forms;
- ❑ Check stubs or pay receipts;
- ❑ Bank records, checking statements, credit card bills;
- ❑ Utility bills;
- ❑ Mortgage or rent payments;
- ❑ Post-marked mail;
- ❑ Affidavits from friends, coworkers, community members, family;
- ❑ Other receipts or evidence of residence.

Documentation on Discretionary Factors

- ❑ Birth certificates or resident alien cards of USC/LPR family members;
- ❑ Marriage certificate;
- ❑ Naturalization certificates for close family members;
- ❑ School records of children (report cards, awards, letters from teachers);
- ❑ Evidence of community involvement of children (sports, church, scouts);
- ❑ Letters from counselors or teachers regarding childrens' progress in school;
- ❑ Documentation on involvement of spouse in community (employment, church, community relations, education);

- ❑ Medical records or doctors' letter of any ill family member showing nature of illness;
- ❑ Evidence of respondent's work history (raises, letters, awards);
- ❑ Evidence of respondent's community involvement (letters, church records, etc.);
- ❑ Evidence of property ties (mortgage papers, business ownership, etc.);
- ❑ Evidence of conditions on home country (unemployment rate, education system, medical system, crime rate, political instability);
- ❑ Psychological evaluation on harm to USC/ LPR children, spouse, parents if separated from respondent, or if taken from their cultural surroundings;
- ❑ Rehabilitation—if there is a criminal record, what evidence is there of change (probation report; letters from probation officer; proof of attendance at counseling sessions; letters from family, coworkers, community members on change; evidence of community involvement; or other evidence of change);
- ❑ Any other evidence of positive character traits, hardship, or rehabilitation;
- ❑ Witness list of any witnesses (family, community, work, experts) who will testify.

Note: Documents in a foreign language must be translated with a certificate of translation. *See* 8 CFR §1003.33.

Preparation and Filing of Application and Documentation

- ❑ Read local court rules to see how the court wants the application packaged (number of copies, tabbing, indexing, highlighting, etc.). Check with local court clerk to see if there are rules, or check EOIR website.
- ❑ Under rules in effect as of April 1, 2005, a copy of the application (EOIR-42), biographic information sheet (G-325A), with the application fee of $100 (or fee waiver), notice of appearance (EOIR-28), and the biometrics fee of $70 (made out to DHS) is sent to the designated USCIS service center. The service center then sends out a receipt with instructions to appear at a designated application support center (ASC). The notice should be received within three weeks or call 1-800-375-5283. (*See* Appendix 19, "Instructions for Submitting Certain Applications in Immigration Court.")
- ❑ The applicant goes to the biometrics interview noted on the receipt with the required documents designated on the receipt. The fingerprints are taken and a "biometrics confirmation" document is given to the applicant.
- ❑ File the original application with the supporting documentation, witness list, proof of fee payment, and biometrics on or before the date set by the court. Make sure a certificate of service proving service on the DHS trial attorney is attached.
- ❑ Mail or deliver a copy of the packet to the DHS trial attorney at the time the court is served. Call trial attorney prior to the hearing to:
  - ❑ Make certain packet was received;
  - ❑ See if FBI background check is completed; and
  - ❑ See if there are any issues which can be negotiated and resolved prior to the hearing.

Appendix 4—INA §212(c) Relief Checklist

Eligibility

- ❑ Seven years' "lawful" unrelinquished domicile (8 CFR §§212.3(f)(2), 1212.3(f)(2)).
- ❑ Lawful admission for permanent resident status (8 CFR §§212.3(f)(1), 1212.3(f)(1)).
- ❑ In deportation proceedings (as opposed to removal proceedings); or in removal proceedings for crime to which he or she pleaded prior to April 24, 1996; (8 CFR §1212.3(g)–(h)).
- ❑ Not subject to inadmissibility for security grounds under INA §§212(a)(3)(A)–(C) or (E).
- ❑ Comparable ground of inadmissibility for which deportable. (*Matter of Blake*, 23 I&N Dec. 722 (BIA 2005)).
- ❑ Not barred for serving term(s) of imprisonment for five or more 5 years.
- ❑ The positive equities outweigh the negative factors. (*Matter of Marin*, 16 I&N Dec. 581 (BIA 1978)).

Application

- ❑ Form I-191 with supporting fee ($265 paid to DHS) or fee waiver (8 CFR §§103.7, 1103.7);
- ❑ Fingerprint (biometric) fee of $70 (fees paid at DHS; fingerprint appointment must be scheduled at the DHS application support center (ASC) before hearing so that fingerprints and background checks can be completed before hearing.);
- ❑ Original application with fee receipt(s) or fee waiver filed with the court with all supporting documentation. Certificate of service proving service on DHS trial attorney must be included. See local court rules for filing procedures.

Documentation

- ❑ Birth certificate of applicant with translation;
- ❑ Copy of resident alien card, passport stamp, or other evidence of lawful status;
- ❑ Proof of domicile in the United States:
  - ❑ Tax returns and W-2 forms;
  - ❑ Employment records or pay stubs;
  - ❑ Bank statements or check stubs;
  - ❑ Utility bills;
  - ❑ Mortgage or rent payments;
  - ❑ Receipts from purchases or donations;
  - ❑ School records;
  - ❑ Postmarked mail;
  - ❑ Affidavits or letters from witnesses;
  - ❑ Other dated materials.
- ❑ Evidence of criminal record:
  - ❑ Local police letter;
  - ❑ Proof that fingerprints and FBI background check are completed;
- ❑ Equities:

- ❑ *Family ties:* birth records, baptismal records, marriage certificates, naturalization certificates, and Green Cards for immediate family members[1] who are U.S. citizens or LPRs.
- ❑ *Health issues:* medical records, letter(s) from physician outlining nature of any illness, treatment needed, and harm resulting if treatment not received or if the applicant is forced to leave. If the applicant's family members are sick, show involvement of applicant in caring for the ill family member.
- ❑ *Employment History:* letters from employers and coworkers regarding type of work performed, quality of work, and character of person on the job; in addition, pay stubs or tax returns.
- ❑ *Property ownership:* mortgage papers, proof of business ownership, bank records, evidence of investment.
- ❑ *Community ties:* letters of recommendation from community members showing contributions and involvement in community organizations, receipts from any charitable contributions, evidence of participation in community efforts;
- ❑ *Hardship to USC/LPR children:* proof of academic achievement—report cards, letters from counselors, proof of participation in school or community organizations (scouts, sports, church, other organizations); evidence of (lack of) foreign language ability; evidence of any awards or prizes won for academics, athletic achievement, or community work; psychological evaluations on the emotional hardship to child if parent removed, or if child forced to move to a new culture; relevant medical records on any health issues (asthma, etc.).
- ❑ *Hardship to USC/LPR spouse or parents:* evidence of health problems; evidence of family member's community and/or property ties; inability to support themselves; lack of support system if the applicant is deported; psychological evaluations on impact of removal on family members.
- ❑ *Conditions in native country:* documentation on poor economic, social, medical, educational, or other conditions in the country that will make life difficult for the alien or the USC/LPR immediate family members.
- ❑ *Rehabilitation:* if a crime has been committed, evidence to show that the applicant has rehabilitated him or herself—proof of compliance with terms of probation; evidence of steady employment; proof of community and family involvement; evidence of change in lifestyle; church attendance.
- ❑ *Other Evidence:* any other evidence that might show good character, rehabilitation, or other factors that favor a positive exercise of discretion; *e.g.*, if separated or divorced, evidence of child support.[2]

Filing the Application

Send the following to the service center

- ❑ Copy of the form I-191 (not the documentation);
- ❑ Filing fee of $265;

[1] All foreign language documents must be filed with a translation and a certificate of translation. 8 CFR §1003.33.

[2] Local court rules may have filing deadlines (*e.g.*, 10 business days before court and filing requirements; review local court rules in preparing or filing documentation). Local court procedures can be found at *www.usdoj.gov/eoir*.

  - ❑ Biometrics fee of $70;
  - ❑ E-28;
  - ❑ Copy of counsel instructions or filing.
- ❑ The service center returns a receipt with the date, place, and time for fingerprinting.
- ❑ Applicant is fingerprinted and given a receipt as proof.
- ❑ The original application is filed with the court with all supporting documentation, fees, and fingerprint receipts.
- ❑ A copy is served on the DHS trial attorney.

Note: If the service center does not accept the filing fee and biometric fee, these will have to be paid at the local USCIS office and the fee receipt will have to be taken to the ASC locally. The original application with documentation is then filed with supporting documentation and proof of payment of fees (or fee waiver request) at the immigration court, and a copy served on the DHS trial attorney.

APPENDIX 5—ADJUSTMENT OF STATUS UNDER INA §245(a) CHECKLIST

Eligibility

Entry/Admission

- ❑ Is the applicant admitted or paroled;
- ❑ If not, is he or she eligible under INA §245(i) (petition filed on or before April 30, 2001);
- ❑ Is he or she a VAWA or SIJ applicant.

Visa Petition

- ❑ Is there an approval of a visa petition;
- ❑ Burden of proof (if filed after NTA issued—must prove by clear and convincing evidence bona fide marriage);
- ❑ If not approved, hearing may be postponed pending adjudication (*Matter of Velarde*, 23 I&N Dec. 253 (BIA 2002));
- ❑ Visa availability (immediate relative or current priority date).

Bars to Adjustment[1]

- ❑ Illegal entry/arriving aliens (unless §245(i), VAWA, SIJ, or other special exception);
- ❑ Failure to maintain lawful status (if not immediate relative, VAWA, or SIJ);
- ❑ Unavailability of visa;
    - ❑ Petition not approved (or filed);
    - ❑ No current priority date
- ❑ Grounds of inadmissibility;
    - ❑ Crime (admissions or convictions—see INA §212(a)(2));
    - ❑ Immigration violations (see INA §212(a)(6));
    - ❑ Public charge (see INA §212(a)(4); must have affidavit of support per 8 CFR §213a.2);
    - ❑ Security (see INA §212(a)(3));
    - ❑ Health (see INA §212(a)(i)).

Application and Documentation

- ❑ I-485;
- ❑ G-325;
- ❑ Filing fee of $325 unless waived;
- ❑ Biometrics fee $70;
- ❑ Proof of lawful entry if under INA §245(a);
- ❑ If under §245(i) (unlawful entry but application filed pre-April 30, 2001), supplement with $1,000 penalty sum;

---

[1] Some of these bars are waived for §245(i)-eligible applicants but the visa petition must have been filed prior to April 30, 2001, and the penalty sum must be paid.

- ❑ Affidavit of support (I-864, last three years' tax returns, proof of current employment);
- ❑ Approval of I-130/I-140;
- ❑ Proof of bona fide relationship; if based on marriage, marriage certificate, divorce or death records, birth certificates; if based on other relationship (siblings, parent/child) proof of that relationship);
- ❑ Originals of official documents (marriage, birth, divorce records); translations with certificate of translator (see 8 CFR §1003.33);
- ❑ Proof of fingerprinting;
- ❑ Passport and copy;
- ❑ Photos;
- ❑ Notice of appearance (EOIR-28, G-28);
- ❑ Work authorization (I-765) (not required).

Filing of Adjustment Packet

As of April 1, 2005, there are new filing procedures for adjustments applications filed with the immigration court. The court at the master calendar hearing still gives a date at which time the original application is to be filed with supporting documentation before the court. However, prior to the filing with the court, a copy of the application is sent with all fees and notices of appearance to the USCIS service center. The service center then sends a receipt and instructions to appear at the appropriate application support center (ASC) for fingerprinting. After the fingerprinting is completed, the applicant files the following with the court:

- ❑ Original application and fee receipt (or fee waiver);
- ❑ Supporting documentation;
- ❑ USCIS notice instructing the person to appear at the ASC for fingerprinting;
- ❑ Evidence of fingerprinting;
- ❑ Witness list;
- ❑ Certificate of service.

Check local court rules to be sure the packet complies with local court requirements as to form, content, and date of filing. Serve a copy on the DHS trial attorney.

Waivers

Any necessary waiver applications to remove or waive a ground of inadmissibility should be filed with the adjustment application before the court because it is the court that will adjudicate all such waivers along with the adjustment application.

- ❑ INA §212(c)—Waives drug crimes and other criminal grounds of Inadmissibility (form I-191);
- ❑ INA §212(h)—Waives crimes involving moral turpitude, prostitution, and possession of marijuana (single offense, 30 grams or less) (form I-601);
- ❑ INA §212(i)—Waives immigration fraud (not including false USC claims (form I-601);
- ❑ INA §212(d)(11)—Waives certain smuggling offenses.

Tips for Court

- ❑ Read local court rules on filing (10-day rule, etc);

- ❑ Be ready to prove bona fide relationship (marriage case);
- ❑ Make sure proof of fees paid;
- ❑ Fingerprint check completed;
- ❑ Affidavit of support plus last three years' tax returns;
- ❑ Be prepared for contested issues (*i.e.*, court and DHS examination) on all issues (petition, relationship, admissibility, waivers, and discretion);
- ❑ Medical exam (completed and in sealed envelope);
- ❑ Have petitioner in court.

VAWA Adjustment

Application and Documentation

- ❑ I-485;
- ❑ G-325;
- ❑ Approval Notice for I-360 (self-petition);
- ❑ Filing fee ($325 or waiver);
- ❑ Biometrics fee ($70);
- ❑ Evidence of public charge (offer or employment, affidavit of support, or other evidence—I-864 not mandated);
- ❑ Photographs (two passport size);
- ❑ Birth certificate (and translation);
- ❑ Copy of passport (if available);
- ❑ Medical exam.

Note: Although the self petition is approved, be ready to present documentation on the bona fides of the marriage and evidence of abuse.

APPENDIX 6—WAIVERS CHECKLIST

INA §212(h)—Crime

Waiver for crimes involving moral turpitude (not torture or murder); single offense for possession of marijuana for own use; prostitution; multiple crimes (not drug related); crimes by diplomats who avoid prosecution through diplomatic immunity. The waiver in removal proceedings is usually filed with an application for adjustment of status. Biometrics (fingerprints) are completed with the adjustment. See adjustment checklist for filing procedures.

Eligibility

Extreme Hardship

- ❑ Must be spouse parent, son, or daughter of USC/LPR;
- ❑ Proof that USC/LPR parent, spouse, son, or daughter would suffer extreme hardship; and
- ❑ Merits positive exercise of discretion—must show extraordinary circumstances if there is a violent or dangerous crime.

or

Fifteen-Year Period

- ❑ The criminal acts occurred more than 15 years prior to the date of application for the visa or adjustment of status; and
- ❑ Admission of alien not contrary to national welfare safety or security;
- ❑ Showing of rehabilitation;
- ❑ Alien meets terms, conditions, and procedures established by regulations; and
- ❑ Alien merits a positive exercise of discretion.

Lawful Permanent Residents are not eligible if:

- ❑ Convicted of aggravated felony after admission; or
- ❑ Have not resided lawfully in United States for seven years.

Application and Documentation

All Applicants

- ❑ I-601 application;
- ❑ Filing fee ($265 or fee waiver);
- ❑ G-325A;
- ❑ Biometrics fee (not necessary if already filed and paid with adjustment application).

Based on Extreme Hardship

- ❑ Birth certificate of applicant;
- ❑ Proof of USC/LPR status of spouse, parent, son, or daughter;

- ❑ Evidence of hardship to USC/LPR relative (exceptional or extremely unusual hardship if there is a violent or dangerous crime);
  - ❑ *Health:* Medical records or doctors' letters showing medical condition;
  - ❑ *Separation:* Letters from family, friends, and/or psychological evaluation or counselors report;
  - ❑ *Residence:* Proof of length of residence in United States (and the community where presently residing);
  - ❑ *Community ties:* Proof of community involvement—membership in community groups; letters from community members;
  - ❑ *Property:* Deeds, mortgages, titles, tax returns, evidence of investment or property;
  - ❑ *Employment:* Letters from employers, tax return, W-2 form, letters from co-workers or employers;
  - ❑ *Education:* Evidence of children's or spouses educational records and achievements;
  - ❑ *Conditions in native country:* Reports from government agencies, international organizations, newspapers, or other sources on medical, social, economic, political, and cultural conditions in native country; letters from family and friends in that country;
  - ❑ Any other evidence of hardship to USC/LPR family member.
- ❑ Discretion
  - ❑ Evidence of rehabilitation including where applicable letters from probation on law enforcement officers, family members, or counselors;
  - ❑ Payment of all taxes;
  - ❑ Letters from friends, family, or neighbors on contributions made by alien;
  - ❑ Any other evidence of good moral character.

Based on Fifteen Years Subsequent to Commission of Crime

- ❑ Proof of date of commission of crime;
- ❑ Proof of rehabilitation
  - ❑ Probation officers or law enforcement officers records;
  - ❑ Letters from friends, family, or neighbors;
  - ❑ Proof of community involvement;
  - ❑ Evidence of counseling;
  - ❑ Evidence of continuous work history;
  - ❑ Educational achievement;
  - ❑ Payment of taxes;
  - ❑ Other evidence of rehabilitation.
- ❑ Admission not contrary to national interest

INA §212(i)—Fraud

Waiver for fraud and for willful misrepresentation of a material fact to gain a benefit under the INA. Like the §212(h) waiver, this waiver is generally filed with an application for adjustment of status. Biometrics are completed as part of the adjustment of status application. The procedure for filing is outlined in the adjustment of status checklist.

Eligibility

- ❑ Must have spouse or parent who is a USC/LPR (not child);
- ❑ Must show extreme hardship to USC/LPR parent or spouse (or to self for VAWA self-petitioner);
- ❑ Merit positive exercise of discretion.

Note: Not available to waive fraudulent claims to U.S. citizenship.

Application/Documentation

- ❑ I-601 application form;
- ❑ Filing fee ($265 or fee waiver)
- ❑ G-325A;
- ❑ Birth certificate of applicant (required to establish relationship to USC/LPR parent);
- ❑ Marriage certificate (required to establish relationship to USC/LPR spouse);
- ❑ Proof of citizenship of USC spouse;
- ❑ Proof of termination of all prior marriages (if hardship based on relationship to USC spouse);
- ❑ Proof of citizenship of USC/LPR parents;
- ❑ Resident alien cards of USC/LPR parents or spouse (where applicable);
- ❑ Extreme hardship documentation;
    - ❑ *Health:* Doctors' letters or medical record of ill USC/LPR family member, evidence of health insurance;
    - ❑ *Residence:* Proof of lengthy residence in the United States and the community where individual presently resides;
    - ❑ *Emotional hardship:* Letters, psychological evaluation to show nature of relationship and emotional hardship if family members were to be separated;
    - ❑ *Community involvement:* Evidence of spouse's or parents' involvement in community events;
    - ❑ *Property ties:* Mortgages, deeds, titles, tax returns, or other evidence of property ownership;
    - ❑ *Employment:* Evidence of continuous employment;
    - ❑ *Children:* Although hardship to USC/LPR children is not a factor under the INA, hardship to the children may impact USC/LPR spouse or parent of alien, and may also weigh as a factor on discretion;
    - ❑ *Conditions in native country:* Reports from government, international organizations, or other sources on economic, social (including educational and medical), and political conditions in native country;
    - ❑ Any other evidence of hardship.

Discretion

- ❑ *Children:* Birth certificates of USC children; report cards; evidence of community involvement; awards or prizes received; evidence of health issues; any other evidence on hardship;
- ❑ *Employment:* Evidence of alien's continuous work history and payment of taxes;

- ❑ *Community:* Evidence of alien's community involvement;
- ❑ *Rehabilitation:* Evidence of change since the commission of the fraud or misrepresentation.

INA §212(g)—Health

Waiver for health grounds of inadmissibility under INA §212(a)(1) including communicable diseases of public health significance; physical or mental disorders; or lack of required vaccinations (does not waive drug abuse or addiction).

Eligibility

Communicable Diseases

- ❑ Must have a USC/LPR parent, spouse, or unmarried son or daughter being issued an immigrant visa.

Vaccinations

- ❑ Evidence that vaccinations are not appropriate at the time visa is sought (because of age, lack of availability, or timing of vaccination);
- ❑ Proof that vaccinations previously were completed;
- ❑ Exemptions on moral or religious grounds (must submit evidence showing the refusal or objection to vaccination is sincerely based on religious grounds and that the opposition is to vaccination in all forms).

Physical or Mental Disorder

- ❑ This waiver is granted by DHS or the Attorney General (if case is in immigration court) after consultation with the Secretary of HHS. It is a discretionary waiver. No USC/LPR family relationship is required to waive the physical or mental disorder bar. Evidence to prove discretionary merit should be submitted.

Form/Documentation

- ❑ I-601;
- ❑ Fee ($265 or fee waiver);
- ❑ G-325A;
- ❑ Evidence of relationship to USC/LPR or principal immigrant if it is a waiver of the communicable disease ground of inadmissibility;
- ❑ Evidence of why vaccinations are not medically appropriate if based on waiver of vaccinations;
- ❑ Evidence of positive discretionary merit if waiver is for a physical or mental disorder.

Unlawful Presence—3/10-Year Bar

Waiver for prior unlawful presence of more than 180 days (three-year bar) or more than one year (10-year bar). This waiver is not required for those unlawfully present who have not deported the United States and are seeking to adjust status.

Eligibility

- ❑ Must have USC/LPR spouse or parent (children not included); and

- ❑ Must show extreme hardship to USC/LPR spouse or parent; and
- ❑ Must prove discretionary merit.

Application/Documentation

- ❑ I-601 application;
- ❑ Filing fee ($265 or fee waiver);
- ❑ Birth certificate of alien (required to establish relationship to USC/LPR parent);
- ❑ Marriage certificate (required to establish relationship to USC/LPR spouse);
- ❑ Translations if foreign language documents;
- ❑ Evidence of USC/LPR status of spouse or parent;
- ❑ Evidence of extreme hardship to USC/LPR spouse or parent including following possible factors:
    - ❑ If there is to be a separation of family members (economic and emotional effect of separation);
    - ❑ If family not to be separated but will return to foreign country, effect of the following:
        - ❑ Loss of employment;
        - ❑ Loss of property;
        - ❑ Separation from community;
        - ❑ Psychological effect of separation from Untied States after long period of residence;
        - ❑ Evidence of long period of residence;
        - ❑ Employment history;
        - ❑ Community ties of USC/LPR family members;
        - ❑ Conditions in foreign country (economic, social, educational, political, health, and other factors impacting family).
- ❑ Evidence of discretionary merit.

APPENDIX 7—SAMPLE MOTION TO CHANGE VENUE

UNITED STATES DEPARTMENT OF JUSTICE
EXECUTIVE OFFICE FOR IMMIGRATION REVIEW
OFFICE OF THE IMMIGRATION JUDGE
HOUSTON, TEXAS

In the Matter of:)
)
(Respondent))
)
File No: A- — ---) **IN REMOVAL PROCEEDINGS**

TO THE HONORABLE IMMIGRATION JUDGE:

MOTION FOR CHANGE OF VENUE

The Respondent, through counsel, hereby submits this motion for change of venue, requesting that venue be changed from the immigration court in Houston, Texas, to the immigration court in Memphis, Tennessee.

1) The Respondent is a juvenile. He is a native and citizen of Haiti born May 4, 1987. He is presently detained by the Department of Homeland Security.

2) He was scheduled for a hearing on the merits of an application for asylum on May 2, 2005, before the immigration court in Houston, Texas. In addition he was given until April 18, 2005, to submit any supplemental documentation in his case. He had been held at the Southwest Key juvenile detention facility on Mesa Road in Houston, Texas.

3) Counsel received notice on April 12, 2005, that the Respondent had been moved from Houston to Jackson Mississippi. (See attached emails). The Respondent will now be held by DHS at the following location under the care of Catholic Charities:

Livingston Group Home
1421 Livingston
Jackson, Mississippi 39202
Phone: 601 960 8644

4) The Respondent will remain at this location for the duration of his immigration case according to the juvenile authorities at the Southwest Key where he was previously detained. In addition, he has been approved for "unaccompanied refugee minor" status (URM) by the Office of Refugee Resettlement (ORR).

5) Counsel is unable to prepare the Respondent for any upcoming hearings and has been unable to complete the supplementation of his application for asylum.

6) The immigration court in Memphis has administrative control over cases from Jackson Mississippi. Counsel has contacted EOIR headquarters in Falls Church, Va. and been informed of this.

Based on the above, counsel requests that venue in this case be transferred from the immigration court in Houston, TX to the immigration court in Memphis, Tennessee. If this request is denied, counsel requests a postponement of the asylum case since he will have to travel to Jackson, Mississippi to prepare the supplemental information for the Respondents asylum claim.

Respectfully Submitted,

____
Joseph A. Vail
University of Houston Law Center
Immigration Clinic

CERTIFICATE OF SERVICE

A copy of this motion was mailed this 15th day of April 2005 by first class mail to the Legal Section, Department of Homeland Security, Immigration and Customs Enforcement, 126 Northpoint, Houston, TX. 77060.

____
Joseph A. Vail

ORDER

The Motion for Change of Venue filed by the Respondent, ________ is **GRANTED**. Venue is changed from the Immigration Court in Houston, TX. to the Immigration Court in Memphis, Tennessee.

____
Immigration Judge
Immigration Court
Houston, TX.

Done this ______ day of April, 2005.

APPENDIX 8—SAMPLE MOTION FOR CONTINUANCE

UNITED STATES DEPARTMENT OF JUSTICE
EXECUTIVE OFFICE FOR IMMIGRATION REVIEW
IMMIGRATION COURT
HOUSTON, TEXAS

In the matter of:	§	**File No.**
	§	
	§	
	§	
	§	
Respondent	§	**In Removal Proceedings**
	§	

MOTION FOR CONTINUANCE OF PROCEEDINGS

To the Honorable Immigration Judge _________:

The Respondent, through counsel, respectfully submits the following Motion for Continuance of Proceedings in the above-referenced case. The basis for this request is the following:

1. Respondent is currently awaiting the final decision of U.S. Citizenship and Immigration Services on her U.S. citizen husband's Immigrant Petition for a Spouse (Form I-130).

2. Respondent received notification of the I-130 denial on February 5, 2005. The Notice of Denial of the I-130 states that Mr. Garcia was scheduled for an interview concerning the I-130 petition and the I-485 application filed by Respondent's husband. However, respondent's husband did not receive notice of the interview.

3. Respondent has filed a Motion to Reconsider Denial of the Petition with USCIS.

4. If USCIS grants the motion, the Respondent will be eligible for adjustment of status as the immediate relative of a U.S. citizen.

5. If USCIS denies the motion, the Court could then go forward with other forms of relief for which the Respondent qualify: cancellation of removal for non–LPRs and, in the alternative, voluntary departure.

6. In making this request Respondent relies on 8 CFR §1240.45, which states that an Immigration Judge may grant a reasonable adjournment for good cause shown. The Respondent has shown good cause for a continuance in these proceedings. The Respondent also relies on *Matter of Velarde,* 23 I&N Dec. 253 (BIA 2002), *Bull v. INS*, 790 F.2d. 869 (11th Cir. 1986), and *Matter of Garcia*, 16 I&N Dec. 623 (BIA 1978), which in pertinent parts state that an Immigration Judge may grant a continuance to permit USCIS to adjudicate an I-130 petition.

7. Respondent is also currently awaiting the final decision of the USCIS on her mother's Application for Naturalization (N-400).

8. Respondent is also waiting for her LPR mother to complete fingerprinting. Respondent's mother was scheduled or fingerprints on March 5, 2005. Respondent's mother was unable to fingerprint, however, because of a cut on her finger. Once the cut is healed, Respondent's mother will reschedule her fingerprinting.

9. If USCIS approves this application, the Respondent will also be eligible for adjustment of status immediately under the 3rd preference category for Mexico as the married daughter. Respondent's March 18, 1993 priority date is current.

10. The likelihood that this application will be approved is high. It would seem a waste of judicial resources and the time of counsel for the DHS and the Respondent to go forward with the scheduling of the merits hearing at this time.

11. INA §245(i) allows an alien to adjust status within the United States even if the alien entered illegally, by grandfathering him or her in. Respondent's LPR mother filed a Visa Petition for Respondent in March of 1993. Accordingly, the Respondent "grandfathered in" under §245(i) and is eligible for adjustment of status within the United States because the Respondent had an application pending prior to April 30, 2001.

Respondent, who is not detained, respectfully requests that the Court reset this Proceeding to a time frame slightly longer then that anticipated for adjudication of the Form I-130, preferably 4–6 months.

Respectfully submitted,

____
Student Representative

____
Attorney at Law

Legal Aid Clinic
University of Houston Law Center
100 Law Center
Houston, Texas 77204-6060
(713) 743-2094
(713) 743-2195 (FAX)

Student Representatives and Attorney for

____

Dated:____________________________

CERTIFICATE OF SERVICE

I hereby certify that on Friday, March 18, 2005, a true and correct copy of the Motion for Continuance of Proceedings and Order was mailed via certified mail to the trial attorney representing the Department of Homeland Security in Immigration Court at 2320 La Branch St., Houston, Texas.

____

Student Attorney
Legal Aid Clinic
University of Houston Law Center
100 Law Center
Houston, Texas 77204-6380
(713) 743-2094
(713) 743-2195 (FAX)

Appendix 9—Sample Motion for Extension of Time

UNITED STATES DEPARTMENT OF JUSTICE
EXECUTIVE OFFICE FOR IMMIGRATION REVIEW
IMMIGRATION COURT
HOUSTON, TEXAS

In the matter of:	§	**File No. A-- --- ---**
	§	
	§	
	§	
Respondent	§	**In Removal Proceedings**
	§	

RESPONDENT'S MOTION FOR EXTENSION OF TIME TO FILE DOCUMENTS

TO THE HONORABLE IMMIGRATION JUDGE:

Respondent, through undersigned counsel, hereby requests an extension of time in which to file her application for adjustment of status in this matter. In support thereof, respondent states the following:

1. Respondent's filing deadline is currently September 30, 2005.
2. Counsel for the respondent was unable to file her application for adjustment of status on the deadline because of the recent hurricane situation.
3. The University of Houston Law Center was closed down from 12 noon on Wednesday, September 22, until Thursday September 29 because of the hurricane.
4. Respondent was unable to meet with counsel during that period in order that all documentation could be finalized. For this reason, the application could not be completed.
5. As a result, counsel seeks a fourteen (14) day extension of time in order to file the application for adjustment of status.

6. Respondent's Hearing on the merits of her application for relief is scheduled for November 1, 2005. Even with the requested extension of time, the application with the supporting documents will be filed three weeks prior to the hearing.

Respectfully submitted this 29th day of September, 2005.

____
Student Representative

____
Attorney at Law
Legal Aid Clinic
University of Houston Law Center
4800 Calhoun
Houston, Texas 77204-6380
(713) 743-2094
(713) 743-2195 (FAX)

Dated: September 29, 2005

CERTIFICATE OF SERVICE

A copy of this motion is being served on the DHS trial attorney by certified mail this 29th day of September, 2005 at the office of the legal section for Immigration Customs and Enforcement (ICE) at 126 Northpoint, Houston, TX. 77060.

____

Signature

Appendix 10—Sample Motion for Prehearing Conference

UNITED STATES DEPARTMENT OF JUSTICE
EXECUTIVE OFFICE FOR IMMIGRATION REVIEW
IMMIGRATION COURT
HOUSTON, TEXAS

In re:	)	
File No: A	)	
	)	
In re:	)	
File No: A	)	
	)	
Respondents	)	**In Removal Proceedings**

REQUEST FOR PREHEARING CONFERENCE

To the Honorable Immigration Judge:

The Respondents are husband and wife. They request a prehearing conference with the Court in accordance with 8 CFR §1003.21 The Respondents are scheduled to go forward on their application for political asylum and request for withholding of removal before the court on March 14, 2000. The Respondents are prepared to go forward. However, the Respondents request to meet with the Court prior to going on the record to discuss the presentation of their cases to the Court.

Each has an individual application; however, each is included in the spouse's application as a possible derivative beneficiary. The applications are based on entirely different facts and legal theories; however, each individual has some information regarding the claim of the spouse and could possibly be called as a witness in the other's case, therefore DHS may wish to invoke the "rule" regarding that spouse's presence in the court during the testimony of the other.

The Respondents request a brief prehearing meeting with the court and DHS counsel prior to going on the record to discuss the following:

a) Order of the presentation of the cases.
b) Whether the cases should be consolidated or separated.
c) The order of the presentation of the witnesses.

It believed that a prehearing conference will shorten the presentation before the court and benefit all parties. If the case of Ms. _____ is approved there would be no need to go forward with the application of Mr. __________ in that he would be eligible (as accompanying or following to join his wife. 8 CFR §208.19. His application will be withdrawn if his wife is approved. It is foreseen that the presentation of his case will last between 2–3 hours.

WHEREFORE, Respondents respectfully request a brief prehearing conference with the court and DHS counsel prior to going on the record on March 14, 2000.

Respectfully Submitted,

____
Student Attorney

____
Student Attorney

____
Joseph A. Vail, Esq.
Supervisory Attorney

CERTIFICATE OF SERVICE

A copy of this motion is being served by certified mail upon the DHS trial attorney (Legal Section) at 126 Northpoint, Houston, TX. 77060 this 13th day of March, 2005.

____
Signature

APPENDIX 11—SAMPLE MOTION FOR PERMISSION TO REPRESENT

UNITED STATES DEPARTMENT OF JUSTICE
EXECUTIVE OFFICE FOR IMMIGRATION REVIEW
IMMIGRATION COURT
HOUSTON, TEXAS

In the matter of:	§	**File No.**
	§	
	§	
	§	
	§	
Respondent	§	**In Removal Proceedings**

MOTION FOR PERMISSION TO REPRESENT RESPONDENT IN REMOVAL PROCEEDINGS BEFORE THE IMMIGRATION COURT

TO THE HONORABLE IMMIGRATION JUDGE:

This motion is submitted in reliance on 8 CFR §292.1(a)(2) to request permission from the Court for __________ to represent __________ in removal proceedings.

In support of this motion, the movant states the following:

1. I, ____________, am enrolled at an accredited law school, the University of Houston Law Center, and enrolled in the Immigration Clinic Program there.
2. I am appearing at the request of Respondent, ______________.
3. I am under the direct supervision of a licensed attorney, ______________, who is also a professor in the Immigration Clinic at The University of Houston Law Center.
4. I am appearing without direct or indirect remuneration from the Respondent.

WHEREFORE, movant prays that the Immigration Judge allow the above named law student to represent the Respondent in the removal proceedings before this court.

Respectfully submitted,

____

Student Representative

____

________________, **ESQ.,** Attorney at Law
TBN ---------
Legal Aid Clinic
University of Houston Law Center
4800 Calhoun
Houston, Texas 77204-6380
(713) 743-2094
(713) 743-2195 (FAX)

Dated: September 25, 2004

CERTIFICATE OF SERVICE

A copy of this motion is being served on the DHS trial attorney by personal service on September 27, 2004, at 15850 Export Plaza, Houston, TX.

____

Signature

APPENDIX 12—SAMPLE MOTION FOR TELEPHONIC TESTIMONY

UNITED STATES DEPARTMENT OF JUSTICE
EXECUTIVE OFFICE FOR IMMIGRATION REVIEW
IMMIGRATION COURT
HOUSTON, TEXAS

In the matter of:	§ § § §	**File No. A -- --- ---**
Respondent	§ §	**In Removal Proceedings**

RESPONDENT'S MOTION FOR WITNESS TO TESTIFY BY TELEPHONE

TO THE HONORABLE JUDGE OF SAID COURT:

Counsel for Respondent hereby files this motion for Witness ___________, M.D. to testify live by telephone at the hearing on the merits, and in support thereof, would respectfully show the Court the following:

1. Dr. _________ is a witness offered for the purposes of: providing his own medical credentials, verifying the authenticity of his medical evaluation of Respondent, providing details as to Respondent's injuries and scarring as observed by him, and offering his medical opinion as to the cause of these injuries.

2. Counsel for the Respondent are providing pro bono representation through the University of Houston Immigration Clinic which has no funds available to pay Dr. __________ for a personal appearance in this Court.

3. Dr. ___________'s testimony is critical to Respondent's case in that it provides evidence to the Court of Respondent's past persecution.

4. Under the INA, aliens in removal proceedings "shall have a reasonable opportunity to…present evidence on the alien's own behalf." INA §240(b)(4)(B). Allowing Respondent's doctor to testify telephonically would be affording Respondent a reasonable opportunity to present medical evidence regarding his persecution suffered.

5. The INA allows for removal proceedings to take place through a telephone conference. INA §240(b)(2)(A)(iii). Thus, it is reasonable for a key witness for Respondent be allowed to testify telephonically—a manner of communication approved under the INA.

6. Oral testimony by telephone has been allowed in federal courts. *See United States v. Sunrhodes*, 831 F.2d 1537, 1539–40 (10th Cir. 1987); *Alderman v. Securities& Exchange Commission*, 104 F.3d 285, 288 n.4 (9th Cir. 1997); *Official Airlines Guides, Inc. v. Chruchfield Publications, Inc.*, 765 F. Supp. 1393, 1398 n.2 (D. Ore. 1990) (overruling objections to telephonic testimony, stating "the telephone testimony was made in open court and under oath. The Court had a greater opportunity to evaluate the credibility of the witness through telephone testimony than through deposition testimony offered by both parties").

7. In immigration proceedings, evidence is not to be admitted where it would be "fundamentally unfair." *Hernandez-Garza v. INS*, 882 F.2d 945 (5th Cir. 1989). Considering that telephonic testimony will provide an opportunity for both direct and cross-examination, under identical circumstances, such testimony is not fundamentally unfair.

WHEREFORE, PREMISES CONSIDERED, Counsel for Respondent respectfully move the Court to allow witness Dr. __________ to testify at Respondent's hearing on the merits by telephone and thus grant this motion. If granted, Dr. ___________ may be reached by dialing XXX-XXX-XXXX.

Respectfully submitted,

____
Student Representative

____
Attorney at Law
Immigration Clinic
100 Law Center, 56 TUII
Houston, Texas 77204
(713) 743-2094

Dated: November 12, 2003

CERTIFICATE OF SERVICE

I hereby certify that a true and correct copy of Respondent's Motion for Witness to Testify by Telephone was served by express mail at the office of the ICE Legal Section 126 Northpoint Houston, TX., 77060 on this 12th day of November 2003.

____
Signature

APPENDIX 13—SAMPLE MOTION TO WITHDRAW

UNITED STATES DEPARTMENT OF JUSTICE
EXECUTIVE OFFICE FOR IMMIGRATION REVIEW
IMMIGRATION COURT
HOUSTON, TEXAS

In the Matter of:	§	**File No. A -- --- ---**
	§	
	§	
	§	
	§	
Respondent	§	**In Removal Proceedings**
	§	

MOTION TO WITHDRAW

To The Honorable Immigration Court:

Counsel for the Respondent, ____________, hereby respectfully requests permission to withdraw as counsel in the above-referenced case pursuant to 8 CFR §1003.17(b). This request is based on the following:

1) Respondent has a merits hearing set for April 5, 2005, on his application for a waiver under §212(h) of the Immigration and Nationality Act (INA) and an application for adjustment of status under §245.

2) The application for relief and available supporting documentation have been timely filed with this Court.

3) Respondent and counsel have had differences of opinion regarding the strategy and procedure to be followed in this case. These differences make it impossible for counsel to effectively represent the Respondent.

4) Counsel has met with Respondent and attempted unsuccessfully to resolve these differences.

5) Counsel has informed Respondent of Counsel's intention to seek permission of this Court to withdraw from Respondent's case. Respondent consents to Counsel's withdrawal.

6) Counsel offered to seek a continuance from this Court should the motion to withdraw be granted. The Respondent does not want a continuance and wishes to proceed with the merits hearing scheduled on

April 5, 2005. He wishes to represent himself on that date if the motion to withdraw is granted.

7) Respondent has been advised of the hearing date and time by Counsel.

8) Respondent has been advised of the need to inform the Court and the Department of Homeland Security of any change of address.

9) Counsel prays therefore that this Honorable Court grant the Motion to Withdraw.

Respectfully Submitted,

____

Attorney for the Respondent
Address

CERTIFICATE OF SERVICE

A copy of this motion is being served upon the DHS trial attorney, Legal Section, at 126 Northpoint, Houston, TX 77060 by certified mail this 17th day of March 2005.

____

Signature

APPENDIX 14—SAMPLE DOCUMENTATION INDEX

UNITED STATES DEPARTMENT OF JUSTICE
EXECUTIVE OFFICE FOR IMMIGRATION REVIEW
IMMIGRATION COURT
HOUSTON, TEXAS

In the matter of:	§	**File No.**
	§	
	§	
	§	
Respondent	§	**In Removal Proceedings**
	§	

DOCUMENTATION INDEX

I. Application for Asylum

- **A. Amended I-589 Application for Asylum, Form E-28, Form G-28** 000008
- **B. Personal Statement of Respondent** 000021
  Respondent details his own past persecution and his well-founded fear of future persecution by the Cameroonian government.
- **C. Witness List** 000035

II. Immigration and Identification Documentation

- **D. Passport and I-94 of Respondent** 000037
  Issued April 17, 2002. Respondent admitted May 1, 2002, in Houston on a visitor's visa.

III. Supporting Personal Documentation

- **E. Psychological Evaluation by Joy Breckenridge, Ph.D.** 000045
  Report dated October 13 and 20, 2003, based on mental health assessment of Respondent. Dr. Breckenridge's Curriculam Vitae is also included.
- **F. Medical Report and Explanation from Patrick McColloster, M.D.** 000053
  Report dated October 22, 2003, based on his physical examination of Respondent on October 1, 2003.
- **G. Medical Certificate from Dr. Fabian Meh-Kum, M.D.** 000056
  Medical report dated April 26, 2002, based on physical examination of Respondent following his release from prison in April of 2002. Respondent admitted on April 21, 2002, and released on April 26, 2002. Report notes a severe cough, respiratory distress, wasted appearance, severe dehydration, scars on back and soles of feet, pneumonia, and gastroenteritis.

H. **SCNC Membership Card** 000057
Membership date, June 19, 1999.

I. **Notification of Release from Jail** 000058
Notification of release from Central Prison Buea for imprisonment of the Respondent from February 10, 2001 until April 21, 2002. Respondent was released on bail and was to appear in court on April 30, 2002.

J. **Statement of Humanitarian Assistance to Respondent from Human Rights Defense Group** 000059
Branch Chairman for the Human Rights Defense Group of the Douala branch states that the Respondent is a Human Rights Activist who investigated and reported on Cameroon prisons in 2000.

K. **Statement of Declaration of Imminent Danger of Persecution of Respondent by the Southern Cameroons National Council Chairman** 000062
S.C.N.C. Douala Chapter Chairman states that Respondent was an active participant in S.C.N.C. activities, was responsible for campaigning in Manyu, and was arrested on February 10, 2001.

L. **Statement from Christopher Besong, Southern Cameroons National Council, Douala Chapter Chairman** 000063
Describes his personal knowledge of Respondent's arrest on February 10, 2001, at a rally where Mr. Besong was also present.

M. **Statement of Kum Peter for the Respondent** 000064
States that he received a call from Respondent, while working in the Human Rights Defense Group office, during which Respondent was crying and said he had been badly injured when his home was attacked by the police.

N. **Statement of Moses Ayuk of the Human Rights Defense Group** 000065
Written to Mr. Ngoh Thomas. States that he was present in the Human Rights Defense Group office when they were notified by phone of the attack on Respondent. States that photos were taken of Respondent, and that a report of the incident was made. Describes the injuries to Respondent and the subsequent hiding of Respondent's family out of fear.

O. **Statement of Ngoh Thomas Mudoh, Douala Chairman for the Human Rights Defense Group** 000067
States that the Human Rights Defense Group went to Respondent's home after he was attacked, took pictures, and made a report. Describes Respondent's participation in documenting and reporting the abuse suffered by prisoners.

P. **Photos of Respondent's Injuries from August 2000 Attack** 000069
Photos of Respondent and his cousin Jonas Mbah taken by members of the Human Rights Defense Group immediately following an attack on Respondent by the police.

Q. Statement from Ashuntantang Tanjong, Esq., Attorney for Respondent 000070
Affidavit states his personal knowledge of Respondent's various arrests and mistreatment. It also states his knowledge of the harm and imprisonment of Respondent's wife after Respondent fled to the United States.

R. Letter from Alvine Angieb, Respondent's Wife 000073
States her knowledge of Respondent's mistreatment, harm, arrest, and imprisonment at the hands of the police loyal to the Biya government.

S. Photo of Alvine Angieb, Respondent's Wife 000074
Photo was taken after Respondent came to the United Stattes and immediately following Ms. Angieb's release from jail where she suffered harm by the police who were looking for Respondent.

T. Bail Form 000075
Shows the application for bail on behalf of Respondent, on April 21, 2002, signed by Mr. Enow Zachius, relative of Respondent.

U. Affidavit of Chief Enow Zachius 000076
Attests that he signed the bail form that allowed for Respondent's release. States that bringing about Respondent's release involved some of his personal friends who are also Government officials. States that a senior police commissioner at the Douala airport helped him get Respondent past normal security so that Respondent could leave the country.

V. Statement of Lefang Ulrich, Respondent's Cousin 000078
Describes his conversations with Respondent's wife during Respondent's imprisonment. States that he advised Respondent's wife to try to get Respondent out of jail before his court date so that he would not be transferred to a higher security prison. Describes Respondent's physical state after being released. States that he advised Respondent to leave the country before his court date.

IV. Southern Cameroons National Council (SCNC) and Members' Treatment in Cameroon

W. Various SCNC Materials 000080
Examples of SCNC materials and publications.

X. Photo of Water Cannons 000086
Photo taken by Lefang Ulrich, witness, of the water cannons used by Cameroonian forces to disperse SCNC rallies.

Y. "Cameroon: Human Rights Defender and Political Activists are Arrested and Held in Prison." 000087

Amnesty International, October 25, 2002
States that a member of the Human Rights Defense Group (HRDG) was arrested for speaking out about the right to self-determination of

Anglophones and for acting as an SCNC advisor; political detainees are routinely tortured or ill-treated; there is severe overcrowding, poor hygiene and ventilation, and inadequate food and medical care in the prisons.

Z. The World Factbook 2002 000089
The Southern Cameroon National Council and the Human Rights Defense Group are political pressure groups in Cameroon.

AA. Fear of Torture and Ill-Treatment; Harsh Prison Conditions 000098

Amnesty International Bulletin, January 20, 2000
Cites several instances over a five-year time period in which SCNC members have been targeted, harmed, and/or arrested. Cites instances of SCNC political prisoners dying due to the harsh prison conditions.

V. Treatment of Dissidents and Political Prisoners in Cameroon, Background Documentation

BB. Amnesty International Report Cameroon 2002 000100
Security forces continued to use excessive, sometimes lethal, force in operations to disperse demonstrations and suppress freedom of expression. Political prisoners suffered from serious health problems as a result of poor prison conditions and prolonged confinement in darkness. They continued to be denied access to adequate medical treatment.

CC. Amnesty International Report Cameroon 2001 000102
In February the UN Special Rapporteur on torture published a report in which he described the practice of torture in Cameroon as "systematic and widespread."

DD. Amnesty International Report Cameroon 2000 000104
Conditions in prisons remained extremely harsh and amounted to cruel, inhuman, and degrading treatment. In most prisons, prisoners under sentence of death were kept with their feet chained. Severe overcrowding, poor hygiene and ventilation, inadequate food and lack of medical care resulted in a high mortality rate. The Central Prison was designed to hold 800 prisoners and held 2,700 prisoners in mid-1999.

EE. "Cameroon: Security forces must respect human rights in reaction to political demonstrations." 000108

Amnesty International, October 4, 2001
States that many people were injured when the police used firearms to disperse a nonviolent demonstration.

FF. "Cameroon: Impunity in face of large-scale extrajudicial executions in Douala." 000110

Amnesty International, December 4, 2000

States that a mass grave was discovered with more than 36 bodies near Douala. Many bodies have been found bearing signs of torture and bullet wounds. Speaks of the Cameroonian government's unwillingness to bring an end to torture and extrajudicial executions.

GG. Protectors or Pretenders? Government Human Rights Commissions in Africa: Cameroon. 000112

Human Rights Watch, 2001
Security forces have been responsible for torture and harassment of the political opposition and local human rights activists.

V. Current Country Conditions

HH. U.S. State Department Human Rights Report, 2002 000114
The Cameroonian government has a poor human rights record. Security forces continue to commit numerous serious abuses, such as use of excessive lethal force, unlawful killings, and limits of freedom of press, speech, and movement. Prison conditions remain harsh and life threatening, such as overcrowded and unsanitary prisons.

II. Amnesty International Report Cameroon 2003 000138
Security forces continue to mistreat political activists in police stations. Members of the SCNC were arrested and detained without trial for weeks. Human rights defenders and independent journalists were harassed and intimidated by the security forces. Offices of human rights defenders and opponents were routinely searched and documents confiscated without explanation. Suspects held in custody were subject to torture, and cruel, inhumane, and degrading treatment such as being beat on the soles of feet. Cites the distribution of leaflets calling for the independence of Southern Cameroon as a reason for arrest.

Respectfully submitted,

____

____

____

JOSEPH A. VAIL, ESQ., Attorney at Law
TBC#
Immigration Clinic
University of Houston Law Center
100 Law Center, 56 TU II
Houston, Texas 77204-6060
(713) 743-2094 / (713) 743-2195 (FAX)
Student Representatives and Attorney for
____

Dated: November 4, 2003

APPENDIX 15—SAMPLE CERTIFICATE OF TRANSLATION

I, ___________________, fluent in English and Spanish, state that the attached is a true and correct translation of the birth certificate included with this translation from the Spanish to the English language.

____
Name

____

____
Address

____
Phone number

Date:

APPENDIX 16—SAMPLE CERTIFICATE OF SERVICE

A copy of the application for adjustment of status for__________ was mailed to the DHS Legal Section at 126 Northpoint, Houston, TX 77060, by certified mail on March 23, 2004.

____
Name
University of Houston
Immigration Law Clinic
Houston, TX 77204-6391

APPENDIX 17—MEISSNER PROSECUTORIAL DISCRETION MEMO

U.S. Department of Justice
Immigration and Naturalization Service

HQOPP 50/4

Office of the Commissioner

425 I Street NW
Washington, DC 20536

NOV 17 2000

MEMORANDUM TO REGIONAL DIRECTORS
DISTRICT DIRECTORS
CHIEF PATROL AGENTS
REGIONAL AND DISTRICT COUNSEL

FROM: Doris Meissner
Commissioner
Immigration and Naturalization Service

SUBJECT: Exercising Prosecutorial Discretion

Since the 1996 amendments to the Immigration and Nationality Act (INA) which limited the authority of immigration judges to provide relief from removal in many cases, there has been increased attention to the scope and exercise of the Immigration and Naturalization Service's (INS or the Service) prosecutorial discretion. This memorandum describes the principles with which INS exercises prosecutorial discretion and the process to be followed in making and monitoring discretionary decisions. Service officers are not only authorized by law but expected to exercise discretion in a judicious manner at all stages of the enforcement process–from planning investigations to enforcing final orders–subject to their chains of command and to the particular responsibilities and authority applicable to their specific position. In exercising this discretion, officers must take into account the principles described below in order to promote the efficient and effective enforcement of the immigration laws and the interests of justice.

More specific guidance geared to exercising discretion in particular program areas already exists in some instances,[1] and other program-specific guidance will follow separately.

[1] For example, standards and procedures for placing an alien in deferred action status are provided in the Standard Operating Procedures for Enforcement Officers: Arrest, Detention, Processing, and Removal (Standard Operating Procedures), Part X. This memorandum is intended to provide general principles, and does not replace any previous specific guidance provided about particular INS actions, such as "Supplemental Guidelines on the Use of Cooperating Individuals and Confidential Informants Following the Enactment of IIRIRA," dated December 29, 1997. This memorandum is not intended to address every situation in which the exercise of prosecutorial discretion may be appropriate. If INS personnel in the exercise of their duties recognize apparent conflict between any of their specific policy requirements and these general guidelines, they are encouraged to bring the matter to their supervisor's attention, and any conflict between policies should be raised through the appropriate chain of command for resolution.

Memorandum for Regional Directors, et al. Page 2
Subject: Exercising Prosecutorial Discretion

However, INS officers should continue to exercise their prosecutorial discretion in appropriate cases during the period before more specific program guidance is issued.

A statement of principles concerning discretion serves a number of important purposes. As described in the "Principles of Federal Prosecution,"[2] part of the U.S. Attorneys' manual, such principles provide convenient reference points for the process of making prosecutorial decisions; facilitate the task of training new officers in the discharge of their duties; contribute to more effective management of the Government's limited prosecutorial resources by promoting greater consistency among the prosecutorial activities of different offices and between their activities and the INS' law enforcement priorities; make possible better coordination of investigative and prosecutorial activity by enhancing the understanding between the investigative and prosecutorial components; and inform the public of the careful process by which prosecutorial decisions are made.

Legal and Policy Background

"Prosecutorial discretion" is the authority of an agency charged with enforcing a law to decide whether to enforce, or not to enforce, the law against someone. The INS, like other law enforcement agencies, has prosecutorial discretion and exercises it every day. In the immigration context, the term applies not only to the decision to issue, serve, or file a Notice to Appear (NTA), but also to a broad range of other discretionary enforcement decisions, including among others: Focusing investigative resources on particular offenses or conduct; deciding whom to stop, question, and arrest; maintaining an alien in custody; seeking expedited removal or other forms of removal by means other than a removal proceeding; settling or dismissing a proceeding; granting deferred action or staying a final order; agreeing to voluntary departure, withdrawal of an application for admission, or other action in lieu of removing the alien; pursuing an appeal; and executing a removal order.

The "favorable exercise of prosecutorial discretion" means a discretionary decision not to assert the full scope of the INS' enforcement authority as permitted under the law. Such decisions will take different forms, depending on the status of a particular matter, but include decisions such as not issuing an NTA (discussed in more detail below under "Initiating Proceedings"), not detaining an alien placed in proceedings (where discretion remains despite mandatory detention requirements), and approving deferred action.

---

[2] For this discussion, and much else in this memorandum, we have relied heavily upon the Principles of Federal Prosecution, chapter 9-27.000 in the U.S. Department of Justice's United States Attorneys' Manual (Oct. 1997). There are significant differences, of course, between the role of the U.S. Attorneys' offices in the criminal justice system, and INS responsibilities to enforce the immigration laws, but the general approach to prosecutorial discretion stated in this memorandum reflects that taken by the Principles of Federal Prosecution.

Courts recognize that prosecutorial discretion applies in the civil, administrative arena just as it does in criminal law. Moreover, the Supreme Court "has recognized on several occasions over many years that an agency's decision not to prosecute or enforce, whether through civil or criminal process, is a decision generally committed to an agency's absolute discretion." Heckler v. Chaney, 470 U.S. 821, 831 (1985). Both Congress and the Supreme Court have recently reaffirmed that the concept of prosecutorial discretion applies to INS enforcement activities, such as whether to place an individual in deportation proceedings. INA section 242(g); Reno v. American-Arab Anti-Discrimination Committee, 525 U.S. 471 (1999). The "discretion" in prosecutorial discretion means that prosecutorial decisions are not subject to judicial review or reversal, except in extremely narrow circumstances. Consequently, it is a powerful tool that must be used responsibly.

As a law enforcement agency, the INS generally has prosecutorial discretion within its area of law enforcement responsibility unless that discretion has been clearly limited by statute in a way that goes beyond standard terminology. For example, a statute directing that the INS "shall" remove removable aliens would not be construed by itself to limit prosecutorial discretion, but the specific limitation on releasing certain criminal aliens in section 236(c)(2) of the INA evidences a specific congressional intention to limit discretion not to detain certain criminal aliens in removal proceedings that would otherwise exist. Personnel who are unsure whether the INS has discretion to take a particular action should consult their supervisor and legal counsel to the extent necessary.

It is important to recognize not only what prosecutorial discretion is, but also what it is not. The doctrine of prosecutorial discretion applies to law enforcement decisions whether, and to what extent, to exercise the coercive power of the Government over liberty or property, as authorized by law in cases when individuals have violated the law. Prosecutorial discretion does not apply to affirmative acts of approval, or grants of benefits, under a statute or other applicable law that provides requirements for determining when the approval should be given. For example, the INS has prosecutorial discretion not to place a removable alien in proceedings, but it does not have prosecutorial discretion to approve a naturalization application by an alien who is ineligible for that benefit under the INA.

This distinction is not always an easy, bright-line rule to apply. In many cases, INS decisionmaking involves both a prosecutorial decision to take or not to take enforcement action, such as placing an alien in removal proceedings, and a decision whether or not the alien is substantively eligible for a benefit under the INA. In many cases, benefit decisions involve the exercise of significant discretion which in some cases is not judicially reviewable, but which is not prosecutorial discretion.

Prosecutorial discretion can extend only up to the substantive and jurisdictional limits of the law. It can never justify an action that is illegal under the substantive law pertaining to the conduct, or one that while legal in other contexts, is not within the authority of the agency or officer taking it. Prosecutorial discretion to take an enforcement action does not modify or waive any legal requirements that apply to the action itself. For example, an enforcement decision to focus on certain types of immigration violators for arrest and removal does not mean that the INS may arrest any person without probable cause to do so for an offense within its jurisdiction. Service officers who are in doubt whether a particular action complies with applicable constitutional, statutory, or case law requirements should consult with their supervisor and obtain advice from the district or sector counsel or representative of the Office of General Counsel to the extent necessary.

Finally, exercising prosecutorial discretion does not lessen the INS' commitment to enforce the immigration laws to the best of our ability. It is not an invitation to violate or ignore the law. Rather, it is a means to use the resources we have in a way that best accomplishes our mission of administering and enforcing the immigration laws of the United States.

Principles of Prosecutorial Discretion

Like all law enforcement agencies, the INS has finite resources, and it is not possible to investigate and prosecute all immigration violations. The INS historically has responded to this limitation by setting priorities in order to achieve a variety of goals. These goals include protecting public safety, promoting the integrity of the legal immigration system, and deterring violations of the immigration law.

It is an appropriate exercise of prosecutorial discretion to give priority to investigating, charging, and prosecuting those immigration violations that will have the greatest impact on achieving these goals. The INS has used this principle in the design and execution of its border enforcement strategy, its refocus on criminal smuggling networks, and its concentration on fixing benefit-granting processes to prevent fraud. An agency's focus on maximizing its impact under appropriate principles, rather than devoting resources to cases that will do less to advance these overall interests, is a crucial element in effective law enforcement management.

The Principles of Federal Prosecution governing the conduct of U.S. Attorneys use the concept of a "substantial Federal interest." A U.S. Attorney may properly decline a prosecution if "*no substantial Federal interest would be served by prosecution.*" This principle provides a useful frame of reference for the INS, although applying it presents challenges that differ from those facing a U.S. Attorney. In particular, as immigration is an exclusively Federal responsibility, the option of an adequate alternative remedy under state law is not available. In an immigration case, the interest at stake will always be Federal. Therefore, we must place particular emphasis on the element of substantiality. <u>How important is the Federal interest in the case, as compared to other cases and priorities</u>? That is the overriding question, and answering it requires examining a number of factors that may differ according to the stage of the case.

Memorandum for Regional Directors, et al. Page 5
Subject: Exercising Prosecutorial Discretion

As a general matter, INS officers may decline to prosecute a legally sufficient immigration case if the Federal immigration enforcement interest that would be served by prosecution is not substantial.[3] Except as may be provided specifically in other policy statements or directives, the responsibility for exercising prosecutorial discretion in this manner rests with the District Director (DD) or Chief Patrol Agent (CPA) based on his or her common sense and sound judgment.[4] The DD or CPA should obtain legal advice from the District or Sector Counsel to the extent that such advice may be necessary and appropriate to ensure the sound and lawful exercise of discretion, particularly with respect to cases pending before the Executive Office for Immigration Review (EOIR).[5] The DD's or CPA's authority may be delegated to the extent necessary and proper, except that decisions not to place a removable alien in removal proceedings, or decisions to move to terminate a proceeding which in the opinion of the District or Sector Counsel is legally sufficient, may not be delegated to an officer who is not authorized under 8 C.F.R. § 239.1 to issue an NTA. A DD's or CPA's exercise of prosecutorial discretion will not normally be reviewed by Regional or Headquarters authority. However, DDs and CPAs remain subject to their chains of command and may be supervised as necessary in their exercise of prosecutorial discretion.

Investigations

Priorities for deploying investigative resources are discussed in other documents, such as the interior enforcement strategy, and will not be discussed in detail in this memorandum. These previously identified priorities include identifying and removing criminal and terrorist aliens, deterring and dismantling alien smuggling, minimizing benefit fraud and document abuse, responding to community complaints about illegal immigration and building partnerships to solve local problems, and blocking and removing employers' access to undocumented workers. Even within these broad priority areas, however, the Service must make decisions about how best to expend its resources.

Managers should plan and design operations to maximize the likelihood that serious offenders will be identified. Supervisors should ensure that front-line investigators understand that it is not mandatory to issue an NTA in every case where they have reason to believe that an alien is removable, and agents should be encouraged to bring questionable cases to a supervisor's attention. Operational planning for investigations should include consideration of appropriate procedures for supervisory and legal review of individual NTA issuing decisions.

---

[3] In some cases even a substantial immigration enforcement interest in prosecuting a case could be outweighed by other interests, such as the foreign policy of the United States. Decisions that require weighing such other interests should be made at the level of responsibility within the INS or the Department of Justice that is appropriate in light of the circumstances and interests involved.

[4] This general reference to DDs and CPAs is not intended to exclude from coverage by this memorandum other INS personnel, such as Service Center directors, who may be called upon to exercise prosecutorial discretion and do not report to DDs or CPAs, or to change any INS chains of command.

[5] Exercising prosecutorial discretion with respect to cases pending before EOIR involves procedures set forth at 8 CFR 239.2 and 8 CFR Part 3, such as obtaining the court's approval of a motion to terminate proceedings.

Memorandum for Regional Directors, et al. Page 6
Subject: Exercising Prosecutorial Discretion

Careful design of enforcement operations is a key element in the INS' exercise of prosecutorial discretion. Managers should consider not simply whether a particular effort is legally supportable, but whether it best advances the INS' goals, compared with other possible uses of those resources. As a general matter, investigations that are specifically focused to identify aliens who represent a high priority for removal should be favored over investigations which, by their nature, will identify a broader variety of removable aliens. Even an operation that is designed based on high-priority criteria, however, may still identify individual aliens who warrant a favorable exercise of prosecutorial discretion.[6]

Initiating and Pursuing Proceedings

Aliens who are subject to removal may come to the Service's attention in a variety of ways. For example, some aliens are identified as a result of INS investigations, while others are identified when they apply for immigration benefits or seek admission at a port-of-entry. While the context in which the INS encounters an alien may, as a practical matter, affect the Service's options, it does not change the underlying principle that the INS has discretion and should exercise that discretion appropriately given the circumstances of the case.

Even when an immigration officer has reason to believe that an alien is removable and that there is sufficient evidence to obtain a final order of removal, it may be appropriate to decline to proceed with that case. This is true even when an alien is removable based on his or her criminal history and when the alien–if served with an NTA–would be subject to mandatory detention. The INS may exercise its discretion throughout the enforcement process. Thus, the INS can choose whether to issue an NTA, whether to cancel an NTA prior to filing with the immigration court or move for dismissal in immigration court (under 8 CFR 239.2), whether to detain (for those aliens not subject to mandatory detention), whether to offer an alternative to removal such as voluntary departure or withdrawal of an application for admission, and whether to stay an order of deportation.

The decision to exercise any of these options or other alternatives in a particular case requires an individualized determination, based on the facts and the law. As a general matter, it is better to exercise favorable discretion as early in the process as possible, once the relevant facts have been determined, in order to conserve the Service's resources and in recognition of the alien's interest in avoiding unnecessary legal proceedings. However, there is often a conflict

---

[6] For example, operations in county jails are designed to identify and remove criminal aliens, a high priority for the Service. Nonetheless, an investigator working at a county jail and his or her supervisor should still consider whether the exercise of prosecutorial discretion would be appropriate in individual cases.

between making decisions as soon as possible, and making them based on evaluating as many relevant, credible facts as possible. Developing an extensive factual record prior to making a charging decision may itself consume INS resources in a way that negates any saving from forgoing a removal proceeding.

Generally, adjudicators may have a better opportunity to develop a credible factual record at an earlier stage than investigative or other enforcement personnel. It is simply not practicable to require officers at the arrest stage to develop a full investigative record on the equities of each case (particularly since the alien file may not yet be available to the charging office), and this memorandum does not require such an analysis. Rather, what is needed is knowledge that the INS is not legally required to institute proceedings in every case, openness to that possibility in appropriate cases, development of facts relevant to the factors discussed below to the extent that it is reasonably possible to do so under the circumstances and in the timeframe that decisions must be made, and implementation of any decision to exercise prosecutorial discretion.

There is no precise formula for identifying which cases warrant a favorable exercise of discretion. Factors that should be taken into account in deciding whether to exercise prosecutorial discretion include, but are not limited to, the following:

- Immigration status: Lawful permanent residents generally warrant greater consideration. However, other removable aliens may also warrant the favorable exercise of discretion, depending on all the relevant circumstances.
- Length of residence in the United States: The longer an alien has lived in the United States, particularly in legal status, the more this factor may be considered a positive equity.
- Criminal history: Officers should take into account the nature and severity of any criminal conduct, as well as the time elapsed since the offense occurred and evidence of rehabilitation. It is appropriate to take into account the actual sentence or fine that was imposed, as an indicator of the seriousness attributed to the conduct by the court. Other factors relevant to assessing criminal history include the alien's age at the time the crime was committed and whether or not he or she is a repeat offender.
- Humanitarian concerns: Relevant humanitarian concerns include, but are not limited to, family ties in the United States; medical conditions affecting the alien or the alien's family; the fact that an alien entered the United States at a very young age; ties to one's home country (e.g., whether the alien speaks the language or has relatives in the home country); extreme youth or advanced age; and home country conditions.
- Immigration history: Aliens without a past history of violating the immigration laws (particularly violations such as reentering after removal, failing to appear at hearing, or resisting arrest that show heightened disregard for the legal process) warrant favorable consideration to a greater extent than those with such a history. The seriousness of any such violations should also be taken into account.

Memorandum for Regional Directors, et al.
Subject: Exercising Prosecutorial Discretion

Page 8

- Likelihood of ultimately removing the alien: Whether a removal proceeding would have a reasonable likelihood of ultimately achieving its intended effect, in light of the case circumstances such as the alien's nationality, is a factor that should be considered.
- Likelihood of achieving enforcement goal by other means: In many cases, the alien's departure from the United States may be achieved more expeditiously and economically by means other than removal, such as voluntary return, withdrawal of an application for admission, or voluntary departure.
- Whether the alien is eligible or is likely to become eligible for other relief: Although not determinative on its own, it is relevant to consider whether there is a legal avenue for the alien to regularize his or her status if not removed from the United States. The fact that the Service cannot confer complete or permanent relief, however, does not mean that discretion should not be exercised favorably if warranted by other factors.
- Effect of action on future admissibility: The effect an action such as removal may have on an alien can vary–for example, a time-limited as opposed to an indefinite bar to future admissibility–and these effects may be considered.
- Current or past cooperation with law enforcement authorities: Current or past cooperation with the INS or other law enforcement authorities, such as the U.S. Attorneys, the Department of Labor, or National Labor Relations Board, among others, weighs in favor of discretion.
- Honorable U.S. military service: Military service with an honorable discharge should be considered as a favorable factor. See Standard Operating Procedures Part V.D.8 (issuing an NTA against current or former member of armed forces requires advance approval of Regional Director).
- Community attention: Expressions of opinion, in favor of or in opposition to removal, may be considered, particularly for relevant facts or perspectives on the case that may not have been known to or considered by the INS. Public opinion or publicity (including media or congressional attention) should not, however, be used to justify a decision that cannot be supported on other grounds. Public and professional responsibility will sometimes require the choice of an unpopular course.
- Resources available to the INS: As in planning operations, the resources available to the INS to take enforcement action in the case, compared with other uses of the resources to fulfill national or regional priorities, are an appropriate factor to consider, but it should not be determinative. For example, when prosecutorial discretion should be favorably exercised under these factors in a particular case, that decision should prevail even if there is detention space available.

Obviously, not all of the factors will be applicable to every case, and in any particular case one factor may deserve more weight than it might in another case. There may be other factors, not on the list above, that are appropriate to consider. The decision should be based on the totality of the circumstances, not on any one factor considered in isolation. General guidance such as this cannot provide a "bright line" test that may easily be applied to determine the "right" answer in every case. In many cases, minds reasonably can differ, different factors may point in different directions, and there is no clearly "right" answer. Choosing a course of action in difficult cases must be an exercise of judgment by the responsible officer based on his or her experience, good sense, and consideration of the relevant factors to the best of his or her ability.

There are factors that may not be considered. Impermissible factors include:

- An individual's race, religion, sex, national origin, or political association, activities or beliefs;[7]
- The officer's own personal feelings regarding the individual; or
- The possible effect of the decision on the officer's own professional or personal circumstances.

In many cases, the procedural posture of the case, and the state of the factual record, will affect the ability of the INS to use prosecutorial discretion. For example, since the INS cannot admit an inadmissible alien to the United States unless a waiver is available, in many cases the INS' options are more limited in the admission context at a port-of-entry than in the deportation context.

Similarly, the INS may consider the range of options and information likely to be available at a later time. For example, an officer called upon to make a charging decision may reasonably determine that he or she does not have a sufficient, credible factual record upon which to base a favorable exercise of prosecutorial discretion not to put the alien in proceedings, that the record cannot be developed in the timeframe in which the decision must be made, that a more informed prosecutorial decision likely could be made at a later time during the course of proceedings, and that if the alien is not served with an NTA now, it will be difficult or impossible to do so later.

Such decisions must be made, however, with due regard for the principles of these guidelines, and in light of the other factors discussed here. For example, if there is no relief available to the alien in a removal proceeding and the alien is subject to mandatory detention if

[7] This general guidance on factors that should not be relied upon in making a decision whether to enforce the law against an individual is not intended to prohibit their consideration to the extent they are directly relevant to an alien's status under the immigration laws or eligibility for a benefit. For example, religion and political beliefs are often directly relevant in asylum cases and need to be assessed as part of a prosecutorial determination regarding the strength of the case, but it would be improper for an INS officer to treat aliens differently based on his personal opinion about a religion or belief. Political activities may be relevant to a ground of removal on national security or terrorism grounds. An alien's nationality often directly affects his or her eligibility for adjustment or other relief, the likelihood that he or she can be removed, or the availability of prosecutorial options such as voluntary return, and may be considered to the extent these concerns are pertinent.

placed in proceedings, that situation suggests that the exercise of prosecutorial discretion, if appropriate, would be more useful to the INS if done sooner rather than later. It would be improper for an officer to assume that someone else at some later time will always be able to make a more informed decision, and therefore never to consider exercising discretion.

Factors relevant to exercising prosecutorial discretion may come to the Service's attention in various ways. For example, aliens may make requests to the INS to exercise prosecutorial discretion by declining to pursue removal proceedings. Alternatively, there may be cases in which an alien asks to be put in proceedings (for example, to pursue a remedy such as cancellation of removal that may only be available in that forum). In either case, the INS may consider the request, but the fact that it is made should not determine the outcome, and the prosecutorial decision should be based upon the facts and circumstances of the case. Similarly, the fact that an alien has not requested prosecutorial discretion should not influence the analysis of the case. Whether, and to what extent, any request should be considered is also a matter of discretion. Although INS officers should be open to new facts and arguments, attempts to exploit prosecutorial discretion as a delay tactic, as a means merely to revisit matters that have been thoroughly considered and decided, or for other improper tactical reasons should be rejected. There is no legal right to the exercise of prosecutorial discretion, and (as stated at the close of this memorandum) this memorandum creates no right or obligation enforceable at law by any alien or any other party.

Process for Decisions

Identification of Suitable Cases

No single process of exercising discretion will fit the multiple contexts in which the need to exercise discretion may arise. Although this guidance is designed to promote consistency in the application of the immigration laws, it is not intended to produce rigid uniformity among INS officers in all areas of the country at the expense of the fair administration of the law. Different offices face different conditions and have different requirements. Service managers and supervisors, including DDs and CPAs, and Regional, District, and Sector Counsel must develop mechanisms appropriate to the various contexts and priorities, keeping in mind that it is better to exercise discretion as early in process as possible once the factual record has been identified.[8] In particular, in cases where it is clear that no statutory relief will be available at the immigration hearing and where detention will be mandatory, it best conserves the Service's resources to make a decision early.

Enforcement and benefits personnel at all levels should understand that prosecutorial discretion exists and that it is appropriate and expected that the INS will exercise this authority in appropriate cases. DDs, CPAs, and other supervisory officials (such as District and

---

[8] DDs, CPAs, and other INS personnel should also be open, however, to possible reconsideration of decisions (either for or against the exercise of discretion) based upon further development of the facts.

Sector Counsels) should encourage their personnel to bring potentially suitable cases for the favorable exercise of discretion to their attention for appropriate resolution. To assist in exercising their authority, DDs and CPAs may wish to convene a group to provide advice on difficult cases that have been identified as potential candidates for prosecutorial discretion.

It is also appropriate for DDs and CPAs to develop a list of "triggers" to help their personnel identify cases at an early stage that may be suitable for the exercise of prosecutorial discretion. These cases should then be reviewed at a supervisory level where a decision can be made as to whether to proceed in the ordinary course of business, to develop additional facts, or to recommend a favorable exercise of discretion. Such triggers could include the following facts (whether proven or alleged):

Lawful permanent residents;
Aliens with a serious health condition;
Juveniles;
Elderly aliens;
Adopted children of U.S. citizens;
U.S. military veterans;
Aliens with lengthy presence in United States (i.e., 10 years or more); or
Aliens present in the United States since childhood.

Since workloads and the type of removable aliens encountered may vary significantly both within and between INS offices, this list of possible trigger factors for supervisory review is intended neither to be comprehensive nor mandatory in all situations. Nor is it intended to suggest that the presence or absence of "trigger" facts should itself determine whether prosecutorial discretion should be exercised, as compared to review of all the relevant factors as discussed elsewhere in these guidelines. Rather, development of trigger criteria is intended solely as a suggested means of facilitating identification of potential cases that may be suitable for prosecutorial review as early as possible in the process.

Documenting Decisions

When a DD or CPA decides to exercise prosecutorial discretion favorably, that decision should be clearly documented in the alien file, including the specific decision taken and its factual and legal basis. DDs and CPAs may also document decisions based on a specific set of facts not to exercise prosecutorial discretion favorably, but this is not required by this guidance.

The alien should also be informed in writing of a decision to exercise prosecutorial discretion favorably, such as not placing him or her in removal proceedings or not pursuing a case. This normally should be done by letter to the alien and/or his or her attorney of record, briefly stating the decision made and its consequences. It is not necessary to recite the facts of the case or the INS' evaluation of the facts in such letters. Although the specifics of the letter will vary depending on the circumstances of the case and the action taken, it must make it clear to the alien that exercising prosecutorial discretion does not confer any immigration status, ability to travel to the United States (unless the alien applies for and receives advance parole), immunity from future removal proceedings, or any enforceable right or benefit upon the alien. If, however, there is a potential benefit that is linked to the action (for example, the availability of employment authorization for beneficiaries of deferred action), it is appropriate to identify it.

The obligation to notify an individual is limited to situations in which a specific, identifiable decision to refrain from action is taken in a situation in which the alien normally would expect enforcement action to proceed. For example, it is not necessary to notify aliens that the INS has refrained from focusing investigative resources on them, but a specific decision not to proceed with removal proceedings against an alien who has come into INS custody should be communicated to the alien in writing. This guideline is not intended to replace existing standard procedures or forms for deferred action, voluntary return, voluntary departure, or other currently existing and standardized processes involving prosecutorial discretion.

Future Impact

An issue of particular complexity is the future effect of prosecutorial discretion decisions in later encounters with the alien. Unlike the criminal context, in which statutes of limitation and venue requirements often preclude one U.S. Attorney's office from prosecuting an offense that another office has declined, immigration violations are continuing offenses that, as a general principle of immigration law, continue to make an alien legally removable regardless of a decision not to pursue removal on a previous occasion. An alien may come to the attention of the INS in the future through seeking admission or in other ways. An INS office should abide by a favorable prosecutorial decision taken by another office as a matter of INS policy, absent new facts or changed circumstances. However, if a removal proceeding is transferred from one INS district to another, the district assuming responsibility for the case is not bound by the charging district's decision to proceed with an NTA, if the facts and circumstances at a later stage suggest that a favorable exercise of prosecutorial discretion is appropriate.

Service offices should review alien files for information on previous exercises of prosecutorial discretion at the earliest opportunity that is practicable and reasonable and take any such information into account. In particular, the office encountering the alien must carefully assess to what extent the relevant facts and circumstances are the same or have changed either procedurally or substantively (either with respect to later developments, or more detailed knowledge of past circumstances) from the basis for the original exercise of discretion. A decision by an INS office to take enforcement action against the subject of a previous documented exercise of favorable prosecutorial discretion should be memorialized with a memorandum to the file explaining the basis for the decision, unless the charging documents on their face show a material difference in facts and circumstances (such as a different ground of deportability).

Memorandum for Regional Directors, et al. Page 13
Subject: Exercising Prosecutorial Discretion

Legal Liability and Enforceability

The question of liability may arise in the implementation of this memorandum. Some INS personnel have expressed concerns that, if they exercise prosecutorial discretion favorably, they may become subject to suit and personal liability for the possible consequences of that decision. We cannot promise INS officers that they will never be sued. However, we can assure our employees that Federal law shields INS employees who act in reasonable reliance upon properly promulgated agency guidance within the agency's legal authority – such as this memorandum–from personal legal liability for those actions.

The principles set forth in this memorandum, and internal office procedures adopted hereto, are intended solely for the guidance of INS personnel in performing their duties. They are not intended to, do not, and may not be relied upon to create a right or benefit, substantive or procedural, enforceable at law by any individual or other party in removal proceedings, in litigation with the United States, or in any other form or manner.

Training and Implementation

Training on the implementation of this memorandum for DDs, CPAs, and Regional, District, and Sector Counsel will be conducted at the regional level. This training will include discussion of accountability and periodic feedback on implementation issues. In addition, following these regional sessions, separate training on prosecutorial discretion will be conducted at the district level for other staff, to be designated. The regions will report to the Office of Field Operations when this training has been completed.

APPENDIX 18—HOWARD PROSECUTORIAL DISCRETION MEMO

Office of the Principal Legal Advisor
U.S. Department of Homeland Security
425 I Street N.W., Room 6100
Washington, DC 20536

U.S. Immigration
and Customs
Enforcement

OCT 6 2005

MEMORANDUM FOR: Chief Counsels

FROM: William J. Howard
Principal Legal Advisor

SUBJECT: Exercising Prosecutorial Discretion To Dismiss Adjustment Cases

PURPOSE:

To set forth the criteria and procedures by which an Immigration and Customs Enforcement (ICE) Office of the Chief Counsel (OCC) may join in or file a motion to dismiss proceedings without prejudice when the ICE OCC determines adjustment applications currently pending before EOIR would be appropriate for approval by Citizenship and Immigration Services (CIS).

The basis for this policy is to reallocate limited ICE resources to priority cases by dismissing appropriate cases where it appears in the discretion of the ICE OCC that relief in the form of adjustment of status appears clearly approvable.

CRITERIA:

Motions to Dismiss Proceedings Without Prejudice pursuant to this memorandum should be predicated on the following threshold criteria.

- EOIR must have jurisdiction to adjudicate the application for adjustment.
- The respondent must demonstrate prima facie eligibility for adjustment of status based on a properly filed application for adjustment under the Immigration and Nationality Act (including but not limited to sections 209, 245, 249, or section 1 of the Act of November 2, 1966). Where the application for adjustment is predicated on a visa petition, the case may be dismissed where the visa petition is approved and immediately available or the record establishes a long-term relative relationship where approval of an immediately available petition is likely.

- Adjustment applications must support a discretionary determination by the ICE OCC that the applications appear clearly approvable.

- There is no asylum application pending adjudication before the Immigration Judge.

- ICE OCC should not generally join in a Motion to Dismiss Without Prejudice or so move sua sponte in removal proceedings involving threats to national security, human rights violators, criminal convictions or conduct necessitating a 212(h) waiver (e.g. Operation Community Shield, Operation ICE Storm, Operation Cornerstone or Operation Predator), immigration fraud necessitating a 212(i) waiver (e.g. Operation Jakarta), or detained aliens. With the approval of the Chief Counsel, dismissal may be permitted in the above cases based upon unique or special circumstances including but not limited to the extent and/or seriousness of criminal conduct, recency and/or significance of immigration fraud, or national security interests. While this is not an exhaustive list, the policy outlined herein should ordinarily be followed absent a competing enforcement interest.

PROCEDURE:

A Motion to Dismiss Without Prejudice must be predicated on the respondent demonstrating prima facie eligibility through an application for adjustment before EOIR. When applicable, the respondent or his/her representative must contact the ICE OCC representing DHS before the Immigration Court to request ICE OCC consent to dismiss proceedings. ICE OCC may require that such request be made in writing, be supported by a true and complete copy of the adjustment application pending before EOIR, and be supported by any other evidentiary material including, but not limited to, a copy of the current DOS Visa Bulletin showing current priority date and respondent's FBI Identification Record accessible at http://www.fbi.gov/hq/cjisd/fprequest.htm. (FAQ's accessible at http://www.fbi.gov/hq/cjisd/faqs.html.)

The ICE OCC may join in a Motion to Dismiss without Prejudice or move sua sponte for dismissal without prejudice if the ICE OCC determines that the respondent's application for adjustment is likely to be granted.

Where appropriate, ICE OCC may request revisions to a proposed motion be made as a precondition for giving its consent. ICE OCC should strive to reply in a timely manner to requests for dismissal of proceedings for adjustment before CIS.

ICE OCC should specifically request that a decision of the Immigration Judge dismissing proceedings will expressly state that dismissal of the matter shall be without prejudice to the Department of Homeland Security (DHS) so that the record will be clear that the re-commencement of removal proceedings will not be barred by the doctrines of res judicata or collateral estoppel. If the Immigration Judge dismisses removal proceedings without prejudice, the OCC should route the administrative file(s) through DRO to CIS for adjudication of adjustment applications and update the General Counsel Electronic Management System (GEMS) including entering "DFA" (Dismissed for Adjustment) within the events note portion of the events tab in GEMS cases manager until "Dismissed for Adjustment" is incorporated as a dropdown order option within the events tab. While the applicant bears the burden of satisfying CIS filing and eligibility requirements, should the immigration court grant a joint request to forward the original adjustment application to the ICE OCC at the time of dismissal of proceedings, the original adjustment application should be placed in the administrative file prior to routing the administrative file to CIS.

Use

This memorandum is intended solely for the guidance of DHS personnel in the performance of their duties. It is not intended to, does not, and may not be relied upon to create any right or benefit, substantive or procedural, enforceable at law or equity by any individual or other party in removal proceedings, in litigation with the United States, or in any other form or manner. Discretionary decisions of the ICE OCC regarding the exercise of prosecutorial discretion under this memorandum are final and not subject to legal review or recourse.

INSTRUCTIONS FOR SUBMITTING CERTAIN APPLICATIONS IN IMMIGRATION COURT AND FOR PROVIDING BIOMETRIC AND BIOGRAPHIC INFORMATION TO U. S. CITIZENSHIP AND IMMIGRATION SERVICES

** If you are filing both an I-589 Form and any additional forms (such as I-485, EOIR-40, EOIR-42A, EOIR-42B, or I-881), you must follow BOTH INSTRUCTIONS A & B.*

❑ A. Instructions for Form I-589 (Asylum and for Withholding of Removal)*

In addition to filing your application for asylum and supporting documents with the Immigration Court, you **must complete the following requirements** before the Immigration Judge can grant relief or protection in your case:

SEND these 3 items to the address below:

(1) A clear copy of the **first three pages** of your completed Form I-589 (Application for Asylum and for Withholding of Removal) that you will be filing or have filed with the Immigration Court, which must include your **full name, your current mailing address, and your alien number (A number)**. (Do Not submit any documents other than the first three pages of the completed I-589),

(2) A copy of Form EOIR–28 (Notice of Entry of Appearance as Attorney or Representative Before the Immigration Court) if you are represented, and

(3) A copy of these instructions.

USCIS Nebraska Service Center
Defensive Asylum Application With Immigration Court
P.O. Box 87589
Lincoln, NE 68501-7589

Please note that there is **no filing fee required** for your asylum application.

After the 3 items are received at USCIS Nebraska Service Center, **you will receive**:

- A **USCIS receipt notice** in the mail indicating that USCIS has received your asylum application, and
- An **ASC notice** for you, and separate Application Support Center (ASC) notices for each dependent included in your application. Each ASC notice will indicate the individual's unique receipt number and will provide instructions for each person to appear for an appointment at a nearby ASC for collection of biometrics (such as your photograph, fingerprints, and signature). If you do not receive this notice in 3 weeks, call (800) 375-5283. If you also mail applications under Instructions B, you will receive 2 notices with different receipt numbers. You must wait for and take both scheduling notices to your ASC appointment.

You (and your dependents) must then:

- **Attend** the biometrics appointment at the ASC, and obtain a **biometrics confirmation** document before leaving the ASC, and
- **Retain** your **ASC biometrics confirmation** as proof that your biometrics were taken, and bring it to your future Immigration Court hearings.

❑ B. Instructions for Form(s) I-485, EOIR-40, EOIR-42A, EOIR-42B, or I-881*

You **must complete the following requirements** before the Immigration Judge can grant relief in your case:

SEND these 5 items to the address below:

(1) A clear copy of the entire application form that you will be filing or have filed with the Immigration Court. (Do not submit any documents other than the completed form itself),

(2) The appropriate application fee. (The fee can be found in the instructions with the application, the regulations, and at www.uscis.gov or for the EOIR forms, at www.usdoj.gov/eoir),

(3) The $70 USCIS biometrics fee,

(4) A copy of Form EOIR–28 (Notice of Entry of Appearance as Attorney or Representative Before the Immigration Court) if you are represented, and

(5) A copy of these instructions.

USCIS Texas Service Center
P.O. Box 852463
Mesquite, Texas 75185-2463

Both fees must be submitted in the form of a check or a money order (or 2 separate checks/money orders) and be made out to: "Department of Homeland Security."

After the 5 items are received at the USCIS Texas Service Center, **you will receive:**

- A **USCIS notice** with your USCIS receipt number and **with instructions** to appear for an appointment at a nearby Application Support Center (ASC) for collection of your biometrics (such as your photographs, fingerprints, and signature). Your dependents will receive separate notices if they are required to provide biometrics. If you do not receive this notice in 3 weeks, call (800) 375-5283. If you also apply for asylum, take both scheduling notices to your ASC appointment (*see* side A).

You (and your dependents) must then:

- **Attend** this biometrics appointment at the ASC, and obtain a **biometrics confirmation** document from the ASC,
- **File** the following with the Immigration Court within the time period directed by the Immigration Judge: (1) the original **application Form**, (2) all **supporting documentation**, and (3) the **USCIS notice** that instructs you to appear for an appointment at the ASC, and serves as a receipt for your filing fees, and
- **Retain** your **ASC biometrics confirmation** as proof that your biometrics were taken, and bring it to your future Immigration Court hearings.

IMPORTANT: Failure to complete these actions and to follow any additional instructions that the Immigration Judge has given you could result in a delay in deciding your application or in your application being deemed abandoned and dismissed by the court.

(Eff. Date 4/1/05)

TABLE OF CASES

A

B

C

D

E

F

G

H

I

J

K

L

M

N

O

P

Q

R

S

T

U

V

W

SUBJECT MATTER INDEX

A

S